The Philokalia

VOLUME III

THE PHILOKALIA

THE COMPLETE TEXT
compiled by

ST NIKODIMOS OF THE HOLY MOUNTAIN
and
ST MAKARIOS OF CORINTH

translated from the Greek
and edited by
G. E. H. PALMER
PHILIP SHERRARD
KALLISTOS WARE

with the assistance of
THE HOLY TRANSFIGURATION MONASTERY
(BROOKLINE)
CONSTANTINE CAVARNOS
BASIL OSBORNE
NORMAN RUSSELL

VOLUME III

faber and faber
LONDON · BOSTON

First published in the UK in 1984
by Faber and Faber Limited

First paperback edition published in the USA in 1986
by Faber and Faber, Inc.
50 Cross Street
Winchester, MA 01890

© *The Eling Trust 1984*

CONTENTS

INTRODUCTORY NOTE

As in the first two volumes, the three editors – whose names appear below – are responsible for rewriting the notes which St Nikodimos placed before each text or series of texts by a single author. We are likewise responsible for the Glossary, which reproduces that in volume ii, and for the footnotes unless otherwise indicated.

We would like once again to thank Mrs Ian Busby for her invaluable work.

G. E. H. Palmer
Philip Sherrard
Bishop Kallistos of Diokleia

Dr G. E. H. Palmer died on 7 February 1984; he had shared in the final editing of the typescript of volume iii, but was not able to correct the proofs. Αἰωνία ἡ μνήμη!

NOTE ON BIBLICAL QUOTATIONS
AND REFERENCES

All Biblical passages have been translated directly from the Greek as given in the original *Philokalia*. This means that quotations from the Old Testament are normally based on the Greek Septuagint text. Where this differs significantly from the Hebrew, we have indicated the fact by adding the Roman numeral LXX after the reference.

Even though we follow the Septuagint text, in giving references we use the numbering and titles of the Hebrew, as reproduced in the Authorized Version (King James Bible), since this is more widely familiar in the Western world. In particular the following differences between the Hebrew and the Septuagint should be noted:

NUMBERING OF PSALMS

Hebrew (Authorized Version)	Greek (Septuagint)
1–8	1–8
9 and 10	9
11–113	Subtract one from the number of each Psalm in the Hebrew
114 and 115	113
116 : 1–9	114
116 : 10–16	115
117–146	Subtract one from the number of each Psalm in the Hebrew
147 : 1–11	146
147 : 12–20	147
148–150	148–150

TITLES OF BOOKS

Hebrew (Authorized Version)	*Greek (Septuagint)*
1 Samuel	1 Kingdoms
2 Samuel	2 Kingdoms
1 Kings	3 Kingdoms
2 Kings	4 Kingdoms

Where authors in the *Philokalia* merely refer to a passage or paraphrase it, but do not quote it exactly, 'cf.' is added before the reference.

ST PHILOTHEOS OF SINAI

Introductory Note

'It is not clear', states St Nikodimos, 'at what date our holy father Philotheos flourished and died.' He is known to us solely as the author of the present work *Forty Texts on Watchfulness*. From his name it is evident that he was a monk of Mount Sinai, while the content of his *Forty Texts* shows that he followed in the tradition of St John Klimakos, abbot of Sinai (sixth–seventh century), whom he quotes (§20; cf. §34). His spiritual teaching is also close to that of another Sinaite author, St Hesychios the Priest (?eighth–ninth century);[1] the three of them may be regarded as forming together a distinctively Sinaite 'school' of ascetic theology. Certainly later in date, then, than Klimakos, and probably likewise later than Hesychios, Philotheos may have lived in the ninth or tenth century.

Clear and concise, the *Forty Texts* are especially valuable for the simple definitions that they give of key concepts. As the title indicates, St Philotheos assigns central significance to the quality of watchfulness or spiritual sobriety (*nipsis*). In common with St Hesychios, he sees this as closely connected with inner attentiveness and the guarding of the intellect: the three notions are virtually synonymous. But he underlines, more explicitly than does Hesychios, the importance of bodily asceticism and the keeping of the commandments; the inner and the outer warfare go together. Like the other two members of the Sinaite 'school', he commends the invocation of the Holy Name, 'the unceasing prayer of Jesus Christ' (§2), which has power to 'concentrate the scattered intellect' (§27), thereby enabling it to maintain continual mindfulness of God. Particularly striking is Philotheos' insistence upon the remembrance of death, which is to be viewed not as something morbid and 'world-denying', but rather as enhancing the unique value of each moment of time.

[1] See *The Philokalia*, vol. i (London & Boston, 1979), pp. 161–98.

Forty Texts on Watchfulness

1. There is within us, on the noetic plane, a warfare tougher than that on the plane of the senses. The spiritual worker has to press on with his intellect towards the goal (cf. Phil. 3 : 14), in order to enshrine perfectly the remembrance of God in his heart like some pearl or precious stone (cf. Matt. 13 : 44–46). He has to give up everything, including the body, and to disdain this present life, if he wishes to possess God alone in his heart. For the noetic vision of God, the divine Chrysostom has said, can by itself destroy the demonic spirits.

2. When engaged in noetic warfare we should therefore do all we can to choose some spiritual practice from divine Scripture and apply it to our intellect like a healing ointment. From dawn we should stand bravely and unflinchingly at the gate of the heart, with true remembrance of God and unceasing prayer of Jesus Christ in the soul; and, keeping watch with the intellect, we should slaughter all the sinners of the land (cf. Ps. 101 : 8. LXX). Given over in the intensity of our ecstasy to the constant remembrance of God, we should for the Lord's sake cut off the heads of the tyrants (cf. Hab. 3 : 14. LXX), that is to say, should destroy hostile thoughts at their first appearance. For in noetic warfare, too, there is a certain divine practice and order. Thus we should force ourselves to act in this way until it is time for eating. After this, having thanked the Lord who solely by virtue of His compassion provides us with both spiritual and bodily food, we should devote ourselves to the remembrance of death and to meditation, on it. The following morning we should courageously resume the same sequence of tasks. Even if we act daily in this manner we will only just manage, with the Lord's help, to escape from the meshes of the noetic enemy. When this pattern of spiritual practice is firmly

established in us, it gives birth to the triad faith, hope and love. Faith disposes us truly to fear God. Hope, transcending servile fear, binds us to the love of God, since 'hope does not disappoint' (Rom. 5 : 5), containing as it does the seed of that twofold love on which hang 'the law and the prophets' (Matt. 22 : 40). And 'love never fails' (1 Cor. 13 : 8), once it has become to him who shares in it the motive for fulfilling the divine law both in the present life and in the life to be.

3. It is very rare to find people whose intelligence is in a state of stillness. Indeed, such a state is only to be found in those who through their whole manner of life strive to attract divine grace and blessing to themselves. If, then, we seek – by guarding our intellect and by inner watchfulness – to engage in the noetic work that is the true philosophy in Christ, we must begin by exercising self-control with regard to our food, eating and drinking as little as possible. Watchfulness may fittingly be called a path leading both to the kingdom within us and to that which is to be; while noetic work, which trains and purifies the intellect and changes it from an impassioned state to a state of dispassion, is like a window full of light through which God looks, revealing Himself to the intellect.

4. Where humility is combined with the remembrance of God that is established through watchfulness and attention, and also with recurrent prayer inflexible in its resistance to the enemy, there is the place of God, the heaven of the heart in which because of God's presence no demonic army dares to make a stand.

5. Nothing is more unsettling than talkativeness and more pernicious than an unbridled tongue, disruptive as it is of the soul's proper state. For the soul's chatter destroys what we build each day and scatters what we have laboriously gathered together. What is more disastrous than this 'uncontrollable evil' (Jas. 3 : 8)? The tongue has to be restrained, checked by force and muzzled, so to speak, and made to serve only what is needful. Who can describe all the damage that the tongue does to the soul?

6. The first gate of entry to the noetic Jerusalem – that is, to attentiveness of the intellect – is the deliberate silencing of your tongue, even though the intellect itself may not yet be still. The second gate is balanced self-control in food and drink. The third is ceaseless mindfulness of death, for this purifies intellect and body. Having once experienced the beauty of this mindfulness of death, I

was so wounded and delighted by it – in spirit, not through the eye –
that I wanted to make it my life's companion; for I was enraptured by
its loveliness and majesty, its humility and contrite joy, by how full of
reflection it is, how apprehensive of the judgment to come, and how
aware of life's anxieties. It makes life-giving, healing tears flow from
our bodily eyes, while from our noetic eyes rises a fount of wisdom
that delights the mind. This daughter of Adam – this mindfulness of
death – I always longed, as I said, to have as my companion, to sleep
with, to talk with, and to enquire from her what will happen after the
body has been discarded. But unclean forgetfulness, the devil's murky
daughter, has frequently prevented this.

7. It is by means of thoughts that the spirits of evil wage a secret
war against the soul. For since the soul is invisible, these malicious
powers naturally attack it invisibly. Both sides prepare their
weapons, muster their forces, devise stratagems, clash in fearful
battle, gain victories and suffer defeats. But this noetic warfare lacks
one feature possessed by visible warfare: declaration of hostilities.
Suddenly, with no warning, the enemy attacks the inmost heart, sets
an ambush there, and kills the soul through sin. And for what
purpose is this battle waged against us? To prevent us from doing
God's will as we ask to do it when we pray 'Thy will be done'. This
will is the commandments of God. If with the Lord's help through
careful watchfulness you guard your intellect from error and observe
the attacks of the demons and their snares woven of fantasy, you
will see from experience that this is the case. For this reason the
Lord, foreseeing the demons' intentions by His divine power, set
Himself to defeat their purpose by laying down His commandments
and by threatening those who break them.

8. Once we have in some measure acquired the habit of self-
control, and have learnt how to shun visible sins brought about
through the five senses, we will then be able to guard the heart with
Jesus, to receive His illumination within it, and by means of the
intellect to taste His goodness with a certain ardent longing. For we
have been commanded to purify the heart precisely so that, through
dispelling the clouds of evil from it by continual attentiveness, we
may perceive the sun of righteousness, Jesus, as though in clear sky;
and so that the principles of His majesty may shine to some extent
in the intellect. For these principles are revealed only to those who
purify their minds.

9. We ought to make ourselves each day such as we should be when we are to appear before God. For the prophet Hosea says: 'Hold fast to mercy and judgment, and always draw close to your God' (Hos. 12 : 6. LXX). Again, Malachi, speaking in God's name, says: 'A son honours his father, and a servant his lord. If I am a father, where is the honour due to me? And if I am Lord, where is the fear? So says the Lord Almighty' (Mal. 1 : 6. LXX). And St Paul states: 'Let us cleanse ourselves from all pollution of the flesh and spirit' (2 Cor. 7 : 1). And again, Wisdom says: 'Guard your heart with all diligence, for on this depends the outcome of life' (Prov. 4 : 23). And our Lord Jesus Christ said: 'Cleanse first the inside of the cup, so that the outside may also be clean' (Matt. 23 : 26).

10. Untimely talk sometimes provokes hatred in those who listen, sometimes – when they note the folly of our words – abuse and derision. Sometimes it defiles our conscience, or else brings upon us God's condemnation and, worst of all, causes us to offend against the Holy Spirit.

11. If with the Lord's help you cleanse your heart and uproot sin – struggling for the knowledge that is more divine and seeing in your intellect things invisible to most people – you must not on this account be arrogant towards anyone. For an angel, being incorporeal, is more pure and full of spiritual knowledge than any other created thing; yet it was an angel who, in exalting himself, fell like lightning from heaven. Thus his pride was reckoned by God as impurity. But those who dig up gold are known to all.

12. St Paul says: 'The person engaged in spiritual warfare exercises self-control in all things' (1 Cor. 9 : 25). For, bound as we are to this wretched flesh, which always 'desires in a way that opposes the Spirit' (Gal. 5 : 17), we cannot when sated with food stand firm against demonic principalities, against invisible and malevolent powers; 'for the kingdom of God is not food and drink' (Rom. 14 : 17), and 'the will of the flesh is hostile to God: for it is not subject to the law of God, nor indeed can it be' (Rom. 8 : 7). It is clear that it cannot be because it is earthly, a compound of humours, blood and phlegm, and always gravitating downwards. Thus it is always attached to earthly things and relishes the corrupting pleasures of the present life. 'For the will of the flesh is death' (Rom. 8 : 6); and 'they that are in the flesh cannot conform to God's will' (Rom. 8 : 8).

13. Guarding the intellect with the Lord's help requires much humility, first in relation to God and then in relation to men. We ought to do all we can to crush and humble the heart. To achieve this we should scrupulously remember our former life in the world, recalling and reviewing in detail all the sins we have committed since childhood (except carnal sins, for the remembrance of these is harmful). This not only induces humility but also engenders tears and moves us to give heartfelt thanks to God. Perpetual and vivid mindfulness of death has the same effect: it gives birth to grief accompanied by a certain sweetness and joy, and to watchfulness of intellect. In addition, the detailed remembrance of our Lord's Passion, the recollection of what He suffered, greatly humbles and abashes our pride, and this, too, produces tears. Finally, to recount and review all the blessings we have received from God is truly humbling. For our battle is against proud demons.

14. Do not reject out of self-love these saving medicines of the soul. If you do, you are no disciple of Christ or imitator of St Paul. For St Paul says: 'I am not fit to be called an apostle' (1 Cor. 15 : 9); and again: 'I was once a blasphemer and a persecutor and a violent, insolent man' (1 Tim. 1 : 13). Do you see, proud man, how the saint was not forgetful of his former life? Indeed, all the saints, from the beginning of creation to the present day, have put on this lowliest holy cloak of God. Our Lord Jesus Christ Himself, being God incomprehensible, unknown and ineffable, wishing to show us the way of eternal life and holiness, was clothed in humility during His whole life in the flesh. Thus holy humility ought truly to be called a divine virtue, a royal robe and commandment. Moreover, the angels and all the radiant and divine powers practise and preserve this virtue, knowing how Satan fell when he became proud, and how he lies in the abyss as a fearful warning of such a fall to both angels and men. Through his pride he proved himself in God's sight more degraded than any other created thing. We also know what fall Adam fell through pride.

Since we have so many examples of this virtue that confers such blessings on the soul, let us follow them as fully as possible and humble ourselves in every way. Let us humble ourselves in soul and body, in thought and will, in words and ideas, in our outer bearing and our inner state. For unless we strive to do this we will turn our advocate, Jesus Christ, the Son of God and God, against us. For the Lord 'ranges himself against the proud, but gives grace to the humble' (Jas. 4 : 6); and: 'Everyone that is arrogant is unclean before the Lord' (Prov. 16 : 5. LXX); and: 'He who humbles himself will be exalted' (Matt. 23 : 12); and: 'Learn from Me, for I am gentle and humble in heart' (Matt. 11 : 29). So we must be careful.

15. Our Saviour says: 'Watch yourselves, lest your hearts be weighed down by dissipation, drunkenness and worldly cares' (Luke 21 : 34); and St Paul says: 'The person engaged in spiritual warfare exercises self-control in all things' (1 Cor. 9 : 25). Aware of all that is said to us in divine Scripture, let us lead our life with self-control, especially in regard to food. Let us accustom our body to virtuous and orderly habits, nourishing it with moderation. For in this way the upsurges of the soul's desiring power are more easily calmed and subdued by its sovereign aspect, the intelligence; and in fact the same is true where the soul's incensive power is concerned, as well as our other faults. For those with experience regard virtue as consisting in an all-inclusive self-control, that is, in the avoidance of every kind of evil. For the pre-eminent source of purity is God, the source and giver of all blessings; but next comes self-control with regard to food, exercised in the same regular manner each day.

16. It is through us that Satan fights God, trying to nullify God's will, embodied as it is in the divine and life-giving commandments, by preventing us from carrying them out. Similarly, it is through us, and through the help which He gives us, that God seeks to accomplish His holy will and so to defeat the devil's lethal purpose. In vain does the devil strive to oppose God by making men disobey the commandments; for God in His turn uses human weakness to overthrow the devil's schemes. And you can see that this is the case. For it is evident that all the commandments of the Gospel legislate for the tripartite soul and make it healthy through what they enjoin. They do not merely seem to make it healthy, but they actually have this effect. The devil, on the other hand, fights day and night against the tripartite soul. But if he fights against it, it is clear that he fights against Christ's commandments, since Christ legislates for the tripartite soul through the commandments. The three parts of

the soul are represented by its incensive power, its desiring power, and its intelligence.

Note how Christ says, 'Whoever is angry with his brother without good cause will be brought to judgment' (Matt. 5 : 22), and then tells us how anger may be healed. But the enemy in his turn tries to subvert this commandment by stirring up strife and thoughts of rancour and envy within us. For he too knows that the intelligence should control the incensive power; and so, by bombarding the intelligence with evil thoughts – with thoughts of envy, strife, contention, guile, self-esteem – he persuades the intelligence to abandon its control, to hand the reins over to the incensive power, and to let the latter go unchecked. And the incensive power, having so to speak unseated its rider, disgorges through the mouth in the form of words all those things stored up in the heart as a result of the devil's wiles and the intellect's negligence. And the heart is then seen to be full, not of the divine Spirit and of godlike thoughts, but of evil. It is as the Lord said: 'The mouth expresses what fills the heart' (Matt. 12 : 34). For if the devil can induce the person he has taken possession of to utter what is harboured within, then that person will not merely call his brother 'dolt' or 'fool' but may well pass from insulting words to murder. It is in these ways that the devil fights against God and the commandment God gave about not being angry with one's brother without good cause. But the insulting words and their consequences could have been avoided had their initial provocations been expelled from the heart through prayer and attentiveness. Thus the devil achieves his purpose when he makes us break God's commandment by means of the thoughts that he insinuates into the heart.

17. What does the Lord command where the appetitive aspect or desiring power of the soul is concerned? 'Whoever looks at a woman with lust has already committed adultery with her in his heart' (Matt. 5 : 28). Aware of this injunction, the devil weaves a kind of mental net in order to undermine its effect. He does not attack us by exciting desire through an actual physical woman, but he operates inwardly by projecting into our intellect lascivious figures and images, and by insinuating words that rouse desire, and by other methods of this kind which those who have experience of the intellect know about.

18. What commandments are directed at the intelligence? 'I tell you, never swear an oath ... but simply say "Yes" and "No" ' (Matt. 5 : 34, 37); and: 'He who does not renounce everything and follow Me is not worthy of Me' (cf. Matt. 10 : 37–38); and: 'Enter through the narrow gate' (Matt. 7 : 13). These are instructions to the intelligence. Again, the enemy – wanting to overpower the intelligence, a skilled commander – first addles its wits with gluttonous and promiscuous thoughts, treating it derisively and dismissing it from its command as though it were a drunken general; then he uses anger and desire as servants of his own will. Free in this way from the control of the intelligence, these powers – the desiring and the incensive powers – use the five senses as aids in sinning openly. And these are the sins into which we then fall: our eyes become inquisitive, not having the intellect controlling them from within; our ears love to hear frivolous things; our sense of smell becomes effeminate and our tongue unbridled, and our hands touch what they ought not to touch. With this goes injustice instead of justice, folly instead of moral judgment, licentiousness instead of self-restraint, slavishness instead of courage. For these four principal virtues – justice, moral judgment, self-restraint and courage – govern the three aspects of the soul. When these aspects are properly guided, they keep the senses away from degrading things. Then the intellect, tranquil, its powers with God's help under control and tractable, fights the noetic battle readily and bravely. But if, being inattentive, it is defeated by the devil's provocations and its powers are thrown into confusion, it breaks the divine commandments. Such violation, if not followed by the appropriate degree of repentance, will certainly lead to chastisement in the future. The intellect, consequently, should always be watchful. In this way it maintains its natural state and is a true guardian of the divine commandments.

19. The soul is walled off, fenced in and bound with chains of darkness by the demonic spirits. Because of the surrounding darkness she cannot pray as she wants to, for she is fettered inwardly, and her inner eyes are blind. Only when she begins to pray to God, and to acquire watchfulness while praying, will she be freed from this darkness through prayer. Otherwise she will remain a prisoner. For through prayer the soul discovers that there

is in the heart another fight and another hidden type of opposition, and a different kind of warfare against the thoughts provoked by the evil spirits. Holy Scripture bears witness to this when it says: 'If the spirit of the ruler rises up against you, do not desert your place' (Eccles. 10 : 4). The place of the intellect is its firm stand in virtue and its watchfulness. For one can take a firm stand with respect to virtue and vice. Thus the psalmist says: 'Blessed is the man who has not walked in the counsel of the ungodly, and has not stood in the path of sinners' (Ps. 1 : 1); and St Paul says: 'Stand, therefore, having girded your loins with truth' (Eph. 6 : 14).

20. With all our strength let us hold fast to Christ, for there are always those who struggle to deprive our soul of His presence; and let us take care lest Jesus withdraws because of the evil thoughts that crowd our soul (cf. John 5 : 13). Yet we will not manage to hold Him without great effort on the soul's part. Let us study His life in the flesh, so that in our own life we may be humble. Let us absorb His sufferings, so that by emulating Him we may endure our afflictions patiently. Let us savour His ineffable incarnation and His work of salvation on our behalf, so that from the sweet taste in our soul we may know that the Lord is bountiful (cf. Ps. 34 : 8). Also, and above all, let us unhesitatingly trust in Him and in what He says; and let us daily wait on His providence towards us. And whatever form it takes, let us accept it gratefully, gladly and eagerly, so that we may learn to look only to God, who governs all things in accordance with the divine principles of His wisdom. If we do all these things, we are not far from God; for godliness is 'perfection that is never complete', as one who was divinely inspired and spiritually perfect has said.[1]

21. He who really redeems his life, always dwelling on the thought and remembrance of death, and wisely withholding the intellect from the passions, is in a far better position to discern the continual presence of demonic provocations than the man who chooses to live without being mindful of death. The latter, by purifying the heart through spiritual knowledge alone, but not keeping in mind any thought of grief, may sometimes appear to control all the destructive passions by his skill; yet he is unwittingly fettered by

[1] See St John Klimakos, *The Ladder of Divine Ascent*, Step 29 (P.G. lxxxviii, 1148c; English translation (E.T.) by Archimandrite Lazarus [London, 1959], p. 259).

one of them, the worst of all – pride, into which, abandoned by God, he sometimes falls. Such a person must be very vigilant lest, deluded by conceit, he becomes deranged. For, as St Paul says (cf. 1 Cor. 4 : 6, 18, 19; 8 : 1), souls that gather knowledge from here and there tend to become haughty and disdainful towards their inferiors, as they regard them; they lack the spark of the love which builds up. But he who all the day long is mindful of death discerns the assaults of the demons more keenly; and he counter-attacks and repels them.

22. The blessed remembrance of God – which is the very presence of Jesus – with a heart full of wrath and a saving animosity against the demons, dissolves all trickeries of thought, plots, argumentation, fantasies, obscure conjectures and, in short, everything with which the destroyer arms himself and which he insolently deploys in his attempt to swallow our souls. When Jesus is invoked, He promptly burns up everything. For our salvation lies in Christ Jesus alone. The Saviour Himself made this clear when He said: 'Without Me you can do nothing' (John 15 : 5).

23. At every hour and moment let us guard the heart with all diligence from thoughts that obscure the soul's mirror; for in that mirror Jesus Christ, the wisdom and power of God the Father (cf. 1 Cor. 1 : 24), is typified and luminously reflected. And let us unceasingly seek the kingdom of heaven inside our heart (cf. Luke 17 : 21), the seed (cf. Luke 13 : 19), the pearl (cf. Matt. 13 : 45) and the leaven (cf. Matt. 13 : 33). Indeed, if we cleanse the eye of the intellect we will find all things hidden within us. This is why our Lord Jesus Christ said that the kingdom of heaven is within us, indicating that the Divinity dwells in our hearts.

24. Watchfulness cleanses the conscience and makes it lucid. Thus cleansed, it immediately shines out like a light that has been uncovered, banishing much darkness. Once this darkness has been banished through constant and genuine watchfulness, the conscience then reveals things hidden from us. Through the intellect it teaches us how to fight the unseen war and the mental battle by means of watchfulness, how we must throw spears when engaged in single combat and strike with well-aimed lances of thought, and how the intellect must escape being hit and avoid the noxious darkness by hiding itself in Christ, the light for which it longs. He who has tasted this light will understand what I am talking about.

The soul is never sated with it, but the more it feeds on it, the more hungry it grows. It is a light that attracts the intellect as the sun the eye. Inexplicable, it yet becomes explicable through experience. This experience I have known or, more precisely, I have been wounded by it; but it commands me to be silent, even though my intellect would delight in speaking of it. 'Pursue peace with all men and the holiness without which no one will see the Lord' (Heb. 12 : 14). Do this in order to acquire love and purity, for these are peace and holiness.

25. You must direct your wrath only against the demons, for they wage war upon us through our thoughts and are full of anger against us. As regards the manner of the hourly warfare within us, listen and act accordingly. Combine prayer with inner watchfulness, for watchfulness purifies prayer, while prayer purifies watchfulness. It is through unceasing watchfulness that we can perceive what is entering into us and can to some extent close the door against it, calling upon our Lord Jesus Christ to repel our malevolent adversaries. Attentiveness obstructs the demons by rebutting them; and Jesus, when invoked, disperses them together with all their fantasies.

26. Be extremely strict in guarding your intellect. When you perceive an evil thought, rebut it and immediately call upon Christ to defend you; and while you are still speaking, Jesus in His gentle love will say: 'Behold, I am by your side ready to help you.' When this whole detachment of the enemy has been put out of action through prayer, again turn your attention to your intellect. There you will see a succession of waves worse than before, with the soul swimming among them. But again, awakened by His disciple, Jesus as God will rebuke the winds of evil (cf. Matt. 8 : 23–27). Having found respite for an hour perhaps, or for a moment, glorify Him who has saved you, and meditate on death.

27. Let us go forward with the heart completely attentive and the soul fully conscious. For if attentiveness and prayer are daily joined together, they become like Elijah's fire-bearing chariot (cf. 2 Kgs. 2 : 11), raising us to heaven. What do I mean? A spiritual heaven, with sun, moon and stars, is formed in the blessed heart of one who has reached a state of watchfulness, or who strives to attain it; for such a heart, as a result of mystical contemplation and ascent, is enabled to contain within itself the uncontainable God. If,

then, you aspire to holiness, try with God's help to invoke the
Lord and wholeheartedly to turn words into actions. By restraining with a certain forcefulness the five senses through which the
soul can be injured, you will certainly make the struggle within
the heart lighter for the intellect. So, by means of certain ploys,
keep out all external enemies, and with incorporeal, God-given
weapons fight against the thoughts which they produce inside
you. Avert sensual pleasure through strenuous vigils, and be
sparing in food and drink. Keep the body properly slim so that
you reduce the burden of the heart's warfare, with full benefit to
yourself. Chastise your soul with the thought of death, and
through remembrance of Jesus Christ concentrate your scattered
intellect. It is particularly at night that the intellect grows lucid in
its radiant contemplation of God and of divine realities.

28. We should not reject the practice of bodily asceticism; for as
wheat comes from the earth, so from such practice grows
spiritual joy and benediction. Nor should we try to evade our
conscience when it speaks to us of things conducive to salvation
that we ought to do, and constantly tells us what is right and
what is our duty. This it does especially when purified through
active, applied, and meticulous watchfulness of intellect; for then,
owing to its pure state, the judgments of the conscience tend to
be all-embracing, to the point, and indisputable. So it should not
be evaded, since it tells us inwardly how to live in conformity to
God's will, and by severely censuring the soul when the mind has
been infected by sins, and by admonishing the erring heart to
repent, it provides welcome counsel as to how our defective state
can be cured.

29. Smoke from wood kindling a fire troubles the eyes; but then
the fire gives them light and gladdens them. Similarly, unceasing
attentiveness is irksome; but when, invoked in prayer, Jesus
draws near, He illumines the heart; for remembrance of Him
confers on us spiritual enlightenment and the highest of all
blessings.

30. Forcing his way into our intellect, our enemy tries to compel
us—created in God's image though we are—to eat the dust and
to creep on our bellies as he does (cf. Gen. 3 : 14). This is why
God says: 'I will put enmity between you and him' (cf. Gen.
3 : 15). Hence we must always breathe God, so that we are

never wounded by the devil's fiery darts (cf. Eph. 6 : 16). 'I shall protect him', He says, 'because he has known My name' (Ps. 91 : 14. LXX); and: 'His salvation is near those who fear Him' (Ps. 85 : 9).

31. St Paul, the 'chosen vessel' (Acts 9 : 15) who spoke 'in Christ' (2 Cor. 2 : 17), out of his great experience of invisible noetic warfare wrote to the Ephesians: 'We do not wrestle against flesh and blood, but against demonic principalities and powers, against the rulers of the darkness of this world, against spiritual wickedness in the celestial regions' (Eph. 6 : 12). And the Apostle Peter says: 'Be watchful, be vigilant, because your adversary, the devil, walks about like a roaring lion, seeking whom he may devour. Stand against him, steadfast in faith' (1 Pet. 5 : 8). And our Lord Jesus Christ, speaking of the various attitudes of those who hear the words of the Gospel, says: 'Then comes the devil, and snatches the word out of their hearts' – that is to say, he steals it by inducing them to forget it – 'lest they should believe and be saved' (Luke 8 : 12). And again Paul says: 'For with the inward man I delight in the law of God; but I see another law . . . warring against the law of my intellect, and bringing me into captivity' (Rom. 7 : 22–23). They said these things to instruct and enlighten us about what we fail to perceive.

32. In the absence of self-reproach and humility, spiritual knowledge puffs us up, making us feel superior to others (cf. 1 Cor. 8 : 1). But if we are aware of our own weakness we will keep in mind Paul's words when he says: 'My brethren, it is not as though I had already grasped it or were already perfect . . . but forgetting what lies behind, and reaching forward to what lies in front, I pursue my purpose, aiming at the prize of the high calling of God' (Phil. 3 : 13–14). And again: 'I do not run aimlessly, nor do I box by beating the air with my fists. But I discipline my body harshly, and bring it into subjection; for I fear lest, after preaching to others, I myself should be cast away' (1 Cor. 9 : 26–27). Do you not see how humility is a road to holiness, and what humility the great St Paul had? He said: 'Christ came into the world to save sinners, of whom I am the worst' (1 Tim. 1 : 15). Should we not humble ourselves, then, because of the lowliness of our nature? For what is more lowly than clay? And we must be mindful of God, since we have been created for this. But we must also practise

self-control, so that with our Lord's help we may advance unhampered in the spiritual life.

33. The person who gives himself over to evil thoughts cannot keep his outer self free from sin; and if evil thoughts have not been uprooted from the heart, they are bound to manifest themselves in evil actions. We look on things adulterously because the inner eye has become adulterous and darkened; and we want to hear about foul things because our soul's ears have listened to what the foul demons inside us have whispered to us. Consequently, with the Lord's help, we must cleanse ourselves within and without. We must guard our senses and free each of them from impassioned and sinful influences. And just as, ignorant and full of futility, we used to live in the world with intellect and senses enslaved to the deceit of sin, so now, having changed to the life according to God, we must dedicate intellect and senses to the service of the living and true God, and of God's justice and will.

34. First there is provocation; then a coupling with the provocation; then assent to it; then captivity to it; then passion, grown habitual and continuous. This is how the holy fathers describe the stages through which the devil gets the better of us.[1]

35. Provocation, they say, is a thought still free from passion, or an image newly engendered in the heart and glimpsed by the intellect. Coupling is to commune with this thought or image, in either an impassioned or a dispassionate way. Assent is the pleasurable acceptance by the soul of the thing seen. Captivity is the forcible and enforced abduction of the heart, or persistent intercourse with the object, disrupting even our best state. Passion, in the strict sense, they define as that which lurks impassionably in the soul over a long period. Of these stages the first is sinless; the second, not altogether free from sin; the sinfulness of the third stage depends on our inner state; and the struggle itself brings us either punishment or crowns of victory.

36. Captivity is one thing at the time of prayer, another when we are not engaged in prayer. Passion, however, incontestably leads either to a corresponding repentance or to future chastisement. But the person who rebuffs the initial provocation, or who regards

---

[1] See in particular St Mark the Ascetic, *On the Spiritual Law*, §§ 138–41 (in vol. i of our translation of *The Philokalia*, pp. 119–20), and St John Klimakos, *Ladder*, Step 15 (896c–897b; E.T., pp. 157–8). Cf. Glossary, pp. 363–5.

it dispassionately, has at one stroke cut off all the sinful stages that follow. Such, then, is the strategy employed by the evil demons in their war against both those who are monks and those who are not; and the issue is either defeat or victory, as we have said. The victors are rewarded with crowns; those who fall and do not repent are punished. So let us wage noetic war against the demons, lest we translate their evil purposes into sinful actions. Let us cut sin out of our heart, and we will find within us the kingdom of heaven (cf. Luke 17 : 21). Let us preserve our heart's purity and always be filled with deep compunction towards God through this best of undertakings.

37. Many monks are not aware how the demons deceive the intellect. Being naïve and undeveloped, they tend to give all their attention to the practice of the virtues and do not bother about the intellect. They move through life, I fear, without having tasted purity of heart, and are totally ignorant of the darkness of the passions within. Such people, unaware of the battle about which Paul speaks (cf. Eph. 6 : 12) and not imbued with personal experience of true goodness, regard as lapses only those sins which are actually put into effect. They do not take into account the defeats and the victories that occur on the plane of thought, for these, being internal, cannot be seen by natural sight and are known only to God our judge, and to the conscience of the spiritual contestant. I take it that the scriptural words, 'They said, "Peace", but there was no peace' (Ezek. 13 : 10), apply to such people. The other brethren pray for them in their simplicity, and as best they can teach them to avoid the actual commission of sin. But for those who have a divine desire to cleanse the vision of the soul there is another form of activity in Christ and another mystery.

38. Vivid mindfulness of death embraces many virtues. It begets grief; it promotes the exercise of self-control in all things; it is a reminder of hell; it is the mother of prayer and tears; it induces guarding of the heart and detachment from material things; it is a source of attentiveness and discrimination. These in their turn produce the twofold fear of God. In addition, the purging of impassioned thoughts from the heart embraces many of the Lord's commandments. The harsh hour-by-hour struggle in which so many athletes of Christ are engaged has as its aim precisely this purging of the heart.

39. An unexpected event or misfortune considerably disrupts the mind's attentiveness; and, by dislodging the intellect from its concentration on higher realities and from its noble state of virtue, it diverts it towards sinful quarrelsomeness and wrangling. The cause of this overthrow is assuredly our lack of attention to the enemy's attacks.

40. None of the painful things that happen to us every day will injure or distress us once we perceive and continually meditate on their purpose. It is on account of this that St Paul says: 'I take delight in weakness, insults and hardships' (2 Cor. 12 : 10); and: 'All who seek to live a holy life in Christ Jesus will suffer persecution' (2 Tim. 3 : 12). To Him be glory through all the ages. Amen.

ILIAS THE PRESBYTER

Introductory Note

'Ilias the Presbyter and Ekdikos', as he is called in the manuscripts, was – so his designation suggests – a lawyer who subsequently entered the ranks of the clergy. The title *ekdikos* signifies a judge attached to the ecclesiastical court at the Great Church of the Holy Wisdom ('St Sophia') in Constantinople. Evidently Ilias resigned from this legal post, becoming in all probability a monk before his ordination to the priesthood. He seems to have lived around the end of the eleventh or the beginning of the twelfth century. It is possible, although not certain, that he knew the writings of St Symeon the New Theologian (949–1022), whose influence some have detected in what Ilias says about tears and the divine light. He cannot in any case be later than the twelfth century, since the earliest manuscript of his work dates from this time. He may be the same person as Ilias, Metropolitan of Crete in the early twelfth century, the author of commentaries on St Gregory of Nazianzos and St John Klimakos.[1]

In the surviving manuscripts *A Gnomic Anthology* appears variously under the names of St John of Karpathos (?seventh century),[2] St Maximos the Confessor (580–662),[3] and Ilias himself. Almost certainly the third of these attributions is correct. Although styled an 'anthology', the work is not in fact a collection of excerpts from other authors but is Ilias' own composition. It is divided into four sections, each preceded by a couplet in verse. (The Greek *Philokalia* provides

---

[1] St Nikodimos suspends judgment here. The identification is accepted by V. Laurent, in *Revue des études byzantines* xvi (1958), pp. 121–3, and in *Dictionnaire d'histoire et de géographie ecclésiastiques* xv (1963), col. 187–8; but it is denied by M.-Th. Disdier, 'Elie l'Ecdicos et les *hetera kephalaia* attribués à saint Maxime le Confesseur et à Jean de Carpathos', *Echos d'Orient* xxxi (1932), pp. 17–43. On the theology of Ilias, see also M.-Th. Disdier, 'La vie spirituelle selon Elie l'Ecdicos', *Echos d'Orient* xxxi (1932), pp. 144–64; J. Darrouzès, in *Dictionnaire de spiritualité* iv (1960), col. 576–8; N. G. Politis, 'The path to contemplation in Ilias the Ekdikos' (in Greek), *Epetiris Hetaireias Vyzantinon Spoudon* xliii (1977–8), pp. 345–64.

[2] See *The Philokalia*, vol. i, p. 297.

[3] Op. cit., vol. ii (London & Boston, 1981), p. 48.

continuous numbering for parts I–II, and likewise for parts III–IV, but there are in reality four parts, not two.) The poetic epigraphs provide a general indication of the contents of each section:

Part I: moral teaching (fasting, ascetic effort, the vices and virtues, with special emphasis on humility).

Part II: prayer.

Part III: spiritual contemplation (with particular reference to 'natural contemplation' or the 'contemplation of nature', that is, knowledge of the inner essences or principles of created things – of what in III, 13 are termed 'the world's foundations').

Part IV: the practice of the virtues (*praxis*) and contemplation (*theoria*) (taking up all the main themes mentioned in the earlier parts).

Ilias delights in vivid imagery taken from the world of nature, and also employs the nuptial symbolism of the Song of Songs. Like St Maximos, he makes a clear distinction between 'thought', on the discursive and rational level, and 'intellection', understood as the non-discursive apprehension of spiritual truth (III, 1–5). Following Evagrios, he speaks about a vision of the innate 'luminosity' of the intellect (II, 82, 89); beyond this, there is the higher vision of the divine light, in which the body also shares (II, 104–6). Here the *Gnomic Anthology* points forward to the teaching of the fourteenth-century Hesychasts, especially St Gregory Palamas. Four times Ilias refers to *evchi monologistos*, 'single-phrased prayer' (II, 94, 104; IV, 65, 75), a term that links him with the Sinaite 'school'. In St John Klimakos this expression, used with the additional word *Iïsou*, 'of Jesus', definitely signifies the Jesus Prayer,[1] and in our translation we have taken the view that Ilias means it in the same sense, although in the Greek he does not actually add the qualification 'of Jesus'.

In making our English version we have compared the text in the Greek *Philokalia* with that found among the works of St Maximos (*P.G.* xc, 1401–61): the latter frequently, but by no means invariably, gives a better sense.

Subtle and highly concentrated, the short paragraphs of the *Gnomic Anthology* disclose their true meaning only if read with unusually close attention. Few other authors have been able, in so short a space, to provide such a comprehensive guide to the spiritual way.

[1] *Ladder*, Step 15 (889D; E.T., p. 154).

A Gnomic Anthology

PART I

Here you will find, if you truly search,
A flowing spring, a pure fount of moral teaching.

1. No Christian believing rightly in God should ever be off his guard. He should always be on the look-out for temptation, so that when it comes he will not be surprised or disturbed, but will gladly endure the toil and affliction it causes, and so will understand what he is saying when he chants with the prophet: 'Prove me, O Lord, and try me' (Ps. 26 : 2. LXX). For the prophet did not say, 'Thy correction has destroyed me', but, 'it has upheld me to the end' (Ps. 18 : 35. LXX).

2. The first step towards excellence is fear of God, the last is loving desire for Him.

3. The first step towards perfection is spiritual knowledge put into practice and practice imbued with spiritual knowledge. For practice without such knowledge is of no value, and so is such knowledge when unaccompanied by practice.

4. Practice where the body is concerned consists of fasting and vigil; where the mouth is concerned it consists of psalmody. But prayer is better than psalmody, and silence is more valuable than speech. In the case of the hands, practice is what they do uncomplainingly; and of the feet, it is what they do as soon as they are urged to do it.

5. Where the soul is concerned, practice is self-control accompanied by simplicity, and simplicity animated by self-control.

6. In the case of the intellect, practice is prayer in contemplation and contemplation in prayer.

7. Mercy and truth precede all the other virtues. They in their turn produce humility and so discrimination; for, according to the fathers,

discrimination comes from humility. Without discrimination, neither practice nor spiritual knowledge can fulfil its purpose. For practice uncontrolled by such knowledge strays here and there aimlessly, like a calf; while knowledge that refuses to clothe itself in the honourable vesture of practice lacks nobility, however much it may pretend to possess it.

8. A courageous soul acts correctly when it is master of both practice and contemplation, like a woman who keeps two lamps burning throughout her life. But a soul debilitated by sensual pleasure fails to do what it should.

9. Suffering deliberately embraced cannot free the soul totally from sin unless the soul is also tried in the fire of suffering that comes unchosen. For the soul is like a sword: if it does not go 'through fire and water' (Ps. 66 : 12. LXX) – that is, through suffering deliberately embraced and suffering that comes unchosen – it cannot but be shattered by the blows of fortune.

10. Trials and temptations subject to our volition are chiefly caused by health, wealth and reputation, and those beyond our control by sickness, material losses and slander. Some people are helped by these things, others are destroyed by them.

11. Desire and distress subsist in the soul; sensual pleasure and pain in the body. Sensual pleasure gives rise to pain, and pain to sensual pleasure (for, wanting to escape the wearisome feeling of pain, we take refuge in sensual pleasure); while desire results in distress.

12. The virtuous may appear to be bad, but essentially they are good; superficially the self-important and pleasure-loving may appear to be good, but basically they are evil.

13. The person who hates evil commits it but seldom and then not intentionally. But the person attached to the causes of evil commits it frequently and deliberately.

14. Those who deliberately refuse to repent sin continually; those who sin without meaning to not only repent with all their heart, but also do not often have cause to repent.

15. Let your words combine insight and self-awareness, so that the peaceable divine Logos may not be ashamed to enshrine Himself in them because of their brashness and lack of restraint.

16. A person may have sullied his soul with words even if he has not degraded it by actions; and he may still be impure in his

thoughts even if he watches over his words. For there are three different ways of sinning.

17. You will not be able to perceive the face of virtue so long as you still look on vice with a feeling of pleasure. But vice will appear hateful to you when you hunger for the taste of virtue and avert your gaze from every form of evil.

18. Demons wage war against the soul primarily through thoughts, not through things; for things fight against us in their own right. Hearing and sight are responsible for the warfare waged through things, habit and the demons for that waged through thoughts.

19. The soul is liable to sin in three ways: in actions, in words, and in thoughts. We attain freedom from sin in six ways: by preserving the purity of the five senses and of the spoken word. Whoever succeeds in doing this is indeed perfect, capable also of keeping every aspect of the body under control.

20. The soul's non-intelligent or passible aspect consists of the five senses and the faculty of speech. When in a state of dispassion, the faculty of speech is preserved fully integrated with the soul's passible aspect; but when in an impassioned state, it receives the evil influences that the passible aspect communicates to it.

21. The body cannot be purified without fasting and vigil, the soul without mercy and truth, and the intellect without contemplation of God and communion with Him. These pairs constitute the principal virtues in these three aspects of the human person.

22. When the soul moves in obedience to these virtues, her citadel – patient endurance – is not disturbed by temptations. 'You will gain possession of your souls through your patient endurance' (Luke 21 : 19), says the Logos. Otherwise the soul will be shaken by fits of cowardice, as an unwalled city is by a distant uproar.

23. Not all those who are discreet in their words are also circumspect in their thought. Nor are all those who are circumspect in their thought also discreet where their external senses are concerned. For although all men are subject to the senses, not all pay them the same amount of tribute. In their artlessness, most men do not know the price the senses demand for what they supply.

24. Although moral judgment is by nature indivisible, there are none the less different degrees of it. One person may be given more of it, another less, so that practical virtue, having grown with the help of the principal virtues, may bring to fruition in each person the

goodness of which he is capable. But most people fail to a greater or lesser degree to practise the virtues, and the degree of moral judgment granted to them varies accordingly.

25. Few are circumspect with regard to what is according to nature, but many with regard to what is contrary to nature. For having expended out of fear all their intrinsic quota of circumspection on what is contrary to nature, they have little left to exercise with regard to what is according to nature. Indeed, they expend most of it on superfluous things and what is by nature worthless.

26. A sense of the right moment and a sense of proportion go hand in hand with an intelligent silence. Truth is the banquet of all the three together. Where there is such a banquet, the father of lies, confronting a soul as it departs from this life, will not find in it any of the things he looks for.

27. A truly merciful person is not one that deliberately gives away superfluous things, but one that forgives those who deprive him of what he needs.

28. Some men through acts of charity acquire spiritual wealth by means of material wealth; others renounce their material wealth altogether on becoming aware of the spiritual wealth that is inexhaustible.

29. Everyone likes to be rich in spiritual blessings, but it is grievous to be rich in such blessings and not to be allowed to enjoy them for long.

30. From the outside a soul may appear to be healthy, while within, in the depths of consciousness, it may suffer from some hidden sickness. It can be healed from the outside through being pierced by reproof, and from within through the renewal of the intellect. Whoever, then, rejects such reproof, and shamelessly continues to lie on his bed in the sickroom of lethargy, is a fool.

31. Do not be angry with a person who unwittingly operates on you like a surgeon. Look rather at the abomination he has removed and, blaming yourself, bless him because through God's grace he has been of such service to you.

32. If you are concerned for your soul's health, do not despair of your sickness as though it were incurable; but apply to it the potent medicine of ascetic effort and you will get rid of it.

33. Do not shun the person who opportunely berates you; but go to him and he will show you how much evil lies hidden from your

consciousness. Once you have swallowed the bitter and nauseous draught, you will taste the sweet nourishment of health.

34. The greater the pain that you feel, the more you should welcome the person whose reproof makes you feel it. For he is bringing about within you that total purification without which your intellect cannot attain the pure state of prayer.

35. When you are reproved, you ought either to remain silent, or else gently to defend yourself to your accuser – not indeed in order to gain his approval, but to help him rise up in case he has stumbled by reproving you in ignorance.

36. If someone is rightly offended with you, but you repent before he calls on you to do so, you lose nothing; but if you repent only after you have been asked to, you forfeit half the harvest. If you never cause estrangement by giving offence to others, you recover all the seed that you sowed; but if you always put the blame on yourself, you gain in addition more than you originally laid out.

37. A haughty person is not aware of his faults, or a humble person of his good qualities. An evil ignorance blinds the first, an ignorance pleasing to God blinds the second.

38. As regards his good qualities, the proud man does not want to be compared with his equals; but as regards his failings, he is quite content to be compared with those worse than himself.

39. Reproof strengthens the soul, whereas praise debilitates it and makes it even more sluggish in its spiritual struggle.

40. The substance of wealth is gold; of virtue, humility. Just as he who lacks gold is poor, even though this may not be outwardly apparent, so the spiritual aspirant who lacks humility is not virtuous.

41. Lacking gold, a merchant is not a merchant, even though he may be very skilful in trading; similarly, lacking humility, a spiritual aspirant will never possess the joys of virtue, however great the confidence he places in his own intelligence.

42. The higher a man ascends in humility, the lower he appears in his own eyes; but if he lacks humility, the higher he appears. The humble man does not wish to be compared even with the most lowly, and is grieved when he is given first place at table (cf. Luke 14 : 7–10).

43. It is good for the spiritual aspirant to regard a task as beyond him, but to be in his actions superior to this diffidence. In this way he will both earn men's respect and in God's sight will be 'a worker who has no cause to be ashamed' (2 Tim. 2 : 15).

44. He who is afraid of being cast out of the bridal chamber as an interloper (cf. Matt. 22 : 11–13) should either carry out all God's commandments, or else should strive to fulfil just one of them – humility.

45. Combine simplicity with self-control, and unite truth with humility, and you will keep house with justice, at whose table every other virtue likes to gather.

46. Truth without humility is blind. That is why it becomes contentious: it tries to support itself on something, and finds nothing except rancour.

47. A good character testifies to the beauty of virtue, just as soundness of body bears witness to a peaceful soul.

48. It is best not to go astray at all. Second best is not to hide your error through shame, or be shameless about it, but to humble yourself and, when reproved, to reprove yourself likewise, gladly accepting the punishment. If you do not do this, everything you offer to God is valueless.

49. In addition to voluntary suffering, you must also accept that which comes against your will – I mean slander, material losses and sickness. For if you do not accept these but rebel against them, you are like someone who wants to eat his bread only with honey, never with salt. Such a man does not always have pleasure as his companion, but always has nausea as his neighbour.

50. He who washes his neighbour's garment with inspired words, or who sews it up by contributing to his needs, has the outward appearance of a servant, but is really a master. But when he acts in this way he must be careful to do so truly as a servant, lest by growing conceited he loses both his reward and his proper rank.

51. Just as faith gives substance to the things for which we hope (cf. Heb. 11 : 1), so moral judgment gives substance to the soul and humility to virtue. And it is extraordinary how things perfect in themselves become imperfect when deprived of the qualities that should be associated with them.

52. 'The Lord will guard your going out and your coming in' (Ps. 121 : 8): that is, He will enable you by means of self-control to watch over the food you take in and the words you give out. For the person who exercises self-control over food and speech escapes the desire that enters through the eyes, and calms the anger that issues from a disordered mind. The spiritual aspirant must exercise the greatest

care and exert himself in every way in relation to these two passions. By so doing he will strengthen his practice of the virtues and put his contemplation on a sound basis.

53. Some are most careful about the food they take in but negligent about the words they give out. To adapt Ecclesiastes (11 : 10. LXX), such men do not know how to remove anger from the heart or desire from the flesh. Only through the removal of these things is a pure heart established within us by the renewing Spirit (cf. Ps. 51 : 10).

54. You can achieve frugality by lowering the quantity of your food, and sinlessness in speech by raising the quality of your silence.

55. Sear your loins by abstaining from food, and prove your heart by controlling your speech, and you will succeed in bringing the desiring and incensive powers of your soul into the service of what is noble and good.

56. Sexual desire diminishes in the spiritual aspirant once the body has passed its prime; but gluttony continues unless properly disciplined. You must try to prevent the disgrace of the effect by removing its cause; otherwise in the life to come you will be found lacking in the virtue of self-control and will be covered with shame.

57. The ascetic has to know when and by means of what foods to treat the body as an enemy, when to encourage it as a friend, and when to succour it as an invalid. Otherwise he may unwittingly offer to the friend what is proper for the enemy, or to the enemy what is proper for the friend, and to the invalid what is proper for either of the other two; and having alienated all three he may find them fighting against him in time of temptation.

58. If, when eating, the nourishment in your food is more important to you than its savour, then the grace of tears will be given to you and you will begin to find spiritual refreshment; and you will forget all other taste, relishing its sweetness beyond that of anything else.

59. The tears of the man who scatters his energies dry up, but they gush forth in the man who keeps to the narrow path (cf. Matt. 7 : 13–14).

60. Neither the sinner nor the righteous man is free from remorse: the first, because he has not altogether abandoned evil; the second, because he has not yet attained perfection.

61. Among the things that lie within our power are the virtues of prayer and silence; among the things that depend for the most part not on us, but on the constitution of the body, are fasting and vigil. Hence

the spiritual aspirant must try to attain whatever is more accessible to him.

62. Patience is the house of the soul, for in it the soul is safeguarded. Humility is the soul's wealth, for the soul is nourished through it.

63. If you do not bear criticism patiently, you will not be honoured with praise. If before indulging in pleasure you reflect on the pain inherent in it, you will escape the distress to which it gives birth.

64. Do not fetter yourself to a small thing and you will not be enslaved to a greater one. For the greater evil is built up only on the basis of the smaller.

65. By being mindful of greater evils, you will also be fearful of smaller ones; but if you give way to the greater evils, you will shamefully indulge in the lesser as well.

66. You will not be able to attain the greater virtues until you have fully achieved those which lie within your power.

67. In those in whom mercy and truth prevail, everything is godlike; for truth judges no one without mercy, while mercy never manifests compassion apart from truth.

68. Having united simplicity and self-control, you will experience the blessing which their union produces.

69. You will not be able to cut down the passions attacking you unless you first leave untilled the soil from which they are fed.

70. Some try to purify only the matter of the body, others that of the soul as well. The first gain a certain control with regard to the actual committing of a sin, the second with regard to the passion behind it. But extremely few gain control over the underlying desire.

71. Passionateness is the evil matter of the body; self-indulgence, that of the soul; impassioned craving, that of the intellect. Touch is responsible for the first; the rest of the senses for the second; and a perverse disposition for the third.

72. The self-indulgent man is close to the impassioned man; and the man of impassioned craving to the self-indulgent man. Far from all three is the dispassionate man.

73. The impassioned man is strongly prone to sin in thought, even though for the time being he does not sin outwardly. The self-indulgent man actually commits the sin suggested in thought, even though he suffers inwardly. The man of impassioned craving is given over freely or, rather, servilely, to the various modes of sinning. The

dispassionate man is not dominated by any of these degrees of passion.

74. Passionateness is removed from the soul through fasting and prayer; self-indulgence through vigil and silence; and impassioned craving through stillness and attentiveness. Dispassion is established through remembrance of God.

75. Words of eternal life drop from the lips of dispassion like honey from the honeycomb (cf. Song of Songs 4 : 11). Who then is worthy of touching her lips with his own, of lying between her breasts (cf. Song of Songs 1 : 13), and smelling the fragrance of her clothes (cf. Song of Songs 4 : 10,11) – that is to say, of rejoicing in the laws of the virtues which are, it is said, superior to all the perfumes perceived by the senses?

76. Many may be stripped of the coat of self-love, but few of the coat of worldly display; while only the dispassionate are free from self-esteem, the last coat of all.

77. Every soul will be stripped of the visible body; but only the soul that has indulged but sparsely in the pleasures of this life will be stripped of the body of sin.

78. All who live will die; but to sin will die only those who have consciously hated it.

79. Who will see himself stripped of sin prior to the ordinary death of the body? And prior to the future stripping, who is there that knows himself and his own nature?

Part II

Prayer unites with the Bridegroom
A soul wounded by nuptial love.

80. The deiform soul, placed as it is on the frontier between sensible and spiritual light, is enabled through the former to see and do what pertains to the body, and through the latter what pertains to the Spirit. But as a result of man's inveterate habit of mind, the light of the Spirit has grown dim within the soul, whereas the light of the sensible world shines more brightly within it. Consequently, it cannot fix its attention totally on things divine unless it is wholly united with intelligible light during prayer. In this way, it is compelled to stand midway between darkness and light, linked to spiritual light through participation, and to sensible light by means of the fantasy.

81. An intellect subject to passion cannot penetrate the narrow gate of prayer until it abandons the cares to which it has attached itself. So long as it remains continually occupied with bodily matters, it will inflict suffering on itself.

82. Let prayer inhere in the intellect as a ray in the sun. If the intellect lacks prayer, then worldly cares, like 'clouds driven about by the wind and bringing no rain' (Jude, verse 12), deprive it of its native luminosity.

83. Strength to pray lies in the deliberate privation of food, and strength to go without food lies in not seeing or hearing about worldly things except when strictly necessary. He who is negligent in this fails to build his fasting on a firm foundation, and so he brings about the collapse of the whole edifice of prayer, which itself is based on fasting.

84. If the intellect does not become detached from all sensible things, it cannot rise upwards and realize its true dignity.

85. Fasting corresponds to daylight, because it is clearly manifest; prayer corresponds to night, because it is invisible. He who practises each of these rightly, the one in conjunction with the other, will attain his goal, the city from which 'pain, sorrow and sighing have fled away' (Isa. 35 : 10. LXX).

86. Spiritual work can exist even without bodily labour. Blessed, therefore, is the man who regards spiritual work as superior to physical work: through the first he makes up for any deficiency where the second is concerned, because he lives the hidden life of prayer that is manifest to God.

87. St Paul exhorts us to persevere in the faith, to rejoice in hope, and to persist steadfastly in prayer (cf. Rom. 12 : 12), so that the blessing of joy may be with us. If this is so, then he who fails to persevere lacks faith, and he who does not rejoice lacks hope. For he has abandoned prayer – the source of joy – by not persisting in it.

88. If the intellect has become so closely attached to worldly thoughts through its inveterate involvement with them, how intimate would it not become with prayer if it prayed unceasingly? For, it is said, the intellect will flourish in whatever it makes its constant occupation.

89. Because of long absence from its true home, the intellect has forgotten the luminosity it enjoyed there; hence it must once more become oblivious to things in this world and hasten back to its true home through prayer.

90. Sometimes prayer will fail to bring spiritual refreshment to the intellect, just as a mother's breasts, when they cease to give milk, will not solace her child. At other times the intellect in prayer is like a child that sleeps contentedly in its mother's arms.

91. In the contrite bridal-bed of the virtuous life the bride – prayer – says to her lover: 'I will give you my breasts if you dedicate yourself wholly to me' (cf. Song of Songs 7 : 12).

92. You cannot become intimate with prayer unless you have renounced all material things.

93. During prayer alienate yourself from everything except life and breath if you want to be with the intellect alone.

94. Evidence of an intellect devoted to God is its absorption in the single-phrased Jesus Prayer; of an adroit intelligence, opportune speech; of a non-attached sense – perception, simplicity in taste. When such evidence is present in all three cases, the soul's powers are said to be in good health.

95. The nature of the person who prays must be supple and malleable, like that of children, so that it is receptive to the development brought about by prayer. Thus, if you want to be united with prayer, do not be negligent.

96. Not all have the same purpose in prayer: one man has one purpose, another has another. One prays that, if possible, his heart may always be absorbed in prayer; another, that he may even transcend prayer; and a third, that he may not be hindered by thoughts during prayer. But all pray either to be preserved in what is good, or not to be carried away by evil.

97. If everyone is humbled by prayer – for he who prays with humility is brought to compunction – it follows that anyone outwardly boastful is not praying in a state of humility.

98. Bearing in mind the widow who persuaded the cruel judge to avenge her (cf. Luke 18 : 2–5), the man who prays will never lose heart because the blessings to be gained through prayer are slow in arriving.

99. Prayer deserts you if you give attention to thoughts within and to conversations without. But if you largely ignore both in order to concentrate on it, it will return to you.

100. Unless the words of prayer penetrate to the soul's depths no tears will moisten your cheeks.

101. Corn will spring up for the farmer who has hidden seed in the earth; tears will flow for the monk who diligently attends to the words of prayer.

102. The key to the kingdom of heaven is prayer. He who uses this key as he should sees what blessings the kingdom holds in store for those who love it. He who has no communion with the kingdom gives his attention merely to worldly matters.

103. The intellect cannot say boldly to God at the time of prayer: 'Thou hast burst my bonds asunder; I will offer to Thee the sacrifice of praise' (Ps. 116 : 16–17. LXX), unless out of a desire for higher things it frees itself from cowardice, indolence, excessive sleep and gluttony, all of which lead it to sin.

104. He who is distracted during prayer stands outside the first veil. He who undistractedly offers the single-phrased Jesus Prayer is within the veil. But he alone has glimpsed the holy of holies who, with his natural thoughts at rest, contemplates that which transcends every intellect, and who has in this way been granted to some extent a vision of the divine light.

105. Whenever the soul, paying no attention to external things, is concentrated in prayer, then a kind of flame surrounds it, as fire surrounds iron, and makes it wholly incandescent. The soul remains the same, but can no longer be touched, just as red-hot iron cannot be touched by the hand.

106. Blessed is he who in this life is granted the experience of this state and who sees his body, which by nature is of clay, become incandescent through grace.

107. To beginners the law of prayer is burdensome, like a despotic master; but to the more advanced it is like an erotic force, impelling those smitten by it as a hungry man is impelled towards a rich banquet.

108. To those who genuinely practise the virtues, prayer is sometimes like an overshadowing cloud (cf. Exod. 13 : 21) that keeps off inflammatory thoughts; at other times, bedewing them as it were with tears, it grants them spiritual visions.

109. The music of the lute sounds sweet to the outer ear; but a soul in which during prayer there is no sound of mystical invocation in the Spirit has not attained true compunction. It is only when 'we do not know how to pray as we should, but the Spirit Himself makes intercession for us' (Rom. 8 : 26), that we are brought to this state of compunction.

Part III

Exalted as it reads these texts
The intellect is radiant with spiritual contemplation.

1. The man of spiritual knowledge must recognize when his intellect is in the realm of intellection, when it is in that of thought, and when in that of sense-perception. And in each case he must recognize whether it is there at the right time or at the wrong time.

2. When the intellect is not in the realm of intellection, it is generally in that of thought. And when it is in the realm of thought, it is not in that of intellection. But when it is in the realm of sense-perception, it is associated with all manner of visible and material things.

3. By means of intellection the intellect attains spiritual realities; through thought the reason grasps what is rational. Sense-perception is involved with practical and material realities by means of the fantasy.

4. When the intellect is self-concentrated, it contemplates neither the objects of sense-perception nor those of the rational faculty; on the contrary, it contemplates pure intellects and the rays of divine light flowing with peace and joy.

5. The intellection of an object is one thing, the rational apprehension of that object is another, and the object perceived is a third. The first constitutes the essence, the second is an attribute of the essence, and the third comprises the distinctive subject matter.

6. Given free rein, the intellect is insatiable. But when it is confined to one path – that of prayer – and has not yet reached its goal, it feels cramped, and implores its partner to let it enjoy the things from which it has been withheld.

7. When the intellect has been drawn down from the realm above,

it will not return thither unless it is completely detached from worldly things through concentration on things divine.

8. If you cannot make your soul dwell only on thoughts kindred to it, at least keep your body to itself, and reflect continually upon the wretchedness to which it is subject. For thus, by God's mercy, you will in time be able to return to your original nobility.

9. The man engaged in ascetic practice can readily submit his intellect to prayer, while the contemplative can readily submit prayer to the intellect. The first restricts his perception of visible forms, while the second directs his soul's attention towards the inner essences concealed in such forms. Alternatively, the first compels the intellect to apprehend the inner essences of corporeal realities, while the second persuades it to grasp those of incorporeal beings. The inner essences of corporeal realities are also incorporeal, with respect both to their specific qualities and to their essential being.

10. When you free your intellect from self-indulgence in the body, in food and possessions, then whatever you do will be regarded by God as a pure offering. In exchange, the eyes of your heart will be opened, and you will be able clearly to meditate on the divine principles inscribed within it; and their sweetness to your spiritual taste will be greater than that of honey.

11. You will not be able to make your intellect rise above physical and material things, and even above the desire for necessary food, until you introduce it into the pure realm of the righteous. Then mindfulness of death and of God will fill the earthy heart and cleanse it of all profligate desire.

12. There is nothing more fearful than the thought of death, or more wonderful than remembrance of God. For the first induces the grief that leads us to salvation, and the second bestows gladness. 'I remembered God,' says the prophet, 'and I rejoiced' (Ps. 77 : 3. LXX). And Sirach says: 'Be mindful of your death and you will not sin' (Ecclus. 7 : 36). You cannot possess the remembrance of God until you have experienced the astringency of the thought of death.

13. Until the intellect has seen God's glory with 'unveiled face' (2 Cor. 3 : 18), the soul cannot say from experience of that glory: 'I shall exult in the Lord, I shall delight in His salvation' (cf. Ps. 35 : 9. LXX). For its heart is still shrouded in self-love, so that the world's foundations – the inner essences of things – cannot be re-

vealed to it. And it will not be free from this shroud until it has undergone both voluntary and involuntary sufferings.

14. The leader of the people of Israel first must flee from Egypt (the actual committing of sin), next must cross over the Red Sea (servitude through attachment), and thirdly must dwell in the desert – the desert lying between the impulses to sin and the outward fulfilment of these impulses. Only then, sending ahead his visual and visionary force, can he spy out the promised land – dispassion (cf. Josh. 2 : 1).

15. Those who dwell in the desert – those who abstain from the actual committing of evil – possess the blessings of the promised land only by hearsay. Those who have spied out these blessings with the soul's perception have attained the contemplation of visible things. But those who have been privileged actually to enter the promised land feed in full consciousness on the milk and honey that flows within it (cf. Exod. 3 : 8) – that is to say, on the inner essences of both corporeal and incorporeal realities.

16. A man still subject to physical impulses has not yet been crucified with Christ (cf. Gal. 2 : 20), and if he still drags natural thoughts along with him he has not yet been buried with Him. How then can he be raised up with Christ, to live in newness of life?

17. The three most comprehensive virtues of the soul are prayer, silence and fasting. Thus you should refresh yourself with the contemplation of created realities when you relax from prayer; with conversation about the life of virtue when you relax from silence; and with such food as is permitted when you relax from fasting.

18. So long as the intellect dwells among divine realities, it preserves its likeness to God, being filled with goodness and compassion. When it descends to the realm of things perceived by the senses – provided its descent has been opportune and apt – it can give and receive experience and then, strengthened by this, it can return to itself. But when its descent has been inopportune and unnecessary, it acts like an inept general who fails to use most of his fighting force.

19. The paradise of dispassion hidden within us is an image of that in which the righteous will dwell. None the less, not all who fail to enter the first will be excluded from the second.

20. The rays of the visible sun cannot penetrate a shuttered house. Nor will the rays of the spiritual sun penetrate the soul unless its senses are closed to visible things.

21. The man of spiritual knowledge is one who descends from the realm of intellection to that of sense-perception in a sublime manner and who raises his soul heavenwards with humility.

22. Traversing the fields a bee gathers the ingredients for honey; traversing the ages the soul infuses sweetness into the mind.

23. A deer that has eaten a snake rushes to water in order to neutralize the poison; but a soul wounded by the arrows of God drinks deep draughts of ceaseless longing for her assailant.

24. Unimpassioned thoughts arise in one living in a state of self-unity; reasoned calculations in one living in a state of self-division. But when all thoughts have been expelled from the fragmented soul, only incorporeal intellects commune with it, revealing to it the principles of providence and judgment that constitute the foundations of the world.

25. One living in a state of self-division cannot avoid the distinction between male and female; but this may be done by one living in a state of self-unity, when the distinction between male and female is suppressed through attaining the divine likeness in Christ Jesus (cf. Gal. 3 : 28).

26. Thoughts pertain neither to the non-rational aspect of the soul (for they do not occur in non-rational animals), nor to its intellectual aspect (since they are not to be found in angels). Being products of the reason, they use the imagination as a ladder, and so ascend from the world of the senses to the intellect, conveying to the latter the observations which they have derived from sense-perception; then they redescend from the intellect down to the world of the senses, communicating to it the intellect's principles.

27. When the ship of sinfulness is overwhelmed by the flood of tears, evil thoughts will react like people drowning in the waves and trying to grasp hold of something so as to keep afloat.

28. Thoughts gather about the soul according to its underlying quality: either they are like pirates and try to sink it, or they are like oarsmen and try to help it when it is in danger. The first tow it out into the open sea of sinful thoughts; the second steer it back to the nearest calm shore they can find.

29. Unless the soul strips itself of the thoughts that lead up to self-esteem – which is the worst of the seven evil thoughts – it will not be able to strip off this seventh thought either; and so it will not be able to clothe itself in the eighth thought, called by St Paul 'our house

that is from heaven'. Only those who have divested themselves of material things are able 'with heartfelt sighs' to clothe themselves in this eighth thought (cf. 2 Cor. 5 : 2–4).

30. Angelic thoughts accompany perfect prayer; spiritual thoughts, intermediate prayer; and thoughts about nature, the prayer of beginners.

31. The quality of the grain is usually evident in the ear of corn; similarly, the purity of contemplation is usually evident in prayer. The grain is surrounded by a spear-like sheath in order to prevent the birds from eating it; contemplation is armed with spiritual thoughts through which to destroy the temptations that attack it.

32. Through the practice of the virtues the outward aspects of the soul become like the silver-coated wings of a dove. Through contemplation its inward and intelligible aspects become golden. But the soul that has not in this way regained its beauty cannot soar aloft and come to rest in the abode of the blessed.

Part IV

Here is a meadow full of the fruits
Of spiritual practice and contemplation.

33. In olden times men were instructed to offer in the temple the firstfruits of the threshing-floor and the wine-press (cf. Num. 18 : 12). Likewise we ought now to offer God self-control and truth as the firstfruits of ascetic practice, and love and prayer as the firstfruits of the virtue of contemplation. Through the first we repulse the assaults of mindless desire and anger; through the second we vanquish empty thoughts and the snares into which they lead us.

34. The first stage of ascetic practice is marked by self-control and truthfulness; the intermediate stage by moderation and humblemind-edness; the final stage by freedom from thoughts and the sanctification of the body.

35. Ascetic practice consists not merely in managing to do what is right, but also in doing it rightly: the doer must concern himself with timeliness and congruity.

36. To contemplate is to perceive not only the existing state of corporeal realities but also the ultimate goal of their inner principles.

37. Ascetic practice cannot be consolidated without contempla-tion, and contemplation cannot be genuine without ascetic practice. For practice must be based on intelligence, and contemplation on practice. In this way evil will be powerless to disrupt practice, and contemplation will be prolific in acts of goodness.

38. The goal of ascetic practice is the mortification of the passions; of spiritual knowledge, the contemplation of the virtues.

39. Ascetic practice is to contemplation as matter is to form; and contemplation is to ascetic practice as the eye is to the face.

40. Many compete for practical virtue, but only one receives the

prize: he who seeks to attain its goal through contemplation.

41. The man engaged in ascetic practice drinks the draught of compunction during prayer, but the contemplative gets drunk with the best cup (cf. Ps. 23 : 5. LXX). The first meditates on things that are according to nature, while the second ignores even himself during prayer.

42. The man engaged in ascetic practice cannot persist in spiritual contemplation for long. He is like a person who is being given hospitality but must shortly leave his host's house.

43. When praying, men engaged in ascetic practice are as it were entering the gate of God's commandments; but contemplatives when praising God stand as though in the courts of the virtues. The first give thanks because they have been freed of their fetters, the second because they have also taken captive those who waged war against them.

44. You must be governed by both ascetic practice and contemplation. Otherwise you will be like a ship voyaging without the right sails: either it risks being overturned by the violence of the winds because its sails are too large, or it fails to take advantage of the breeze because they are too small.

45. By the oarsmen of the spiritual ship understand devout thoughts. By oars understand the vital powers of the soul: the incensive and the desiring powers, and the will and free choice. The man engaged in ascetic practice is always in need of these, whereas the contemplative does not always need them. For during prayer the contemplative bids farewell to everything: himself holding the tiller of discernment he keeps awake throughout the night of contemplation, offering praises to Him who holds all things together. And perhaps he sings some love-song to his soul as he watches the swell of the salty sea and the tumult of the waves, and marvels at the righteous judgments of God.

46. The person at a stage intermediate between ascetic practice and contemplation does not make the voyage entirely by means of oars, nor entirely by means of spiritual sails, but with the aid of both. Because he possesses a measure of contemplation, he gladly endures the hardships of ascetic practice; and because he is assisted by ascetic practice, he equally accepts the reasons for the shortcomings of his contemplation.

47. The contemplative, with his will assisted by nature as though by a current, voyages without difficulty. But the man engaged in

ascetic practice, finding his resolution undermined by his attachment to sensible things, is much troubled by the waves of his thoughts; indeed, he almost falls into despair because of their violence.

48. Land that is not well tilled is unlikely to yield a good crop of clean grain; and unless the man engaged in ascetic practice proceeds diligently and without ostentation, he will not enjoy a bountiful harvest of good clean fruit as the result of his prayer.

49. The mind engaged in the unremitting practice of prayer is like well-trodden earth: such earth will be smooth and welcoming to tender feet, while the mind will then be untarnished and receptive to pure prayer.

50. In relation to material things, the intellect is assisted by thought; but in relation to immaterial things, thought, unless repudiated, will be like 'a thorn in the flesh' (2 Cor. 12 : 7) to the intellect.

51. The man engaged in ascetic practice finds that during prayer the knowledge of sensible things covers his heart like a veil, which he is unable to remove because of his attachment to these things. Only the contemplative man, owing to his non-attachment, can to some degree see the glory of God 'with unveiled face' (2 Cor. 3 : 18).

52. Prayer combined with spiritual contemplation constitutes the promised land in which there flows, like 'milk and honey' (Exod. 3 : 8), the spiritual knowledge of the principles of God's providence and judgment. Prayer combined with a certain measure of natural contemplation is Egypt, in which those who pray still encounter the memory of their grosser desires. Simple prayer is manna in the desert (cf. Num. 11 : 7). Since it is unvarying, this manna does not disclose to the impatient the promised blessings for which they long; but for those who persevere with such restricted food, it imparts most excellent and abiding nourishment.

53. Ascetic practice combined with contemplation is like the body united to its ruling spirit. Without contemplation, it is like flesh dominated by a spirit of self-will.

54. Sense-perception is the forecourt of the deiform soul; the reason is her temple; and the intellect, her high priest. The intellect is to be found in the forecourt when held captive by inept thoughts; in the temple when circumscribed by thoughts that are apposite. When it is free from both, it is privileged to enter the holy sanctuary.

55. There is a sound of grief and lamentation in the house of the

soul still at the stage of ascetic practice, because of the suffering it endures; but in the house of the contemplative soul 'a voice of exultation and thanksgiving' (cf. Ps. 42 : 4. LXX) is heard, because of its spiritual knowledge.

56. On account of his sufferings, the man engaged in ascetic practice wants to leave this life and to be with Christ; the contemplative, on the contrary, is quite content to remain in the flesh, both because of the joy that he receives from prayer, and because of the use that he can be to his fellow-men (cf. Phil. 1 : 23–24).

57. Where people of greater intelligence are concerned, contemplation precedes ascetic practice, whereas in the case of the more obtuse, ascetic practice precedes contemplation. Both contemplation and ascetic practice lead to the same auspicious conclusion; but this is attained more quickly by those in whom contemplation precedes ascetic practice.

58. Paradise is the contemplation of intelligible realities. During prayer the man of spiritual understanding enters into it as into his own home; but the man engaged in ascetic practice is like a passer-by: he wants to look in, but is prevented by the wall of his spiritual immaturity.

59. Bodily passions are like wild animals, while passions of the soul are like birds. The man engaged in ascetic practice can keep the animals out of the noetic vineyard; but unless he enters into a state of spiritual contemplation, he cannot keep the birds away, however much he strives to guard himself inwardly.

60. The man engaged in ascetic practice cannot rise above ethical propriety, unless he goes beyond the natural law – as Abraham went forth from his own land – and beyond his own limited state of development – as Abraham left his kinsmen (cf. Gen. 12 : 1). In this way, as a mark of God's approval, he will be liberated from the all-embracing hold of pleasure; for it is this veil of pleasure, wrapped around us from our birth, that prevents us from receiving complete freedom.

61. When spring comes, a colt cannot bear being confined to the stable and feeding out of the manger. Similarly, the newly-initiated intellect cannot long bear being confined to prayer: like the colt, it would gladly go out into the fields of natural contemplation, there to devote itself to psalmody and spiritual reading.

62. Ascetic practice girds the soul's vital powers with fasting and vigil, while contemplative virtue keeps the spiritual powers burning like lamps by means of silence and prayer. The vital powers have the reason as their tutor, the spiritual powers have the indwelling Logos as their bridal escort.

63. The uninitiated intellect is not permitted to enter the ripe vineyard of prayer. It is given access only – and barely – to the literal repetition of the psalms, as a poor man is allowed to glean the small grapes left on the vines.

64. Just as not all those who have audience with a king can also dine with him, so not all those who have attained a certain familiarity with prayer will rise to contemplation during it.

65. Apt silence bridles anger; moderation in food bridles mindless desire; and the single-phrased Jesus Prayer bridles unruly thought.

66. The man who dives into the sea for pearls will fail in his efforts unless he first strips off his clothes; similarly, the man who plunges into the sea of spiritual knowledge in search of the pearl of wisdom will fail to find it unless he strips himself of his attachment to the world of the senses.

67. The intellect that encloses itself within the mind during prayer is like a bridegroom conversing with the bride inside the bridal chamber. But the intellect that is not allowed to enter stands dejectedly outside, crying: ' "Who will lead me into the walled city?" (Ps. 60 : 9). Who will guide me until I no longer see vanities and delusions during prayer?'

68. As food without salt is to the taste, so is prayer without compunction to the intellect.

69. The soul still in pursuit of prayer is like a woman in the pains of childbirth; but the soul that has attained prayer is like a woman who has given birth and is full of joy on account of her child.

70. In olden times the Amorites used to come down from the mountain and attack those trying to force their way through (cf. Deut. 1 : 44). In our days evil forgetfulness repulses those who, before attaining purity, attempt to rise to higher form-free prayer.

71. The demons are extremely hostile to pure prayer. Moreover, it is not the host of psalms that can terrify them, as an army might terrify an external enemy; it is the alliance of the intellect with the reason and of the reason with sense-perception.

72. Prayer free from passion is like sustaining bread to those who

pray; prayer combined with some degree of contemplation is like nourishing oil; and prayer that is free of forms is like sweet-smelling wine. Those who drink deeply of this wine are rapt out of themselves.

73. It is said of the wild ass that it scorns the crowds in the city, and of the unicorn that it cannot be fettered by anyone (cf. Job 39 : 7–9). Similarly, the intellect, having mastered thoughts both natural and contrary to nature, mocks their vanity, and during prayer cannot be dominated by any of the objects of sense-perception.

74. Shaking a stick at dogs provokes their fury; forcing oneself to pray in purity provokes the fury of the demons.

75. The spiritual aspirant must restrain his senses through frugality and his intellect through the single-phrased Jesus Prayer. Having in this way detached himself from the passions, he will find himself caught up to the Lord during prayer.

76. Those who indulge their passions, being materially-minded, are distracted during prayer by their thoughts as by frogs. Those who restrain their passions are gladdened during prayer by the changing forms of contemplation, which are like nightingales moving from one branch to another. But in the dispassionate there is silence and great quiescence of both thought and intellection during prayer.

77. In olden times, when Miriam, the sister of Moses, saw the fall of the enemy, she took up a timbrel and led the women who sang the victory-songs (cf. Exod. 15 : 20–21). In our days, when the soul overcomes the passions, love – the highest of the virtues – rises up to praise it. As though taking up the lyre, it embarks upon the contemplation that long ago has been appointed for it as a hard-won addition to its beauty; and it ceaselessly glorifies God, rejoicing with its sister-virtues.

78. When through continuous prayer the words of the psalms are brought down into the heart, then the heart like good soil begins to produce by itself various flowers: roses, the vision of incorporeal realities; lilies, the luminosity of corporeal realities; and violets, the many judgments of God, hard to understand.

79. A flame gives light so long as it is wedded to matter. But the soul becomes God's shrine only when free ·from matter. The flame rises up so long as it has something to burn on; the soul is raised upward until it is consummated in divine love.

80. A soul that has denied itself completely, and has been raised above creation wholly to the realm of prayer, does not descend whenever it wishes: it descends when He who weighs and measures all our affairs judges it to be right.

81. When listlessness is expelled from the soul, and malice from the mind, then the intellect, naked in simplicity, innocent and totally stripped of the veil of shame, sings a new song to God, with joyful gratitude celebrating the forefeast and inauguration of the life to come.

82. When the soul that prays begins to respond to the higher divine realities, then, like the bride in the Song of Songs, it sings to its companions: 'My Beloved stretched His hand through the opening, and my womb trembled because of Him' (Song of Songs 5 : 4).

83. As a soldier returning from war unburdens himself of his arms, so the man engaged in ascetic practice unburdens himself of thoughts when he attains to contemplation. For as the first has no need of arms except in time of war, so the second has no need of thoughts unless he reverts to the things apprehended by the senses.

84. The man engaged in ascetic practice sees corporeal realities in terms of their relations; the contemplative sees them in terms of their nature. Only the spiritually illumined grasps the inner principles of what the other two perceive.

85. Incorporeal realities may be apprehended in the *logoi* or inner principles of corporeal realities; but in incorporeal realities may be apprehended the supraessential Logos to whom every diligent soul urgently strives to return.

86. The inner principles of corporeal realities are concealed like bones within objects apprehended by the senses: no one who has not transcended attachment to sensible things can see them.

87. A soldier casts off his arms when he has ceased fighting; the contemplative casts off thoughts when he returns to the Lord.

88. A general becomes despondent when he fails to capture any booty in war; so does the man engaged in ascetic practice when he fails to attain spiritual contemplation in prayer.

89. When bitten by some wild animal, a deer runs swiftly to earthly springs of water; a soul wounded by the most tender arrow of prayer hastens towards the light of incorporeal realities.

90. Just as the eye cannot see a grain of wheat unless the eyelids are open, so the practical intellect cannot see its own nature unless stripped of the attachment to sensible things that obscures its vision.

91. The stars are hidden when the sun rises, and thoughts vanish when the intellect returns to its own realm.

92. When the stage of ascetic practice has been fulfilled, spiritual visions flood the intellect like the sun's rays coming over the horizon; even though they are native to it, and embrace it because of its purity, they appear to come from outside.

93. If on descending from the realm of vision to attend to practical matters the contemplative intellect were to speak of what it has experienced, it would say such things as: 'What is more wondrous than divine beauty, or more lovely than the sense of God's magnificence? What longing is so keen and unbearable as that engendered by God in a soul purified of every vice and truly able to say: "I am wounded with love"?' (Song of Songs 2 : 5. LXX).

94. 'My heart grew warm within me and a fire was kindled during my meditation' (Ps. 39 : 3. LXX). So may speak the man who has no difficulty in following God through prayer and who has no desire for temporal life.

95. When it has rejected evil, let the soul still engaged in ascetic struggle repeat the words of the Song to the malicious demons and thoughts that forcibly try to turn its attention once more to vanities and delusion: 'I have taken off my coat; how can I put it on again? I have washed my feet; how can I make them dirty?' (Song of Songs 5 : 3).

96. The soul that enjoys God's love is bold enough to say to Him: 'Tell me, Good Shepherd, where You graze Your Sheep, and where You rest Your lambs at noon, so that by following them I may avoid becoming like one encircled by the flocks of Your companions' (cf. Song of Songs 1 : 7. LXX).

97. The soul still engaged in ascetic struggle, trying to hold fast to the words of prayer and not being able to do so, cries out like the soul in the Song: 'By night on my bed I sought Him whom I love; I sought Him but I did not find Him; I called Him, but He did not listen to me. I will rise now through more strenuous prayer and will go about the city, in the wide streets and the market-places, and will look for my Beloved. Perhaps I shall find Him who is present in all things and beyond all things; and I will feast on the vision of His glory' (cf. Song of Songs 3 : 1–2. LXX).

98. When the soul begins to be all tears from the joy that accompanies prayer, it grows bold and, like a bride to her bridegroom, cries: 'Let my Beloved come down into His garden, and let Him feed on

the hard-won consolation of my tears as though on choice fruit' (cf. Song of Songs 5 : 1. LXX).

99. When the soul still engaged in ascetic struggle begins to be struck with wonder at the Creator because of the magnificence and beauty of created things, and to savour the delight that comes from them, it too cries in astonishment: 'How beautiful You are, my Bridegroom, paradise of Your Father: You are a flower of the field and a cedar of His, like the cedars of Lebanon. I yearned for His shadow, and I sat down, and His fruit was sweet in my mouth' (cf. Song of Songs 2 : 1–3. LXX).

100. If someone who receives a king in his house becomes in this way illustrious, admired of all and full of joy, how much more so will the soul that, when purified, receives the King of kings, according to His unfailing promise? But it must guard itself with great care, casting out everything that does not seem to please Him, and introducing everything that does.

101. If a person is expecting to be summoned tomorrow by the king, will he have any concern other than to consider what he will say in order to please the king? A soul that takes careful note of this will not be found unprepared when it comes before the future judgment seat.

102. Blessed is the soul that, because it expects its Lord daily, thinks nothing of the day's toil or of the night's, since He is going to appear in the morning.

103. God sees all men, but only those see God who perceive nothing during prayer. God listens to those who see Him, while those to whom He does not listen do not see Him. Blessed is the man who believes that he is seen by God; for his foot will not slip (cf. Ps. 73 : 2) unless this is God's will.

104. The blessings of the kingdom within us – which the world-loving eye has not seen, and the presumptuous ear has not heard, and which have not entered into a heart empty of the Holy Spirit (cf. 1 Cor. 2 : 9) – are a pledge and foretaste of the blessings to be given by God to the righteous in the kingdom that is to come. If we do not savour the first, which are the fruits of the Spirit (cf. Gal. 5 : 22), we will not be able to enjoy the second.

105. The thoughts of those engaged in ascetic practice are like deer. Deer sometimes go up into the mountains because they are frightened of hunters, and sometimes down to the valleys because they want

what they can find there. Similarly those engaged in ascetic practice can neither be constantly in a state of spiritual contemplation, for they are still immature, nor be constantly in a state of natural contemplation, for they do not always seek relaxation. The thoughts of contemplatives, however, disdain inferior forms of contemplation.

106. Raindrops moisten the furrows, and tear-laden sighs rising from the heart soften the soul's state during prayer.

107. No one can contemplate the Triune Divinity unless his vision transcends the material dyad as well as the material monad; and he will not transcend the latter unless he has integrated the intellections of his intellect.

108. It is less hard to check the downward flow of a river than for one who prays to check the turbulence of the intellect when he wishes, preventing it from fragmenting itself among visible things and concentrating it on the higher realities kindred to it. This is so in spite of the fact that to check the flow of a river is contrary to nature, while to check the turbulence of the intellect accords with nature.

109. Those who inwardly purify the intellect by ignoring what is visible are filled with such wonder and such joy that they would not be able to find room for anything earthly, even though they were to be flooded with all the things over which people fight.

110. Simply to speak of the laws of nature is enough to arouse deep admiration. But when they are fully understood, they are as fields full of flowers, whose lavish blossoms give out a spiritual sweetness like nectar from heaven.

111. Bees surround their queen among fresh meadow-flowers; and the soul that is unceasingly in a state of compunction is surrounded and assisted by the angelic powers, for it is kindred to them.

112. Within the visible world, man is as it were a second world; and the same is true of thought within the intelligible world. For man is the herald of heaven and earth, and of all that is in them; while thought interprets the intellect and sense-perception, and all that pertains to them. Without man and thought both the sensible and the intelligible worlds would be inarticulate.

113. A person released from long captivity is not so full of joy as the intellect freed from its attachment to sensible things and winging its way towards the heavenly realm that is its native land.

114. A person who prays, not with attention, but distractedly, will regard the psalms as uncouth; and from the point of view of the psalms he will appear equally uncouth. Both will be considered mad by the demons.

115. Those to whom the world is crucified are not the same as those who are crucified to the world (cf. Gal. 6 : 14). For the first, the nails are fasting and vigils; for the second, they are to shed every possession and to be treated with contempt. Without the second, the sufferings involved in the first are useless.

116. No one can pray purely if he is constrained by the passions of ostentation and ambition. For the attachments and frivolous thoughts in which these passions involve him will twine around him like ropes, and during prayer will drag his intellect down like a fettered bird that is trying to fly.

117. The intellect cannot be peaceful during prayer unless it has acquired self-control and love. With God's help the first strives to put an end to the body's hostility towards the soul, the second to our hostility towards our fellow-men. Upon the man who has in this way established peace within himself, 'the peace that surpasses the intellect' (Phil. 4 : 7) then descends and, according to God's promise, takes up its abode in him.

118. The person struggling to enter the kingdom of God must excel in works of righteousness: in almsgiving, by providing out of his own paucity; and in suffering for the sake of peace, by responding to trials with patient endurance in the Lord.

119. Neither one who falls short of virtue because of negligence nor one who out of presumption oversteps it will reach the harbour of dispassion. Indeed, no one will enjoy the blessings of righteousness who tries to attain them by means of either deficiency or excess.

120. Land cannot make a farmer wealthy merely by yielding the equivalent to the grain which he has sown, or even by adding to it slightly; it can do so only by multiplying it. Similarly, the achievements of one engaged in ascetic practice cannot make him righteous unless his diligence towards God exceeds his natural propensity.

121. Not everyone who does not love his neighbour actually hates him, and not everyone who does not hate his neighbour is able to love him. It is one thing to envy one's neighbour's progress, and another to refrain from hindering it. The height of malice consists not simply in

being galled at one's neighbour's superiority, but also in traducing his good qualities by saying that they are not good at all.

122. Bodily passions are one thing, passions of the soul another. Passions according to nature are other than those which are contrary to nature. The person who repulses the former, but does not take account of the latter, is like a man who sets up a high thick fence to keep wild animals out, but wishes joy to the birds eating the finest grapes in his spiritual vineyard.

123. First the soul imagines evil, then desires it, then feels pleasure or pain with respect to it, then becomes fully conscious of it, and finally unites with it either outwardly or inwardly. Thoughts accompany all these phases, except that of the initial stimulus. If this is repudiated, none of the evil that follows will be actualized.

124. Those who are approaching dispassion will be troubled only by fantasies; those who restrain their passions, by desires; those who indulge their passions, by entanglements. Those who misuse what they have to meet their needs, but feel remorse for it, are conscious of the evil they do; those who feel no remorse unite with evil.

125. Pleasure has its seat in every part of the body, but does not disturb everyone in the same way. In some people, it disturbs more the desiring aspect of the soul; in others, the incensive aspect; and in others, the intelligence. It does this through gluttony, bad temper and malice, the source of all the unholy passions.

126. Like the gates of a city, we have to open the organs of sense-perception in order to satisfy essential needs; but in so doing we must take care not to give access at the same time to warlike tribes that seek to attack us.

127. Pleasure is the mother of desire; bad temper, of anger; malice, of jealousy. Whoever does not struggle against the ringleaders will not be left in peace by their subordinates; nor can you restrain the passions if you practise the commandments only because you are forced to do so.

128. Those who repulse provocations prevent thoughts from entering the spiritual vineyard like marauding animals and ruining it. Those who couple with provocations, but do not take pleasure in them, simply allow the animals to enter, though not to touch any of the things inside. Those who enjoyably commune with the passions through thoughts, yet do not reach the point of giving assent to them, are like men who, after allowing a wild boar to come through the

fence into the vineyard, have stopped him from taking his fill of the grapes but then have found him more than they can control. Such people often end by giving assent to the passions.

129. If you still have to give thought to the exercising of self-control you have not yet attained simplicity. Only one engaged in ascetic struggle, it is said, has to exercise self-control (cf. 1 Cor. 9 : 25), not one who is spiritually perfect. A person engaged in ascetic struggle is like a man who has a vineyard or corn-land not among other vineyards or other farms, but somewhere out on its own, and which for this reason needs much guarding and watching. No one, however, touches the vineyard of the person who has attained simplicity: it is like that of a king or some other awesome potentate, whose very name is enough to make thieves and passers-by shudder at the thought of trying to enter it.

130. Many ascend the cross of mortification, but few consent to be nailed to it. For many submit to hardships and afflictions of their own choosing; but only those who have died completely to this world and to the respite it offers readily submit to the sufferings that come against their will.

131. Many have removed all their 'coats of skin' (Gen. 3 : 21) except the last, that of self-esteem. This is cast off only by those who are disgusted with what produces it: their own self-satisfaction.

132. The person who is offered bodily comfort and men's praise, but refuses to accept them, has been stripped of the final coat, that of self-esteem. To him is granted the grace of being clothed, even in this present life, with the splendour of the heavenly dwelling-place, longed for with so many sighs.

133. The energy or capacity for an action is one thing, and the action or thing energized is another. A sin actually committed is an example of the second, while some form of self-indulgence that is activated only inwardly, not outwardly, is an example of the first. Someone dominated by such self-indulgence is like a person who, although not turned out of his own property, yet has to pay tribute to others who control what he holds dear.

134. When the sense of taste is the chief purveyor of pleasure, the other senses are bound to follow in its wake. This is so even if the reproductive organs of those who are less hot-blooded, such as the elderly, appear to be unmoved and free from excitement because they have dried up. Yet the sterile woman who commits adultery will not

be judged chaste from the fact that she does not produce children. We would say that only the person free from passion within, and not seduced by what he sees, is entirely chaste.

135. The state of the desiring aspect of the soul is revealed through food, gestures and speech; through what appeals and what does not appeal; through taste, sight and hearing, both by the use it makes of them and by the way it misuses them, and even by the neutral attitude it adopts towards them.

136. Where fear does not lead the way, thoughts will be in a state of confusion, like sheep that have no shepherd. Where fear leads the way or goes with them, they will be under control and in good order within the fold.

137. Fear is the son of faith and the shepherd of the commandments. He who is without faith will not be found worthy to be a sheep of the Lord's pasture.

138. Some possess only the rudiments of spiritual qualities, some possess them partially, while others possess them in a complete form. The first are like an ordinary soldier, the second like an officer without any money: the soldier can barely defend his home from those who try to damage it, while the officer is not treated with due respect when he meets others.

139. Those who exhort us, imperfect as we are, to indulge the pleasures of the palate, act like people who encourage us to reopen wounds that are healed, or to scratch an itch because of the enjoyment it gives, or to eat foods which increase fever, or to fence off our spiritual vineyard but to allow the impulses of the flesh to enter like a wild boar and devour our good thoughts like grapes. We must not give way to them; nor must we yield to the importunate flattery of men and passions. Rather, we must strengthen the fence through self-control, until the wild animals – the carnal passions – stop their howling, and vain thoughts no longer descend like birds and despoil the vineyard of our soul, rich as it is with the contemplative vision bestowed on it by our Lord Jesus Christ. To Him be glory throughout the ages. Amen.

THEOPHANIS THE MONK

Introductory Note

In the Greek *Philokalia* this poem appears without any introductory note, and nothing is known concerning its author. He lays particular emphasis upon the need for direct personal experience. Eternal life, he also insists, has to begin here and now, in this present world; but at the same time, like St Gregory of Nyssa, he sees perfection as an endless progress in the age to come, 'a step that has no limit'.

The Ladder of Divine Graces
*which experience has made known to those
inspired by God*

The first step is that of purest prayer.
From this there comes a warmth of heart,
And then a strange, a holy energy,
Then tears wrung from the heart, God-given.
Then peace from thoughts of every kind.
From this arises purging of the intellect,
And next the vision of heavenly mysteries.
Unheard-of light is born from this ineffably,
And thence, beyond all telling, the heart's illumination.
Last comes – a step that has no limit
Though compassed in a single line –
Perfection that is endless.
The ladder's lowest step
Prescribes pure prayer alone.
But prayer has many forms:
My discourse would be long
Were I now to speak of them:
And, friend, know that always
Experience teaches one, not words.
A ladder rising wondrously to heaven's vault:
Ten steps that strangely vivify the soul.
Ten steps that herald the soul's life.
A saint inspired by God has said:
Do not deceive yourself with idle hopes
That in the world to come you will find life
If you have not tried to find it in this present world.
Ten steps: a wisdom born of God.
Ten steps: fruit of all the books.
Ten steps that point towards perfection.

Ten steps that lead one up to heaven.
Ten steps through which a man knows God.
The ladder may seem short indeed,
But if your heart can inwardly experience it
You will find a wealth the world cannot contain,
A god-like fountain flowing with unheard-of life.
This ten-graced ladder is the best of masters,
Clearly teaching each to know its stages.
If when you behold it
You think you stand securely on it,
Ask yourself on which step you stand,
So that we, the indolent, may also profit.
My friend, if you want to learn about all this,
Detach yourself from everything,
From what is senseless, from what seems intelligent.
Without detachment nothing can be learnt.
Experience alone can teach these things, not talk.
Even if these words once said
By one of God's elect strike harshly,
I repeat them to remind you:
He who has no foothold on this ladder,
Who does not ponder always on these things,
When he comes to die will know
Terrible fear, terrible dread,
Will be full of boundless panic.
My lines end on a note of terror.
Yet it is good that this is so:
Those who are hard of heart – myself the first –
Are led to repentance, led to a holy life,
Less by the lure of blessings promised
Than by fearful warnings that inspire dread.
'He who has ears to hear, let him hear.'
You who have written this, hear, then, and take note:
Void of all these graces,
How have you dared to write such things?
How do you not shudder to expound them?
Have you not heard what Uzzah suffered
When he tried to stop God's ark from falling?[1]

[1] 2 Sam. 6 : 6–7.

Do not think that I speak as one who teaches:
I speak as one whose words condemn himself,
Knowing the rewards awaiting those who strive,
Knowing my utter fruitlessness.

ST PETER OF DAMASKOS

Introductory Note

The works of St Peter of Damaskos occupy more space in the
Philokalia than those of any other author, with the one exception of St
Maximos the Confessor. Of the author's life and identity nothing
definite is known apart from the information to be gleaned from his
own writings. St Nikodimos identifies him with a certain Bishop Peter
the Hieromartyr, commemorated on 9 February, who suffered in
defence of the holy ikons around the middle of the eighth century: his
tongue, so it is recounted, was cut out at the orders of the Arab ruler
Walid, and he died in exile in southern Arabia. The Peter whose
works are included in the *Philokalia*, however, must be several
centuries later than this, since he refers by name to Symeon
Metaphrastis the Logothete, who died in the late tenth century.[1] But,
although often quoting from earlier authors, Peter nowhere cites
eleventh-century writers such as St Symeon the New Theologian or
Nikitas Stithatos. A thirteenth-century manuscript of his works dates
him to 1096–7, and another of the fourteenth century to 1156–7.[2] It
seems, then, that he belongs to the eleventh or more probably to the
twelfth century; he is in any event definitely earlier than the
fourteenth-century Hesychast controversy. Although he lived at a
time of worsening relations between Orthodoxy and Rome, he never
alludes to this.

From his name it appears St Peter's family was connected with
Damaskos, but it does not necessarily follow that Peter himself was
born or lived there. He is evidently a monk, writing for other monks.
He speaks of the three main types of monasticism – 'bodily obedience'
in a fully organized community, the hermit life, and the intermediate
or semi-eremitic path, with two or three monks pursuing a 'life of
silence' together in a *kellion* – and, following St John Klimakos, he

---

[1] See below, p. 103; on Symeon Metaphrastis, see also p. 283.
[2] See J. Gouillard, 'Un auteur spirituel byzantin du XIIᵉ siècle. Pierre Damascène', *Echos
d'Orient* xxxviii (1939), pp. 257–78.

commends above all the third of these forms, terming it the 'royal way'.[1] Perhaps, then, this was the form of monasticism which he himself was following. The content of his work confirms this: he says little about the social or communal aspects of the monastic vocation, little about visitors, hospitality or liturgical services. He is concerned throughout with the personal ascesis and prayer of the individual hesychast; and yet he does not envisage the situation of one who is entirely solitary, for he often mentions 'the brethren'.

St Peter himself explains how his work came to be written. 'Devout friends, who also cater for my physical needs', lent him Biblical and Patristic books (had he been living in a fully organized community, the monastery would have met his physical needs, and he would have been able to borrow books from the monastic library). As he read, he noted down passages that caught his attention, in the first instance for his personal use, as a safeguard against his own forgetfulness.[2] He also added connecting comments of his own, writing quickly, almost automatically, and – as he tells us – not knowing what he was going to say before he put pen to paper.[3] The resulting book, he believes, is based entirely on Scripture and the fathers: 'what is said here ... is not mine'.[4] He adds that he has sometimes, although by no means invariably, identified his sources by name, so as to encourage his readers to look up the author for themselves.[5] Of the sources named, the most frequent are St Basil the Great and St John Chrysostom, each mentioned 47 times; next come St John Klimakos (38 times), St Isaac of Nineveh ('the Syrian', 34 times), the Gerontikon or Sayings of the Desert Fathers (about 30 times), St John of Damaskos (28 times), and St Gregory of Nazianzos (23 times). There are fewer references to St Maximos the Confessor (19) and to Neilos/Evagrios (15), but Peter's work as a whole clearly stands in the Evagrian-Maximian tradition. Dionysios is cited only nine times, the Makarian Homilies no more than three times, and St Mark the Ascetic and St John Cassian only twice each. There are nine references to St Dorotheos of Gaza, but none to St Isaiah of Sketis/Gaza or to St Varsanuphios. Probably Peter had not consulted the original works of all the authors whom he cites, but relied at any rate in part on existing anthologies. We have tried to identify the more obvious of

[1] See p. 87. [2] pp. 74, 102–3, 182–3.
[3] p. 211–12. [4] p. 193. [5] p. 193.

his quotations, but have not attempted to provide exhaustive references; some of the allusions are very vague, and probably he does not always have a precise passage in mind. Where there is good reason to believe that a particular ascription is wrong, and the true author can be identified, we have changed the text accordingly.

As might be expected from the manner of composition, St Peter's work is not systematic. Although he makes use of various general schemes – the four cardinal virtues, the eight evil thoughts, the seven bodily actions, the eight stages of contemplation – there are constant digressions, repetitions and changes of theme. Book Two, with its *Twenty-Four Discourses* corresponding to the twenty-four letters of the Greek alphabet, possesses a more coherent structure than Book One; but even in Book Two, especially towards the end, there is often no clear sequence of thought. Chapter headings sometimes refer only to the opening sentence or paragraph of the section, while the rest deals with other matters.[1] But this outward lack of order would not greatly have troubled St Peter's monastic readers, who were interested not in abstract systems but in practical advice; and this the author has undoubtedly provided. Drawing as it does on such a wide range of earlier authorities, the work constitutes, in St Nikodimos' words, 'a recapitulation of holy watchfulness ... a circle within a circle, a concentrated *Philokalia* within the more extended *Philokalia*'.

In his spiritual teaching St Peter is balanced and moderate. Although writing for monks, he insists that salvation and spiritual knowledge are within the reach of everyone; continual prayer is possible in all situations without exception.[2] While emphasizing the need for ascetic effort on the human side, he never underestimates the supreme importance of divine aid: all that we have is a gift of God's grace. Tears, compunction and inward grief are often mentioned, especially in the first three of the eight stages of contemplation; but the predominant note is one of hope, and he has much to say about the universal scope of God's love and the sovereign liberty of the human will.

In common with many of his predecessors, St Peter is reserved about dreams and visions. He prefers, like Evagrios, to recommend imageless prayer – 'pure' prayer of the intellect, on a level above

---

[1] In our translation chapter headings are sometimes abbreviated or modified.
[2] pp. 83–4, 173, 193.

discursive thought. At the same time, however, he follows St Mark the Ascetic[1] in advocating a vivid and detailed meditation upon the incarnate life and more particularly the Passion of Christ; imageless prayer and imaginative meditation are in fact mentioned side by side in the ninth of the *Twenty-Four Discourses*.[2] While urging the repetition of the words 'Lord, have mercy',[3] he nowhere refers specifically to the Jesus Prayer. On frequent occasions he draws attention to the need for spiritual direction. In these and many other ways St Peter of Damaskos proves a faithful guide upon the spiritual way: as St Nikodimos justly claims, his work is a 'treasury of divine knowledge and wisdom'.[4]

[1] *Letter to Nicolas the Solitary* (*The Philokalia*, vol. i, pp. 155–6).

[2] pp. 234–6.

[3] pp. 145, 199.

[4] We have borrowed Nikodimos' phrase to provide a title for Book One, which in the original Greek is simply styled 'The Book of our Holy and God-bearing Father Peter of Damaskos'.

BOOK I

A Treasury of Divine Knowledge

INTRODUCTION

Because by God's grace I have been granted many great gifts and yet have never done anything good myself, I became frightened lest in my laziness and sloth I would forget His blessings – as well as my own faults and sins – and not even offer Him thanks or show my gratitude in any way. I have therefore written this treatise as a rebuke to my unhappy soul, putting in it whatever I have come across from the lives and writings of the holy fathers, citing them by name, so that I might have it by me as a reminder of their words, even though it is incomplete.

As I myself neither own nor ever have owned any books, I have borrowed them from devout friends, who also cater for my physical needs; and going through these books with great care out of love for God, I have then given them back to their owners. These books include first of all the Old and the New Testaments, that is, the Pentateuch, the Psalter, the Four Books of Kings, the Six Books of Wisdom, the Prophets, the Chronicles, the Acts of the Apostles, the Holy Gospels and the commentaries on all these; and then all the writings of the great fathers and teachers – Dionysios, Athanasios, Basil, Gregory the Theologian, John Chrysostom, Gregory of Nyssa, Antony, Arsenios, Makarios, Neilos, Ephrem, Isaac, Mark, John of Damaskos, John Klimakos, Maximos, Dorotheos, Philimon, as well as the lives and sayings of all the saints.

I went through all these slowly and diligently, trying to discover the root of man's destruction and salvation, and which of his actions or practices does or does not bring him to salvation. I wanted to find what it is that everyone seeks after, and how people served God in the past, and still serve Him today, in wealth or poverty, living among many sinners or in solitude, married or celibate: how, quite simply, in every circumstance and activity we find life or death, salvation or destruction. Even among us monks there are different situations: obedience to a spiritual father in all matters pertaining to body or soul; the stillness that purifies the soul; spiritual counsel in the place of obedience; the offices of abbot and bishop. In each of these situations, some find salvation and others perish.

This in itself astonished me; but I was astonished also by the fall of that erstwhile angel in heaven, immaterial by nature, clothed with wisdom and every virtue, who suddenly became a devil, darkness and ignorance, the beginning and end of all evil and malice. And then there was Adam, who enjoyed such honour and so many blessings, such familiarity with God, who was adorned with wisdom and virtue, alone in paradise with Eve: he suddenly became an exile, filled with passions, mortal, forced to labour with sweat and affliction. From him sprang the only two brothers in the world, Cain and Abel; and between them jealousy triumphed, and deceit, and these gave rise to murder, cursing and terror. I was astonished, too, by their descendants, whose sins were so many that they provoked the flood; and then, after God in His compassion had saved those in the ark, one of them – Canaan – was cursed, although it was his father Ham who had sinned: for in order not to abrogate God's blessing, righteous Noah cursed the son instead of the father (cf. Gen. 9 : 22–27). Then there were the tower of Babel, the people of Sodom, the Israelites, Solomon, the Ninevites, Gehazi, Judas, and all those who were endowed with blessings and yet turned to sin.

I was also astonished how God, who is good beyond all goodness and full of compassion, permits all the many and various trials and afflictions of the world. Some He allows as sufferings conducive to repentance. These include hunger, thirst, grief, privation of life's needs, abstinence from pleasure, the wasting of the body through asceticism, vigils, labours, hardships, prolific bitter tears, anguish, fear of death, of cross-examination, of being called to account, of living in hell with demons, the appalling day of judgment, the ignominy that is to fall on the whole world, the terror, the bitter searching out and assessment of one's acts, words and thoughts, the threats and the wrath; and in addition to these, the various agelong punishments, the useless lamenting and the ceaseless tears; the unrelieved darkness, the fear, the pain, the exile, the dismay, the oppression, the throttling of the soul in this world and in the next. And then there are all the dangers facing one in this world: shipwrecks, illnesses of every kind, lightning, thunder, hail, earthquake, famine, tidal waves, untimely deaths – all the painful things that God allows to happen to us against our will.

Other things are willed not by God but by ourselves or by the demons. These include battles, passions, the whole range of sins from folly to despair and final destruction, of which our treatise will speak as it goes on; the attack of demons, wars, the tyranny of the passions; the derelictions, dislocations and vicissitudes of life; the anger, slander and all the affliction that we of our own will bring upon ourselves and one another against God's will. Again I was astonished how, though beset by such evils, many have been saved, and that nothing has been able to prevent this. On the other hand, many have perished against God's will.

When from my laborious study of the Scriptures I became aware of all these things, and many more, my soul was shattered and often I felt quite helpless, like spilt water. I did not fully grasp the significance of what I read; indeed, had I done so, I would not have been able to remain in this life, filled as it is with sin and disobedience to God, which produce all the evils of this world and the next. Nevertheless, through God's grace, I came upon the answers I sought for, and saw, from my reading of the holy fathers, that we have to make certain distinctions.

First, we must recognize that the starting-point of all our spiritual development is the natural knowledge given us by God, whether this comes through the Scriptures by human agency, or by means of the angel that is given in divine baptism to guard the soul of every believer, to act as his conscience and to remind him of the divine commandments of Christ. If the baptized person keeps these commandments, the grace of the Holy Spirit is preserved in him.

Then, alongside this knowledge, there is our capacity to choose. This is the beginning of our salvation; by our free choice we abandon our own wishes and thoughts and do what God wishes and thinks. If we succeed in doing this, there is no object, no activity or place in the whole of creation that can prevent us from becoming what God from the beginning has wished us to be: that is to say, according to His image and likeness, gods by adoption through grace, dispassionate, just, good and wise, whether we are rich or poor, married or unmarried, in authority and free or under obedience and in bond-age – in short, whatever our time, place or activity. That is why, alike before the Law, under the Law and under grace, there have been many righteous men – men who preferred the knowledge of God and His will to their own thoughts and wishes. Yet there were also many who have perished in these same times and in the same circumstances, because they preferred their own thoughts and wishes to those of God.

This, then, is the general picture. But situations and pursuits vary, and one needs to acquire discrimination, either through the humility given by God or through questioning those who possess the gifts of discrimination. For without discrimination nothing that comes to pass is good, even if we in our ignorance think that it is. But when through discrimination we learn how it lies in our power to attain what we wish, then what we do begins to conform to God's will.

Only, as has been said, in all things we ought to renounce our own will so as to attain the goal God has set for us and to pursue whatever He wishes. Unless we do this we can never be saved. For since Adam's transgression we are all subject to the passions because of our constant association with them. We do not gladly pursue goodness, nor do we long for the knowledge of God, nor do we do good out of love, as the dispassionate do; instead we cling to our passions and our vices and do not aspire at all to do what is good unless constrained by the fear of punishment. And this is the case with those who receive God's word with firm faith and purpose. The rest of us do not even aspire to this extent, but we regard the afflictions of this life and the punishments to come as of no account and are wholeheartedly enslaved to our passions. Some of us do not even perceive our desperate plight, and only under constraint and reluctantly engage in the struggle for virtue. And in our ignorance we long for what merits our hatred.

Just as sick people need surgery and cautery to recover the health they have lost, so we need trials, and toils of repentance, and fear of death and punishment, so that we may regain our former health of soul and shake off the sickness which our folly has induced. The more the Physician of our souls bestows upon us voluntary and involuntary suffering, the more we should thank Him for His compassion and accept the suffering joyfully. For it is to help us that He increases our tribulation, both through the sufferings we willingly embrace in our repentance and through the trials and punishments not subject to our will. In this way, if we voluntarily accept affliction, we will be freed from our sickness and from the punishments to come, and perhaps even from present punishments as well. Even if we are not grateful, our Physician in His grace will still heal us, although by means of chastisement and manifold trials. But if we cling to our disease and persist in it, we will deservedly bring upon ourselves agelong punishment. We will have made ourselves like the demons and so will justly share with them the agelong punishments prepared for them; for, like them, we will have scorned our Benefactor.

We do not all receive blessings in the same way. Some, on receiving the fire of the Lord, that is, His word, put it into practice and so become softer of heart, like wax, while others through laziness become harder than clay and altogether stone-like. And no one compels us to receive these blessings in different ways. It is as with the sun whose rays illumine all the world: the person who wants to see it can do so, while the person who does not want to see it is not forced to, so that he alone is to blame for his lightless condition. For God made both the sun and man's eyes, but how man uses them depends on himself. Similarly, then, God irradiates knowledge to all and at the same time He gives us faith as an eye through which we can perceive it.

If we choose to grasp this knowledge firmly by means of faith, we can keep ourselves mindful of it by putting it into practice; and God then gives us greater ardour, knowledge and power. For our pursuit of natural knowledge kindles our ardour, and this ardour increases our capacity to put the knowledge into practice. By putting it into practice we keep ourselves mindful of it, and this in its turn induces us to practise it to an even greater extent. Greater practice is rewarded by greater knowledge; and from the understanding thus acquired we gain control of the passions and learn how to endure our sufferings patiently. Sufferings produce devotion to God and a recognition of His gifts and our faults. These give birth to gratitude, and gratitude inculcates the fear of God which leads us to the keeping of the commandments, to inward grief, gentleness and humility. These three virtues produce discrimination, which gives us spiritual insight and makes it possible for the intellect in its purity to foresee coming faults and to forestall them through its experience and recollection of what has happened in the past; in this way it can protect itself against stealthy attacks. All this generates hope, and from hope come detachment and perfect love.

Once we have advanced thus far we shall not wish for anything except the will of God; rather we will joyfully abandon this transitory life out of love for God and for our fellow-men. Through the wisdom and indwelling of the Holy Spirit and through adoption to sonship, we are crucified with Christ and buried with Him, and we rise with Him and ascend with Him spiritually by imitating His way of life in this world. To speak simply, we become gods by adoption through grace, receiving the pledge of eternal blessedness, as St Gregory the Theologian says.[1] In this way, with regard to the eight evil thoughts,[2] we become dispassionate, just, good and wise, having God within ourselves – as Christ Himself has told us (cf. John 14 : 21–23) – through the keeping of the commandments in order, from the first to the last. I will speak below about how the commandments should be practised.

Since we have spoken of the knowledge of the virtues, we will also speak about the passions. Knowledge comes like light from the sun. The foolish man through lack of faith or laziness deliberately closes his eyes – that is, his faculty of choice – and at once consigns the knowledge to oblivion because in his indolence he fails to put it into practice. For folly leads to indolence, and this in turn begets inertia and hence forgetfulness. Forgetfulness breeds self-love – the love of one's own will and thoughts – which is equivalent to the love of pleasure and praise. From self-love comes avarice, the root of all evils (cf. 1 Tim. 6 : 10), for it entangles us in worldly concerns and in this way leads to complete unawareness of God's gifts and of our own faults. It is now that the eight ruling passions take up residence: gluttony, which leads to unchastity, which breeds avarice, which gives rise to anger when we fail to attain what we want – that is, fail to have our own way. This produces dejection, and dejection engenders first listlessness and then self-esteem; and self-esteem leads to pride. From these eight passions come every evil, passion and sin. Those consumed by them are led to despair and utter destruction; they fall away from God and become like the demons, as has already been said.

Man stands at the crossroads between righteousness and sin, and chooses whichever path he wishes. But after that the path which he has chosen to follow, and the guides assigned to it, whether angels and saints or demons and sinners, will lead him to the end of it, even

[1] Gregory of Nazianzos, *Orations* 29, 19; 45, 3 and 7 (*P.G.* xxxvi, 100A, 628A, 632B).
[2] Cf. *The Philokalia*, vol. i, p. 73.

if he has no wish to go there. The good guides lead him toward God and the kingdom of heaven, the evil guides toward the devil and agelong punishment. But nothing and no one is to blame for his destruction except his own free will. For God is the God of salvation, bestowing on us, along with being and well-being, the knowledge and strength that we cannot have without the grace of God. Not even the devil can destroy a man, compelling him to choose wrongly, or reducing him to impotence or enforced ignorance, or anything else: he can only suggest evil to him.

Thus he who acts rightly should ascribe the grace of so doing to God, for along with our being He has given us everything else. But the person who has opted for the path of evil, and actually commits evil, should blame only himself, for no one can force him to commit it, since God created him with free will. Hence he will merit God's praise when he chooses the path of goodness; for he does so, not from any necessity of his nature, as is the case with animals and inanimate things that participate passively in goodness, but as befits a being that God has honoured with the gift of intelligence. We ourselves deliberately and wilfully choose to do evil, being coached in it by its discoverer. God, who is good beyond goodness, does not force us, lest being forced and still disobeying we should be even more culpable. Nor does He take from us the freedom that in His goodness He has bestowed upon us.

Let him who wants to act rightly entreat God in prayer, and at once knowledge and power will be given him. In this way it will be evident that the grace bestowed by God was justly given; for it was given after prayer, although it could have been given without prayer. No praise, however, is due to the man who accepts the air by means of which he lives, knowing that without it life is impossible; rather he himself owes thanks to his Creator, who has given him a nose and the health to breathe and live. Similarly, we also should rather thank God because in His grace He has created our prayer, our knowledge, our strength, our virtue, all our circumstances and our very selves. And not only has He done all this, but He ceaselessly does whatever He can to overcome our wickedness and that of our enemies, the demons.

Even the devil, having lost the knowledge of God, and so inevitably becoming ignorant in his ingratitude and pride, cannot of himself know what to do. On the contrary, he sees what God does to save us and maliciously learns from this and contrives similar things for our destruction. For he hates God and, being unable to fight Him directly, he fights against us who are in God's image, thinking to avenge himself on God in this way; and, as St John Chrysostom says, he finds us obedient to his will. For instance, he sees how God created Eve as a helpmate for Adam, and so he enlists her co-operation to bring about disobedience and transgression. Or, again, God gave a commandment so that by keeping it Adam might be mindful of the great gifts he had received and thank his Benefactor for them; but the devil made of this commandment the starting-point for disobedience and death. Instead of prophets, he promotes false prophets; instead of apostles, false apostles; instead of law, lawlessness; instead of virtues, vice; instead of commandments, transgressions; instead of righteousness, foul heresies.

In addition, when the devil saw Christ descending in His extreme goodness to the holy martyrs and revered fathers, appearing either in Himself or through angels or in some other ineffable form, he began to fabricate numerous delusions in order to destroy people. It is on account of this that the fathers, in their discrimination, wrote that one should not pay any attention to such diabolic manifestations, whether they come through images, or light, or fire, or some other deceptive form.[1] For the devil can deceive even in sleep or through the senses. If we accept such delusions, he makes the intellect, in its utter ignorance and self-conceit, depict various shapes or colours so that we think that this is a manifestation of God or of an angel. Often in sleep, or to our senses when awake, he shows us demons that are apparently defeated. In short, he does all he can to destroy us by making us succumb to these delusions.

In spite of all this, the devil will fail in his purpose if we apply the counsel of the holy fathers: that during the time of prayer we should keep our intellect free from form, shape, and colour,[2] and not give access to anything at all, whether light, fire or anything else; and that we should do all we can to confine our mind solely to the words we are saying,[3] since he who prays only with his mouth prays to the wind and not to God. For, unlike men, God is attentive to the intellect and not to the words spoken. We must worship, it is said, 'in spirit and in

---

[1] Cf. Diadochos, On Spiritual Knowledge 36–7 (The Philokalia, vol. i, pp. 263–4).
[2] Cf. Evagrios, On Prayer 67, 114, 117 (The Philokalia, vol. i, pp. 63, 68).
[3] Cf. John Klimakos, Ladder, Step 28 (1132C; E.T., p. 252).

truth' (John 4 : 24); and again, 'I had rather speak five words whose
meaning I understand than ten thousand words in a strange tongue' (1
Cor. 14 : 19).

It is now that the devil, having failed in all his other schemes,
tempts us with thoughts of despair: he tries to persuade us that in the
past things were different and that the men through whom God
performed wonders for the strengthening of the faith were not like
us. He also tells us that there is now no need for such exertion. For
are we not now all of us Christians and all baptized? 'He who believes
and is baptized shall be saved' (Mark 16 : 16). What more do we
need? But if we succumb to this temptation and remain as we are, we
will be completely barren. We will be Christians only in name, not
realizing that he who has believed and been baptized must keep all
Christ's commandments; and even when he has succeeded in doing
this, he should say, 'I am a useless servant' (Luke 17 : 10), as the
Lord told His apostles when He instructed them to carry out all He
had laid down for them.

Everyone who is baptized renounces the devil, saying, 'I renounce
Satan and all his works, and I join myself to Christ and all His works.'
But where is our renunciation, if we do not abandon every passion
and desist from every sinful act that the devil promotes? Rather, let us
hate such things with all our soul and show our love for Christ
through the keeping of His commandments. And how shall we keep
His commandments unless we relinquish our own will and thought –
the will and thought, that is to say, which are opposed to the
commandments of God?

There are often people who because of personal temperament or
out of habit do in fact choose what is good in certain situations and
hate what is evil. And there are also good thoughts, as the Scriptures
attest, although they require the discrimination of those who possess
experience; for without discrimination even those thoughts that seem
good are not in fact good, either because they come at the wrong
time, or are unnecessary, or unworthy, or are not properly understood. For unless both the questioner and he who is questioned are
attentive not only to the Scriptures but also to the question raised,
they will miss the meaning of what has been said, and the resulting
damage will be serious. I myself have often found this, both when
asking and when being asked; and when afterwards I have understood the true sense of the passage under discussion, I have been

amazed to learn how the words can be the same, but the meaning very different.

Thus we need discrimination in all things if we are to know how to act so as to do the will of God. For God, as the creator of all things, knows our nature thoroughly and has ordered all things for our benefit; and He has laid down laws that accord with our nature and are not alien to it, even though they are not capable of leading to perfection those who voluntarily aspire to attain God in a way that transcends nature. For that requires the more than natural qualities of virginity, deliberate poverty, humility – not of gratitude, for this is natural. Humility is more than natural, since the humble man pursues every virtue and, though not a debtor, he regards himself as the greatest debtor of all. The grateful person, on the other hand, will simply acknowledge the debt he owes. Similarly, the merciful man who performs his acts of charity by drawing on his possessions remains within the bounds of nature, and does not go beyond them as does the person who deliberately gives away all he possesses. Again, marriage is natural, while virginity is a more than natural grace. The person who remains within the bounds of nature is saved if he abandons his own will and fulfils that of God; but to the person who transcends these bounds God will give the crown of endurance and glory, because he has renounced not only what is forbidden by the law but also, with God's help, his own nature. He loves the supranatural God with all his soul and imitates His dispassion with all his strength.

Yet since we are ignorant not merely of ourselves and of what we do, but also of the purpose of what is done and of the true goal of everything, the divine Scriptures and the words of the saints, whether prophets and righteous men of old or more recent holy fathers, appear to us to be contradictory. Those who wish to be saved appear to disagree with one another. But in reality this is not the case.

Briefly, we may say that in the nature of things, if someone wants to be saved, no person and no time, place or occupation can prevent him. He must not, however, act contrary to the objective that he has in view, but must with discrimination refer every thought to the divine purpose. Things do not happen out of necessity: they depend upon the person through whom they happen. We do not sin against our will, but we first assent to an evil thought and so fall into captivity. Then the thought itself carries the captive forcibly and against his wishes into sin. The same is true of sins that occur through ignorance: they arise from sins consciously committed. For unless a man is drunk with either wine or desire, he is not unaware of what he is doing; but such drunkenness obscures the intellect and so it falls, and dies as a result. Yet that death has not come about inexplicably: it has been unwittingly induced by the drunkenness to which we consciously assented. We will find many instances, especially in our thoughts, where we fall from what is within our control to what is outside it, and from what we are consciously aware of to what is unwitting. But because the first appears unimportant and attractive, we slip unintentionally and unawares into the second. Yet if from the start we had wanted to keep the commandments and to remain as we were when baptized, we would not have fallen into so many sins or have needed the trials and tribulations of repentance.

If we so wish, however, God's second gift of grace – repentance – can lead us back to our former beauty. But if we fail to repent, inevitably we will depart with the unrepentant demons into agelong punishment, more by our own free choice than against our will. Yet God did not create us for wrath but for salvation (cf. 1 Thess. 5 : 9), so that we might enjoy His blessings; and we should therefore be thankful and grateful towards our Benefactor. But our failure to get to know His gifts has made us indolent, and indolence has made us forgetful, with the result that ignorance lords it over us.

We have to make strenuous efforts when we first try to return to where we fell from. For we resent abandoning our own desires, and we think that we can carry out both God's wishes and our own – which is impossible. Our Lord Himself said, 'I have come to do, not My own will, but the will of the Father who sent Me' (cf. John 6 : 38), even though the will of Father, Son and Holy Spirit is one, since they constitute a single inseparable nature. But He said this on our account and with respect to the will of the flesh. For if the flesh is not consumed and if a man is not wholly led by the Spirit of God, he will not do the will of God unless he is forced to. But when the grace of the Spirit rules within him, then he no longer has a will of his own, but whatever he does is according to God's will. Then he is at peace. Men like that will be called sons of God (cf. Matt. 5 : 9), because they will the will of their Father, as did the Son of God who is also God.

Yet it is impossible to discover the will of God unless we keep the commandments, thereby cutting off all pleasure or personal will, and unless we endure all the pain that this involves. As has been said, pleasure and pain are born of folly, and they give rise to all evil. For the foolish man loves himself and cannot love his brother or God; he can neither refrain from pleasure or from the desires that give him satisfaction, nor can he endure pain. Sometimes he gets what he wants, and then he is filled with pleasure and elation; sometimes he does not get it and, completely dominated by the pain which this engenders, he is cast down and dejected, experiencing a foretaste of hell.

From knowledge, or understanding, is born self-control and patient endurance. For the man of understanding restrains his own will and endures the resulting pain; and, regarding himself as unworthy of anything pleasant, he is grateful and thankful to his Benefactor, fearing lest because of the many blessings that God has given him in this world he should suffer punishment in the world to come. Thus through self-control he practises the other virtues as well. He looks on himself as in God's debt for everything, finding nothing whatsoever with which to repay to his Benefactor, and even thinking that his virtues simply increase his debt. For he receives and has nothing to give. He only asks that he may be allowed to offer thanks to God. Yet even the fact that God accepts his thanks puts him, so he thinks, into still greater debt. But he continues to give thanks, ever doing what is good and reckoning himself an ever greater debtor, in his humility considering himself lower than all men, delighting in God his Benefactor and trembling even as he rejoices (cf. Ps. 2 : 11).

As he advances through this humility towards divine and unfailing love, he accepts sufferings as though he deserved them. Indeed, he thinks he deserves more suffering than he encounters; and he is glad that he has been granted some affliction in this world, since through it he may be spared a portion of the punishments which he has prepared for himself in the world to be. And because in all this he knows his own weakness, and that he should not exult, and because he has been found worthy of knowing and enduring these things by the grace of God, he is filled with a strong longing for God.

Humility is born of spiritual knowledge, and such knowledge is born of trials and temptations. To the person who knows himself is given knowledge of all things,[1] and he who subjects himself to God

---

[1] Cf. Clement of Alexandria, *Pedagogue* III, i. 1.

brings every material thought under his control; and then all things are subject to him, for he is completely humble. According to St Basil and St Gregory,[1] he who knows himself – who knows, that is to say, that he stands midway between nobility and baseness, in that he has a soul capable of spiritual knowledge and a mortal, earthly body – never exults or despairs. Rather, with a feeling of shame before his noetic soul he rejects everything shameful and, knowing his weakness, he shrinks from all sense of elation.

Thus he who knows his own weakness as a result of the many temptations and trials that he undergoes through the passions of soul and body, understands the measureless power of God and how He redeems the humble who cry out to Him through persistent prayer from the depths of their hearts. For such a person prayer becomes a delight. He knows that without God he can do nothing (cf. John 15 : 5), and in his fear lest he fall he strives to cleave to God and is amazed as he considers how God has rescued him from so many temptations and passions. He gives thanks to his Saviour, and to his thanksgiving he adds humility and love; and he does not dare to judge anyone, knowing that as God has helped him, so He can help all men when He wishes, as St Maximos says. He knows, too, that if a person realizes his weakness he may be able to fight and conquer many passions; for in such a case God swiftly comes to his assistance, lest his soul be utterly destroyed. And for many other reasons as well the person who recognizes his own weakness does not fall. No one can attain this recognition unless he first suffers many temptations of soul and body, and gains experience by enduring them patiently and so overcoming them with God's strength.

Such a man does not dare to act according to his own volition or to depend on his own ideas without first questioning those with experience. For what does a person gain by choosing to do or to think something that does not contribute to his bodily life or to the salvation of his soul? And if he does not know what wish he should abandon and what thought he should put aside, let him test every action and every thought by holding back from it with self-control and by seeing how that affects him. If its realization brings pleasure, but resisting it brings pain, then it is something bad and he should reject it before it takes root; otherwise he will find it hard to overcome it

[1] Gregory of Nazianzos, *Oration* 45, 7 (*P.G.* xxxvi, 632AB).

later, when he sees what damage it does. This applies to every action or thought which does not help us to keep ourselves alive and to conform to God's will. For a long-standing habit assumes the strength of nature; but if you do not give way to it, it loses strength and is gradually destroyed. Whether a habit is good or bad, time nourishes it, just as wood feeds a fire. Thus, so far as we can, we should cultivate and practise what is good, so that it becomes an established habit operating automatically and effortlessly when required. It was through victories in small things that the fathers won their great battles.

For if a man refuses to satisfy even the basic needs of the body, but rejects them in order to travel along the strait and narrow road, how can he ever fall victim to the love of possessions? Love of possessions consists not merely in owning many things, but also in attachment to them, or in their misuse or excessive use. For many of the saints of old, such as Abraham, Job, David and many others, had extensive possessions, but they were not attached to them: they held them as a gift from God and sought to please Him all the more through their use of them. Nevertheless the Lord, being beyond perfection and being wisdom itself, strikes at the root: for He urges those who would follow Him through the imitation of supreme virtue to renounce not only material goods or possessions, but even their own soul (cf. Luke 14 : 26), that is to say, their own thoughts and will.

Because they knew this, the fathers fled from the world as a hindrance to perfection; and not only from the world but also from their own will for the same reason. No one of them ever did what he himself wanted. Some lived in bodily obedience, so that in the place of Christ they would have a spiritual father guiding their every thought. Others, fleeing totally from human society, lived in the desert and had God himself as their teacher, for whose sake they chose to undergo a voluntary death. Others pursued the 'royal way',[1] leading a life of silence with one or two companions: these had one another as counsellors in doing God's will. And those who, after being subject to a spiritual father, were then appointed by him to take charge of other brethren, carried out their task as if they were themselves still under obedience, keeping the traditions of their own spiritual fathers. Thus all their efforts were blessed by God.

[1] Cf. John Klimakos, *Ladder*, Step 1 (641D; E.T., p. 56).

Nowadays, however, whether we are under obedience or in authority, we are not willing to abandon our own will, and so none of us makes any progress. None the less, it is still possible to escape from human society and from worldly affairs, and to take the 'royal way' through living the life of stillness with one or two others, studying the commandments of Christ and all the Scriptures day and night. By this means, through being tested in all things by our conscience and application, by reading and by prayer, we may perhaps attain the first commandment, the fear of God, which comes through faith and the study of the Holy Scriptures; and through this we may achieve inward grief, and so arrive at the commandments of which St Paul spoke: faith, hope and love (cf. 1 Cor. 13 : 13). For he who has faith in the Lord fears chastisement; and this fear prompts him to keep the commandments. The keeping of the commandments leads him to endure affliction; and the enduring of affliction produces hope in God. Such hope separates the intellect from all material attachment; and the person freed from such attachment possesses love for God. Whoever follows this sequence will be saved.

Stillness, which is the basis of the soul's purification, makes the observance of the commandments relatively painless. 'Flee,' it has been said, 'keep silence, be still, for herein lie the roots of sinlessness.' Again it has been said: 'Flee men and you will be saved.'[1] For human society does not permit the intellect to perceive either its own faults or the wiles of the demons, so as to guard itself against them. Nor, on the other hand, does it allow the intellect to perceive God's providence and bounty, so as to acquire in this way knowledge of God and humility.

That is why whoever wishes to travel the shortest road to Christ – the road of dispassion and spiritual knowledge – and joyfully to attain perfection, should not turn either to the right or to the left, but in his whole way of life should journey diligently along the royal way. He should steer a middle course between excess and insufficiency, as both engender pleasure. He should not obscure the intellect with excessive food and conviviality, making himself blind through such distractions; but neither should he cloud his mind through prolonged fasts and vigils. Rather, he should carefully and patiently practise the seven forms of bodily discipline as though climbing a ladder,

[1] *Apophthegmata*, alphabetical collection, Arsenios 1–2; E.T. Sister Benedicta Ward, *The Sayings of the Desert Fathers: The Alphabetical Collection* (2nd ed., London/Oxford, 1981), p. 9.

mastering them once and for all and advancing towards that moral state in which, as the Lord has said (cf. Matt. 13 : 11–12), by God's grace the different stages of spiritual contemplation are given to the believer.

All Scripture is inspired by God and profitable (cf. 2 Tim. 3 : 16), and no one can thwart someone who wishes to be saved. Only God who made us has power over us, and He is ready to help and protect from every temptation those who cry out to Him and want to do His holy will. Without Him we can do nothing (cf. John 15 : 5): we cannot even suffer evil against our will unless God permits it in order to chastise us and save our souls. But the evil that we commit ourselves is our own responsibility and arises from our own laziness with the help of the demons. On the other hand, all knowledge, strength and virtue are the grace of God, as are all other things. And through grace He has given all men the power to become sons of God (cf. John 1 : 12) by keeping the divine commandments. Or, rather, these commandments keep us, and are the grace of God, since without His grace we cannot keep them. We have nothing to offer Him except our faith, our resolution and, in brief, all the true dogmas that we hold with firm faith through the teaching we have heard (cf. Rom. 10 : 17). With all this in mind, let us set to work undistractedly, as though beginning lessons at school, and in this way carefully learn about the seven forms of discipline to which we have referred.

THE SEVEN FORMS OF BODILY DISCIPLINE

The first of these forms of discipline consists in stillness,[1] or in living a life without distraction, far from all worldly care. By removing ourselves from human society and distraction, we escape from turmoil and from him who 'walks about like a roaring lion, seeking whom he may devour' (1 Pet. 5 : 8) through idle talk and the worries of life. Instead, we have but one concern: how to do God's will and to

---

[1] Stillness (*hesychia*) means in Greek not only inner tranquillity (see the Glossary) but also exterior withdrawal into solitude: hence its inclusion, at first sight somewhat unexpectedly, among the forms of *bodily* discipline.

prepare our soul so that it is not condemned when we die; and how with complete attention to learn about the snares of the demons and our own faults which, being more in number than the sands of the sea and like dust in their fineness, pass unrecognized by most people. Ever mourning, we grieve over human nature but are comforted by God. For in our gratitude we are encouraged because we have come to see what we could never have hoped to perceive had we lived outside our cell. Having recognized our own weakness and the power of God, we are filled with fear and hope, so that we neither lapse through ignorance because we are too sure of ourselves nor, when some misfortune befalls us, fall into despair because we have forgotten God's compassion.

The second form of bodily discipline consists in moderate fasting. We should eat once a day and then not to the point of satiety. We should eat one kind of simple and readily accessible food – if possible, the kind of food that we do not relish particularly. In this way we can overcome gluttony, greed and desire, and live without distraction. But we should not refuse any kind of food completely, lest thereby we wrongly reject things that, being created by God, are 'wholly good and beautiful' (Gen. 1 : 31).[1] Nor should we gulp everything down at once, indulgently and without restraint; but each day we should eat one kind of thing, with self-control. We should use all things for the glory of God, and we should not refuse anything on the grounds that it is evil, as the accursed heretics do. We may drink wine when appropriate: in old age, sickness and cold weather it is most helpful, but must be drunk only in small quantities. When we are young and in good health, and the weather is warm, water is better, though we should drink it as little as possible. For thirst is the best of all bodily disciplines.

The third form of discipline consists in keeping moderate vigils. We should sleep for half the night and the other half we should

---

[1] The Greek word used here is not *agathos* (good) but *kalos*, a term that in the Septuagint, and in the Greek patristic tradition as a whole, denotes the beautiful no less and sometimes more than the good. To speak of creation and created things as beautiful does not of course mean only that they are pleasing to look at. What is implicit in this context is the understanding that physical beauty is an epiphany of divine beauty: physical beauty is related to moral beauty, and both are related to their origin in the world of incorporeal essences (*logoi*: see *Logos* in the Glossary) and its principle, the Good itself, or God. It is with these connotations in mind that the term should be read, as indeed it should be read in the actual title of *The Philokalia* (cf. vol. i, p. 13).

devote to the recital of psalms and to prayer, compunctive sorrow, and tears. Through this judicious fasting and vigil the body will become pliable to the soul, healthy and ready for every good work; while the soul will gain in fortitude and illumination, so as to see and to do what is right.

The fourth form of discipline consists in the recital of psalms – that is to say, in prayer expressed in a bodily way through psalms and prostrations. This is in order to gall the body and humble the soul, so that our enemies the demons may take flight and our allies the angels come to us, and we may know from where we receive help. Otherwise in ignorance we may grow arrogant, thinking that what we do is due to ourselves. If that happens, we will be forsaken by God so that we may recognize our own weakness.

The fifth form of discipline consists in spiritual prayer, prayer that is offered by the intellect and free from all thoughts. During such prayer the intellect is concentrated within the words spoken and, inexpressibly contrite, it abases itself before God, asking only that His will may be done in all its pursuits and conceptions. It does not pay attention to any thought, shape, colour, light, fire, or anything at all of this kind; but, conscious that it is watched by God and communing with Him alone, it is free from form, colour and shape. Such is the pure prayer appropriate for those still engaged in ascetic practice; for the contemplative there are yet higher forms of prayer.

The sixth form of discipline consists in reading the writings and lives of the fathers, paying no attention to strange doctrines, or to other people, especially heretics. In this way we learn from the divine Scriptures and from the discrimination of the fathers how to conquer the passions and acquire the virtues. Our intellects will be filled with the thoughts of the Holy Spirit, and we will forget the unseemly words and conceptions to which we gave our attention before we became monks. Moreover, through deep communion in prayer and reading we will be able to grasp precious meanings; for prayer is helped by reading in stillness, and reading is helped by pure prayer, so long as we attend to what is being said and do not read or recite carelessly. It is true, however, that we cannot properly understand the full significance of what we read because of the darkness induced by the passions; our presumption often leads us astray, especially when we rely on the wisdom of this world which we think we possess, and do not realize that we need knowledge based on experience to understand these things, and that if we wish to attain knowledge of God mere reading or listening is not enough. For reading and listening are one thing and experience is another. One cannot become a craftsman simply by hearsay: one has to practise, and watch, and make numerous mistakes, and be corrected by those with experience, so that through long perseverance and by eliminating one's own desires one eventually masters the art. Similarly, spiritual knowledge is not acquired simply through study but is given by God through grace to the humble. That a person on reading the Scriptures may think that he partially understands their meaning need cause no surprise, especially if that person is at the stage of ascetic practice. But he does not possess the knowledge of God; he simply hears the words of those who do possess this knowledge. Writers like the prophets often did indeed possess divine knowledge, but as yet the ordinary reader does not. So it is in my own case: I have collected material from the Holy Scriptures, but have not been found worthy of learning directly from the Holy Spirit; I have learnt only from those who did learn directly from the Holy Spirit. It is like learning about a person or a city from those who have actually seen them.

The seventh form of bodily discipline consists in questioning those with experience about all our thoughts and actions, in case we go astray because of our inexperience and self-satisfaction, thinking and doing one thing after another, and so become presumptuous, imagining that we know as we should, although we still know nothing, as St Paul says (cf. 1 Cor. 8 : 2).

In addition to practising these seven bodily disciplines, we should patiently endure all that God allows to happen to us so that we may learn and gain experience and knowledge of our weaknesses. We should neither grow too bold nor fall into despair, whatever happens to us, whether good or bad. We should repudiate every dream and every idle word or action, and should always meditate on God's name, at every moment, in every place, in all we do, as something more precious than breath itself. And we should sincerely abase ourselves before God, withdrawing the intellect from all worldly thoughts, seeking only that God's will may be done. Then the intellect will begin to see that its faults are like the sand of the sea. This is the beginning of the soul's illumination and a sign of its health: the soul becomes contrite and the heart humble, and truly regards itself as the least of things. Then we begin to understand God's blessings, whether particular or all-embracing, of which the Holy Scriptures speak; and we begin to understand also our own offences. We start to keep all the commandments, from the first to the last, fully aware of what we are doing. For the Lord has established them like a ladder, and we cannot miss one out and go on to the next: as with steps, we must go from the first to the second, from the second to the third, and so on. In the end they make man a god, through the grace of Him who has given the commandments to those who choose to keep them.

THE SEVEN COMMANDMENTS

If we want to make a start, we must concentrate on the practice of these seven forms of bodily discipline and on nothing else: otherwise we will fall over a precipice or, rather, into chaos. In the case both of the seven gifts of the Spirit and of the Lord's Beatitudes, we are taught that if we do not begin with fear, we can never ascend to the rest. For, as David says, 'the fear of the Lord is the beginning of wisdom' (Ps. 111 : 10). Another inspired prophet describes the seven gifts as 'the spirit of wisdom and understanding, the spirit of counsel and strength, the spirit of knowledge and reverence, the spirit of the fear of God' (cf. Isa. 11 : 2–3). Our Lord Himself began his teaching by speaking of fear; for He says, 'Blessed are the poor in spirit' (Matt. 5 : 3), that is, those who quail with fear of God and are inexpressibly contrite in soul. For the Lord has established this as the basic commandment, knowing that without this even living in heaven would be profitless, for one would still possess the same madness through which the devil, Adam and many others have fallen.

If, then, we wish to keep the first commandment – that is, to possess fear of the Lord – we should meditate deeply upon the contingencies of life already described and upon God's measureless and unfathomable blessings. We should consider how much He has done and continues to do for our sake through things visible and invisible, through commandments and dogmas, threats and promises; how He guards, nourishes and provides for us, giving us life and saving us from enemies seen and unseen; how through the prayers and intercessions of His saints He cures the diseases caused by our own disarray; how He is always long-suffering over our sins, our irreverence, our delinquency – over all those things that we have done, are doing, and will do, from which His grace has saved us; how He is patient over our actions, words and thoughts that have provoked His anger; and how He not only suffers us, but even bestows greater blessings on us, acting directly, or through the angels, the Scriptures, through righteous men and prophets, apostles and martyrs, teachers and holy fathers.

Moreover, we should not only recall the sufferings and struggles of the saints and martyrs, but should also reflect with wonder on the self-abasement of our Lord Jesus Christ, the way He lived in the world, His pure Passion, the Cross, His death, burial, resurrection and ascension, the advent of the Holy Spirit, the indescribable miracles that are always occurring every day, paradise, the crowns of glory, the adoption to sonship that He has accorded us, and all the things contained in Holy Scripture and so much else. If we bring all this to mind, we will be amazed at God's compassion, and with trembling will marvel at His forbearance and patience. We will grieve because of what our nature has lost – angel-like dispassion, paradise and all the blessings which we have forfeited – and because of the evils into which we have fallen: demons, passions and sins. In this way our soul will be filled with contrition, thinking of all the ills that have been caused by our wickedness and the trickery of the demons.

So it is that God grants us the blessing of inward grief, which constitutes the second commandment. For, as Christ says, 'Blessed are those who grieve' (Matt. 5 : 4) – who grieve for themselves and also, out of love and compassion, for others as well. We become as one who mourns a dead person, because we perceive the terrible consequences that the things we have done before our death will have for us after we are dead; and we weep bitterly, from the depths of our heart and with inexpressible sorrow. Worldly honour or dishonour no longer concerns us; we become indifferent to life itself, often forgetting even to eat because of the pain in our heart and our ceaseless lamentation.

In this way God's grace, our universal mother, will give us gentleness, so that we begin to imitate Christ. This constitutes the third commandment; for the Lord says, 'Blessed are the gentle' (Matt. 5 : 5). Thus we become like a firmly-rooted rock, unshaken by the storms and tempests of life, always the same, whether rich or poor, in ease or hardship, in honour or dishonour. In short, at every moment and whatever we do we will be aware that all things, whether sweet or bitter, pass away, and that this life is a path leading to the future life. We will recognize that, whether we like it or not, what happens happens; to be upset about it is useless, and moreover deprives us of the crown of patience and shows us to be in revolt against the will of God. For whatever God does is 'wholly good and beautiful' (Gen. 1 : 31), even if we are unaware of this. As the psalm puts it: 'He will teach the gentle how to judge' (Ps. 25 : 9. LXX) or, rather, how to exercise discrimination. Then, even if someone gets furious with us, we are not troubled; on the contrary, we are glad to have been given an opportunity to profit and to exercise our understanding, recognizing that we would not have been tried in this way were there not some cause for it. Unwittingly or wittingly we must have offended God, or a brother, or someone else, and now we are being given a chance to receive forgiveness for this. For through patient endurance we may be granted forgiveness for many sins. Moreover, if we do not forgive others their debts, the Father will not forgive us our debts (cf. Matt. 6 : 15). Indeed, nothing leads more swiftly to the forgiveness of sins than this virtue or commandment: 'Forgive, and you will be forgiven' (cf. Matt. 6 : 14).

This, then, is what we realize when we imitate Christ, growing gentle through the grace of the commandment. But we are distressed for our brother, because it was on account of our sins that this brother was tempted by the common enemy and so became a remedy for the healing of our weakness. Every trial and temptation is permitted by God as a cure for some sick person's soul. Indeed, such trials not only confer on us forgiveness of our past and present sins, but also act as a check on sins not yet committed. But this is not to the credit either of the devil, or of the person who tempts, or of the person tempted. The devil, being maleficent, deserves our hatred, for he acts with no concern for our welfare. The person who tempts us merits our compassion, not because he tempts us out of love but because he is deluded and oppressed. The person tempted, finally, endures affliction because of his own faults, not on behalf of someone else. If the latter were the case, he would deserve praise; but as it is, he is not without sin. Were he without sin – which is impossible – he would still endure the affliction in hope of reward and out of fear of punishment. Such, then, is the situation of these three. But God, being self-sufficient and giving to each what is to his profit, does indeed deserve our thanks, since He patiently suffers both the devil and the wickedness of men, and yet bestows His blessings upon those who repent both before and after they sin.

Thus the person who has been granted the grace of keeping the third commandment, and so has acquired full discrimination, will no longer be deceived either wittingly or unwittingly. Instead, having received the grace of humility, he will regard himself as nothing. For gentleness is the substance of humility, and humility is the door leading to dispassion. Through dispassion a man enters into perfect unfaltering love; for he understands his own nature – what it was before birth and what it will be after death. For mortal man is nothing but a slight, short-lived stench, baser than any other created being. For no created being, animate or inanimate, has ever subverted the will of God except man who, although loaded with blessings, endlessly angers God.

That is why man has been given the fourth commandment, that is, longing to acquire the virtues: 'Blessed are they that hunger and thirst after righteousness' (Matt. 5 : 6). He becomes as one who hungers and thirsts for all righteousness, that is, both for bodily virtue and for the moral virtue of the soul. He who has not tasted something, says Basil the Great, does not know what he is missing; but once he has tasted it, he is filled with longing. Thus he who has tasted the sweetness of the commandments, and realizes that they lead him gradually towards the imitation of Christ, longs to acquire them all, with the result that he often disdains even death for their sake. Glimpsing the mysteries of God hidden in the Holy Scriptures, he thirsts to grasp them fully; and the more knowledge he gains, the more he thirsts, burning as though drinking flames. And because the Divine cannot be grasped fully by anyone, he continues to thirst for ever.

What health and sickness are to the body, virtue and wickedness are to the soul, and knowledge and ignorance to the intellect. The greater our devotion to the practice of the virtues, the more our intellect is illumined by knowledge. It is in this way that we are accounted worthy of mercy, that is, through the fifth commandment: 'Blessed are the merciful, for they will receive mercy' (Matt. 5 : 7). The merciful person is he who gives to others what he has himself received from God, whether it be money, or food, or strength, a helpful word, a prayer, or anything else that he has through which he can express his compassion for those in need. At the same time he considers himself a debtor, since he has received more than he is asked to give. By Christ's grace, both in the present world and in the world to come, before the whole of creation he is called merciful, just as God is called merciful (cf. Luke 6 : 36). Through his brother, it is God Himself who has need of him, and in this way God has become his debtor. Although his needy brother can live without him giving what he is asked for, he himself can neither live nor be saved if he does not do what he can to show mercy. If he is not willing to show mercy to his own kind, how can he ask God to show mercy to him? Bearing these and many other things in mind, the person to whom it is granted to keep the commandments gives not only his possessions but even his very life for his neighbour. This is perfect mercy; for just as Christ endured death on our behalf, giving to all an example and a model, so we should die for one another, and not only for our friends, but for our enemies as well, should the occasion call for it.

Not that it is necessary, of course, to have property in order to show mercy. Possessions, rather, are a great weakness. Indeed, it is better to have nothing to give and still to be full of sympathy for all. And if we do have something to give to those in need, we should ourselves be detached from the things of this life, and yet feel deeply involved with our fellow men. Neither should we, in our arrogance, take it upon ourselves to teach others when we have not yet proved ourselves by our own actions; though we make the excuse that we are thereby helping the souls of the weak, the truth is that we are ourselves weaker than those we claim to be helping. For every action must be done at the right time and with discrimination, so that it is not inopportune or detrimental. For a weak person flight is always best, while the total shedding of possessions is far superior to giving alms.

It is through detachment that one is enabled to fulfil the sixth commandment: 'Blessed are the pure in heart' (Matt. 5 : 8). The pure in heart are those who have accomplished every virtue reflectively and reverently and have come to see the true nature of things. In this way they find peace in their thoughts. For, as the seventh commandment puts it, 'Blessed are the peacemakers' (Matt. 5 : 9), that is, those who have set soul and body at peace by subjecting the flesh to the spirit, so that the flesh no longer rises against the spirit (cf. Gal. 5 : 17). Instead, the grace of the Holy Spirit reigns in their soul and leads it where it will, bestowing the divine knowledge whereby man can endure persecution, vilification and maltreatment 'for righteousness' sake' (Matt. 5 : 10), rejoicing because his 'reward is great in heaven' (Matt. 5 : 12).

All the Beatitudes make man a god by grace; he becomes gentle, longs for righteousness, is charitable, dispassionate, a peacemaker, and endures every pain with joy out of love for God and for his fellow men. For the Beatitudes are gifts from God and we should thank Him greatly for them and for the rewards promised: the kingdom of heaven in the age to be, spiritual refreshment in this world, the fulness of all God's blessings and mercies, His manifestation when we contemplate the hidden mysteries found in the Holy Scriptures and in all created things, and the great reward in heaven (cf. Matt. 5 : 12). For if we learn while on earth to imitate Christ and receive the blessedness inherent in each commandment, we shall be granted the highest good and the ultimate goal of our desire. As the apostle says, God, who dwells in unapproachable light, alone is blessed (cf. 1 Tim. 6 : 15–16). We, for our part, have the duty of keeping the commandments – or, rather, of being kept by them; but through them God in His compassion will give to the believer rewards both in this world and in the world to be.

When through blessed inward grief all this has been realized, then the intellect finds relief from the passions; and through the many bitter tears that it sheds over its sins it is reconciled to God. It is crucified with Christ spiritually through moral practice, that is, through the keeping of the commandments and the guarding of the five senses, so that they do not do anything contrary to their nature. Restraining mindless impulses, the intellect begins to curb the passions of anger and desire that encompass it. Sometimes it assuages tempestuous anger with the gentleness of desire; and at other times it calms desire with the severity of anger. Then, coming to itself, the intellect recognizes its proper dignity – to be master of itself – and is able to see things as they truly are; for its eye, made blind by the devil through the tyranny of the passions, is opened. Then man is granted the grace to be buried spiritually with Christ, so that he is set free from the things of this world and no longer captivated by external beauty. He looks upon gold and silver and precious stones, and he knows that like other inanimate things such as wood and rock they are of the earth, and that man, too, is after death a bit of dust and mould in the tomb. Regarding all the delectations of this life as nothing, he looks upon their continual alteration with the judgment that comes from spiritual knowledge. Gladly he dies to the world, and the world becomes dead to him: he no longer has any violent feeling within him, but only calmness and detachment.

Thus, by virtue of his soul's purity, he is found worthy to be resurrected with Christ spiritually, and receives the strength to look without passion on the exterior beauty of visible things and to praise through them the Creator of all. Contemplating in these visible things God's power and providence, His goodness and wisdom, as St Paul says (cf. Rom 1 : 20–21), and perceiving the mysteries hidden in the divine Scriptures, his intellect is given the grace to ascend with Christ through the contemplation of intelligible realities, that is, through the knowledge of intelligible powers. Perceiving, after tears of under-standing and joy, the invisible through the visible (cf. Rom. 1 : 20) and the eternal through the transitory, he realizes that if this ephemeral world, which is said to be a place of exile and punishment for those who have transgressed the commandments of God, is so beautiful, how much more beautiful must be the eternal, inconceiv-able blessings 'that God has prepared for those who love Him' (1 Cor. 2 : 9). And if these blessings are beyond our conception, how much more so must be the God who created all things from nothing.

If you turn from all other activity and give yourself entirely to the cultivation of the virtues of soul and body, which is what the fathers mean by religious devotion; and if you disregard any dream or private thought not confirmed by Scripture, and avoid all pointless company, not hearing or reading anything fruitless, and especially anything that involves heresy, then the tears of joy and understanding will well up copiously within you and you will drink from their plenitude. In this way you will attain another form of prayer, the form of pure prayer that is proper to the contemplative. For just as previously you had one form of reading, one form of tears and prayer, so now you have another. Since your intellect has moved into the sphere of spiritual contemplation, you should now read all parts of the Scriptures, no longer fearing the more difficult and obscure passages, as is the case with those still at the stage of ascetic practice, who are weak in their ignorance.

By your persistent struggle in practising the virtues of body and soul, you have been crucified with Christ and buried with Him through the knowledge of created things, both of their nature and of the changes they undergo; and you have been raised with Him through dispassion and through the knowledge of the mysteries of God inherent in the visible world. As a result of this knowledge you have ascended with Christ into the transcendent world through the knowledge of intelligible realities and of the mysteries hidden in the divine Scriptures. You move from fear to religious devotion, from which springs spiritual knowledge; from this knowledge comes judgment, that is, discrimination; from discrimination comes the strength that leads to understanding; from thence you come to wisdom.

By passing through all these levels of practice and contemplation you are granted pure and perfect prayer, established within you through the peace and love of God and through the indwelling of the Holy Spirit. This is what is meant by saying, 'Gain possession of God within yourself'; and, as St John Chrysostom has said, this manifestation and indwelling of God is realized when your body and soul become so far as is possible sinless, like those of Christ; and when you possess, by virtue of Christ, an intellect that apprehends, through the grace and wisdom of the Holy Spirit, the knowledge of things both human and divine.

THE FOUR VIRTUES OF THE SOUL

There are four forms of wisdom: first, moral judgment, or the knowledge of what should and should not be done, combined with watchfulness of the intellect; second, self-restraint, whereby our moral purpose is safeguarded and kept free from all acts, thoughts and words that do not accord with God; third, courage, or strength and endurance in sufferings, trials and temptations encountered on the spiritual path; and fourth, justice, which consists in maintaining a proper balance between the first three. These four general virtues arise from the three powers of the soul in the following manner: from the intelligence, or intellect, come moral judgment and justice, or discrimination; from the desiring power comes self-restraint; and from the incensive power comes courage.

Each virtue lies between two unnatural passions. Moral judgment lies between craftiness and thoughtlessness; self-restraint, between obduracy and licentiousness; courage, between overbearingness and cowardice; justice between over-frugality and greed. The four virtues constitute an image of the heavenly man, while the eight unnatural passions constitute an image of the earthly man (cf. 1 Cor. 15 : 49).

God possesses a perfect knowledge of all these things, just as He knows the past, the present and the future; and they are known to some extent by him who through grace has learned from God about His works, and who through this grace has been enabled to realize in himself that which is according to God's image and likeness (cf. Gen. 1 : 26). But if someone claims that, simply by hearing about these things, he knows them as he should, he is a liar. Man's intellect can never rise to heaven without God as a guide; and it cannot speak of what it has not seen, but must first ascend and see it. On the level of hearsay, you should speak only of things that you have learnt from the Scriptures, and then with circumspection, confessing your faith in the Father of the Logos, as St Basil the Great puts it, and not imagining that through hearsay you possess spiritual knowledge; for that is to be worse than ignorant. As St Maximos has said, 'To think that one knows prevents one from advancing in knowledge.'[1] St John Chrysostom points out that there is an ignorance which is praiseworthy: it consists in knowing consciously that one knows nothing. In addition, there is a form of ignorance that is worse than any other: not to know that one does not know. Similarly, there is a knowledge that is falsely so called, which occurs when, as St Paul says, one thinks that one knows but does not know (cf. 1 Cor. 8 : 2).

ACTIVE SPIRITUAL KNOWLEDGE

There is such a thing as true spiritual knowledge, and there is total ignorance; but best of all is active spiritual knowedge. For of what use is it to possess all knowledge, or, rather, to receive it from God by grace, as did Solomon (cf. 1 Kgs. 3 : 12) – and there will never be

[1] *On Love* III, 81 (*The Philokalia*, vol. ii, p. 96).

another man like him – and yet go into agelong punishment? What good is such knowledge to you unless, as a result of your actions and firm faith, your conscience assures you that you are delivered from future punishment, and that you have no reason to condemn yourself for neglecting anything you should and could have done? As St John the Theologian says: 'If our heart does not condemn us, then we can approach God with confidence' (1 John 3 : 21). But it may be, St Neilos says, that our conscience itself deceives us, overcome by the darkening of the passions, as St John Klimakos observes.[1] For evil can by itself darken the intellect, as St Basil the Great puts it, and presumption can make it blind, not allowing it to become what it supposes itself to be. What, then, shall we say of those who are enslaved to the passions, and yet think they have a clear conscience? Even the Apostle Paul, in whom Christ dwelt in word and act, said: 'Though I have nothing on my conscience' – no sin, that is to say – 'yet I am not thereby acquitted' (1 Cor. 4 : 4).

Because of our great insensitivity most of us think that we are something while in fact we are nothing (cf. Gal. 6 : 3): as St Paul says, 'When they are talking about peace . . . calamity falls on them' (1 Thess. 5 : 3). For they did not in fact possess peace but, as St John Chrysostom explains, only talked about it, thinking in their great insensitivity that they did possess it. Such people, as James the brother of the Lord points out, have forgotten about their sins (cf. Jas. 1 : 24), and most of them in their pride deceive themselves, as St John Klimakos says, into thinking that they are dispassionate.[2]

Indeed, I myself am terrified of those three giants of the devil about whom St Mark the Ascetic has written: laziness, forgetfulness and ignorance.[3] For I am always dominated by them, and I am afraid that in my unawareness of my own limitations I will stray from the straight path, as St Isaac puts it. It is for this reason that I have compiled this present collection. The person who hates being rebuked is obviously subject to the passion of pride, St John Klimakos says; but the person who puts behind him the fault for which he was rebuked is loosed from his bonds.[4] As Solomon says, 'When a fool enquires about wisdom, he is regarded as wise' (cf. Prov. 17 : 28. LXX).

---

[1] *Ladder*, Step 5 (780B; E.T., p. 108).
[2] *Ladder*, Step 23 (969C; E.T., p. 182).
[3] *Letter to Nicolas the Solitary* (*The Philokalia*, vol. i, pp. 158–60).
[4] *Ladder*, Step 23 (968A; E.T., p. 180).

I have given the names of books and saints at the beginning, so as not to overburden my work by specifying to whom each saying belongs. Indeed, the holy fathers often copied out the words of the divine Scriptures just as they are, as St Gregory the Theologian did with those of Solomon; and Symeon Metaphrastis the Logothete said with reference to St John Chrysostom that it would be wrong not to use the saint's words and to substitute his own. And yet he could have done so; for all the fathers were inspired by the same Holy Spirit. Sometimes they do cite their authors, adorning their works with their names, and in their humility preferring the words of the Scriptures to their own; at other times, because of the great number of citations, they quote anonymously, so as not to overload their texts.

THE BODILY VIRTUES AS TOOLS FOR THE ACQUISITION OF THE VIRTUES OF THE SOUL

It is good to be reminded of certain things frequently, and so I will begin by quoting for the most part from the writings of others. For what I say is not my own invention but comes from the words and discernment of the divine Scriptures and the holy fathers.

St John of Damaskos affirms that the bodily virtues – or, rather, tools of virtue – are essential, for without them the virtues of the soul cannot be acquired.[1] But one must pursue them in humility and with spiritual knowledge. If they are not pursued in this way, but only for themselves, then they serve no purpose, just as plants are useless if they do not bear any fruit. Moreover, no one can fully master any art without long application and the excision of his own desires. Hence, after ascetic practice we need spiritual knowledge, total devotion to God in all things, and careful study of the divine Scriptures; for without these things no one can ever acquire virtue. The person enabled by grace to devote himself utterly and always to God has achieved the highest good; he who has not reached this point should take care not to grow negligent in any way. Blessed are they who are completely devoted to God, either through obedience to someone

[1] *On the Virtues and the Vices* (*The Philokalia*, vol. ii, p. 334).

experienced in the practice of the virtues and living an ordered life in stillness, or else through themselves living in stillness and total detachment, scrupulously obedient to God's will, and seeking the advice of experienced men in everything they say or think. Blessed above all are those who seek to attain dispassion and spiritual knowledge unlaboriously through their total devotion to God: as God Himself has said through His prophet, 'Devote yourselves to stillness and know that I am God' (Ps. 46 : 10).

Those who live in the world – or rather who live after the fashion of the world, for this includes many so-called monks – should try to attain a measure of devotion, as did the righteous men of old, so as to examine their unhappy souls before their death and to amend or humble them, and not to bring them to utter destruction through their total ignorance and their conscious or unconscious sins. David, indeed, was a king; but every night he watered his bed with tears because of his sense of the divine presence (cf. Ps. 6 : 6). And Job says: 'The hair of my flesh stood up' (Job 4 : 15). Let us then, like those living in the world, devote at least a small part of the day and night to God; and let us consider what we are going to say in our defence before our righteous Judge on the terrible day of judgment. Let us take trouble over this, for it is essential in view of the threat of agelong punishment; and let us not be troubled about how we shall live if we are poor or how we can grow rich so as to give alms, thus stupidly devoting all our attention to worldly matters. We have to work, St John Chrysostom says; but we need not concern or trouble ourselves about many things, as our Lord told Martha (cf. Luke 10 : 41). For concern with this life prevents that concern with one's own soul and its state which is the purpose of the man who devotes himself to God and is attentive to himself. It is said in the Law, 'Be attentive to yourself' (Deut. 15 : 9. LXX). St Basil the Great has written about this text with marvellous wisdom.[1]

[1] Cf. *Sermon on the words 'Be attentive to yourself'* (P.G. xxxi, 197–217).

THE GUARDING OF THE INTELLECT

As St John of Damaskos says, without attentiveness and watchfulness of the intellect we cannot be saved and rescued from the devil, who walks about 'like a roaring lion, seeking whom he may devour' (1 Pet. 5 : 8). For this reason the Lord often said to His disciples, 'Watch and pray; for you do not know at what hour your Lord is coming' (Matt. 26 : 41; 24 : 42). Through them He was giving a warning to us all about the remembrance of death, so that we should be prepared to offer a defence, grounded in works and attentiveness, that will be acceptable to God. For the demons, as St Hilarion has said, are immaterial and sleepless, concerned only to fight against us and to destroy our souls through word, act and thought. We lack a similar persistence, and concern ourselves now with our comfort and with ephemeral opinion, now with worldly matters, now with a thousand and one other things. We are not in the least interested in examining our life, so that our intellect may develop the habit of so doing and may give attention to itself unremittingly.

As Solomon says, 'We walk among many snares' (Ecclus. 9 : 13); and St John Chrysostom has written about them, explaining what they are with great precision and wisdom. The Lord Himself, wishing to purge us of all worldly care, exhorts us not to bother about what we eat or wear, but to have only a single concern: how to be saved 'as a roe from the snare and as a bird from the net' (Prov. 6 : 5. LXX), in this way gaining the quick-sightedness of the roe and the soaring flight of the bird. It is truly remarkable that these things are said by King Solomon; and his father, too, said the same. Both of them lived in virtue and wisdom with great attentiveness and many ascetic struggles. Yet, after being granted so many gifts of grace and even the manifestation of God, they were overcome, alas, by sin: the first lamented both murder and adultery, while the second committed many terrible acts (cf. 2 Sam. chs. 11–12; 1 Kgs. ch. 11). As St John Klimakos[1] and Philimon the Ascetic[2] put it, does this not fill anyone of understanding with fear and

---

[1] *Ladder*, Step 25 (1001B; E.T., pp. 199–200).
[2] *A Discourse on Abba Philimon* (*The Philokalia*, vol. ii, p. 353).

terror? In our weakness, how can we not shudder and try to escape from the distractions of this life, we who are nothing and who are as insensate as brutes? Wretched as I am, would that I had been true to my nature, as animals are; for the dog is better than I.

OBEDIENCE AND STILLNESS

If we want to perceive our lethal condition, we must abandon our own desires and all the preoccupations of this life. Through this flight from everything, let us assiduously devote ourselves to God with a devotion that is truly blessed and divine. Let each of us seek his own soul through studying the divine Scriptures, either in perfect obedience of soul and body or in stillness following the angelic way. This is especially important for those who are as yet subject to the passions and cannot control their own desires, whether great or small.

'Sit in your own cell', it has been said, 'and your cell will teach you all things.'[1] Or as St Basil puts it, 'Stillness initiates the soul's purification'.[2] It is also true that Solomon says, 'God has given noxious distraction to the sons of men, so that they may be distracted by vain things' (cf. Eccles. 1 : 13). This is to prevent their mindless and impassioned inertia from dragging them down into what is even worse.

What, however, are we to say about one who has by God's grace been rescued from both these pitfalls and has become a monk, wearing the angelic habit of the solitary or monastic life, and thereby, as St Dionysios the Areopagite says, showing himself to be, in word and action, so far as this is possible, an image of the one and only God?[3] Should not such a person always devote himself to God and be attentive with his intellect in everything he undertakes, meditating continually on God in accordance with the state he has attained? This is what Ephrem and other holy fathers recommend to those setting out on the spiritual path. One man should have a psalm on his

---

[1] *Apophthegmata*, Moses 6; E.T., p. 139.
[2] *Letter* ii, 2 (*P.G.* xxxii, 228A).
[3] *The Ecclesiastical Hierarchy* VI, i, 3; iii, 2–3 (*P.G.* iii, 533A, 533D–536A).

lips, another a verse of a hymn; all those who have not yet been found worthy of entering the realm of contemplation and spiritual knowledge, the fathers tell us, should attend with the intellect to psalms and troparia.[1] In this way each will be engaged in some kind of meditation, whether working or travelling or lying down before sleep. As soon as each has finished his appointed rule of prayer, he should at once enclose his intellect in some form of meditation, lest the enemy find him unoccupied in the remembrance of God and attack him with vanities or worse. This counsel is given to all.

By means of the virtues of soul and body, and after many struggles, a person is enabled to rise noetically, by Christ's grace, and to engage in spiritual labour – the labour of the intellect – so that he begins to grieve inwardly for his own soul. When this happens, he should guard as the apple of his eye the thought that induces pain-laden tears, to use the words of St John Klimakos.[2] He should continue to do this until God in His providence, to prevent him growing proud, withdraws the fire and the water. The fire is the heart's pain and its burning faith; the water is tears. And they are not given to all, says St Athanasios the Great,[3] but only to those enabled by grace to see the terrible things that occur before and after death, and who in stillness bear them constantly in mind. As Isaiah says: 'The ear of the hesychast hears strange wonders' (cf. Job 4 : 12); and again: 'Devote yourself to stillness and know' (Ps. 46 : 10).

Stillness alone engenders knowledge of God, for it is of the greatest help even to the weakest and to those most subject to the passions. It enables them to live without distraction and to withdraw from human society, from the cares and encounters that darken the intellect. I mean not simply worldly cares but also those that appear insignificant and sinless. As St John Klimakos says, 'A small hair will irritate the eye.'[4] And St Isaac says, 'Do not think that avarice consists simply in the possession of silver or gold; it is present whenever our thought is attached to something.' The Lord Himself has said, 'Where your treasure is, there will your heart be also' (Matt. 6 : 21) – either in divine or in worldly thoughts and concerns. For this reason all should be detached and should devote themselves to God. If they live in

---

[1] Troparion: a short stanza in rhythmic prose, occurring in the service books of the Church.
[2] *Ladder*, Step 7 (808A; E.T., p. 117).
[3] Athanasios (?), *On Virginity* 17 (*P.G.* xxviii, 272CD).
[4] *Ladder*, Step 27 (1109D; E.T., p. 245).

the world, they can in this way attain at least some measure
of understanding and spiritual knowledge. Or they may devote
themselves wholly to God, making it their one concern to conform to
His will; and then God, seeing their intention, will grant them rest
through spiritual knowledge. By this means He confers on them the
meditation that belongs to the first stage of contemplation, which
enables them to acquire inexpressible contrition of soul and to
become poor in spirit (cf. Matt. 5 : 3). Leading them in this way
gradually through the other stages of contemplation, He will make it
possible for them to keep the Beatitudes until they attain peace in
their thoughts. This peace is the 'realm' or 'dwelling-place of God', as
Evagrios says, referring to the Psalter: 'In peace is His dwelling-place'
(Ps. 76 : 2. LXX).[1]

THE EIGHT STAGES OF CONTEMPLATION

The stages of contemplation are, it seems to me, eight in number.
Seven pertain to this present age, while the eighth is the pursuit of the
age to come, as St Isaac says.[2]

The first stage, according to St Dorotheos,[3] is knowledge of the
tribulations and trials of this life. This fills us with grief for all the
damage done to human nature through sin.

The second is knowledge of our own faults and of God's bounty, as
St John Klimakos, St Isaac and many other fathers express it.

The third is knowledge of the terrible things that await us before
and after death, as revealed in the Holy Scriptures.

The fourth is deep understanding of the life led by our Lord Jesus
Christ in this world, and of the words and actions of His disciples and
the other saints, the martyrs and the holy fathers.

The fifth is knowledge of the nature and flux of things, as St
Gregory and St John of Damaskos put it.

---

[1] *Gnostic Centuries* V, 39; cf. *On Prayer* 58 (*The Philokalia*, vol. i, p. 62).

[2] Isaac of Nineveh (Isaac the Syrian), *Mystic Treatises*, E.T. from the Syriac by A. J.
Wensinck (Amsterdam, 1923), p. 136; Greek translation, ed. N. Theotokis/I. Spetsieris
(Athens, 1895), p. 292. Cf. Basil, *On the Six Days of Creation* II, 8 (*P.G.* xxix, 49–52); Maximos
the Confessor, *On Theology* I, 51–6 (*The Philokalia*, vol. ii, pp. 124–5).

[3] *Instructions* I, 8 (ed. Regnault, p. 158).

The sixth is contemplation of created beings, that is to say, knowledge and understanding of God's visible creation.

The seventh is understanding of God's spiritual creation.

The eighth is knowledge concerning God, or what we call 'theology'.

These are the eight stages of contemplation. The first three are suitable for one still engaged in ascetic practice, so that with many bitter tears he may purify his soul from all the passions and may be allowed through God's grace to proceed to the remaining stages.

The last five stages pertain to the contemplative or gnostic. Through them he maintains a careful watch over the activities of both body and soul, and performs them rightly. As a result he is enabled to grasp these later stages clearly with his intellect.

Thus the man engaged in ascetic practice begins to enter the path of spiritual knowledge by way of the first three stages; and by concentrating on his task and by meditating on the thoughts produced within him, he progresses in them until they are established in him. In this way the next stage of knowledge enters automatically into his intellect. The same happens with all the remaining stages.

To make things quite clear, I will speak, despite my incompetence, about each stage of contemplation, and about what is understood and said at each stage. In this way we can discover how we ought to act when grace begins to open the eyes of our soul and we come with astonishment to understand thoughts and words that instil in us fear of God or, in other words, contrition of soul.

THE FIRST STAGE OF CONTEMPLATION

The first stage of contemplation is that which leads the seeker to all the later stages. The person who is called to this first stage should act as follows. He should seat himself facing the east, as once did Adam, and meditate in this way:

'Adam then sat and wept because of his loss of the delights of paradise, beating his eyes with his fists and saying: "O Merciful One, have mercy on me, for I have fallen."'

'Seeing the angel driving him out and closing the door to the divine garden, Adam groaned aloud and said: "O Merciful One, have mercy on me, for I have fallen." '[1]

After that, reflecting on what then took place, he should begin to lament in this way, grieving with all his soul and shaking his head and saying with great sorrow of heart:

Woe is me, a sinner! What has happened to me? Alas, what was I and what have I become! What have I lost, what found? Instead of paradise, this perishable world. Instead of God, and life in the company of the angels, the devil and the demons of impurity. In the place of rest, hard labour; in the place of gladness and joy, the sorrows and tribulations of this world; instead of peace and endless felicity, fear and tears of sorrow. In the place of virtue and justice, injustice and sin. Instead of goodness and dispassion, evil and passion; instead of wisdom and intimacy with God, ignorance and exile; instead of detachment and freedom, a life full of worries and the worst kind of slavery. Woe, woe is me! How, created a king, have I become in my folly a slave of passion? How can I have embraced death instead of life through my disobedience? Alas! What has happened to me, pitiful that I am, because of my thoughtlessness? What shall I do? War and confusion beset me, illness and temptation, danger and shipwreck, fear and sorrow, passion and sin, bitterness and distress. What shall I do? Where shall I flee? 'All doors are closed to me', as Susanna said (Sus. 1 : 22).

I do not know what to ask for. If I ask for life, I fear the trials of life, its ups and downs, its conflicts. I see how Satan, the angel who once rose as the morning star (cf. Isa. 14 : 12), has now become the devil, as we call him. I see how the first-created man was sent into exile (cf. Gen. 3 : 23); how Cain became his brother's murderer (cf. Gen. 4 : 8); how Canaan was cursed (cf. Gen. 9 : 25); I see the citizens of Sodom burned by fire (cf. Gen. 19 : 24–25); Esau banished (cf. Gen. 25 : 33); I see the Israelites subjected to God's wrath (cf. Num. 14 : 34); I see Gehazi and Judas, the apostle, cast out because they were sick with avarice (cf. 2 Kgs. 5 : 26–27; Matt. 26 : 15,24); I see David, the great prophet and king, lamenting his double sin (cf. Ps. 51); I see Solomon, for all his wisdom, fallen (cf. 1 Kgs. 11 : 9–11);

---

[1] Sunday of Forgiveness, Canon, ikos after Canticle 6: see Mother Mary and Archimandrite Kallistos Ware, *The Lenten Triodion* (London, 1978), p. 175. The sections on the eight stages of contemplation are full of quotations or reminiscences from the service books.

I see how one of the seven deacons and one of the forty martyrs lapsed, as St Basil the Great says. Gleefully the prince of evil entrapped the mean-spirited Judas, one of the twelve; he snatched man from Eden, and ensnared one of the forty martyrs. Grieving for him the same Basil the Great says, 'Foolish and worthy of our tears is he, for he went astray in both lives: in this life he was destroyed by fire and in the next went to eternal fire.'[1] And I see many others, numberless, who fell; not only unbelievers, but also many of the fathers, in spite of all their labours.

Yet who am I, who am worse and more obdurate and weaker than them all? What shall I call myself? For Abraham says that he is 'but dust and ashes' (Gen. 18 : 27); David calls himself 'a dead dog' (2 Sam. 9 : 8) and 'a flea' (1 Sam. 24 : 14) in Israel; Solomon calls himself 'a little child, not knowing left from right' (cf. 1 Kgs. 3 : 7); the three holy children say, 'We have become a shame and a reproach' (Song of the Three Children, verse 10); Isaiah the prophet says, 'Woe is me, for I am undone, because I am a man of unclean lips' (Isa. 6 : 5); the prophet Habakkuk says, 'I am a child' (Jer. 1 : 6); St Paul calls himself the chief of sinners (cf. 1 Tim. 1 : 15); and all the rest said that they were nothing. What then should I do? Where shall I hide myself from my many crimes? What will become of me, who am nothing, worse than nothing? For that which is nothing has not sinned, nor has it received God's blessings as I have. Alas, how shall I pass the rest of my life? And how shall I escape the snares of the devil? For the demons are sleepless and immaterial, death is at hand, and I am weak. Lord, help me; do not let Thy creature perish, for Thou carest for me in my misery. 'Make known to me, Lord, which way I should go; for I lift up my soul to Thee' (Ps. 143 : 8). 'Forsake me not, O Lord my God, be not far from me; make haste to help me, O Lord of my salvation' (Ps. 38: 21–22).

By such words the soul is made contrite, if it has at least some sensibility. By persisting in this way, and growing accustomed to the fear of God, the intellect begins to understand and meditate on the second stage of contemplation.

---

[1] *Sermon on the Forty Martyrs* 7 (*P.G.* xxxi, 520c).

THE SECOND STAGE OF CONTEMPLATION

Woe is me, unhappy that I am! What shall I do? I have sinned greatly; many blessings are bestowed on me; I am very weak. Many are the temptations: sloth overwhelms me, forgetfulness benights me and will not let me see myself and my many crimes. Ignorance is evil; conscious transgression is worse; virtue is difficult to achieve; the passions are many; the demons are crafty and subtle; sin is easy; death is near; the reckoning is bitter. Alas, what shall I do? Where shall I flee from myself? For I am the cause of my own destruction. I have been honoured with free will and no one can force me. I have sinned, I sin constantly, and am indifferent to any good thing, though no one constrains me. Whom can I blame? God, who is good and full of compassion, who always longs for us to turn to Him and repent? The angels, who love and protect me? Men, who also desire my progress? The demons? They cannot constrain anyone unless, because of negligence or despair, he chooses to destroy himself. Who is then to blame? Surely it is myself?

I begin to see that my soul is being destroyed, and yet I make no effort to embark on a godly life. Why, O my soul, are you so indifferent about yourself? Why, when you sin, are you not as ashamed before God and His angels as you are before men? Alas, alas, for I do not feel the shame before my Creator and Master that I feel before a man. Before a man I cannot sin, but do all I can to appear to be acting righteously; yet standing before God I think evil thoughts and often am not ashamed to speak of them. What madness! Though I sin, I have no fear of God who watches me, and yet I cannot tell to a single man what I have done so as to give him a chance to correct me. Alas, for I know the punishment and yet am unwilling to repent. I love the heavenly kingdom, and yet do not acquire virtue. I believe in God and constantly disobey His commandments. I hate the devil, and yet do not stop doing what he wants. If I pray, I lose interest and become unfeeling. If I fast, I become proud, and damn myself all the more. If I keep vigil, I think I have achieved something, and so I have no profit from it. If I read, I do one of two evil things in my obduracy: either I read for the sake of profane learning and self-esteem, and so am further benighted; or by reading, and not acting in the spirit of what I read,

I simply increase my guilt. If by God's grace I happen to stop sinning in outward action, I do not stop sinning continually in what I say. And if God's grace should protect me also from this, I continue to provoke His wrath by my evil thoughts. Alas, what can I do? Wherever I go, I find sin. Everywhere there are demons. Despair is worst of all. I have provoked God, I have saddened His angels, I have frequently injured and offended men.

I would like, Lord, to erase the record of my sins by tears, and through repentance to live the rest of my life according to Thy will. But the enemy deceives me and battles with my soul. Lord, before I perish completely, save me.

I have sinned against Thee, Saviour, like the prodigal son; receive me, Father, in my repentance and have mercy on me, O God.

I cry to Thee, O Christ my Saviour, with the voice of the publican: be gracious to me, as to him, and have mercy upon me, O God.[1]

What will happen in the last days? What is to come afterwards? How hapless I am! 'Who will give water to my head and a fountain of tears to my eyes?' (Jer. 9 : 1. LXX). Who can grieve for me as I deserve? I cannot do so. Come, mountains, cover me in my abjectness. What have I to say? O how many blessings has God bestowed on me, blessings that only He knows of, and how many terrible things in act, word and thought have I done in my ingratitude, always provoking my Benefactor. And the more long-suffering He is, the more I disdain Him, becoming harder in heart than lifeless stones. Yet I do not despair, but acknowledge Thy great compassion.

I have no repentance, no tears. Therefore I entreat Thee, Saviour, to make me turn back before I die and to grant me repentance, so that I may be spared punishment.[2]

O Lord my God, do not abandon me, though I am nothing before Thee, though I am wholly a sinner. How shall I become aware of my many sins? For unless I become aware, severe is my condemnation. For me Thou hast created heaven and earth, the four elements and all that is formed from them, as St Gregory the Theologian says.[3] I shall keep silence as to the rest, for I am unworthy to say anything

[1] Sunday Vespers, stichira of repentance, Tone 2: *The Lenten Triodion*, pp. 184–5.
[2] Ibid., Tone 6: p. 186.
[3] Cf. *Oration* 14, 23 (*P.G.* xxxv, 888AB).

because of my many crimes. Who, even if he had the intellect of an
angel, could grasp all the countless blessings I have been given? Yet
because I do not change my ways I shall lose them all.

By meditating in this way, a man gradually advances to the third
stage of contemplation.

THE THIRD STAGE OF CONTEMPLATION

Again he laments:[1] Alas, what agony the soul experiences when it is
separated from the body. How many tears it sheds then, and there is
no one to take pity on it. Turning its eyes to the angels, it entreats in
vain. Stretching its hands towards men, it finds no one to help it.

I weep and grieve when I think of death and see man's beauty,
created by God in His own image, lying in the grave, ugly, abject, its
physical form destroyed. What is this mystery that has befallen us?
How have we been given over to corruption? How have we been
yoked to death? Truly it is by God's command, as it is written. Ah,
what will I do at the moment of my death, when the demons encircle
my unhappy soul, bearing the indictment of the sins I have
committed, consciously or unconsciously, in word, act and thought,
and demanding from me my defence? But alas, even without any
other sin, I am already condemned – and rightly so – for not having
kept the commandments.

Tell me, my wretched soul, where are your baptismal promises?
What has happened to your covenant with Christ and your
renunciation of Satan? Where is your keeping of God's commandments, your imitation of Christ through the virtues of body and soul?
Because of this you were called a Christian. What has happened to
your profession of the monastic habit? Should you blame bodily
weakness, where is the faith that casts all care upon the Lord, the
faith by which, even had it been no bigger than a mustard seed, you
would have been able to move mountains (cf. Matt. 17 : 20)? Where
is the complete repentance that repels every evil word or action?

[1] From the Funeral Service: see I. F. Hapgood, *Service Book of the Holy Orthodox-Catholic
Apostolic Church* (2nd ed., New York, 1922), pp. 385–6.

Where is the contrition of soul and the deep inward grief? Where is the gentleness, the generosity, the heart's freedom from evil thoughts, the all-embracing self-control that restrains each member of the body and every thought and desire that is not indispensable for the soul's salvation or for bodily life? Where is the patience that endures so many tribulations for the sake of the kingdom of heaven? Where is the gratitude in all things? The ceaseless prayer? The recollection of death? The tears of distress for my failure to love? Where is the moral judgment attuned to God, that keeps the soul from the snares of our enemies? Where is the self-restraint that prevents anything contrary to the will of God from being done or deliberately thought? Where is the courage that endures terrible sufferings and that advances full of hope against the adversary? Where is the justice that gives to each thing its due, the humility that knows its own weakness and ignorance, and the godlike compassion that would have saved me from all the wiles of the demons? Where is dispassion and perfect love, the peace that excels all intellect (cf. Phil. 4 : 7), whereby I should have been called a son of God (cf. Matt. 5 : 9)? Even without bodily strength he who wishes can possess all these things simply through his own resolution.

What can I say about all this? What can I do? If in my uncertainty I lose heart for a while because I have completely failed to do what I should to the limits of my power, I shall fall lower than Hades, as St Athanasios the Great says. How wretched I am! What have I brought upon myself, not only through my sins, but rather through my refusal to repent! For if like the prodigal son I had repented, my loving Father would have received me back (cf. Luke 15 : 11–32). And if I had been as honest as the publican (cf. Luke 18 : 13), condemning myself alone and no one else, I too would have received forgiveness of sins from God, especially if I had called upon Him with all my soul as the publican did. As it is, I still do not regard myself in this way. Because of this, I fear that I shall dwell in Hades with the demons, and I live in dread of the coming judgment, with the river of fire, the thrones, and the open books (cf. Dan. 7 : 9–12), angels running ahead, all humankind standing by, everything naked and exposed (cf. Heb. 4 : 13) before the fearsome and righteous Judge.

How shall I endure the examination, the displeasure of the awe-inspiring impartial Judge, the gathering of numberless angels, the retribution demanded with terrible threats, the decision that cannot be altered? How shall I bear the ceaseless lamenting and the useless tears, the pitch darkness and the worm that does not sleep, the unquenchable fire and many torments? How bear exclusion from the kingdom and separation from the saints, the departure of the angels and the alienation from God, the soul's enfeeblement and eternal death, the fear, the pain, the distress, the shame, the torture of the conscience?

Woe is me, a sinner. What has happened to me? Why should I destroy myself so wrongly? I still have time for repentance. The Lord calls me: shall I procrastinate? How long, my soul, will you remain in your sins? How long will you put off repentance? Think of the judgment to come, cry out to Christ your God: Searcher of hearts, I have sinned; before Thou condemnest me, have mercy upon me! At Thy awesome coming, O Christ, may I not hear: 'I know you not' (Matt. 25 : 12). For we have placed our hope in Thee, our Saviour, even though in our negligence we fail to keep Thy commandments. But, we pray Thee, spare our souls. Alas, Lord, for I have grieved Thee and did not perceive it; yet behold, through Thy grace I have begun to perceive, and so am filled with confusion. My unhappy soul is shaken with fear.

Shall I be allowed to live for a short time longer, so as to weep bitter tears and cleanse my defiled body and soul? Or, after sorrowing for a while, shall I then stop once more, obdurate as always? What shall I do to acquire unceasing pain of soul? Shall I fast and keep vigil? Yet without humility I will gain nothing. Shall I read and sing psalms with my mouth only? For my passions have darkened my intellect and I cannot understand the meaning of what is said. Shall I fall prostrate before Thee, the giver of all blessings? But I have no confidence. My life is without hope; I have destroyed my soul. Lord, help me and receive me as the publican; for like the prodigal I have sinned against heaven and before Thee (cf. Luke 15 : 18). I have sinned like the harlot who came to Thee weeping, and of whom it is written: 'Full of despair on account of life, her ways well known, she came to Thee bearing myrrh and crying: "O virgin-born, do not cast me away, harlot though I am; do not spurn my tears, O joy of the angels; but receive me in my repentance, O Lord, and in Thy great mercy do not reject me, a sinner." '[1] For I, too, am in despair because of my many sins, yet I am well known to Thine ineffable compassion and the boundless sea of Thy mercies.

[1] Wednesday in Holy Week, Mattins, aposticha: *The Lenten Triodion*, p. 540.

Casting my soul's despair into this sea, I dare to concentrate my intellect in holy remembrance of Thee; and, rising up, in fear and trembling I make this one request: that unworthy though I am I may be found worthy to be Thy servant; that by grace I may have an intellect that is free from all form, shape, colour or materiality; that, as Daniel once bowed down before Thy angel (cf. Dan. 10 : 9), I may fall on hands and knees before Thee, the only God, Creator of all, and offer Thee first thanksgiving and then confession. In this way shall I begin to seek Thy most holy will, confessing Thy grace in all the blessings that Thou hast granted me, who am but dirt, dust and ashes, and knowing that, being wholly a creature of earth, it is only through the intellect that I am enabled to approach Thee.

Then, conscious that Thy look is upon me, with all my soul I will cry out and say: O most merciful Lord, I thank Thee, I glorify Thee, I hymn Thee, I venerate Thee, for unworthy though I am Thou hast found me worthy in this hour to give thanks to Thee and to be mindful of the wonders and blessings – numberless and unfathomable, visible and invisible, known and unknown – that Thy grace has bestowed and still bestows on our souls and bodies. I confess Thy gifts; I do not hide Thy blessings; I proclaim Thy mercies; I acknowledge Thee, O Lord my God, with all my heart, and glorify Thy name for ever. 'For great is Thy mercy towards me' (Ps. 86 : 13), and inexpressible is Thy forbearance and long-suffering over my many sins and iniquities, over the heinous and godless things that I have done, and still do, and will do in the future. From these Thy grace has saved me, whether they were committed consciously or unconsciously, in word, in action, or in thought. Thou knowest them all, O Lord, Searcher of hearts, from my birth until my death; and, abject that I am, I dare to confess them before Thee. 'I have sinned, I have transgressed, I have acted godlessly' (cf. Dan. 9 : 5), 'I have done evil in thy sight' (Ps. 51 : 4), and I am not worthy to gaze upon the height of heaven.

Yet, finding courage in Thy inexpressible compassion, in Thy goodness and tender mercy that excel our understanding, I fall before Thee and entreat Thee, Lord: 'Have mercy upon me, O Lord, for I am weak' (Ps. 6 : 2), and forgive me my many crimes. Do not allow me to sin again or to stray from Thy straight path, or to injure or offend anyone, but check in me every iniquity, every evil habit, every mindless impulse of soul and body, of anger and desire; and teach me to act according to Thy will.

Have mercy on my brethren and fathers,[1] on all monks and priests everywhere, on my parents, my brothers and sisters, my relatives, on those who have served us and those who serve us now, on those who pray for us and who have asked us to pray for them, on those who hate us and those who love us, on those whom I have injured or offended, on those who have injured or offended me or who will do so in the future, and on all who trust in Thee. Forgive us every sin whether deliberate or unintentional. Protect our lives and our departure out of this world from impure spirits, from every temptation, from all sin and malice, from presumption and despair, from lack of faith, from folly, from self-inflation and cowardice, from delusion and unruliness, from the wiles and snares of the devil. In Thy compassion grant us what is good for our souls in this age and in the age to be. Give rest to our fathers and brethren who have departed this life before us, and through the prayers of them all have mercy on my unhappy self in my depravity. See how feeble I am in all things: rectify my conduct, direct my life and death into the paths of peace, fashion me into what Thou wilt and as Thou wilt, whether I want it or not. Grant only that I shall not fail to find myself at Thy right hand on the day of judgment, Lord Jesus Christ my God, even though I am the least of all Thy servants to be saved.

Give peace to Thy world, and in ways best known to Thee have mercy on all men. Count me worthy to partake of Thy pure body and Thy precious blood, for the remission of sins, for communion in the Holy Spirit, as a foretaste of eternal life in Thee with Thine elect, through the intercessions of Thy most pure Mother, of the angels and the celestial powers and of all Thy saints; for Thou art blessed through all the ages. Amen.

Most holy Lady, Mother of God, all celestial powers, holy angels and archangels, and all saints, intercede for me a sinner.

God our Master, Father almighty, Lord Jesus Christ, the Only-begotten Son, and Holy Spirit, one Godhead, one Power, have mercy on me a sinner.[2]

After praying in this way you should immediately address your own thoughts and say three times: 'O come, let us worship and fall down before God our King.' Then you should begin the psalms,

---

[1] Cf. the prayers at the end of Compline: Hapgood, *Service Book*, pp. 162–3.
[2] Prayer at the Third Hour: Hapgood, *Service Book*, pp. 47–8.

reciting the *Trisagion* after each subsection of the Psalter,[1] and enclosing your intellect within the words you are saying. After the *Trisagion*[2] say 'Lord, have mercy' forty times; and then make a prostration and say once within yourself, 'I have sinned, Lord, forgive me'. On standing, you should stretch out your arms and say once, 'God, be merciful to me a sinner'. After praying in this way, you should say once more, 'O come, let us worship . . .' three times, and then another sub-section of the Psalter in the same way.

When, however, God's grace kindles a sense of deep penitence in the heart, you should allow your intellect to be bathed in tears of compunction, even if this means that your mouth stops reciting psalms and your mind is made captive to what St Isaac the Syrian calls 'blessed captivity'. For now is the time to harvest, not to plant (cf. Eccles. 3 : 2).[3] You should therefore persist in such thoughts, so that your heart grows more full of compunction and bears fruit in the form of godly tears. St John Klimakos says that if a particular word moves you to compunction, you should linger over it.[4] Every bodily activity – by which I mean fasting, vigils, psalmody, spiritual reading, stillness and so on – is directed towards the purification of the intellect; but without inward grief the intellect cannot be purified, and so be united to God through the pure prayer that transports it beyond all conceptual thought, and sets it free from all form and figure. Yet all that is good in bodily activities has good results – and the reverse is also true. Everything, however, demands discrimination if it is to be used for the good; without discrimination we are ignorant of the true nature of things.

Many of us may be shocked when we see disagreement in what was said and done by the holy fathers. For instance, the Church has received through its tradition the practice of singing many hymns and troparia; but St John Klimakos, in praising those who have received from God the gift of inward grief, says that such people do not sing hymns among themselves.[5] Again, while speaking of those in a state of

---

[1] Literally, 'after each antiphon'. In Orthodox usage the Psalter is divided into twenty sections, each called 'kathisma', and every 'kathisma' is divided into three subsections, each called 'stasis' or 'antiphon'.

[2] The *Trisagion* ('Holy God, Holy and Strong, Holy and Immortal, have mercy upon us') is presumably to be followed by the prayer 'Most Holy Trinity, have mercy upon us . . .', and then by the Lord's Prayer, according to the usual Orthodox practice.

[3] *Mystic Treatises*, E.T., pp. 113, 115; Greek, pp. 135, 137.

[4] *Ladder*, Step 28 (1132B; E.T., p. 252).

[5] *Ladder*, Step 7 (813A; E.T., p. 121).

pure prayer, St Isaac says that often it happens that a person so concentrates his intellect during prayer that, like Daniel the prophet (cf. Dan. 10 : 9), he falls unbidden to his knees, his hands outstretched and his eyes gazing at Christ's Cross; his thoughts are changed and his limbs are made weak because of the new thoughts that arise spontaneously in his intellect.[1] Many of the holy fathers write similarly about such persons, how in the rapt state of their intellect they not only pass beyond hymns and psalmody but, as Evagrios says, even become oblivious of the intellect itself.[2] Yet, because of the feebleness of our intellect, the Church is right to commend the singing of hymns and troparia; for by this means those of us who lack spiritual knowledge may willy-nilly praise God through the sweetness of the melody, while those who possess such knowledge and so understand the words are brought to a state of compunction.

Thus, as St John of Damaskos puts it, we are led as though up a ladder to the thinking of good thoughts. The more habitual these thoughts become, the more the longing for God draws us on to understand and worship the Father 'in Spirit and in truth' (John 4 : 24), as the Lord said. St Paul also indicates this when he says: 'I had rather speak five words whose meaning I understand than ten thousand words in a strange tongue' (1 Cor. 14 : 19); and again: 'I wish that men would pray everywhere, lifting up holy hands without anger and without quarrelling' (1 Tim. 2 : 8). Thus hymns and troparia are remedies for our weakness, while the experiences of rapture mark the perfection of the intellect. This is the solution to such questions. For 'all things are good in their proper time' (cf. Ecclus. 39 : 34); and, as Solomon says, 'For each thing there is a proper time' (Eccles. 3 : 1). But to those ignorant of this proper time everything will appear discordant and untimely.

When one has attained the level of good thoughts, one should take extreme care to keep these points in mind, lest out of negligence or conceit one is deprived of God's grace, as St Isaac says. When God-given thoughts increase in a man's soul and lead him toward greater humility and compunction, he should always give thanks, acknowledging that only by God's grace does he know such things, and regarding himself as unworthy of them. If good thoughts

---

[1] *Mystic Treatises*, E.T., p. 40; Greek, p. 102.
[2] Cf. *On Prayer* 120 (*The Philokalia*, vol. i, p. 68); also John Cassian, *Conferences* IX, 31.

cease and his mind is once more darkened, losing its awe and its sense of inward grief, he should be greatly distressed and humble himself in word and deed; for grace has already abandoned him, so that he may realize his own weakness, acquire humility and try to amend his life, as St Basil the Great says. For had he not neglected that inward grief which is so dear to God he would not have lacked tears when he wished for them. That is why we should always be conscious of our own weakness and the power of God's grace, and should neither lose hope if something happens to us, nor be emboldened to think that we are anything whatsoever. Rather we should always hope in God with humility. This applies particularly to those who in thought and action are seeking to regain the gift of tears: they had once been granted this providential grace, but they failed to preserve it because of past, present or future negligence or self-elation, as we have explained.

If someone has deliberately relinquished these gifts of grace – inward grief, tears and radiant thoughts – what does he deserve if not deep distress? For what greater folly is there than that of the man who, after starting from what is contrary to nature and attaining through grace a state above nature – by which I mean tears of understanding and love – then reverts through some trivial act or extraneous thought and his own wilfulness to the ignorance of a beast, as a dog to its own vomit? Yet if such a man decides once more to devote himself to God, reading the divine Scriptures with attentiveness and the remembrance of death, and keeping his intellect, so far as he can, free from vain thoughts during prayer, he can regain what he has lost. And he can do this all the more readily if he is never angry with anyone, however greatly he suffers at the other's hands, and if he never allows anyone to be angry with him, but does all he can through his actions and his words to remedy things. When this happens his intellect exults still more, being released from the turbulence of anger; and he learns by practice never to neglect his own soul, fearing lest he should be once again abandoned. And because of his fear he is kept from falling, and is blessed always with tears of repentance and inward grief until he attains the tears of joy and love, whereby through Christ's grace his thoughts are set at peace.

Yet we who are still impassioned and obdurate should always meditate on words of grief, and should examine ourselves daily, both before our set rule of prayer, during it, and afterwards. We should do this if we are still struggling, despite our weakness, to devote ourselves to God and to turn away from everything else, as St Isaac puts it; and we should do it even if we have so turned away and remain concentrated, our eyes sleepless and our minds watchful, as St John Klimakos says. Consider what progress you are making in these things, so that your soul may be chastened and may begin to experience the gift of tears, as St Dorotheos says.

Such, then, are the first three stages of contemplation, by means of which we are enabled to go forward to the further stages.

THE FOURTH STAGE OF CONTEMPLATION

The fourth stage of contemplation consists in the understanding of our Lord's incarnation and His manner of life in this world, to the point that we practically forget even to eat, as St Basil the Great writes. This, according to St John Klimakos, is what happened to King David (cf. Ps. 102 : 4) when his mind was rapt in ecstasy at God's marvels.[1] As St Basil says, he was at a loss as to what to do in return: 'What shall I give to the Lord in return for all His benefits towards me?' (Ps. 116 : 12). For our sakes God lived among men; because of our corrupted nature the Logos became flesh and dwelt among us. The Source of Blessing visited the ungrateful, the Liberator the captives, the Sun of Righteousness those sitting in darkness. The Man of Dispassion came to the Cross, Light to Hades, Life to death, Resurrection to the fallen. To Him let us cry: 'Our God, glory to Thee!'[2] St John of Damaskos says: 'Heaven was amazed, and the earth's ends were astounded, that God should appear in bodily form to men and that your womb, O Mother of God, became capable of containing the heavens; because of this the orders of angels and of men magnify you.'[3] And again: 'All who heard shuddered at the ineffable condescension of God: how the Most High of His own will descended even to the body, born man from a virgin womb. Because of this we the faithful magnify the pure Mother of our God.'[4]

'Come, all peoples, and believe. Let us climb the holy and heavenly

[1] *Ladder*, Step 7 (801D; E.T., p. 114).
[2] *Paraklitiki*, Tone 7, Sunday Mattins, stichiron at Lauds.
[3] *Paraklitiki*, Tone 8, Sunday Mattins, Canon, Canticle 9, irmos.
[4] *Paraklitiki*, Tone 8, Sunday Mattins, Canon, Canticle 9, another irmos.

mountain; free from materiality, let us stand in the city of the living God and behold with our intellect the immaterial godhead of the Father and the Spirit blazing forth in the Only-begotten Son. Thou hast enraptured me with longing for Thee, O Christ, and hast transformed me with the intensity of Thy divine love; with immaterial fire consume my sins and fill me with delight in Thee, so that in my joy, O Lord, I may praise Thy first and second coming.[1] Thou art all tenderness, O Saviour, all my desire, truly the goal of my insatiable longing; Thou art all beauty irresistible.'

If anyone through the virtues of body and soul has received knowledge of these things, and of the mysteries hidden in the words of the holy fathers, of the divine Scriptures, and especially of the Holy Gospels, he will never lose his longing or cease from shedding the tears that come to him unbidden. And we, too, who do no more than listen to the Scriptures, should devote ourselves to them and meditate on them so constantly that through our persistence a longing for God is impressed upon our hearts, as St Maximos says. For this is what the holy fathers did before they acquired direct spiritual knowledge. All the longing of the martyrs was directed solely toward God. They were united to Him through love and sang His praises, as St John of Damaskos says of the three holy children: 'These most blessed children, risking their lives in Babylon for their ancestral laws, disdained the foolish commandment of their king; cast into the flames yet not consumed, they sang a hymn worthy of the One who kept them safe.'[2] This is quite natural; for when a person truly perceives God's marvels he is wholly beside himself and is oblivious of this transient life because he has understood the divine Scriptures, as St Isaac puts it.[3]

Such a man is not like us: for though we may for a while be slightly stirred by the Scriptures, we are again plunged into darkness by laziness, forgetfulness and ignorance, and become obdurate because of our passions. But he who has been purified of the passions through inward grief perceives the hidden mysteries in all the Scriptures and is astonished by them all, especially by the words and actions recorded in the Holy Gospels. He is amazed to see how the wisdom of God

[1] Feast of the Transfiguration, Mattins, Second Canon, Canticle 9, troparia: see Mother Mary and Archimandrite Kallistos Ware, *The Festal Menaion* (London, 1969), p. 494.

[2] Tone 6, Mattins, Canon, Canticle 8, irmos.

[3] *Mystic Treatises*, E.T., p. 3; Greek, p. 4.

renders what is difficult easy, so that gradually it deifies man. He is filled with goodness, so that he loves his enemies; he is merciful, as his Father is merciful (cf. Luke 6 : 36); he is dispassionate, as God is dispassionate; he is endowed with every virtue and is perfect, as the Father is perfect (cf. Matt. 5 : 48). In short, the Holy Bible teaches us that what befits God befits man as well, so that he becomes god by divine adoption.

Who would not marvel at the teaching of the Holy Gospel? For, simply on condition that we choose rightly, God grants us complete rest in both this world and the next, and confers on us great honours. It is as the Lord said: 'He who humbles himself will be exalted' (Luke 18 : 14). St Peter bears this out when he leaves his nets and receives the keys of heaven (cf. Matt. 16 : 19); and each of the other disciples, leaving behind what little he had, received into his charge the whole world in this age and in the age to come. 'The eye has not seen, and the ear has not heard, and man's heart has not grasped the things that God has prepared for those who love Him' (1 Cor. 2 : 9). This is true not only of the apostles, but also of all those who up to the present time have elected to pursue the spiritual life. As one of the fathers says: 'Even though they struggled in the desert they had much repose.' He said this with reference to the life that is tranquil and trouble-free.

Who has greater repose and honour, the person who devotes himself to God and acts accordingly, or the person involved in hustle, law courts and worldly cares? The person who always converses with God through meditation on the Holy Scriptures and undistracted prayer and tears, or the person who is always on the go, who devotes himself to fraud and lawless actions which, when they come to nothing, leave him only with his exhaustion and perhaps twofold death? Consider how some of us endure even painful and dishonourable death all for nothing. Indeed, some for purely destructive ends have inflicted the greatest injury on their own souls. I have in mind robbers, pirates, fornicators, instigators of quarrels – all of them people who refused salvation and the repose, honour and rewards that go with it. How blind we are! We endure death for the sake of destruction, but do not love life for the sake of salvation. And if we prefer death to the kingdom of heaven, in what do we differ from the thief or grave-robber or soldier? These, simply for the sake of food, have often endured the death that is to come as well as death in this present life.

We must make Christ our primary goal; for on those who choose Him He confers the kingdom of heaven. This means that in this present life we must rise spiritually above all things, subjecting them all to Him. We must rule not only over external things but also over the body, through our non-attachment to it, and over death, through the courage of our faith; then in the life to come we shall reign in our bodies eternally with Christ through the grace of the general resurrection. Death comes both to the righteous and to the sinner, but there is a great difference. As mortals both die, and there is nothing extraordinary in that. But the one dies without reward and possibly condemned; the other is blessed in this world and in the next.

What is the point of amassing riches? Despite his unwillingness, the seeming possessor will have to surrender them, not just at the moment of his death, but often before this, with much shame, tribulation and pain. Wealth breeds innumerable trials – fear, anxiety, constant worry and troubles sought and unsought – and yet many have endured even death for its sake. But God's holy commandment saves every man from all this and gives him complete freedom from anxiety and fear; often, indeed, it confers inexpressible delight on those who deliberately choose to rid themselves of possessions. For what brings more delight than to achieve dispassion, and no longer to be under the sway of anger or the desire for worldly things? Regarding as nothing the things that most people value and rising above them, we live as in paradise, or rather as in heaven, set free from all constraints through our untroubled devotion to God.

Because a person in such a state joyfully accepts all that happens to him, all things bring him repose; because he loves everyone, everyone loves him; because he is detached from all things, he rises above them all. Moreover, he has no wish for the things that other people fight about and which cause them distress when they fail to acquire them, even though they would only be condemned if they did acquire them. This detachment frees an acquisitive person from all sufferings in this present life and in the life to come. Because he does not want anything that he does not possess, he is above and beyond all comfort and wealth; while to desire what one lacks is the greatest torment a man can suffer prior to agelong torment. A person in this condition is a slave, even though he may appear to be a rich man or a king. The commandments of the Lord are not burdensome (cf. 1 John 5 : 3).

Yet, abject as we are, we do not carry them out with any eagerness unless we are rewarded for it.

He who can partially understand the grace of the Holy Gospel and the things that are in it – that is to say, the actions and teachings of the Lord, His commandments and His doctrines, His threats and His promises – knows what inexhaustible treasure he has found, even if he cannot speak about such things as he should, since what is heavenly is inexpressible. For Christ is hidden in the Gospel, and he who wishes to find Him must first sell all that he has and buy the Gospel (cf. Matt. 13 : 44). It is not enough merely to find Christ through one's reading, but one should also receive Him in oneself by imitating His way of life in the world. For he who seeks Christ, says St Maximos, should seek him not outside but inside himself.[1] Like Christ he should become sinless in body and soul, in so far as a human being can do this; and he should guard the testimony of his conscience (cf. 2 Cor. 1 : 12) with all his strength. In this way, even though in the eyes of the world he is poor and of no consequence, he will rule as a king over his will at all times, rising above it and rejecting it. For what is the use of appearing to be a king if you are a slave to anger and desire in this world, while in the next you will receive agelong punishment because you would not keep the commandments?

How witless we are when, for the sake of things that are paltry and transient, we do not aspire to receive great and eternal blessings. We reject what is good and pursue the opposite. What can be simpler than giving a glass of cold water or a piece of bread, or than refraining from one's own desires and petty thoughts? Yet through such things the kingdom of heaven is offered to us, by the grace of Him who said: 'Behold, the kingdom of heaven is within you' (Luke 17 : 21). For, as St John of Damaskos says, the kingdom of heaven is not far away, not outside us, but within us. Simply choose to overcome the passions, and you will possess it within you because you live in accordance with God's will. But if you do not choose to do this, you will end up with nothing. For the kingdom of God, say the fathers, is to live in conformity to God; and this is also the meaning of Christ's first and second coming.

We spoke of the second coming when dealing with inward grief. As for the first coming, he who through grace and with full

---

[1] *On Theology* II, 35 (*The Philokalia*, vol. ii, p. 146).

consciousness of soul grasps the significance of the incarnation should in his astonishment exclaim: Great art Thou, O Lord, and marvellous are Thy works; and no word suffices to hymn Thy wonders.[1] Behold, dear Lord, I Thy servant stand before Thee, speechless, motionless, awaiting the light of spiritual knowledge that comes from Thee. For Thou hast said, Lord, 'Without Me you can do nothing' (John 15 : 5). Teach me, therefore, about Thyself. For this reason I have dared, like the sister of Thy friend Lazarus (cf. Luke 10 : 39), to sit at Thy most pure feet, so that I too may hear through my intellect, if not about Thy incomprehensible divinity, then at least about the manner of Thy incarnate life in the world. In this way I shall gain some slight awareness of the meaning of what in Thy grace Thou hast said in the Holy Gospel; and of how Thou hast dwelt among us, 'gentle and humble in heart' (Matt. 11 : 29), as Thou Thyself hast said, so that we might learn from Thee to be the same. Thou hast lived in poverty, though Thou art rich in mercy; by Thy own free choice Thou hast endured toil and thirst, though Thou hast offered to the Samaritan woman living water (cf. John 4 : 10), and hast said: 'If any man thirst, let him come to Me and drink' (John 7 : 37). For Thou art the source of healing, and who can hymn Thy manner of life in this world?

I am earth, ashes, dust, a transgressor, a suicide, who have sinned many times against Thee and continue to do so; yet Thou hast enabled me to grasp something of Thy actions and words; and I dare to ask Thee about them, hoping to see Thee by faith, although Thou art invisible to the whole of creation. Forgive me my boldness. For Thou knowest, O Lord, Searcher of hearts, that I do not ask out of idle curiosity, but seek to learn. I believe that if I am found worthy of Thy spiritual knowledge, then in Thy compassion Thou wilt grant to me, as Thou dost to all who long for Thee, the strength to imitate Thy life in the flesh; for it is by virtue of Thy incarnation that I by grace am called a Christian. Although, unlike Thy disciples, none of us is capable of enduring death for the sake of his enemies, or of acquiring the poverty and virtue which Thou and they possessed, yet each of us does what he can according to the strength of his resolve. For even if we were to die for Thy sake daily, still we could not repay Thee what we owe. For Thou, O Lord, being perfect God and perfect man, hast lived in this world without sin and endured all things on our behalf;

[1] Cf. the prayer at the Great Blessing of the Waters on the Feast of Epiphany: *The Festal Menaion*, p. 356.

while we, even if we do endure something, suffer on our own account and for our own sins. Who is not amazed when he thinks of Thy inexpressible self-abasement? For being God, inscrutable, all-powerful and ruling all things, enthroned above the cherubim – who are figures of wisdom in its multiplicity – on account of us, who have provoked Thy anger from the beginning, Thou hast humbled Thyself, accepting to be born and brought up among us. Thou hast endured persecution, stoning, mocking, insults, cuffs and blows, ridicule and spitting, then the Cross and the nails, the sponge and reed, vinegar and gall, and all the rest that I am unworthy to hear about. Then a spear pierced Thy most pure side, and from this wound Thou hast poured forth for us eternal life: Thy precious blood and water.

I hymn Thy birth and her who gave Thee birth: she whom Thou didst preserve a virgin after she gave birth as she was before she gave birth. I worship Thee in the cave, swaddled in the manger. I glorify Thee, who hast gone down into Egypt with Thy virginal and most pure Mother; who hast lived in Nazareth in obedience to Thy mortal parents, Thy putative father and Thy true mother. I hymn Thee, baptized in Jordan by John the Forerunner – Thee, Lord, and Thy Father who bore witness to Thee, and Thy Holy Spirit who manifested Thee. I hymn Thy baptism and Thy baptizer John, Thy prophet and Thy servant. I glorify Thee who didst fast for us, who hast voluntarily accepted temptation and triumphed over the enemy in the body which Thou didst take from us, giving us victory over him in Thy inexpressible wisdom. I glorify Thee as Thou hast lived together with Thy disciples, cleansed lepers, made cripples stand erect, given light to the blind, speech and hearing to the dumb and the deaf; as Thou hast blessed the loaves and walked upon the sea as upon dry land, taught the crowds about the practice of the virtues and about contemplation, proclaimed the Father and the Holy Spirit, foretold the threats and promises to come, and spoken of all that brings us to salvation. I praise Thee who hast already vanquished the enemy; who dost pull up the passions by their roots with Thy wise teaching; who dost make fools wise and dost overthrow crafty idiots by thy boundless wisdom; who dost raise the dead with Thy inexpressible might and dost cast out demons with Thy authority as God of all. And not only dost Thou do these things in Thy own person, but Thou givest Thy servants the power to do even greater things (cf. John 14 : 12), so that we may be still more astonished, as

Thou Thyself hast said. Great is Thy Name, for through Thee Thy saints perform all their miracles.

Lord Jesus Christ, Son and Logos of God, the most tender name of our salvation, great is Thy glory, great are Thy works, marvellous are Thy words, 'sweeter also than honey and the honeycomb' (Ps. 19 : 10). Glory to Thee, O Lord, glory to Thee. Who can glorify and hymn Thy coming in the flesh, Thy goodness, power, wisdom, Thy life in this world and Thy teaching? And how is it that Thy holy commandments teach us the life of virtue so naturally and so easily? As Thou didst say, Lord: 'Forgive, and you will be forgiven' (cf. Matt. 6 : 14); and again: 'Seek and you will find, knock and it will be opened to you' (Matt. 7 : 7); and: 'Whatever you would that men should do to you, do also to them' (Matt. 7 : 12). Who, having understood Thy commandments and other sayings, will not be astonished when he perceives Thy boundless wisdom? For Thou art the wisdom of God, the life of all, the joy of angels, the ineffable light, the resurrection of the dead, the good shepherd 'who gives His life for the sheep' (John 10 : 11). I hymn Thy transfiguration, crucifixion, burial, resurrection, ascension, Thy enthronement at the right hand of God the Father, the descent of the Holy Spirit and Thy future advent, when Thou wilt come with power and great, incomprehensible glory.

I grow weak, my Lord, before Thy wonders and, at a loss, I long to take refuge in silence. Yet I do not know what to do. For if I keep silence, amazement overwhelms me; but if I dare to say something, I am struck dumb and rapt away. I regard myself as unworthy of heaven and earth, and as deserving every punishment, not simply because of the sins I have committed, but much more because of the blessings I have received without my showing any gratitude, contemptible as I am. For Thou, Lord, who dost transcend all goodness, hast filled my soul with every blessing. I dimly perceive Thy works and my mind is amazed. Merely to look on what is Thine reduces me to nothing. Yet the knowledge is not mine, nor the endeavour, for it is Thy grace. Therefore I will lay my hand on my mouth, as Job once did (cf. Job 40 : 4), and will take refuge in Thy saints, for I am bewildered.

Blessed Queen of the universe, you know that we sinners have no intimacy with the God whom you have borne. But, putting our trust in you, through your mediation we your servants prostrate ourselves before the Lord: for you can freely approach Him since He is your son and our God. Thus I, too, unworthy believer that I am, entreat you, holy Queen, that I may be allowed to perceive the gifts of grace bestowed on you and on the other saints, and to understand how you display so many virtues. Simply your giving birth to the Son of God shows that you excel all other beings. For He who, as creator of all, knows all things before they come into existence, found your womb worthy of His indwelling. No one can question you about your mysteries, for they transcend nature, thought and intellect. Rightly do we, who have been saved through you, pure Virgin, confess that you are the Mother of God, extolling you with the angelic choirs.[1] For God, whom men cannot see, on whom the ranks of angels do not dare to look, has through you become visible to men as the Logos made flesh. Glorifying Him with the heavenly hosts we proclaim you blessed.[2] And what shall we call you, who are full of grace? Heaven, for you have made the Sun of Righteousness shine forth? Paradise, for you have put forth the flower of immortality? Virgin, for you have remained inviolate? Pure mother, for you have held in your holy embrace the God of all?[3] Mother of God, you are the true vine, for you have borne the fruit of life. We entreat you, intercede in your glory with the apostles and all the saints, that God may have mercy on our souls.[4] For with the true faith we confess that you are the Mother of God and we bless you, the ever-blessed. All generations proclaim you blessed as the only Mother of God, more honoured than the cherubim and incomparably more glorious than the seraphim.

Unable to grasp the mysteries of the Mother of God, I marvel at the lives of the other saints, and ask: How did you dwell, Baptist and Forerunner of the Lord, in the desert? What shall we call you, O prophet: angel, apostle, martyr? Angel, because you lived as though bodiless; apostle, because you caught the nations in your net; martyr, because you were beheaded for Christ's sake. Pray to Him for the salvation of our souls.[5] 'The memory of the just is praised', as Solomon says (cf. Prov. 10 : 7. LXX); but the Lord's testimony

[1] Tone 8, Mattins, Canon, Canticle 9, irmos.
[2] *Paraklitiki*, Tone 6, Sunday Mattins, Canon, Canticle 9, irmos.
[3] Theotokion at the First Hour: Hapgood, *Service Book*, p. 39.
[4] Theotokion at the Third Hour: Hapgood, *Service Book*, p. 46.
[5] Feast of the Beheading of St John the Baptist (29 August), Vespers, stichiron at the Lity.

suffices you, Forerunner: truly you were proclaimed greater in honour than the prophets, for you were found worthy to baptize Him whom they prophesied.[1]

Holy apostles and disciples of the Saviour, eyewitnesses of His mysteries, you have proclaimed Him whom none can contemplate and who has no origin, saying, 'In the beginning was the Logos' (John 1 : 1). You were not created before the angels, nor did you learn this from men, but from the wisdom that is from above. We beseech you, then, since you have communion with God, intercede for our souls. I marvel at your love of God. It is as the ancient troparia say: 'Lord, because the apostles truly longed for Thee on earth, they considered all things to be dung, so that they might gain Thee alone (cf. Phil. 3 : 8). For Thee they gave their bodies over to torture and, glorified because of this, they intercede for our souls.'[2] How is it that, being men, as we are, and wearing flesh of clay, you displayed such virtues, so that you even endured death for the sake of those who slew you? How, few though you were, did you conquer the whole world? How, though simple and unlettered, did you overcome kings and rulers? How, though unarmed, naked and poor, enclosed in weak flesh, did you defeat the invisible demons? And what was the great strength, or rather faith, which enabled you to receive the power of the Holy Spirit – you and the holy martyrs who fought the good fight and received their crowns? Apostles, martyrs, prophets, hierarchs, holy men, we beseech you to intercede with Christ so that in His goodness He will save our souls.[3]

Who is not astounded when he sees, O holy martyrs, the good fight that you fought? Being in the body you conquered the bodiless enemy, confessing Christ and armed with the Cross. In this way justly you were revealed to be expellers of demons and enemies of barbaric powers. Intercede unceasingly for the salvation of our souls.[4] For, like the three children in the fiery furnace, you did not endure your trials in the hope of a reward, but out of love for God, as you yourselves have declared: 'For even if He does not deliver us, yet we will not for that reason deny Him as one who does not save' (cf. Dan. 3 : 17–18). I marvel at your extreme humility, holy children, for even though you

[1] Feast of the Beheading of St John the Baptist, dismissal hymn at Vespers.
[2] *Paraklitiki*, Tone 8, Wednesday Vespers, aposticha.
[3] *Paraklitiki*, Tone 2, Saturday Mattins, kathisma after the first stichology.
[4] *Paraklitiki*, Tone 4, Monday Mattins, aposticha.

were surrounded by flames, you declared that you did not know how to give thanks to God. 'There is at this time no prince, prophet, leader or burnt offering', you said, '. . . but because we come with a contrite heart and humble spirit, accept us' (Song of the Three Children, verses 15–16). I marvel at the power of God that has filled you, and that also filled Elijah the prophet; as St John of Damaskos has said: 'Out of the flame hast Thou made dew fall upon Thy saints (cf. Song of the Three Children, verse 27), and hast burnt up with water the sacrifice of the Righteous One (cf. 1 Kgs. 18 : 38). For Thou doest all things, O Christ, simply by Thy will alone.'[1] Yet which shall I contemplate first? The testimonies found in the Gospel, or the Acts of the Apostles? The contests of the martyrs, or the struggles of the holy fathers, or of the saints ancient and recent, both men and women? Their lives and sayings, or their power of interpretation and discernment? I am at a loss and stand amazed.

But I pray Thee, compassionate Lord, do not allow me to be condemned because of the unworthy and ungrateful manner in which I contemplate the great mysteries that Thou hast revealed to Thy saints and through them to me, a sinner and Thy unworthy servant. For see, Lord, Thy servant stands before Thee, idle in everything, speechless, as one who is dead; and I do not dare to say anything more or presumptuously to contemplate further. But as always I fall down before Thee, crying from the depths of my soul and saying, 'Master, rich in mercy, Lord Jesus Christ . . .' and the rest of the prayer.[2] (Here you should meditate on the second prayer[3] and the psalms, watching over the conduct of your soul and body, so that you develop a disposition receptive to divine thoughts. Then you will be able with full consciousness to understand all the mysteries and miracles hidden within the Holy Scriptures. Astounded in this way at God's gifts, you will come to love Him alone and to suffer for His sake with joy, as all the saints have done. For the Holy Scriptures are full of astonishing things, as Solomon says.)

Along with the other marvels, I wonder at God's power as it was manifest in the manna. For the manna did not preserve the same form until the following day, but dissolved and was found to be full of

---

[1] Sunday of Forgiveness, Mattins, Canon, Canticle 8, katavasia: *The Lenten Triodion*, p. 177.

[2] Prayer at the end of Great Compline: Hapgood, *Service Book*, p. 162.

[3] Perhaps the prayer after Compline, 'Forgive, O Lord who lovest man, those who hate and wrong us . . .': Hapgood, *Service Book*, p. 163.

worms (cf. Exod. 16 : 20). This was to prevent those who lacked faith from concerning themselves about the next day. But in the pitcher that was in the tabernacle it remained unchanged (cf. Exod. 16 : 32–34). Again, when cooked with fire the manna was not burnt; yet it dissolved at the faintest ray of sunlight, so that the greedy should not collect more than they needed to keep alive. How marvellously God works everywhere for the salvation of men, as the Lord says with regard to divine providence: 'My Father goes on working and I work too' (John 5 : 17). He who reverently meditates on this is outwardly taught by the Holy Scriptures, and inwardly by divine providence. He begins to see things as they are in their true nature, as St Gregory of Nyssa and St John of Damaskos say. He is no longer deceived by the exterior attractiveness of the things of this world, such as physical beauty, wealth, transient glory and so on; nor is he seduced by the shadows they cast, as are those still subject to the passions.

THE FIFTH STAGE OF CONTEMPLATION

Through the fifth stage of contemplation, that called 'counsel' by the prophet (cf. Isa. 11 : 2), one comes to understand, as the final Beatitude indicates, the changeable nature of visible created things: how they derive from the earth and return again to the earth, thus confirming the words of Ecclesiastes: 'Vanity of vanities; all is vanity' (Eccles. 1 : 2). St John of Damaskos says the same thing: 'All human affairs, all that does not exist after death, are vanity. Riches vanish, glory leaves us. When death comes, all such things disappear.' And again, 'Truly all things are vanity; life is but a shadow and a dream, and every man born of the earth troubles himself in vain, as the Scriptures say (cf. Ps. 39 : 6. LXX). By the time we have gained the whole world we shall be in the grave, where king and pauper are one.'[1]

[1] From the Funeral Service: Hapgood, *Service Book*, pp. 381, 385.

THE SIXTH STAGE OF CONTEMPLATION

When a person has acquired the habit of detachment, then he is granted access to the sixth stage of contemplation, that known as 'strength' (cf. Isa. 11 : 2). At this stage one begins to look without passion on the beauty of created things.

There are three categories of thought: human, demonic, and angelic.[1] Human thought consists in the abstract conception, arising in the heart, of some created thing, such as a man, or gold, or some other sensible object. Demonic thought consists in a conceptual image compounded with passion. One thinks, for example, of a human being, but this thought is accompanied by mindless affection, that is to say, by the desire for a relationship not blessed by God but involving unchastity; or else it is accompanied by unreasoning hatred, that is to say, by rancour or spite. Again, one thinks of gold avariciously or with the intention of stealing or seizing it; or else one is roused to hatred and blasphemy against God's works, thus causing one's own perdition. For if we do not love things as they should be loved, but love them more than we love God, then we are no different from idolators, as St Maximos says.[2] But if, on the other hand, we hate and despise things, failing to perceive that they were created 'wholly good and beautiful' (Gen. 1 : 31), we provoke the anger of God.

Angelic thought, finally, consists in the dispassionate contemplation of things, which is spiritual knowledge proper. It is the mid-point between two precipices, protecting the intellect and enabling it to distinguish between its true goal and the six diabolic pitfalls that threaten it. These pitfalls lie above and below, to the right and left, and on the near side and on the far side of the intellect's true goal. Thus spiritual knowledge proper stands as though at the centre, surrounded by these pitfalls. It is the knowledge taught by those earthly angels who have made themselves dead to the world, so that their intellect has grown dispassionate and hence sees things as it

---

[1] Cf. Evagrios, *Texts on Discrimination* 7 (*The Philokalia*, vol. i, pp. 42–3); also Maximos the Confessor, *On Love* II, 84 (*The Philokalia*, vol. ii, p. 79).

[2] *On Love* I, 7 (*The Philokalia*, vol. ii, p. 53).

should. In this way, the intellect does not go above its true goal out of pride or self-esteem, thinking it understands things merely through its own power of thought; nor does it fall below its true goal, prevented by ignorance from attaining perfection. It does not veer to the right through rejecting and hating created things, or to the left through mindless affection for them and attachment to them. It does not remain on the near side of its true goal because of its utter ignorance and sloth, nor trespass on its far side, lured by the spirit of meddlesomeness and senseless curiosity that arises from contempt or maliciousness. Rather, it accepts spiritual knowledge with patience, humility and the hope that is born of a deep faith. In this way, through its partial knowledge of things the intellect is led upwards towards divine love. But, even though it possesses some knowledge, it is aware that it is still ignorant; and this awareness keeps it in a state of humility. Thus through persistent hope and faith it reaches its goal, neither hating anything completely as evil, or loving anything beyond measure.

We should look on man with wonder, conscious that his intellect, being infinite, is the image of the invisible God; and that even if it is for a time limited by the body, as St Basil says, it can embrace all form, just as God's providence embraces the whole universe. For the intellect has the ability to transform itself into everything, and is dyed with the form of the object it apprehends. But when it is taken up into God, who is formless and imageless, it becomes formless and imageless itself. Then we should marvel at how the intellect can preserve any thought or idea, and how an earlier thought need not be modified by later thoughts, or a later thought injured by earlier ones. On the contrary, the mind like a treasure-house tirelessly stores all thoughts. And these thoughts, whether new or long held in store, the intellect when it wishes can express in language; yet although words are always coming from it, it is never exhausted.

When we come to consider the body, we should marvel at the way in which eyes, ears and tongue are used externally according to the soul's wish, eyes through the medium of light, and ears and tongue through the medium of air; and how no one sense impedes any of the others or can do anything the soul does not intend. We should marvel, too, at how the body, that is not its own animating principle, is, at God's command, commixed with the noetic and deiform soul, created by the Holy Spirit breathing life into it (cf. Gen. 2 : 7), as St John of Damaskos says.[1] Yet it is wrong to think, as some do, that the soul is an emanation from the supraessential Godhead, for this is impossible. As St John Chrysostom says, 'In order to prevent the human intellect from thinking that it is God, God has subjected it to ignorance and forgetfulness, so that in this way it may acquire humility.' He also says that the Creator willed that there should be a separation in this natural intermixture of soul and body. The deiform soul, as St John Klimakos says, either ascends upward to heaven, or goes downward to Hades, while the earthly body returns to the earth from which it was taken.[2] But through the grace of our Saviour Jesus Christ these two separated elements are once more joined together at His second coming, so that each of us may receive the due reward for his works. Who can grasp but an inkling of this mystery without being astonished? God raises man again from the earth after he has committed so many terrible crimes, despising the divine commandments, and He bestows on man the same immortality that he possessed originally, even though man has disobeyed the commandment which preserves him from death and corruption, and in his arrogance has drawn death upon himself.

Enlightened spiritually through angelic inspiration, man marvels at these and many other things concerning human nature. Again, he contemplates the beauty and use of gold, and marvels at how such a thing has come out of the earth for our sake, so that the weak may distribute their wealth in acts of charity, while those unwilling to exercise such charity are helped to do so by various unsought trials which, so long as they are thankfully accepted, lead to salvation. Thus both groups are saved. Those, however, who choose to shed all their possessions will be crowned with glory, for – like those who live in virginity – they accomplish what transcends nature. In so far as gold is a perishable and earthly thing, it is not to be preferred to the commandments of God; yet as something created by God and useful for bodily life and for salvation, it deserves, not our hatred, but our love and self-control.

By thus contemplating dispassionately the beauty and use of each thing, he who is illumined is filled with love for the Creator. He surveys all visible things in the upper and lower worlds: the sky, the

---

[1] *Exposition of the Faith* II, 12 (ed. Kotter, §26, p. 76).
[2] *Ladder*, Step 26 (1036B; E.T., p. 217).

sun, the moon, stars and clouds, water-spouts and rain, snow and hail, how in great heat liquids coagulate, thunder, lightning, the winds and breezes and the way they change, the seasons, the years, the days, the nights, the hours, the minutes, the earth, the sea, the countless flocks, the four-legged animals, the wild beasts and reptiles, all the kinds of bird, the springs and rivers, the many varieties of plant and herb, both wild and cultivated. He sees in all things the order, the equilibrium, the proportion, the beauty, the rhythm, the union, the harmony, the usefulness, the concordance, the variety, the delightfulness, the stability, the motion, the colours, the shapes, the forms, the reversion of things to their source, permanence in the midst of corruption.

Contemplating thus all created realities, he is filled with wonder. He marvels how the Creator by a simple command brought the four elements forth out of nothing; how, by virtue of His wisdom, opposites do not destroy one another; and how out of the four elements God made all things for our sake. Yet, as St Gregory the Theologian says, these things are insignificant in comparison with Christ's incarnation and with the blessings to come. He perceives, too, how God's goodness and wisdom, His strength and forethought, which are concealed in created things, are brought to light by man's artistic powers. It is as God Himself said to Job (cf. Job 12 : 13). Similarly he sees how by means of words and letters – through fragments of inanimate ink – God has revealed such great mysteries to us in the Holy Scriptures; and how, even more wonderfully, the holy prophets and apostles gained such blessings through their great labour and love of God, while we can learn about these matters simply by reading. For, inspired by the Logos, the Scriptures speak to us of the most astonishing things.

Whoever is aware of all this recognizes that there is nothing incidental or evil in creation, and that even what takes place against God's will is miraculously changed by God into something good. For example, the fall of the devil was not God's will, yet it has been turned to the advantage of those being saved. For the devil is permitted to tempt the elect – according to the strength of each, as St Isaac says – so that he may be mocked and, with God's help, defeated by them.[1] And these people, who have achieved equality with the

---

[1] *Mystic Treatises*, E.T., p. 186; Greek, p. 216.

angels, include not only men, but also great numbers of women. Because of their patient endurance and faith in the divine Judge they receive, by His grace and compassion, crowns of immortality: for God has defeated and continues to defeat the murderous and insolent snake.

The person who has received the grace of spiritual knowledge knows that all things are 'wholly good and beautiful' (Gen. 1 : 31); but he who possesses only the first glimmerings of such knowledge should recognize in all humility that he is ignorant and, as St John Chrysostom advises, he should admit on every occasion, 'I do not know'. For, as Chrysostom says, 'if someone asserts that the height of the sky is such and such, and I say that I do not know, at least I have told the truth, whereas the other person is deceived into thinking that he knows while in fact he does not know, as St Paul says' (cf. 1 Cor. 8 : 2).[1] It is on this account that with firm faith and by questioning those with experience we should accept the doctrines of the Church and the decisions of its teachers, both concerning the Holy Scriptures and concerning the sensible and spiritual worlds. Otherwise we may quickly fall because we walk according to our own understanding, as St Dorotheos puts it.[2] We should admit our own ignorance in all things, so that by searching and with distrust in our own opinions we may aspire to learn and, at a loss in spite of great knowledge, may realize our own ignorance through recognizing the infinite wisdom of God.

The intellect, being spiritual, is capable of every spiritual perception when it purifies itself for God, according to St Gregory the Theologian. Yet we should regard such knowledge with the greatest apprehension, lest there be hidden in our soul a single evil doctrine able to destroy it without our committing any other sin, as St Basil the Great says. For this reason we should not try, through contempt or arrogant zeal, to attain this kind of contemplative knowledge prematurely; rather we should practise the commandments of Christ in due order and proceed undistracted through the various stages of contemplation previously discussed. Once we have purified the soul through patient endurance and with tears of fear and inward grief, and have reached the state of seeing the true nature of things, then – initiated spiritually by the angels – the intellect spontaneously attains this contemplative knowledge.

[1] Cf. On the Incomprehensibility of God II, 6–7; V, 5 (P.G. xlviii, 717–18, 742–3).
[2] Instructions V, 61 (ed. Regnault, p. 250).

But if a person is presumptuous and tries to reach the second stage before having reached the first, then not only will he fail to conform to God's purpose, but he will provoke many battles against himself, particularly through speculating about the nature of man, as we have learnt in the case of Adam. Those still subject to the passions gain nothing by attempting to act or think as if they were dispassionate: solid food is not good for babies, even though it is excellent for the mature (cf. Heb. 5 : 14). Rather they should exercise discrimination, yearning to act and think like the dispassionate, but holding back, as being unworthy. Yet when grace comes they should not reject it out of despair or laziness; neither should they presumptuously demand something prematurely, lest by seeking what has its proper time before that time has come, as St John Klimakos says, they fail to attain it in its proper time, and fall into delusion, perhaps beyond the help of man or the Scriptures.[1]

If a person's purpose is fixed in God with all humility and he patiently endures the trials that come upon him, God will resolve for him any question that perplexes him and perhaps even leads him into delusion. Then, greatly ashamed but full of joy, he turns back, seeking the path of the fathers. For, as St John Klimakos states, we should regard what happens according to God's will, and nothing else, as coming from grace for our good, even though in itself it is not very good. Without such patience and humility a person will suffer what many have suffered, perishing in their stupidity, trusting to their own opinions and thinking they can get along very well without either a guide or the experience that comes from patience and humility. For experience transcends tribulation, trials and even active warfare. Should a person of experience be subject to some slight attack on the part of the demons, this trial will be a source of great joy and profit to him; for it is permitted by God so that he may gain yet further experience and courage in facing his enemies.

The signs that he has done this are tears, contrition of soul before God, flight into stillness and patient recourse to God, a diligent enquiry into the Scriptures and a desire, based on faith, to accomplish God's purpose. When, on the other hand, a person lacks patience and humility, the signs of this are doubt with regard to God's help, being ashamed to ask questions humbly, avoidance of stillness and the

---

[1] *Ladder*, Step 26 (1032C; E.T., p. 214).

reading of Scripture, a love of distraction and of human company, with the idea – entirely misguided – that one will attain a state of repose in this way. On the contrary, it is now that the passions find an opportunity to put down roots, and that trials and temptations grow stronger, while one's own pusillanimity, ingratitude and listlessness wax because of one's abounding ignorance.

The trials imposed by spiritual fathers in order to discipline and instruct their spiritual children are one thing; but the trials brought on by our enemies for our destruction are another. This is especially true when we are deluded by pride; for 'God opposes the proud, but gives grace to the humble' (cf. Jas. 4 : 6; Prov. 3 : 34. LXX). Every tribulation that we accept patiently is good and profitable; but if we do not accept it patiently, it drives us away from God and serves no useful purpose. When this happens, there is only one cure – humility. The humble man censures and blames himself and no one else when he suffers affliction. Consequently, he patiently awaits for God to release him, and when this happens he rejoices and gratefully endures whatever comes; and through his experience of these things he gains spiritual knowledge. Recognizing his own ignorance and weakness, he seeks diligently for the Physician and, seeking, he finds Him, as Christ himself has said (cf. Matt. 7 : 8). Having found God, he longs for Him; and the more he longs, the more God longs for him. Then, purifying himself as much as he can, he struggles to make room in himself for the Beloved for whom he longs. And the Beloved for whom he longs, finding room for Himself in this man, takes up His abode there, as the *Gerontikon* says. Dwelling there, He protects His home, and fills it with light. And the person thus filled with light knows and, knowing, he is known, as St John of Damaskos says.

In all this, and in what has been said above, one should keep a proper order, and one should work on whatever one understands. For what one cannot understand one should give silent thanks, as St Isaac says, but should not presumptuously assume that one has understood it. And St Isaac, borrowing his words from Sirach, also says: 'When you find honey, eat moderately, lest by over-indulging you make yourself sick' (cf. Prov. 25 : 16).[1] As St Gregory the Theologian says, 'Uncontrolled contemplation may well push us

---

[1] *Mystic Treatises*, E.T., pp. 35–6; Greek, pp. 96–7.

over the edge, when we seek for what is beyond our strength and are unwilling to say, "God knows this; but who am I?" '[1] And as St Basil observes, we must believe that He who made the mountains and the great sea-monsters has also hollowed out the sting of the bee.[2]

Thus he who is strong enough to attain understanding apprehends the spiritual from the sensible, and the invisible and eternal from what is visible and transient. Having grasped, through grace, a knowledge of the higher powers, he sees that a single righteous man is worth more than the whole world. 'Consider how many tongues and nations the righteous man excels', says St John Chrysostom. 'Yet an angel is greater than man, and the vision of a single angel is enough to fill us with astonishment. Remember what happened to Daniel, the equal of the angels, when he saw the angel' (cf. Dan. 10 : 5–21).[3]

THE SEVENTH STAGE OF CONTEMPLATION

A person given grace to attain the seventh stage of contemplation marvels at the multitude of incorporeal powers: authorities, thrones, dominions, seraphim and cherubim, the nine orders mentioned in all the divine Scriptures, whose nature, power and other good qualities, as well as their hierarchical disposition, are known to God their Creator. But the heavenly hosts have also other ranks, about which St John Chrysostom speaks. He says that the words 'Lord of Sabaoth' mean 'Lord of the celestial powers', and that these powers transmit illumination to one another. The angels, he says, illumine man, while they in turn are illumined by the archangels; these are illumined by the principalities. Thus each order receives illumination and knowledge from another.[4] He also tells us that humankind constitutes as it were but a single sheep, lost not by God but through its own choice, and that the ninety-nine other sheep are the orders of angels (cf. Matt. 18 : 12–14).[5]

---

[1] *Oration* 39, 8 (*P.G.* xxxvi, 344A).

[2] Cf. *On the Six Days of Creation* IX, 5 (*P.G.* xxix, 201D).

[3] *On the Incomprehensibility of God* III, 4 (*P.G.* xlviii, 722).

[4] Op. cit., II, 4; III, 5–6 (*P.G.* xlviii, 714, 724–5). Cf. Dionysios the Areopagite, *The Celestial Hierarchy* IV, 2; VII, 2 (*P.G.* iii, 180B, 208A).

[5] Cf. Gregory of Nyssa, *Against Eunomios* 10 (ed. Jaeger, vol. ii, p. 293; *P.G.* xlv, 889A).

Considering the wisdom and power of the Creator and how He has produced such multiple states of being simply by summoning them into existence, St Gregory the Theologian says that God conceived first the angelic powers and then the states sequent to them.[1] As St Isaac says, on passing spiritually beyond the threshold – that is to say, beyond the veil of the temple – one becomes immaterial. The outer part of the temple represents this world; the veil or the threshold represents the firmament of heaven; the holy of holies represents the supracosmic realm where the bodiless and immaterial powers ceaselessly hymn God and intercede for us, as St Athanasios the Great says. In that realm one's thoughts are at peace and one becomes a son of God by grace, initiated into the mysteries hidden in the Holy Scriptures, as St John of Damaskos puts it: 'The divine veil of the temple was rent by the Cross of the Creator, revealing to the faithful the truth concealed beneath the literal sense of Scripture; and they cry: God of our fathers, blessed art Thou.'[2] As St Kosmas the Hymnographer says, 'When the first man tasted the tree, he was commixed with corruption: cast out ignobly from life and with a body subject to corruption, he passed on this punishment to all mankind. But we, the earth-born, restored through the wood of the Cross, cry aloud: Blessed art Thou and praised above all for ever.'[3]

THE EIGHTH STAGE OF CONTEMPLATION

Through the eighth stage of contemplation we are led upwards to the vision of what pertains to God by means of the second kind of prayer, the pure prayer proper to the contemplative. In it the intellect is seized during the transport of prayer by a divine longing, and it no longer knows anything at all of this world, as both St Maximos[4] and St John of Damaskos confirm. Not only does the intellect forget all things, but it forgets itself as well. Evagrios says that so long as the

---

[1] *Oration* 45, 5–6 (*P.G.* xxxvi, 629ABC).

[2] *Paraklitiki*, Tone 3, Sunday Mattins, Canon, Canticle 7, troparion.

[3] Feast of the Exaltation of the Cross (14 September), Mattins, Canon, Canticle 7, troparion: *The Festal Menaion*, p. 149.

[4] *On Love* I, 10 (*The Philokalia*, vol. ii, p. 54).

intellect is still conscious of itself, it abides, not in God alone, but also in itself. According to St Maximos, it is only when it abides in God alone that it is granted direct vision of what pertains to God and, through the indwelling of the Holy Spirit, becomes in the true sense a theologian.[1]

In our ignorance, however, we should not identify God in Himself with His divine attributes, such as His goodness, bountifulness, justice, holiness, light, fire, being, nature, power, wisdom and the others of which St Dionysios the Areopagite speaks.[2] God in Himself is not among any of the things that the intellect is capable of defining, for He is undetermined and undeterminable. In theology we can speak about the attributes of God but not about God in Himself, as St Dionysios explains to St Timothy, invoking St Hierotheos as witness.[3] It is indeed more correct to speak of God in Himself as inscrutable, unsearchable, inexplicable, as all that it is impossible to define. For He is beyond intellection and thought, and is known only to Himself, one God in three hypostases, unoriginate, unending, beyond goodness, above all praise. All that is said of God in divine Scripture is said with this sense of our inadequacy, that though we may know that God is, we cannot know what He is; for in Himself He is incomprehensible to every being endowed with intellect and reason.[4]

The same applies to the incarnation of the Son of God and to the hypostatic union, as St Cyril says. We can only marvel at the way in which the flesh He assumed from us is taken up into His divinity, as St Basil the Great puts it. The union is like that of fire and iron, and it is on this model that we are to conceive of the two natures in the single person of Christ. As St John of Damaskos says in his hymn to the Mother of God: 'O most holy Lady, you have given birth to the incarnate God as one hypostasis in two natures; and to Him we all sing: Blessed art Thou, O God.'[5] And again: 'Without changing, He who is beyond determination was in you, all-holy Lady, united hypostatically to our flesh; for He is compassionate and He alone is blessed.'[6]

---

[1] Cf. *On Theology* I, 39 (*The Philokalia*, vol. ii, p. 122).

[2] *The Divine Names* I, 6 (*P.G.* iii, 596AB); *Mystical Theology* 3–5 (1032D–1048B).

[3] Cf. *The Divine Names* II, 10 (*P.G.* iii, 648CD).

[4] Cf. Basil, *Against Eunomios* I, 12 (*P.G.* xxix, 540A); Gregory of Nazianzos, *Oration* 28, 17 (*P.G.* xxxvi, 48c).

[5] *Paraklitiki*, Tone 5, Sunday Mattins, Canon, Canticle 7, Theotokion.

[6] *Paraklitiki*, Tone 5, Sunday Mattins, Canon to the Theotokos, Canticle 7, troparion.

THAT THERE ARE NO CONTRADICTIONS
IN HOLY SCRIPTURE

Whenever a person even slightly illumined reads the Scriptures or
sings psalms he finds in them matter for contemplation and
theology, one text supporting another. But he whose intellect is still
unenlightened thinks that the Holy Scriptures are contradictory. Yet
there is no contradiction in the Holy Scriptures: God forbid that
there should be. For some texts are confirmed by others, while
some were written with reference to a particular time or a
particular person. Thus every word of Scripture is beyond reproach.
The appearance of contradiction is due to our ignorance. We ought
not to find fault with the Scriptures, but to the limit of our capacity
we should attend to them as they are, and not as we would like
them to be, after the manner of the Greeks and Jews. For the
Greeks and Jews refused to admit that they did not understand, but
out of conceit and self- satisfaction they found fault with the
Scriptures and with the natural order of things, and interpreted
them as they saw fit and not according to the will of God. As a
result they were led into delusion and gave themselves over to every
kind of evil.

The person who searches for the meaning of the Scriptures will
not put forward his own opinion, bad or good; but, as St Basil the
Great and St John Chrysostom have said, he will take as his teacher,
not the learning of this world, but Holy Scripture itself. Then if his
heart is pure and God puts something unpremeditated into it, he
will accept it, providing he can find confirmation for it in the
Scriptures, as St Antony the Great says.[1] For St Isaac says that the
thoughts that enter spontaneously and without premeditation into
the intellects of those pursuing a life of stillness are to be accepted;
but that to investigate and then to draw one's own conclusions is an
act of self-will and results in material knowledge.[2]

This is especially the case if a person does not approach the
Scriptures through the door of humility but, as St John Chrysostom
says, climbs up some other way, like a thief (cf. John 10 : 1), and
forces them to accord with his allegorizing. For no one is more

[1] *Apophthegmata*, Antony 3; E.T., p. 2.
[2] Cf. *Mystic Treatises*, E.T., p. 351.

foolish than he who forces the meaning of the Scriptures or finds fault with them so as to demonstrate his own knowledge – or, rather, his own ignorance. What kind of knowledge can result from adapting the meaning of the Scriptures to suit one's own likes and from daring to alter their words? The true sage is he who regards the text as authoritative and discovers, through the wisdom of the Spirit, the hidden mysteries to which the divine Scriptures bear witness.

The three great luminaries, St Basil the Great, St Gregory the Theologian and St John Chrysostom, are outstanding examples of this: they base themselves either on the particular text they are considering or on some other passage of Scripture. Thus no one can contradict them, for they do not adduce external support for what they say, so that it might be claimed that it was merely their own opinion, but refer directly to the text under discussion or to some other scriptural passage that sheds light on it. And in this they are right; for what they understand and expound comes from the Holy Spirit, of whose inspiration they have been found worthy. No one, therefore, should do or mentally assent to anything if its integrity is in doubt and cannot be attested from Scripture. For what is the point of rejecting something whose integrity Scripture clearly attests as being in accordance with God's will, in order to do something else, whether good or not? Only passion could provoke such behaviour.

THE CLASSIFICATION OF PRAYER ACCORDING TO THE EIGHT STAGES OF CONTEMPLATION

Where the first four of the eight stages of contemplation are concerned, we should say the traditional written prayers daily; where the last four are concerned, like St Philimon we should continuously utter the words 'Lord, have mercy', keeping our intellect completely free from thoughts.[1] Those who are advanced on the spiritual way should direct their intellect now to the contemplation of sensible

---

[1] *A Discourse on Abba Philimon* (*The Philokalia*, vol. ii, p. 346).

realities, and now to the cognition of intelligible realities and to that which is formless; now to the meaning of some passage of the Scriptures, and now to pure prayer. On the bodily level they should engage sometimes in reading, sometimes in prayer, sometimes in shedding tears over their own state or, out of divinely-inspired sympathy, on behalf of others; or they should undertake some task in order to assist someone unwell either mentally or physically.

Thus at all times they will fulfil the work of the angels, never concerning themselves with the things of this world. For God, who has chosen them, who has set them apart to be His companions, and has granted them this way of life and this freedom from anxiety, will Himself look after them and nourish them in soul and body: 'Cast your burden upon the Lord, and He will nourish you' (Ps. 55 : 22. LXX). The more they place their hope in the Lord with regard to all things that concern them, whether of soul or body, the more they will find that the Lord provides for them. In the end they will regard themselves as lower than all other creatures because of God's many gifts, visible and invisible, bestowed on both soul and body. So great grows their debt that they cannot feel proud about anything because of their shame at God's generosity. The more they give thanks to Him and try forcibly to exert themselves for the sake of His love, the more God draws near to them through His gifts and longs to fill them with peace, making them value stillness and voluntary poverty more than all the kingdoms of this earth, without even taking account of any reward in the world to come.

The holy martyrs suffered when tormented by their enemies, but their longing for the kingdom and their love of God conquered the pain. They even regarded the strength they were given to overcome their enemies as a further great blessing that added to their debts. As a result, when found worthy of enduring death for Christ's sake, they had in many cases lost all sense of pain. In the same way the holy fathers at first exerted themselves forcibly in many forms of asceticism, as well as in their warfare against the spirits of evil; but their longing and aspiration for the state of dispassion was triumphant.

After his struggles the person who attains the state of dispassion is relieved of all worry and anxiety, because he has conquered the passions. A person still subject to the passions may also think that all is well, but he does so merely because of his blindness. It is only the spiritual contestant who wants to conquer the passions but finds he cannot do so that suffers tribulation and warfare. Sometimes God allows a person in this situation to be defeated by his enemies so that he may acquire humility. On account of this he ought to recognize his own weakness and flee vigorously from what harms him, so that he forgets his former habits. For if one does not first flee from distraction and acquire complete quietude, one will never be dispassionate with regard to anything, or be able always to say what is right and good. In short, this total flight from distraction is of prime importance in all things, if one is not to be dragged back by one's former habits. But let no one, on hearing about humility, dispassion and other such things, think in his ignorance that he possesses them. He should search for the signs of these things in himself and see if he can find them.

HUMILITY

The following are the signs of humility: when possessing every virtue of body and soul, to consider oneself to be the more a debtor to God because, though unworthy, one has received so much by grace; when tried or tempted by the demons or by men, to regard oneself as deserving such things – and much more – so that a small part of one's debt may be taken away and one may find some mitigation of the punishment one expects on the day of judgment; when not suffering any such trial, to be extremely troubled and afflicted, and to look for some way in which to exert oneself more forcibly; on achieving this, again to take it as a gift from God and so to humble oneself further; and, not discovering anything to give God in return, to continue to labour and to consider oneself to be all the more a debtor.

DISPASSION

This, surely, is the sign of dispassion: to remain calm and fearless in all things because one has received by God's grace the strength to do anything, as St Paul puts it (cf. Phil. 4 : 13). Such a person is totally unconcerned about his material life, but exerts himself in ascetic labours as forcibly as he can, and so attains a state of repose. Full of thanksgiving, he exerts himself still more forcibly, thus finding himself always engaged in battle and triumphing with the help of humility. It is by this means that a person advances; for, as St Isaac says, things accomplished without forcefulness are not works but gifts of God. If one were to find repose after one's first efforts, it would be the prize of defeat and not a reason for boasting. It is not those who receive a reward who are to be praised, but those who exert themselves forcibly in their labours and who receive nothing.

What can we say? The more we act and the more we give thanks to our Benefactor, the more we are His debtors; for He is without need and wants nothing, while without Him we are not able to do anything good (cf. John 15 : 5). The person found worthy of praising God gains more by it than God, for he has received a great and marvellous gift of grace. The more he praises God, the more he becomes a debtor, until finally he finds no limit or interruption to his knowledge of God or to thanksgiving or humility or love. For these things belong, not to this world – which would mean that they had an end – but to that eternal world which does not have an end and in which there is on the contrary an increase in knowledge and in gifts of grace. He who in thought and practice is found worthy of that world is freed from all the passions.

In order to attain all this we must focus our attention on God, have no concern for this world, and must not be dismayed by any trial or temptation. Starting from this world, we must continually advance, ascending to a higher level of reality. We should not be distracted by anything: neither by dreams, whether evil or seemingly good, nor by the thought of anything, whether good or bad, nor by distress or deceitful joy, nor by self-conceit or despair, nor by depression or elation, nor by a sense of abandonment or by illusory help and strength, nor by negligence or progress, nor by laziness or seeming zeal, nor by apparent dispassion or passionate attachment. Rather with humility we should strive to maintain a state of stillness, free from all distraction, knowing that no one can do us harm unless we ourselves wish for it.

Because of our conceit and our failure constantly to have recourse to God, we should cast ourselves down before Him, asking that His will should be done in all things and saying to every thought that comes to us: I do not know who you are; God knows if you are good or not; for I have thrown myself, as I shall continue to throw myself, into His hands, and He looks after me (cf. 1 Pet. 5 : 7). For just as He created me out of what was not, so it is within His power to save me by His grace if He so chooses. May His holy will be done in this world and in the next, as He wishes and when He wishes. I have no will of my own. I know but one thing: that, though I have sinned greatly, I receive great blessings; and yet I do not even thank God for His goodness through my actions and my thoughts, so far as it is in my power to do so. In spite of this He is able and willing to save all men, myself included, as He wishes. How do I know, being a man, whether He wants me to be this or that? Thus, through fear of sinning, I have fled to this stillness; and because of my sins and my many weaknesses I sit doing nothing in my cell, like a prisoner, awaiting the Lord's decision.

Yet even if we see that we are doing nothing and are altogether lost, let us not be afraid; for if we do not leave our cell, we will learn contrition of soul and will shed heartfelt tears. But again, should we find ourselves eager to undertake spiritual labours and should we be granted such tears, let us not rejoice over this but be on our guard against fraud and prepare ourselves for war.

In short, we should be detached from all things, whether good or bad, so that nothing perturbs us and we reach a state of stillness, struggling as much as we can and, if we have someone to advise us, doing what we are told to do. If we do not have anyone to advise us, we should take Christ as our counsellor, asking Him with humility and through pure heartfelt prayer about every thought and undertaking. Let us not presume that we are fully-tested monks until we have encountered Christ in the world to be, as Abba Agathon[1] and St John Klimakos tell us. If our sole purpose is to do God's will, God Himself will teach us what it is, assuring us of it either directly, through the intellect, or by means of some person or of Scripture. And if for God's sake we amputate our own will, God will enable us to reach, with inexpressible joy, a perfection that we have never known; and when we experience this we will be filled with wonder at seeing how joy and spiritual knowledge begin to pour forth from everywhere. We will derive some profit from everything and God will reign in us, since we have no will of our own, but have submitted ourselves to the holy will of God. We become like kings, so that whatever we desire we receive effortlessly and speedily from God, who has us in His care.

---

[1] *Apophthegmata*, Agathon 29; E.T., pp. 24-5.

This is the faith with which the Lord said it is possible to move mountains (cf. Matt. 21 : 21); upon it, according to St Paul (cf. Col. 1 : 23), the other virtues are founded. For this reason the enemy does everything he can to disrupt our state of stillness and make us fall into temptation. And if he finds us in some way lacking in faith, wholly or partially trusting in our own strength and judgment, he takes advantage of this to overcome us and to take us captive, pitiful as we are. Once we have truly grasped this, we will abandon all the delights and comforts of this world, and will free ourselves as fast as possible from its preoccupations and anxieties. We will do this either through the way of obedience, setting our spiritual father in the place of Christ and referring every idea, thought and action to him, so that we have nothing we can call our own; or by following the path of stillness in resolute faith, fleeing from all things.

Then for us Christ takes the place of all things and becomes all things for us, in this world and in the world to come, as St John Chrysostom and St John of Damaskos say. Christ feeds us, clothes us, brings us joy, encourages us, gladdens us, gives us rest, teaches and enlightens us. In short, Christ cares for us as He cared for His disciples; and even if we do not have to toil as they did, yet we have their firmness of faith, which frees us from the self-concern that dominates other people. Like the apostles in their fear of the Jews, we sit in our cells out of fear of the spirits of evil, and we await our Teacher. We await Him so that through contemplation in the full sense, or through the spiritual knowledge of His creatures, we may be helped to rise noetically from the passions and be given peace, as happened according to St Maximos to the apostles when the doors were closed (cf. John 20 : 19).[1]

A FURTHER ANALYSIS OF THE SEVEN FORMS
OF BODILY DISCIPLINE

We should always carry out what was said at the beginning of this work with regard to the seven forms of bodily and moral discipline, not doing either more or less than was recommended there.

---

[1] *On Theology* II, 46 (*The Philokalia*, vol. ii, p. 148).

Exceptions may be made if a person is too young to engage in bodily warfare, or if he possesses excessive bodily strength which requires a correspondingly severe degree of discipline. Again, exceptions may be made in cases of bodily frailty: here a certain relaxation can be allowed, but not a total suspension of discipline, for this according to St Isaac can harm even the dispassionate. The relaxation must be no more than is necessary as a remedy for the sickness; then the soul will not take it as an excuse for slackening its own exertions. This is the right course when a person desperately wants some relaxation. Yet such relaxation, they say, can be dangerous for the young and the healthy.

The holy fathers St Basil and St Maximos state that, to relieve hunger and thirst, only bread and water are needed, while for health and bodily strength we require other foods that God in His compassion has given us. But so that the constant eating of the same thing does not produce a feeling of revulsion in the sick person, he should eat different foods, one at a time, as already said. It is abstention and dissipation that bring on illness, while self-control and a change of foods each day are conducive to health. The body then remains impervious to pleasure and sickness, and co-operates in the acquisition of the virtues.

As has been said, all this is intended for those who are still engaged in the struggle for purification. As for those who have attained the state of dispassion, they often do not eat for days on end, since they have become like children in their devotion to Christ and forget about their bodies. St Sisois was such a person: in the ecstasy of his love for God he asked to take communion after he had eaten.[1] As St Paul said for the good of us all, 'If we go out of ourselves in ecstasy, it is for God; if we are restrained, it is for your sake' (2 Cor. 5 : 13). Among others, St Basil the Great has also spoken of these things. Certain people in this state, even after eating plentifully, have not been aware of it: it is as if they had eaten nothing. For their intellect is not in the body, and so is not aware of the body's ease or its pain.

This is clear from many of the fathers and holy martyrs, as well as from the saint whom Evagrios described.[2] A certain elder living in the desert, he tells us, used to pray noetically; and it happened – for his benefit as well as for that of many others – that God permitted the

---

[1] *Apophthegmata*, Sisois 4; E.T., p. 213.
[2] *On Prayer* 111 (*The Philokalia*, vol. i, p. 68).

demons to seize him hand and foot and fling him down from a high place; yet so that he would not be harmed by falling from such a height, they would catch him on a rush-mat. This they did for some time, trying to see if his intellect would descend from the heavens; but they were not able to make it do so. When would such a man be aware of food or drink or of anything bodily? Or take the case of St Ephrem: after he had conquered all the passions of soul and body by the grace of Christ, he asked in his immense humility that the gift of dispassion might be taken away from him, so that he would not fall into idleness and be condemned because he no longer had to fight the enemy. St John Klimakos was amazed at this and wrote that there are some, like St Ephrem, who are more dispassionate than those who have attained the state of dispassion.[1]

DISCRIMINATION

We therefore need discrimination in all things so that we may rightly assess every form of action. For him who possesses it, discrimination is a light illuminating the right moment, the proposed action, the form it takes, strength, knowledge, maturity, capacity, weakness, resolution, aptitude, degree of contrition, inner state, ignorance, physical strength and temperament, health and misery, behaviour, position, occupation, upbringing, faith, disposition, purpose, way of life, degree of fearlessness, skill, natural intelligence, diligence, vigilance, sluggishness, and so on. Then discrimination reveals the nature of things, their use, quantity and variety, as well as the divine purpose and meaning in each word or passage of Holy Scripture. An example of how to discern such a meaning occurs in the Gospel of St John. When the Greeks came wanting to see the Lord, He said, 'The hour is come' (John 12 : 23). Clearly He meant that the moment for the calling of the Gentiles had arrived; for the time of His passion had begun, and He used this request from the Greeks as a sign. Discrimination clarifies all these things and also the significance of the interpretation given by the fathers. As St Neilos says, it is not what happens that is the object of our enquiry, but why it happens.

[1] *Ladder*, Step 29 (1148D; E.T., p. 259).

If we act in ignorance of all this we may expend much effort but will accomplish nothing. That is what St Antony the Great[1] and St Isaac say about those who struggle to attain bodily virtues but neglect the work proper to the intellect, though such work should be our main concern. In the words of St Maximos, 'Engage the body in ascetic practice according to its capacity, but apply your whole effort to the intellect.'[2] As he points out, the person disciplining his body is sometimes overcome by gluttony and somnolence, by distraction and· talkativeness, and through these he darkens his intellect; at other times he clouds his mind through extended fasting, vigils and excessive labours. But he who cultivates the intellect contemplates, prays and engages in theology, and is able to achieve every virtue.

A sensible person struggles intelligently to minimize, so far as he can, the needs of his body, so that he may devote himself to the keeping of the commandments with few or no material preoccupations. Indeed, the Lord Himself says, 'Do not worry about your life, what you will eat, or what you will drink, or about your body, what you will put on' (Matt. 6 : 25). When a person is full of such anxiety he cannot even see himself: how then can he perceive the long-prepared snares of the enemy? For, as St John Chrysostom remarks, the enemy does not always fight in the open. If he did, so many of us would not have fallen so readily into his snares, leaving but a few that are saved, as the Lord says (cf. Luke 13 : 23–24). On the contrary, when he wants to plunge a person into some great sin, the enemy prepares the ground by making him negligent in trivial, unnoticed things. For example, before adultery, there are frequent licentious glances; before murder, moments of anger; before the clouding of the mind, small distractions; and, before these, concern for what appear to be the needs of the body. Because of this the Lord who, as the Wisdom of the Father (cf. 1 Cor. 1 : 24), foreknows all things and so anticipates the devil's tricks, commands us to frustrate the impulses to sin by cutting them off before they can develop, lest by thinking that little things may readily be condoned we fall calamitously into great and terrible sins. This He emphasizes in the Sermon on the Mount, when He says, 'It was said by the men of old', that is, by those under the Law, and then continues, 'But I say to you' (cf. Matt. 5 : 21–48).

[1] *Apophthegmata*, Antony 8; E.T., p. 8.
[2] *On Love* IV, 63 (*The Philokalia*, vol. ii, p. 108).

The true student of the Holy Gospels should therefore pay attention to what the Saviour teaches him and do all he can to escape from the enemy's traps. He should regard the commandments as a privilege and a great blessing, since through their deep wisdom he can save his soul. The commandments are a gift from God and, as St James, the brother of God, rightly says, 'All good giving and every perfect gift comes from above' (Jas. 1 : 17). And St John of Damaskos says, 'Thou hast appointed her who gave Thee birth as an infallible ambassador for us, O Christ; through her intercession grant us Thy merciful Spirit, the bestower of all goodness, who comes through Thee from the Father.'[1]

The man who has received the grace of being attentive to Holy Scripture will find, as the fathers say, all benediction hidden everywhere within it. 'He who is instructed in the kingdom of heaven', says the Lord, 'is like a householder who produces from his storeroom things new and old' (Matt. 13 : 52); and this means someone who has learnt how to read Scripture with devoted attention. For Scripture presents one aspect to most people, even if they think that they understand its meaning, and another to the person who has dedicated himself to continual prayer, that is, who keeps the thought of God always within him, as if it were his breathing. As St Basil the Great says, this is true even if in a worldly sense the person is ignorant and uneducated with regard to secular and merely human knowledge. God reveals Himself, as St John Klimakos states, to simplicity and humility, and not to those who engage in laborious study and superfluous learning.[2] Indeed, God turns away from such learning if it is not allied to humility: as St Paul says, it is better to be ignorant in speech rather than in spiritual knowledge (cf. 2 Cor. 11 : 6). Spiritual knowledge is a gift of grace, but skill in speaking is a matter of human learning, as are the other forms of worldly education: they do not contribute to the salvation of the soul. The example of the pagan Greeks makes this clear.

Reading serves as a reminder for those who know from experience about what is being said, while to those who lack ex-perience it provides instruction. As St Basil remarks, when God finds a heart free from all worldly matters and worldly learning, He then writes on it His own thoughts as if it were a clean slate. I say this

[1] *Paraklitiki*, Tone 3, Sunday Mattins, Canon to the Theotokos, Canticle 9, troparion.
[2] *Ladder*, Step 26 (1024C; E.T., p. 209).

so that no one will read what does not assist him to conform to God's will. But if in ignorance of this he does read something unprofitable, let him quickly try to erase it from his mind through spiritual reading in the Holy Scriptures, and especially in those that contribute to the salvation of his soul at the particular point which he has reached in his development. If he is still engaged in ascetic practice, let him read the lives and sayings of the fathers; if grace has raised him to the sphere of divine knowledge, let him read in all the Holy Scriptures, since, in the words of St Paul, this is able to destroy 'all the self-esteem that exalts itself against the knowledge of God' (2 Cor. 10 : 5), and to correct all disobedience and transgression through active virtue and true knowledge of the divine commandments and teachings of Christ. Read nothing other than these; for what is the use of giving admittance to an unclean spirit rather than to the Holy Spirit? For our aim is to grasp the spirit of whatever text we study, even though that does not appear so difficult to us as it does to those with experience.

SPIRITUAL READING

The purpose of spiritual reading is to keep the intellect from distraction and restlessness, for this is the first step towards salvation. Solomon says that the enemy 'hates the sound of steadfastness' (Prov. 11 : 15. LXX), while the wandering of the mind is the first step towards sinning, as St Isaac states.[1] If you want to be completely free from distraction, keep to your cell. Should you become listless, work a little for the benefit of others and to help the sick, for this is what the man of dispassion and the man of spiritual knowledge do. This, indeed, is what the greatest of the fathers did, allowing themselves for the sake of humility to act in the same way as those enslaved to the passions. For they were always able to hold God within themselves and to devote themselves to contemplation in Him, whether working with their hands or in the market place. As St Basil the Great says, even when in a crowd the truly perfect are always alone with themselves and God.

[1] Cf. *Mystic Treatises*, E.T., p. 222; Greek, p. 290.

If you have not yet reached this stage, but want to get rid of your listlessness, you should give up all talk with other people and all sleep beyond what is necessary, allowing the listlessness to smelt you in body and soul, until such time as it grows exhausted and retreats in the face of your patient uninterrupted devotion to God, your reading, and the purity of your prayer. For every enemy assailant, if he sees that he can accomplish something, continues to fight; but when he sees that he cannot, he withdraws, either for good or for a short while. Thus, if you want to defeat your assailants you should endure with all patience: 'He who endures to the end will be saved' (Matt. 10 : 22). According to St Paul, it is right to afflict those who vex us, and to bring relief to ourselves when we are afflicted (cf. 2 Thess. 1 : 6–7).

Nothing done in humility for the sake of God is bad. But things and pursuits differ. Everything not strictly necessary is a hindrance to salvation – everything, that is to say, that does not contribute to the soul's salvation or to the body's life. For it is not food, but gluttony, that is bad; not money, but attachment to it; not speech, but idle talk; not the world's delights, but dissipation; not love of one's family, but the neglect of God that such love may produce; not the clothes worn only for covering and protection from cold and heat, but those that are excessive and costly; not the houses that also protect us from heat and cold, as well as from anything human or animal that might harm us, but houses with two or three floors, large and expensive; not owning something, but owning it when it has no vital use for us; not the possession of books on the part of those who have embraced total poverty, but the possession of books for some purpose other than spiritual reading; not friendship, but the having of friends who are of no benefit to one's soul; not woman, but unchastity; not wealth, but avarice; not wine, but drunkenness; not anger used in accordance with nature for the chastisement of sin, but its use against one's fellow-men.

Again, it is not authority that is bad, but the love of authority; not glory, but the love of glory and – what is worse – vainglory; not the acquisition of virtue, but to suppose that one has acquired it; not spiritual knowledge, but to think that one is wise and – worse than this – to be ignorant of one's own ignorance; not true knowledge but what is falsely called knowledge (cf. 1 Tim. 6 : 20); not the world, but the passions; not nature, but what is contrary to nature; not agreement, but agreement to do what is evil and does not contribute to the soul's salvation; not the body's members, but their misuse. For sight was given us, not so that we should desire what we ought not to desire, but so that on seeing God's creatures we might because of them glorify the Creator and thus nourish our soul and our body. The ears were given us, not to listen to slander and stupidities, but to hear the word of God and every form of speech – of men, birds or anything else – that leads us to glorify the Creator. The nose was given us, not so that we might debilitate and unbrace our soul with delectable perfumes, as St Gregory the Theologian puts it, but so that we might breathe the air bestowed on us by God, and glorify Him because of it; for without it neither man nor beast can live bodily.

I marvel at God's wisdom, at how the most indispensable things – air, fire, water, earth – are readily available to all. And not simply this, but things conducive to the soul's salvation are more accessible than other things, while soul-destroying things are harder to come by. For example, poverty, which anyone can experience, is conducive to the soul's salvation; while riches, which are not simply at our command, are generally a hindrance. It is the same with dishonour, humiliation, patience, obedience, submission, self-control, fasting, vigils, the cutting off of one's will, bodily enfeeblement, thankfulness for all things, trials, injuries, the lack of life's necessities, abstinence from sensual pleasure, destitution, forbearance – in short, all the things conducive to the spiritual life are freely available. No one fights over them. On the contrary, everyone leaves them to those who choose to accept them, whether they have been sought for or have come against our will. Soul-destroying things, on the other hand, are not so readily within our grasp – things like wealth, glory, pride, intolerance, power, authority, dissipation, gluttony, excessive sleep, having one's own way, health and bodily strength, an easy life, a good income, unrestricted hedonism, lavish and costly clothes, and so on. People struggle greatly for these things, but only a few attain them, and in any case the benefit they confer is fleeting. In short, they produce a great deal of trouble and very little enjoyment. For they bring to those who possess them, as well as to those who do not possess them but desire to do so, all manner of distress.

None the less, it is not the thing itself, but its misuse, that is evil. For we were given hands and feet, not so that we might steal and plunder and lay violent hands on one another, but so that we might use them in ways agreeable to God. The weaker among us should use what we have in acts of compassion towards the poor, so as to help our own spiritual development and to assist the needy; while those who are stronger in soul and body should give away all their possessions in imitation of Christ and His holy disciples. In this way we can glorify God and at the same time learn to look with wonder at the divine wisdom hidden in our limbs. For through God's providence our hands and fingers are apt for every skill and activity, whether writing or anything else. From God, too, comes the knowledge of numberless arts and scripts, of healing and medicine, of languages and the various other branches of learning. In short, all things, whether past, present or future, have been and are always being given to us by God in His great goodness, so that our bodies may live and our souls may be saved, provided we use all these things according to His purpose, glorifying Him through them with all thankfulness. If we fail to do this, we will fall and perish, and all things will cause us affliction in this present age, while in the age to be they will bring on us agelong punishment, as has been said.

TRUE DISCRIMINATION

If by the grace of God you have received the gift of discrimination, you should in great humility do everything you can to guard it, so that you do nothing without it. Otherwise you will bring on yourself greater chastisement by sinning knowingly because of your negligence. If you have not received this gift you should not think, say or do anything without consulting others about it, and without a basis of firm faith and pure prayer. Without such faith and such prayer you will never truly achieve discrimination.

Discrimination is born of humility. On its possessor it confers spiritual insight, as both Moses and St John Klimakos say:[1] such a man foresees the hidden designs of the enemy and foils them before they are put into operation. It is as David states: 'And my eyes looked down upon my enemies' (Ps. 54 : 7. LXX). Discrimination is

---

[1] *Ladder*, Step 25 (1004A; E.T., p. 201).

characterized by an unerring recognition of what is good and what is not, and the knowledge of the will of God in all that one does. Spiritual insight is characterized, first, by awareness of one's own failings before they issue in outward actions, as well as of the stealthy tricks of the demons; and, second, by the knowledge of the mysteries hidden in the divine Scriptures and in sensible creation.

As has been already explained, humility, the mother of discrimination and spiritual insight, likewise has its own characteristic by which it is known. The humble person must possess every virtue and yet truly think himself the greatest of debtors and inferior to everything else in creation. If, however, a person does not think in this way, then he can be assured that he is in fact inferior to everything else in creation, even though he seems to lead a life like that of the angels. For even a true angel possessing so many virtues and so much wisdom cannot conform to the Creator's will unless he also possesses humility. What, then, can a person who thinks that he is an angel say for himself if he lacks humility, source of all present and future blessings, begetter of that discrimination which illumines the ends of the earth and without which all things are obscure?

Discrimination is not only called light; it truly is light. We need this light before we say or do anything. When it is present we are able to view everything else with wonder. We can marvel at how God, on the first and greatest of days, began by creating light, so that what was subsequently created might not be invisible and as if it did not exist, as St John of Damaskos says.[1] Let it be said again: discrimination is light; and the spiritual insight it generates is more necessary than all other gifts. For what is more necessary than to perceive the wiles of the demons and with the help of God's grace to protect one's soul? Other things most necessary to us include, according to St Isaac, purity of conscience;[2] and, according to the apostle, the sanctification of the body (cf. Rom. 12 : 1; 1 Cor. 6 : 19–20) without which 'no one will see the Lord' (Heb. 12 : 14).

---

[1] *Exposition of the Faith* II, 7 (ed. Kotter, §21, p. 54).
[2] Cf. *Mystic Treatises*, Greek, p. 354.

THAT WE SHOULD NOT DESPAIR
EVEN IF WE SIN MANY TIMES

Even if you are not what you should be, you should not despair. It
is bad enough that you have sinned; why in addition do you wrong
God by regarding Him in your ignorance as powerless? Is He, who
for your sake created the great universe that you behold, incapable
of saving your soul? And if you say that this fact, as well as His
incarnation, only makes your condemnation worse, then repent; and
He will receive your repentance, as He accepted that of the prodigal
son (cf. Luke 15 : 20) and the prostitute (cf. Luke 7 : 37–50). But if
repentance is too much for you, and you sin out of habit even when
you do not want to, show humility like the publican (cf. Luke
18 : 13): this is enough to ensure your salvation. For he who sins
without repenting, yet does not despair, must of necessity regard
himself as the lowest of creatures, and will not dare to judge or
censure anyone. Rather, he will marvel at God's compassion, and
will be full of gratitude towards his Benefactor, and so may receive
many other blessings as well. Even if he is subject to the devil in
that he sins, yet from fear of God he disobeys the enemy when the
latter tries to make him despair. Because of this he has his portion
with God; for he is grateful, gives thanks, is patient, fears God, does
not judge so that he may not be judged. All these are crucial
qualities. It is as St John Chrysostom says about Gehenna: it is
almost of greater benefit to us than the kingdom of heaven, since
because of it many enter into the kingdom of heaven, while few
enter for the sake of the kingdom itself; and if they do enter it, it is
by virtue of God's compassion. Gehenna pursues us with fear, the
kingdom embraces us with love, and through them both we are
saved by Christ's grace.[1]
    If those attacked by many passions of soul and body endure
patiently, do not out of negligence surrender their free will, and do
not despair, they are saved. Similarly, he who has attained the state
of dispassion, freedom from fear and lightness of heart, quickly falls
if he does not confess God's grace continually by not judging

[1] *Homilies on 1 Timothy* 15, 3 (P.G. lxii, 583).

anyone. Indeed, should he dare to judge someone, he makes it evident that in acquiring his wealth he has relied on his own strength, as St Maximos states. St John of Damaskos says that if someone still subject to the passions, and still bereft of the light of spiritual knowledge, is put in charge of anyone, he is in great danger;[1] and so is the person who has received dispassion and spiritual knowledge from God but does not help other people.

Nothing so benefits the weak as withdrawal into stillness, or the man subject to the passions and without spiritual knowledge as obedience combined with stillness. Nor is there anything better than to know one's own weakness and ignorance, nor anything worse than not to recognize them. No passion is so hateful as pride, or as ridiculous as avarice, 'the root of all evils' (1 Tim. 6 : 10): for those who with great labour mine silver, and then hide it in the earth again, remain without any profit. That is why the Lord says, 'Do not store up treasures on earth' (Matt. 6 : 19); and again: 'Where your treasure is, there will your heart be also' (Matt. 6 : 21). For the intellect of man is drawn by longing towards those things with which it habitually occupies itself, whether these be earthly things, or the passions, or heavenly and eternal blessings. As St Basil the Great says, a persistent habit acquires all the strength of nature.[2]

A weak person especially ought to pay attention to the promptings of his conscience, so that he may free his soul from all condemnation. Otherwise at the end of his life he may repent in vain and mourn eternally. The person who cannot endure for Christ's sake a physical death as Christ did, should at least be willing to endure death spiritually. Then he will be a martyr with respect to his conscience, in that he does not submit to the demons that assail him, or to their purposes, but conquers them, as did the holy martyrs and the holy fathers. The first were bodily martyrs, the latter spiritual martyrs. By forcing oneself slightly, one defeats the enemy; through slight negligence one is filled with darkness and destroyed.

[1] Cf. Neilos, *Ascetic Discourse* (*The Philokalia*, vol. i, pp. 215, 221).
[2] *Longer Rules* 6 (*P.G.* xxxi, 925B).

SHORT DISCOURSE ON THE ACQUISITION OF THE VIRTUES AND ON ABSTINENCE FROM THE PASSIONS

According to St Basil the Great, nothing so darkens the mind as evil, and nothing so enlightens the intellect as spiritual reading in stillness. Nor does anything so quickly fill the soul with sorrow as the thought of death, or so contribute to our secret progress as self-reproach and the excising of our own will. On the other hand, nothing so abets our secret destruction as conceit and self-satisfaction, or so cuts us off from God and provokes our chastisement at the hands of other men as grumbling, or so disposes us to sin as a disorderly life and talkativeness. Again, nothing so quickly fosters the acquisition of virtue as the solitary life and meditation, or so rapidly promotes gratitude and thankfulness as reflection on God's gifts and our own wickedness. Nothing so augments the blessings bestowed on us as our recognition of them, or so contributes to our salvation, even against our will, as trials and temptations. There is no shorter way to Christ – that is to say, to dispassion and the wisdom of the Spirit – than the royal way that avoids both excess and deficiency in all things; nor is any virtue more capable of comprehending the divine will than humility and the abandoning of every personal thought and desire. Nothing so contributes to every good action as pure prayer, and nothing so impedes the acquisition of the virtues as even the slightest mental distraction and day-dreaming.

The greater one's purity, the more clearly one sees how much one sins; and the more one sins, the more benighted one is, even though one may appear to be pure. Again, the more knowledge one has, the more one thinks oneself ignorant; and the more one is ignorant of one's ignorance and of the shortcomings in one's spiritual knowledge, the more one thinks one knows. The more the spiritual contestant endures afflictions, the more he will defeat the enemy; and, lastly, the more one tries for one day to do something good, the more one is a debtor all the days of one's life, as St Mark has said;[1] for even if the ability and desire to do good are one's own,

[1] Mark the Ascetic, *On those who think that they are made righteous by works* 43–4 (*The Philokalia*, vol. i, p. 129).

the grace to do it comes from God. It is only because of this grace that we are able to do anything good; when we do it, then, what have we to boast about? If we boast, it shows that we imagine we have done something good simply through our own strength, and that we unjustly condemn those incapable of doing the same. But he who demands something of others should more rightfully demand it of himself.

If sinners should tremble because they have angered God, those who have been shielded by His grace because of their weakness and proneness to despair should tremble even more, since they are deeply in His debt. St Epiphanios says that ignorance of the Scriptures is a huge abyss; worse still is evil consciously committed; while great is the benefit that the soul receives through Scripture and through prayer. To bear with our neighbour; not to distress him when he wrongs us but to help him to be at peace when he is troubled, as St Dorotheos puts it;[1] to show compassion towards him, sharing his burden and praying for him, full of longing that he may be saved and may enjoy every other blessing of body and soul – this is true forbearance; and it purifies the soul and leads it towards God.

To heal a person is the greatest thing one can do and excels all other virtue, because among the virtues there is nothing higher or more perfect than love for one's neighbour. The sign of this love is not just that one does not keep for oneself anything of which another has need, but also that, as the Lord enjoins, one should joyfully endure death for his sake (cf. John 15 : 13), looking on it as a debt we have to pay. And this is as it should be: for we should love our neighbour to the point of dying for him, not only because nature requires this of us, but also because of the precious blood poured out for us by Christ who commanded us to love in this way. Do not love yourself, says St Maximos, and you will love God;[2] do not pander to your ego, and you will love your brother. Such love comes through hope; and to hope is to believe unhesitatingly that one will surely attain what one hopes for. This in turn is born of a firm faith, where one has no concern whatsoever for one's own life or death, but casts all care upon God (cf. 1 Pet. 5 : 7), as I said when speaking about the person who wants to acquire the signs of

[1] *Instructions* III, 44 (ed. Regnault, p. 214).
[2] *On Love* IV, 37 (*The Philokalia*, vol. ii, p. 104).

dispassion, of which faith is the foundation. He who has faith should reflect that since God in His extreme goodness has created all things – ourselves included – out of non-existence, He is certainly capable of providing as He thinks fit for our souls and bodies.

HOW TO ACQUIRE TRUE FAITH

If we desire to acquire faith – the foundation of all blessings, the door to God's mysteries, unflagging defeat of our enemies, the most necessary of all the virtues, the wings of prayer and the dwelling of God within our soul – we must endure every trial imposed by our enemies and by our many and various thoughts. Only the inventor of evil, the devil, can perceive these thoughts or uncover and describe them. But we should take courage; because if we forcibly triumph over the trials and temptations that befall us, and keep control over our intellect so that it does not give in to the thoughts that spring up in our heart, we will once and for all overcome all the passions; for it will not be we who are victorious, but Christ, who is present in us through faith. It was with regard to this that Christ said, 'If you have faith no bigger than a mustard-seed . . .' (Luke 17 : 6). Yet even if our thought, in a moment of weakness, should succumb, we should not be afraid or despair, or ascribe to our own soul what is said to us by the devil. On the contrary, we should patiently and diligently, to the limit of our strength, practise the virtues and keep the commandments, in stillness and devotion to God, freeing ourselves from all thoughts subject to our volition.

In this way the enemy, who day and night promotes every kind of fantasy and deceit, will not find us worried about his tricks and illusions and all the thoughts within which he lurks, presenting to us as truth what are really deceits and falsehoods; and so he will lose heart and go away. Through such experience of the devil's weakness, the man who practises Christ's commandments will no longer be alarmed by any of his tricks. On the contrary, he will do whatever accords with God's will joyfully and without hindrance, strengthened by faith and assisted by God in whom he has believed. As the Lord

Himself has said, 'All things are possible for the person who believes' (Mark 9 : 23). For it is not he who fights the enemy, but God, who watches over him on account of his faith. As the Prophet said, 'You have made the Most High your refuge' (Ps. 91 : 9. LXX). Such a person no longer feels anxiety about anything, for he knows that 'though the horse is made ready for battle, salvation comes from the Lord' (Prov. 21 : 31). Because of his faith he faces everything boldly. As St Isaac says, 'Acquire faith within you and you will trample on your enemies.'

The man of faith acts, not as one endowed with free will, but as a beast that is led by the will of God. He says to God: 'I became as a beast before Thee; yet I am continually with Thee' (Ps. 73 : 22–23). If Thy desire is that I should be at rest in Thy knowledge, I shall not refuse. If it is that I should experience temptation so as to learn humility, again I am with Thee. Of myself, there is absolutely nothing I can do. For without Thee I would not have come into existence from non-existence; without Thee I cannot live or be saved. Do what Thou wilt to Thy creature; for I believe that, being good, Thou bestowest blessings on me, even if I do not recognize that they are for my benefit. Nor am I worthy to know, nor do I claim to understand, so as to be at rest: this might not be to my profit.

I do not dare to ask for relief in any of my battles, even if I am weak and utterly exhausted: for I do not know what is good for me. 'Thou knowest all things' (John 21 : 17); act according to Thy knowledge. Only do not let me go astray, whatever happens; whether I want it or not, save me, though, again, only if it accords with Thy will. I, then, have nothing: before Thee I am as one that is dead; I commit my soul into Thy pure hands, in this age and in the age to be. Thou art able to do all things; Thou knowest all things; Thou desirest every kind of goodness for all men and ever longest for my salvation. This is clear from the many blessings that in Thy grace Thou hast bestowed and always bestowest on us, visible and invisible, known to us and unknown; and from that gift of Thyself to us, O Son and Logos of God, which is beyond our understanding. Yet who am I that I should dare to speak to Thee of these things, Thou searcher of hearts? I speak of them in order to make known to myself and to my enemies that I take refuge in Thee, the harbour of my salvation. For I know by Thy grace that 'Thou art my God' (Ps. 31 : 14).

I do not dare to say many things, but only wish to set before Thee an intellect that is inactive, deaf and dumb. It is not myself but Thy grace that accomplishes all things. For, knowing that I am always full of evil, I do not attribute such things to my own goodness; and because of this I fall down as a servant before Thee, for Thou hast found me worthy of repentance, and 'I am Thy servant, and the son of Thy handmaid' (Ps. 116 : 16). But do not allow me, my Lord Jesus Christ, my God, to do, say or think anything contrary to Thy will: the sins I have already committed are enough. But in whatever way Thou desirest have mercy on me. I have sinned: have mercy on me as Thou knowest. I believe, Lord, that Thou hearest this my pitiable cry, 'Help Thou my unbelief' (Mark 9 : 24), Thou who hast granted me, not only to be, but also to be a Christian. 'It is a great thing', St John of Karpathos has said, 'for me to be called a monk and a Christian.'[1] As Thou hast said, Lord, to one of Thy servants, 'It is no light thing for you to be called by My name' (cf. Isa. 49 : 6. LXX). This is more to me than all the kingdoms of heaven or of earth. Let me always be called by Thy most sweet name. O Master, full of compassion, I give thanks to Thee.

Just as certain readings and certain words, tears and prayers are appropriate for one engaged in ascetic practice, so his is a different kind of faith from that superior faith which gives birth to stillness. The former is the faith of hearsay, the latter is the faith of contemplation, as St Isaac says.[2] Contemplation is more sure than hearsay. For the ordinary initial faith of the Orthodox is born of natural knowledge, and from this faith are born devotion to God, fasting and vigil, reading and psalmody, prayer and the questioning of those with experience. It is such practices that give birth to the soul's virtues, that is, to the constant observance of the commandments and of moral conduct. Through this observance come great faith, hope, and the perfect love that ravishes the intellect to God in prayer, when one is united with God spiritually, as St Neilos puts it.

The words of prayer are written once and for all, so that he who wishes to present his intellect motionless before the Holy and Life-giving Trinity may always pray one and the same prayer. The intellect itself has the sense that it is seen, even though at that time it is utterly impossible for it to see anything, for it is imageless, formless,

[1] For the Encouragement of the Monks in India 44 (The Philokalia, vol. i, p. 308).
[2] Mystic Treatises, E.T., p. 214; Greek, p. 65.

colourless, undisturbed, undistracted, motionless, matterless, entirely transcending all the things that can be apprehended and perceived in the created world. It communes with God in deep peace and with perfect calm, having only God in mind, until it is seized with rapture and found worthy tò say the Lord's Prayer as it should be said. This is what we are told by St Philimon[1] and St Irene, as well as by the holy apostles, the martyrs and other holy men. Anything other than this is illusion born of self-conceit. For the Divine is infinite and uncircumscribed, and the intellect that returns to itself must be in a similar state, so that through grace it may experience the indwelling of the Holy Spirit. 'For we walk by faith, not by sight,' says St Paul (2 Cor. 5 : 7).

For this reason we should persist in our ascetic practice, so that through this enduring persistence our intellect is drawn in longing towards the Divine. For if the intellect does not find something that is superior to sensible realities it cannot direct its desire towards it, abandoning the things to which it has been so long accustomed. Just as the compassionate and the dispassionate are not greatly harmed by the affairs of this life, since they manage them well, so those who have received great gifts of grace are not harmed, since they ascribe their achievements to God.

THAT STILLNESS IS OF GREAT BENEFIT TO THOSE SUBJECT TO PASSION

Stillness and withdrawal from men and human affairs are of benefit to all, but especially to those who are weak and subject to the passions. For the intellect cannot attain dispassion by means of ascetic practice alone; such practice must be followed by spiritual contemplation. Nor will anyone escape unharmed from distraction and from exercising authority over others unless he has first acquired dispassion through withdrawal. The cares and confusion of this life are liable to harm even the perfect and the dispassionate. Human effort is profitless, says St John Chrysostom, without help from above; but no one receives

---

[1] A Discourse on Abba Philimon makes no special reference to the Lord's Prayer, but commends the use of the Jesus Prayer (The Philokalia, vol. ii, pp. 347–8).

such help unless he himself chooses to make an effort.[1] We need always both things; we need the human and the divine, ascetic practice and spiritual knowledge, fear and hope, inward grief and solace, fearfulness and humility, discrimination and love. For, he says, all things in life are twofold: day and night, light and dark, health and sickness, virtue and vice, ease and adversity, life and death. Through the help from above we in our weakness come to love God, while through our own effort we flee sin out of our fear of trials. But if we are strong we can love God as our Father in all things, knowing that all things are 'wholly good and beautiful' (Gen. 1 : 31) and that God orders them for our benefit. We will restrain ourselves from pleasures and long for adversity, knowing that through such self-restraint our bodies are imbued with life for the glory of the Creator, while through adversity our souls are helped towards salvation by the ineffable mercy of God.

Men are of three kinds: slaves, hirelings or sons. Slaves do not love the good, but refrain from evil out of fear of punishment; this, as St Dorotheos observes,[2] is a good thing, but not fully in accord with God's will. Hirelings love what is good and hate what is evil, out of hope of reward. But sons, being perfect, refrain from evil, not out of fear of punishment, but because they hate evil violently; and they do what is good, not because they hope for reward, but because they consider it their duty. They love dispassion because it imitates God and leads Him to dwell in them; through it they refrain from all evil, even if no punishment threatens them. For unless we are dispassionate God in His holiness does not send down His Holy Spirit upon us, lest we violate His indwelling because out of habit we are still drawn towards the passions, and so incur greater condemnation. But when we are established in virtue, and are no longer friendly with our enemies or pulled this way and that by our impassioned habits, then we receive grace and are not liable to condemnation through receiving it. It is for this reason, according to St John Klimakos,[3] that God does not reveal His will to us lest, after learning it, we disobey Him and so incur greater condemnation, failing like children to recognize in our ingratitude His limitless mercy towards us. For if we want to learn the divine will, he says, we must die to the whole world and to our every wish.

---

[1] *Homilies on Matthew* 82, 4 (P.G. lviii, 742).
[2] *Instructions* IV, 47–48 (ed. Regnault, pp. 220–2).
[3] *Ladder*, Step 26 (1060B; E.T., pp. 219–20).

We should not do anything about which we feel hesitation, nor should we consider something good unless we cannot live or be saved without it. That is why we should question men of experience. In this way, through prayer and firm faith we receive a sense of assurance, until such time as we attain the perfect dispassion that makes our intellect invulnerable and invincible in every good activity. Thus the battle is great, but we remain unharmed. 'For My power comes to its fulness in your weakness', says the Lord to St Paul; and St Paul adds, 'When I am weak, then I am strong' (2 Cor. 12 : 9–10). It is not good to be free from warfare. For the demons retreat for many reasons, as St John Klimakos explains:[1] it may be in order to set an ambush, or to make one presumptuous; and they leave behind self-elation or some other evil, contenting themselves with this on the grounds that it can take the place of the other passions.

The fathers, says the *Gerontikon*, kept the commandments; their successors wrote them down; but we have placed their books on the shelves.[2] And even if we want to read them, we do not have the application to understand what is said and to put it into practice; we read them either as something incidental, or because we think that by reading them we are doing something great, thus growing full of pride. We do not realize that we incur greater condemnation if we do not put into practice what we read, as St John Chrysostom says. And we should remember what the Lord says about the servant who knew his master's will but failed to carry it out (cf. Luke 12 : 47).

Thus reading and spiritual knowledge are good, but only when they lead to greater humility; and to seek advice is good so long as one is not inquisitive about the life of one's teacher. As St Gregory the Theologian says: 'Do not question the authority of him who teaches you or preaches to you.'[3] The Lord Himself commands us to carry out what the priests tell us to do (cf. Matt. 23 : 3). For the actions of those from whom we ask advice do not harm us; nor, on the other hand, does their advice help us if we fail to put it into practice. Each will have to give account for himself: the teacher, for his words; the disciple, for his obedience in doing what he is told. Everything apart from this is contrary to nature and merits condemnation. As

[1] *Ladder*, Step 15 (893B; E.T., p. 156).
[2] *Apophthegmata*, anonymous collection (ed. F. Nau), §228 (96); E.T. Sister Benedicta Ward, *The Wisdom of the Desert Fathers* (Fairacres Publication 48: Oxford, 1975), p. 31.
[3] *Oration* 19, 10 (*P.G.* xxxv, 1053C).

St Evstratios said: 'God is good and righteous, and in His goodness He gives us every good thing, so long as we are grateful, acknowledging through our thanksgiving the good we have received. But if we are ungrateful, we are condemned by the righteous judgment of God.' Thus God's goodness and righteousness by nature supply us with every good thing; if we misuse His gifts, they procure our agelong punishment.

THE GREAT BENEFIT OF TRUE REPENTANCE

It is always possible to make a new start by means of repentance. 'You fell,' it is written, 'now arise' (cf. Prov. 24 : 16).[1] And if you fall again, then rise again, without despairing at all of your salvation, no matter what happens. So long as you do not surrender yourself willingly to the enemy, your patient endurance, combined with self-reproach, will suffice for your salvation. 'For at one time we ourselves went astray in our folly and disobedience', says St Paul. '. . . Yet He saved us, not because of any good things we had done, but in His mercy' (Tit. 3 : 3,5). So do not despair in any way, ignoring God's help, for He can do whatever He wishes. On the contrary, place your hope in Him and He will do one of these things: either through trials and temptations, or in some other way which He alone knows, He will bring about your restoration; or He will accept your patient endurance and humility in the place of works; or because of your hope He will act lovingly towards you in some other way of which you are not aware, and so will save your shackled soul. Only do not abandon your Physician, for otherwise you will suffer senselessly the twofold death because you do not know the hidden ways of God.

What has been said in relation to spiritual knowledge also applies to ascetic practice. Every action of soul and body is beset by six snares: to the left and right lie excess and deficiency of effort; above and below lie self-elation and despair; on the near side and the far side lie cowardice and over-boldness which, as St Gregory the Theologian says, is very different from boldness, even though the words them-

---

[1] *Apophthegmata*, Sisois 38; E.T., pp. 219–20.

selves are similar.[1] At the mid-point between these six snares lies action accomplished with due measure and with patience and humility.

It is remarkable how the human intellect sees things differently according to its own light, even when these things are unalterable and in themselves remain what they are. It is because of this that we do not all have the same attitude to things, but each of us uses them as he wishes, whether for good or for ill. We use sensible things in our practical activity, and intelligible things in thought and disputation.

It seems to me that there are four ways of viewing men and that these correspond to the four states of which St Gregory the Theologian speaks. Some, such as the saints and those who attain dispassion, flourish both in this world and in the world to be. Others, such as the rich man in the Gospel (cf. Matt. 19 : 22), prosper only in this world, in that, though they are blessed in soul or body, they are unworthy of it, since they are without gratitude towards their Benefactor. Others, such as the paralytic (cf. Matt. 9 : 2), who are subject to prolonged illness and gladly embrace afflictions, are punished only in this world. Others, finally, such as those tempted like Judas by their own selfish desires, are punished both in this world and in the world to be.

Moreover, men also have four different attitudes towards sensible realities. Some, like the demons, hate God's works, and they commit evil deliberately. Others, like the irrational animals, love these works because they are attractive, but their love is full of passion and they make no effort to acquire natural contemplation or to show gratitude. Others, in a way that befits men, love God's works in a natural manner, with spiritual knowledge and gratitude, and they use everything with self-control. Finally, others, like the angels, love these works in a manner that is above and beyond nature, contemplating all things to the glory of God and making use of them only in so far as they are necessary for life, as St Paul puts it (cf. 1 Tim. 6 : 8).

[1] *Oration* 5, 8 (*P.G.* xxxv, 673A).

GOD'S UNIVERSAL AND PARTICULAR GIFTS

We ought all of us always to give thanks to God for both the universal and the particular gifts of soul and body that He bestows on us. The universal gifts consist of the four elements and all that comes into being through them, as well as all the marvellous works of God mentioned in the divine Scriptures. The particular gifts consist of all that God has given to each individual. These include wealth, so that one can perform acts of charity; poverty, so that one can endure it with patience and gratitude; authority, so that one can exercise righteous judgment and establish virtue; obedience and service, so that one can more readily attain salvation of soul; health, so that one can assist those in need and undertake work worthy of God; sickness, so that one may earn the crown of patience; spiritual knowledge and strength, so that one may acquire virtue; weakness and ignorance, so that, turning one's back on worldly things, one may be under obedience in stillness and humility; unsought loss of goods and possessions, so that one may deliberately seek to be saved and may be helped when incapable of shedding all one's possessions or even of giving alms; ease and prosperity, so that one may voluntarily struggle and suffer to attain the virtues and thus become dispassionate and fit to save other souls; trials and hardship, so that those who cannot eradicate their own will may be saved in spite of themselves, and those capable of joyful endurance may attain perfection. All these things, even if they are opposed to each other, are nevertheless good when used correctly; but when misused, they are not good, but are harmful for both soul and body.

Better than them all, however, is the patient endurance of afflictions; and he who has been found worthy of this great gift should give thanks to God in that he has been all the more blessed. For he has become an imitator of Christ, of His holy apostles, and of the martyrs and saints: he has received from God great strength and spiritual knowledge, so that he may voluntarily abstain from pleasure and may readily embrace hardship through the eradication of his own will and his rejection of unholy thoughts, and may thus always do and think what is in accordance with God's will. Those who have been found worthy of using things as they ought to be used should in all humility give heartfelt thanks to God, for by His grace they have been freed from what is contrary to nature and from the transgression of the commandments. We, however, who are still subject to the passions and who still misuse things, and who therefore act in a manner that is contrary to nature, should tremble and in all gratitude should give heartfelt thanks to our Benefactor, astonished at His unutterable forbearance, in that though we have disobeyed His commandments, misused His creation and rejected His gifts, He endures our ingratitude and does not cease to confer His blessings on us, awaiting until our last breath for our conversion and repentance.

Thus we should all give thanks to Him, as it is said: 'In everything give thanks' (1 Thess. 5 : 18). Closely linked to this phrase is another of St Paul's injunctions: 'Pray without ceasing' (1 Thess. 5 : 17), that is, be mindful of God at all times, in all places, and in every circumstance. For no matter what you do, you should keep in mind the Creator of all things. When you see the light, do not forget Him who gave it to you; when you see the sky, the earth, the sea and all that is in them, marvel at these things and glorify their Creator; when you put on clothing, acknowledge whose gift it is and praise Him who in His providence has given you life. In short, if everything you do becomes for you an occasion for glorifying God, you will be praying unceasingly. And in this way your soul will always rejoice, as St Paul commends (cf. 1 Thess. 5 : 16). For, as St Dorotheos explains, remembrance of God rejoices the soul; and he adduces David as witness: 'I remembered God, and rejoiced' (cf. Ps. 77 : 3. LXX).[1]

HOW GOD HAS DONE ALL THINGS FOR OUR BENEFIT

God has done all things for our benefit. We are guarded and taught by the angels; we are tempted by the demons so that we may be humbled and have recourse to God, thus being saved from self-elation and delivered from negligence. On the one hand, we are led to

[1] *Instructions* XII, 126 (ed. Regnault, p. 384).

give thanks to our Benefactor through the good things of this world, by which I mean health, prosperity, strength, rest, joy, light, spiritual knowledge, riches, progress in all things, a peaceful life, the enjoyment of honours, authority, abundance and all the other supposed blessings of this life. We are led to love Him and to do what good we can, because we feel we have a natural obligation to repay God for His gifts to us by performing good works. It is of course impossible to repay Him, for our debt always grows larger. On the other hand, through what are regarded as hardships we attain a state of patience, humility and hope of blessings in the age to be; and by these so-called hardships I mean such things as illness, discomfort, tribulation, weakness, unsought distress, darkness, ignorance, poverty, general misfortune, the fear of loss, dishonour, affliction, indigence, and so on. Indeed, not only in the age to be, but even in this present age these things are a source of great blessing to us.

Thus God in His unutterable goodness has arranged all things in a marvellous way for us; and if you want to understand this and to be as you should, you must struggle to acquire the virtues so as to be able to accept with gratitude everything that comes, whether it is good or whether it appears to be bad, and to remain undisturbed in all things. And even when the demons suggest some pride-provoking thought in order to fill you with self-elation, you should remember the shameful things they have said to you in the past and should reject this thought and become humble. And when they again suggest to you something shameful, you should remember that pride-provoking thought and so reject this new suggestion. Thus, through the co-operation of grace and by means of recollection, you make the demons cast out the demons, and are not brought to despair because of their shameful suggestions, or driven out of your mind because of your own conceit. On the contrary, when your intellect is exalted, you take refuge in humility; and when your enemies humble you before God, you are raised up through hope. In this way until your last breath you will never become confused and fall, or through fear succumb to despair.

This, according to the *Gerontikon*, is the great work of the monk. When his enemies suggest one thing, he suggests something else; when they put forward this something else, he introduces the first thing again, knowing that nothing in this life is exempt from change, and that 'he who endures to the end will be saved' (Matt. 10 : 22). But the person who wants things to come about as he himself wills does not know where he is going and, like a blind man thrown hither and thither by the wind, he is entirely dominated by whatever befalls him. Like a slave he fears what produces distress, and he is led captive by his own conceit; in his inane joy he thinks he possesses things he has never seen and of whose origin he is completely ignorant – and if he says he is not ignorant of it, then he is all the more blind. This happens because he does not censure himself. Such lack of self-criticism is a form of self-satisfaction and leads imperceptibly to destruction, as St Makarios says in his discourses about the monk who saw the heavenly Jerusalem:[1] while this monk was praying with some of the brethren, his intellect was ravished in ecstasy, but he perished because he thought that he had achieved something by his own efforts and did not realize that he had become an even greater debtor. Just as those dominated by the passions do not even know what is obvious to all because of the obfuscation produced by their passions, so the dispassionate, because of the purity of their intellect, know things of which most are ignorant.

HOW GOD'S SPEECH IS NOT LOOSE CHATTER

God's speech, says St Maximos, is not loose chatter,[2] for though we were all to speak at length, we still would not have uttered the equivalent of a single word of God. For example, God says, 'You shall love the Lord your God with all your heart, and with all your soul, and with all your might' (Deut. 6 : 5); yet how much have the fathers said and written – and still say and write – without equalling what is contained in that single phrase? For, as St Basil the Great has said, to love God with all your soul means to love nothing together with God; for if someone loves his own soul, he loves God, not with all his soul, but only partially; and if we love ourselves and innumerable other things as well, how can we love God or dare to claim that we love Him? It is the same with love of one's neighbour. If we are not willing to sacrifice this temporal life, or perhaps even the life to come, for the

[1] Makarios/Symeon, *Reden und Briefe. Die Sammlung I des Vaticanus Graecus 694 (B)*, ed. H. Berthold (Berlin, 1973), Logos 16, 3, 6 (vol. i, p. 184). See below, p. 321.
[2] *On Theology* II, 20 (*The Philokalia*, vol. ii, p. 142).

sake of our neighbour, as were Moses and St Paul, how can we say that we love him? For Moses said to God concerning his people, 'If Thou wilt forgive their sins, forgive; but if not, blot me as well out of the book of life which Thou hast written' (Exod. 32 : 32. LXX); while St Paul said, 'For I could wish that I myself were severed from Christ for the sake of my brethren' (Rom. 9 : 3). He prayed, that is to say, that he should perish in order that others might be saved – and these others were the Israelites who were seeking to kill him.

Such are the souls of the saints: they love their enemies more than themselves, and in this age and in the age to come they put their neighbour first in all things, even though because of his ill-will he may be their enemy. They do not seek recompense from those whom they love, but because they have themselves received they rejoice in giving to others all that they have, so that they may conform to their Benefactor and imitate His compassion to the best of their ability; 'for He is bountiful to the thankless and to sinners' (cf. Luke 6 : 35). Indeed, the more a man is found worthy to receive God's gifts, the more he ought to consider himself a debtor to God, who has raised him from the earth and bestowed on dust the privilege of imitating to some degree its Creator and God. For to endure injustice with joy, patiently to do good to one's enemies, to lay down one's own life for one's neighbour, and so on, are gifts from God, bestowed on those who are resolved to receive them from Him through their solicitude in cultivating and protecting what has been entrusted to them, as Adam was commanded to do (cf. Gen. 2 : 15). In this way they hold fast to the gifts through their gratitude towards their Benefactor. For we have never achieved anything good on our own, but all good things are ours from God by grace, and come as it were from nothingness into being. For 'what do you have which you did not receive?' asks St Paul – receive, that is, freely from God; 'and if you received it, why do you boast as if you had not received it' (1 Cor. 4 : 7), but had achieved it by yourself? Yet by yourself you cannot achieve anything, for the Lord has said: 'Without Me, you can do nothing' (John 15 : 5).

HOW IT IS IMPOSSIBLE TO BE SAVED
WITHOUT HUMILITY

Because of the great obscurity produced by the passions, a person may become so demented as to imagine in his lack of humility that he is the equal of the angels, or even greater than they. It was precisely this lack of humility on Lucifer's part that was enough without any other sin to turn him into darkness. What, then, will be the fate of a man who is without humility, since he is but dust and mortal, not to say a sinner? Perhaps in his blindness he does not believe that he has sinned. St John Chrysostom says that the perfect man will certainly become the equal of the angels, as the Lord affirms; but he will do so in the resurrection of the dead, and not in this present world. Even then the perfect will not be angels, but 'equal to the angels' (Luke 20 : 36). This means that men cannot forsake their own nature, though like the angels they can become changeless through grace and released from all necessity, free in everything they do, possessing ceaseless joy, love of God, and all that 'the eye has not seen, and the ear has not heard' (1 Cor. 2 : 9).

In this present life, however, it is impossible for anyone to become perfect, though he may receive as it were a pledge of the blessings promised him. For just as those who have not received God's gifts should humble themselves because of their indigence, so those who have received them should likewise humble themselves, since they have received them from God; otherwise they will be condemned for their lack of gratitude. And just as the wealthy ought to confess God's grace because of the gifts He has given them, so those who are rich in virtues ought to do so all the more. Just as the poor should give thanks to God and return rich love to those who assist them, so all the more should the wealthy give thanks, for through God's providence they are able to perform acts of charity and so are saved both in this age and in the age to be. For without the poor they cannot save their souls or flee the temptations of wealth.

Just as disciples should love their masters, so masters should love their disciples, and on behalf of each other they should mutually acknowledge the grace of God who has given to all men spiritual knowledge and every other good thing. For these good things we ought all of us always to give thanks to Him, especially those who have received from Him the power to renew their holy baptism through repentance, because without repentance no one can be saved. For the Lord has said, 'Why do you call me, Lord, Lord, yet fail to do the things I tell you?' (Luke 6 : 46). But let no one be so stupid as to think, on hearing these or similar words, that if he does not call upon the Lord he will not be culpable. On the contrary, he will be all the more condemned; for, as the Lord has said, 'If they do these things when the wood is green, what will happen when it is dry?' (Luke 23 : 31); and as Solomon says, 'If the righteous man is only just saved, where will the ungodly and the sinner appear?' (Prov. 11 : 31. LXX).

Yet when a person sees himself beset on all sides by the divine commandments he should not despair and so suffer greater condemnation than one who commits suicide. Rather, he should marvel at how the divine Scriptures and the commandments urge a man from this side and that towards perfection, so that he cannot find a way to escape from the good by seeking relief in what is inferior. As soon as he wishes to do something bad, he finds himself face to face with threatening dangers, and so he turns towards the good. God in His love arranges all this in a marvellous manner, so that every man may somehow become perfect, even in spite of himself, if only he will take himself in hand. Those who feel gratitude, filled with a sense of shame because of the blessings they have received, embark on the spiritual contest like people crossing over a river while asleep, as St Ephrem puts it. God has multiplied our trials, says St Isaac, so that out of fear of them we may take refuge in Him.[1] He who does not understand this, but through self-indulgence rejects this gift, has slain and destroyed himself: having received arms for use against his enemies, he has used them to kill himself. For just as God, says St Basil the Great, wants to do good to all because He Himself is good, so the devil, because he himself is evil, desires to involve everyone in his own depravity, even though he cannot do this. And just as loving parents, impelled by their love, turn upon their children with threats when they do foolish things, so God permits trials and temptations because they are a rod that turns those who are worthy away from the devil's maleficence. 'He who spares his rod hates his son; but he who loves him chastens him diligently' (Prov. 13 : 24).

---

[1] *Mystic Treatises*, E.T., p. 336; Greek, p. 204.

Self-indulgent and self-centred as we are, peril besets us on both sides. Those who love God are saved through the trials and temptations He allows them to undergo; but despite such trials we are threatened with destruction because of our pride and because we fail to remain faithful to God, as children who are 'chastened and not killed' (2 Cor. 6 : 9). Let us therefore choose the less perilous course. For it is better to take refuge in God by patiently enduring whatever befalls us than to turn away from Him in fear of facing the trials and temptations He may send; for if we do the latter, we fall into the hands of the devil – which means eternal destruction – or, rather, we bring punishment upon ourselves along with him. For we are faced with this alternative: we must endure either temporary trials and temptations, or else agelong punishment. The righteous, on the other hand, are free from both the perils which beset us, for they welcome joyfully what seems to us painful, and they embrace trials and temptations as an opportunity for profit, while remaining invulnerable to them. For if a man is hit by an arrow but not wounded he will not die; it is the man who receives a mortal wound who perishes from it. In what way did the plague harm Job? Did it not rather add to his glory? Or did calamity perturb the apostles and martyrs? Rather they rejoiced in it, because 'they were found worthy to suffer disgrace for the sake of His name' (Acts 5 : 41).

The more the victor has to struggle, the more he is honoured, and from this he derives great joy. When such a person hears the sound of the trumpet, he does not feel fear because it summons him to face death, but rather he rejoices because it foretells the glory that awaits him. For there is nothing that so readily prepares one for victory as bravery combined with a firm faith; and nothing so readily prepares one for defeat as self-centredness and the cowardice that comes from lack of faith. And there is no better instructor in courage than diligence and experience; nor in clarity of thought than spiritual reading in stillness. Nor is there any cause of forgetfulness so great as indolence, or any swifter path to the forgiveness of sins than the patient endurance of evil. There is no surer way to attain forgiveness of sins than repentance and the eradication of evil, and no more rapid progress of soul than that achieved by cutting off one's own desires and thoughts. Nor is there anything greater than casting oneself down before God day and night and asking that His will be done in all things; or anything worse than loving the licence and distraction of soul or body. For such licence is in no way beneficial to those of us who cleave to the good because we are still frightened of trials and punishment. On the contrary, we are helped by watchfulness and by turning away from worldly affairs, so that, at least by renouncing those things that harm us because of our weakness, we may be able to struggle with our thoughts.

The dispassionate rule over the ruling spirits because they have already triumphed over their shameful passions, while those still under obedience to a spiritual father must struggle with the spirits that are subordinate. Both St Makarios and Abba Kronios say that there are ruling demons and demons that are subordinate. The ruling demons are self-esteem, presumption and so on; the subordinate demons are gluttony, unchastity and similar things. Those who have attained perfect love have the power to do what is good without having to force themselves: they rejoice in doing it and never wish to cease. Should they encounter some unsought obstacle, they act under complete control: drawn by their love for God they resort at once to stillness and spiritual work as though to a familiar and delightful pursuit. It is to such men that the fathers say: 'Pray a little, read a little, meditate a little, work a little, watch over your intellect a little, and in this way pass your time.' They can say this because the dispassionate have control over themselves and are not sinfully led captive by their own desires. When they want, they control the intellect and command the body as though it were their servant.

We, however, ought to be subject to a rule of life, so that we are under an obligation to do what is good, even against our will. For we still pander to our passions and our pleasures, to the comfort of our bodies and to our own desires; and so the enemy leads our intellect where he wills. In the same way our body, dominated by disordered impulses, does whatever it likes uncontrollably. This is only to be expected; for where the intellect is not in command, everything is out of control and contrary to nature. It is altogether different with the true Israelites. When the Lord says to Nathanael, 'Behold, a true Israelite, in whom there is no guile' (John 1 : 47), he thereby proclaims the virtue of the man; for Nathanael means 'zeal for God'. The name given him by his family was 'Simon'; he was called 'the Canaanite' because he came from Cana of Galilee, and 'Nathanael' because of his virtue. Thus the Israelite – that is to say, the intellect that sees God – is without guile. For, according to St Basil the Great, it is usual in the divine Scripture to call a man by a name expressing his particular virtue, rather than by the name given him at birth. So it is in the case of the two chief apostles, Peter and Paul: Peter was first called Simon and then given the name Peter because of his steadfastness (cf. Mark 3 : 16), while Saul, which means 'stormy', was changed to Paul, which means 'rest', 'repose' (cf. Acts 13 : 9). And this was fitting: for at first Paul troubled and disturbed the faithful, but later he gave rest to their souls by word and act, as St John Chrysostom says of him.[1]

Consider the reverence shown by St Paul. When he wished to speak about God, he did not begin until he had offered to Him the prayer and thanksgiving that befits Him, thus showing that it was from God that he had his knowledge and strength. And this is the right order, for counsel comes after prayer. Likewise St Luke did not leave the Acts of the Apostles incomplete because of negligence or some worldly constraint, but because he departed this life to be with God. We, however, leave our tasks unfinished because of our negligence or debility, for we do not carry out the work of God diligently and do not regard it as our main task; on the contrary, we disdain it as a kind of incidental chore. Because of this we fail to prosper, or indeed often regress, like those others who 'turned back' and no longer followed Jesus (cf. John 6 : 66). And yet, says St John Chrysostom, what Jesus said was nothing harsh, as they thought, for he was speaking to them about doctrine. None the less, where a resolute disposition and desire are lacking, even easy things appear difficult – though the reverse is true as well.[2]

ON BUILDING UP THE SOUL THROUGH THE VIRTUES

According to St Basil the Great, the chief thing that every man needs is endurance, just as the earth needs water. On this earth he should lay the foundation of faith (cf. 2 Pet. 1 : 5). Then discrimination, like an experienced builder, can set about slowly building the house of the soul with clay taken from the earth of humility, successively binding one stone to another – that is, one virtue to another – until the roof,

---

[1] On the Change of Names II, 2; IV, 3 (P.G. li, 127, 149).
[2] Homilies on John 47, 2 (P.G. lix, 264).

which is perfect love, is put in place. Then, when it has posted good doorkeepers, always bearing arms – that is to say, luminous thoughts and godlike actions capable of protecting the king from being disturbed – the master of the house comes and takes up residence in it. It should not have a female doorkeeper, one who is busy with her own handiwork, as St Neilos says in his interpretation of the Old Testament:[1] he explains how it was for this reason that the Patriarch Abraham did not appoint a female porter, but rather someone who was manly – swift, incisive thought – armed with, among other things, 'the sword of the Spirit, which is the word of God' (Eph. 6 : 17), so that he might fight off and slay those who try to enter. For such a doorkeeper is sleepless and stands at his post slaying alien thoughts with retaliatory action and confuting speech. He repels everything that enters the heart contrary to God's purpose, disdaining and rejecting it, so that the illumined intellect may never stop contemplating God or be empty of divine thoughts. This is the work of stillness, as St Neilos remarks. Elsewhere, referring to Holy Scripture, St Neilos explains that distraction is the cause of the intellect's obscuration. This is to be expected; for if the intellect is not completely confined like water in a pipe, then the mind cannot be gathered into itself, and so rise to God. And if one does not rise spiritually and taste something at least of what is above, how can one readily be detached from what is below?

Thus, as St Paul says (cf. 2 Cor. 5 : 7), we should press forward on the basis of faith, patiently striving to conform ourselves to God's will. And, with time, those who make good progress succeed in attaining a partial knowledge and in overthrowing the enemy. They will then receive the fulness of this knowledge in the world to be, when the mirror – this mortal life – has been broken (cf. 1 Cor. 13 : 12), and when the soul no longer desires against the flesh, or the flesh against the Spirit (cf. Gal. 5 : 17), and when sloth does not engender forgetfulness or forgetfulness ignorance. This is what most of us experience in this present life, which is why we need a written text to remind us. Indeed, often a thought has spontaneously occurred to me, and it was by writing it down that I committed it to memory. Thus in time of spiritual struggle I had it as a source of aid or relief or gratitude, supported as it was by the testimony of divine Scripture.

[1] *Ascetic Discourse* (*The Philokalia*, vol. i, p. 210).

Had I been negligent about writing it down, I would not have found it when I had need of it, and I would have been deprived of its help by that greatest of evils, forgetfulness.

For this reason we ought to learn the virtues through practising them, not merely through talking about them, so that by acquiring the habit of them we do not forget what is of benefit to us. 'The kingdom of God', as St Paul says, 'resides not in words but in power' (1 Cor. 4 : 20). For he who tries to discover things through actual practice will come to understand what gain or loss lies in any activity that he pursues, as St Isaac says; and he can also give advice to others, for he has often suffered and has thereby gained experience. For some things, St Isaac tells us, appear good, but conceal no small harm; while others appear bad, but contain within themselves the greatest profit.[1] For this reason, he states, not every man can be trusted when giving advice to those who seek it. We can trust only him who has received from God the grace of discrimination and who, as St Maximos says, has acquired through great humility and long practice of the virtues an intellect blessed with spiritual insight. Such a man is in a position to advise, not everyone, but at least those who seek him out voluntarily and who question him by their own choice; for he has learned things in their true order. It is because of his humility, and because his questioners seek him out voluntarily, that what he says is stamped on the soul of his listeners: they are filled with the warmth of faith, regarding their good adviser as if he were that 'wonderful counsellor' of whom the prophet Isaiah speaks, calling him 'mighty God, ruler, prince of peace' (Isa. 9 : 6. LXX).

This refers of course to our Lord Jesus Christ, who said to the man who appealed to Him, 'Who set me up as a judge or arbitrator over you?' (Luke 12 : 14). Yet He also says, 'The Father has committed all judgment to the Son' (John 5 : 22). Through His holy humility, He shows us here, as everywhere, the path to salvation, and how He does not constrain anyone. 'If any man will come after Me,' He says, 'let him deny himself and follow Me' (Matt. 16 : 24), that is, let him not worry about his own life in any way, but just as I actively undergo My visible and voluntary death for the sake of all, so should he follow Me in word and action, as did the apostles and martyrs; and if he cannot do this outwardly, then let him endure death so far as the probity of

---

[1] *Mystic Treatises*, E.T., p. 198; Greek, p. 191.

his intention is concerned. Again, to the rich young man He said: 'If you want to be perfect, go and sell all you have and come and follow Me' (Matt. 19 : 21).

It is with reference to this incident that St Basil the Great observes that the young man lied when he said that he had kept the commandments; for if he had kept them, he would not have acquired many possessions, since the first commandment in the Law is, 'You shall love the Lord your God with all your soul' (Deut. 6 : 5).[1] The word 'all' forbids him who loves God to love anything else to such an extent that it would make him sad were it to be taken away. After this the Law says, 'You shall love your neighbour as yourself' (Lev. 19 : 18), that is, 'you shall love every man'. But how can he have kept this commandment if, when many other men lacked daily nourishment, he had many possessions and was passionately attached to them? If, like Abraham, Job and other righteous men, he had regarded those possessions as the property of God, he would not have gone away sorrowing. St John Chrysostom says the same thing:[2] the young man believed that what was said to him by the Lord was true, and this was why he went away full of sorrow, for he had not the strength to carry it into effect. For there are many who believe the sayings of the Scriptures, but have not the strength to fulfil what is written.

THE GREAT VALUE OF LOVE AND OF ADVICE GIVEN WITH HUMILITY

The Lord, then, gives us these and many other similar counsels, as also do the apostles when they say, 'We exhort you, beloved, to do this thing or that.' We, however, are unwilling to encourage those who seek advice from us. Yet, if they saw us humble and full of respect for them, they would listen to us with joy, feeling assured because we speak the words of Holy Scripture with great humility and love. They would eagerly pursue the honour and love which they receive from us and, together with this honour and love, they would also accept what is difficult, since because of our love it would appear easy to them.

[1] *Sermon to the Rich* 1 (*P.G.* xxxi, 281AB).
[2] Cf. *Homilies on Matthew* 63, 2 (*P.G.* lviii, 605).

This was the case with the holy apostle Peter, who repeatedly heard of death and the cross and yet rejoiced (cf. John 21 : 18–20); they were as nothing to him, for he was filled with the love he felt towards his Master. He was not concerned about miracles, as unbelievers are, but said to the Lord: 'Thy words are the words of eternal life. We believe and are assured that Thou art Christ, the Son of the living God' (John 6 : 68–69). It was not thus with Judas, who died twice; for he hanged himself, yet did not die, but lived on unrepentant, fell ill, and 'burst open', as the Apostle Peter says (Acts 1 : 18). Then again, the holy Apostle Paul says in one place to the brethren: 'So great is our affection for you that we wished to share with you not the Gospel of Christ only, but also our own souls' (1 Thess. 2 : 8); and elsewhere he says, 'We are your servants for Christ's sake' (2 Cor. 4 : 5). Again, writing to Timothy, he tells him to treat the elders as fathers and the younger men as brethren (cf. 1 Tim. 5 : 1). Who is capable of grasping the humility of the saints and the burning love they felt toward God and their neighbour? Indeed, we should be attentive not only to God and our neighbour, but to everyone to whom we speak or write.

For he who wishes to admonish someone or to give him advice – or, rather, to refresh his memory, as St John Klimakos says – should first be purified of the passions, so that he may truly understand God's purpose and the state of the person who asks for his counsel. For the same medicine is not suited for all, even when the illness is the same.[1] Then we must ascertain from the person who is seeking advice whether he does this because he has once and for all committed himself to obedience in soul and body; or whether he has made his request spontaneously and with fervent faith, seeking counsel from us before questioning his own teacher; or whether there is something else that forces him to pretend that he longs for such counsel. For if this last is the case both teacher and disciple will succumb to falsehood and idle talk, deceitfulness and many other things. The disciple, forced by his supposed teacher to speak against his will, feels ashamed and tells lies, pretending that he wants to do good; and the teacher also acts deceitfully, flattering his disciple in order to discover what is hidden in his mind, and in general employing every kind of trick and speaking at length, in spite of the

[1] *Ladder*, Step 26 (1020B; E.T., p. 206).

fact that Solomon has said, 'Through talkativeness you will not escape sin' (Prov. 10 : 19). St Basil the Great has also described the sins that come from talkativeness.

All this has been said, not so that we should refuse to advise those who come to us readily and with firm faith, especially if we have attained a state of dispassion; it is said so that we should not, out of self-esteem, presumptuously teach those who do not express the wish to hear us either through their actions or through their fervent faith. While we are still subject to the passions we should not do this even if we feel we have the authority to do so. Rather, as the fathers have said, unless questioned by the brethren we should not say anything by way of giving help, so that any benefit is a consequence of their own free choice. Both St Paul and St Peter followed this principle (cf. Philem., verse 14; 1 Pet. 5 : 2); and St Peter adds that we should not lord it over the members of our flock but be an example to them (cf. 1 Pet. 5 : 3). And St Paul wrote to St Timothy, 'The farmer who does the work should be the first to eat of the produce' (2 Tim. 2 : 6): that is to say, first practise what you intend to preach. Again, he writes, 'Let no one slight you because you are young' (1 Tim. 4 : 12): that is, do nothing that is immature or childish, but rather be as one who is perfect in Christ. Similarly, it is said in the *Gerontikon* that unless questioned by the brethren the fathers said nothing that might contribute to the soul's salvation; they regarded unsolicited advice as vain chatter.[1] This is quite right; for it is because we think that we know more than others that we speak unbidden. And the more we are guilty of this, the greater the freedom before God we assume we possess, although the closer the saints draw to God, the more they regard themselves as sinners, as St Dorotheos says;[2] they are astounded by the knowledge of God that they have been granted and are reduced to helplessness.

So, too, the holy angels in their infinite happiness and wonder can never satisfy their longing to glorify God; and because they have been found worthy of celebrating so great a Master, they sing His praises ceaselessly, marvelling at what He has brought to pass, as St John Chrysostom says, and advancing to still greater knowledge, as St Gregory the Theologian states. It is the same with all the saints, in this world and in the next. Just as the angels transmit illumination to each

---

[1] *Apophthegmata*, Poimin 45; E.T., p. 173.
[2] *Instructions* II, 33 (ed. Regnault, p. 196).

other, so intelligent beings are instructed by each other. Some derive their knowledge from the divine Scriptures and teach those who are more in need, while others are taught spiritually by the Holy Spirit and make known to their brethren in writing the mysteries that have been revealed to them.

Therefore we all need to humble ourselves before God and before each other, in that we have received from God our being and all other things, and from one another, through Him, our knowledge. He who humbles himself is illumined all the more, while he who refuses to humble himself remains in darkness, as was the case with him who was the Morning-star and is now the devil. For Lucifer originally belonged to the lowest angelic order, the one closest to the earth and the furthest from the supreme order that stands beside the unapproachable throne; but because of his self-elation he and those who obeyed him became lower not only than the nine orders of angels and than us who inhabit the earth, but lower even than the subterranean powers: for he was cast into Tartarus because of his senseless arrogance.

Because of this it is often said that presumption alone, without any other sin, is enough to destroy the soul; for he who regards his sins as trivial is allowed to fall into those that are greater, as St Isaac says.[1] And he who has received a gift from God, and is ungrateful for it, is already on the way to losing it; for, as St Basil the Great says, he has made himself unworthy of God's gift. For gratitude is a form of intercession. Only it must not be like the gratitude of the Pharisee, who condemned others and justified himself (cf. Luke 18 : 11). On the contrary, it must make one regard oneself as a greater debtor than all other men; one gives thanks in astonished bewilderment because one understands God's unutterable restraint and forbearance. Moreover, one ought to marvel that God, who is without need, who is praised above all, accepts this gratitude from us in spite of the way we anger and embitter Him constantly after He has bestowed on us so many and so varied blessings, both universal and particular.

These blessings, of both body and soul, have been described by St Gregory the Theologian and the other fathers, and they take numberless forms. One of them consists in the fact that in the Holy Scriptures some things are obvious and easy to grasp, while others are

[1] *Mystic Treatises*, E.T., p. 43; Greek, p. 20.

unclear and difficult to grasp. Through the first category God draws the slower amongst us towards faith and towards the investigation of more difficult things; and in this way He ensures that we do not fall into despair and lose our faith because of our utter failure to understand what is said. Through the second category He preserves us from incurring even greater condemnation by disdaining the passages that we can understand. He desires that those who want to do so should labour willingly to search out and put into effect what is unclear – and for this they will receive praise, as St John Chrysostom says.

THAT THE FREQUENT REPETITION FOUND IN DIVINE SCRIPTURE IS NOT VERBOSITY

Divine Scripture often repeats the same words, yet this is not to be regarded as verbosity. On the contrary, by means of this frequent repetition it unexpectedly and compassionately draws even those who are very slow in grasping things to an awareness and understanding of what is being said; and it ensures that a particular saying does not escape notice because of its fleetingness and brevity. This can happen especially when we are much involved in the affairs of this life, and know nothing save in part – though, as St John Chrysostom says, we do not know wholly even what is given 'in part', but know only a part of a part.[1] This part itself will be 'done away with' (1 Cor. 13 : 10), not in the sense that it disappears and is reduced to nothing – for then we would have no knowledge at all and would not be human – but in the sense that it will give place to the knowledge that comes from meeting 'face to face', in the same way as childhood disappears when one grows up, to use the analogy given by St Paul (cf. 1 Cor. 13 : 11–12). This again is what St John Chrysostom means when he says that now we know that heaven exists, though not what it is;[2] but that later the lesser will be 'done away with' by the greater, that is, by our knowing what heaven is, so that our knowledge increases.

---

[1] *On the Incomprehensibility of God* I, 3 (*P.G.* xlviii, 703).
[2] Op. cit., II, 7 (*P.G.* xlviii, 718).

For there are many mysteries hidden in the divine Scriptures, and we do not know God's meaning in what is said there. 'Do not be contemptuous of our frankness', says St Gregory the Theologian, 'and find fault with our words, when we admit our ignorance.' It is stupid and uncouth, declares St Dionysios the Areopagite, to give attention not to the meaning intended but only to the words.[1] But he who seeks with holy grief will find. This is a task to be undertaken in fear, for through fear things hidden are revealed to us.

Thus in one passage the prophet Isaiah says, 'The dead shall not see life' (Isa. 26 : 14. LXX); in another he says, 'The dead shall rise' (Isa. 26 : 19. LXX). But this is not contradiction, as they think who fail to understand the meaning disclosed by a spiritual interpretation of divine Scripture. For he was referring to the idols of the Gentiles when he said, 'They shall not see life', because they are soulless; while when he said, 'The dead shall rise', he was referring to the general resurrection and the blessedness of the righteous – though he was also prophesying the rising of the dead together with our Saviour Jesus Christ. Similarly, in the Holy Gospels, in the accounts of the transfiguration of the Lord, one of the Evangelists says 'after six days' (Matt. 17 : 1; cf. Mark 9 : 2) and another speaks of 'eight days' (Luke 9 : 28) – meaning, in each case, after the preceding miracles and teaching of the Lord. But the one leaves out of the reckoning the first and last days and counts only the six days that lie between, while the other includes both of these and so speaks of eight days.

Again, in his Gospel St John the Theologian says at one point, 'And there are many other signs that Jesus performed in the presence of His disciples which are not recorded in this book' (John 20 : 30); while at another he says, 'And there are also many other things which Jesus did' (John 21 : 25), without saying 'in the presence of His disciples'. Concerning these passages St Prochoros, who wrote them both down, says that in the first case the Evangelist is referring to the miracles and other things the Lord did, which he did not record because they had been previously written down by the other Evangelists; and that is why he added 'in the presence of His disciples'. In the second case he is referring to the creation of the world, when the Logos of God was in His incorporeal state, and when together with Him the Father created all things out of non-existence,

---

[1] *The Divine Names* IV, 11 (P.G. iii, 708C).

saying, 'Let this thing be, and it was' (cf. Gen. 1 : 3–14). 'If all these things were to be recorded individually,' says the Theologian, 'I suppose that even the world itself could not contain the books that would be written' (John 21 : 25).[1]

Generally speaking, every scriptural passage and every word of God, or of any saint, refers in a hidden way to the purpose of created things, whether they belong to the sensible or to the intelligible realm. The same is also true of any human statement. And no one knows the meaning of the passage in question except by revelation. As the Lord said, 'The wind blows where it wills' (John 3 : 8). Commenting on this, St John Chrysostom observes that the Lord did not mean that the wind has a power of its own;[2] but, making allowances for Nikodimos' weakness, He spoke of the wind so that Nikodimos might understand what was being said to him. The Lord was in fact referring to the Holy Spirit when He spoke of the wind. He was trying to tell Nikodimos and others that what He said to them was spirit or spiritual and not what they thought it was. He was not speaking about bodily things, in a way that could be understood simply by earthly-minded people. For this reason St John of Damaskos writes that, if the speaker does not disclose to us the meaning of what he says, we cannot know what it means. And how can anyone dare to say, 'I know the purpose of God that is hidden in divine Scripture', unless it has been revealed to him by the Son?

Christ Himself has said that He reveals the truth to whomsoever He wishes (cf. Matt. 11 : 27). This means that He reveals it only if we have previously resolved to receive this knowledge from Him spiritually through the keeping of His divine commandments; because without this anyone who claims to possess knowledge is lying. For, as St John Klimakos says, he speaks from conjecture, not learning authoritatively from God, even though in his conceit he boasts immeasurably. It is such a person that St Gregory the Theologian has in mind when he uses the phrases 'O you great lover of wisdom' or 'O you wonderful scholar', reproaching him for his presumption in thinking he knows something when in fact he is ignorant. In such cases, even what he thinks he has will be taken away from him (cf. Matt. 13 : 12), because he is unwilling to say, 'I do not know', as all

---

[1] We cannot find this passage in the *Acts of John* attributed to Prochoros (ed. T. Zahn, Erlangen, 1880).

[2] *Homilies on John* 26, 1 (*P.G.* lix, 154).

the saints have said. Had he said that, what he lacks might have been given to him because of his humility, and given abundantly, as it was to the saints. For the saints, though they knew, said that they did not know. As St John Chrysostom observes, St Paul did not say, 'I have never known anything yet', but that he had never known anything yet 'as he ought to know it' (cf. 1 Cor. 8 : 2). Thus he knew, but not as he should know.[1]

SPURIOUS KNOWLEDGE

Spurious knowledge, or 'knowledge falsely so called' (1 Tim. 6 : 20), is that which a man possesses when he thinks he knows what he has never known. It is worse than complete ignorance, says St John Chrysostom, in that its victim will not accept correction from any teacher because he thinks that this worst kind of ignorance is in fact something excellent. For this reason the fathers say that we ought to search the Scriptures assiduously, in humility and with the counsel of experienced men, learning not merely theoretically but by putting into practice what we read; and that we ought not to inquire at all into what is passed over in silence by Holy Scripture.

Such enquiry is senseless, St Antony the Great tells us, speaking with reference to those who want to know about the future rather than renouncing any claim to such knowledge on the grounds of their unworthiness.[2] If God in His providence does impart such knowledge, as He did to Nebuchadnezzar (cf. Dan. 2 : 31–45) and Balaam (cf. Num. 23 : 8–10), He imparts it for the benefit of all, even if some of the recipients are unworthy of the gift. In such cases, it does not come from the demons, especially when it is given through dreams and certain forms of imagination. We are not told much about these things, lest we search the Scriptures simply with our minds and then out of pride think that we have grasped something. For the Lord commands that we should search the Scriptures above all by means of bodily and moral actions, and in this way find eternal life (cf. John 5 : 39–40). In particular we

[1] *On the Incomprehensibility of God* II, 6 (*P.G.* xlviii, 717).
[2] Cf. *Apophthegmata*, Antony 2; E.T., p. 2.

should bear in mind that things have been hidden from us for our greater humility, and so that we may not be condemned for sinning knowingly.

The man who has been enabled by grace to acquire spiritual knowledge should struggle to study the divine Scriptures and this knowledge with deep dedication, humility, attention and fear of God; for unless he does this he will be deprived of his knowledge and threatened with punishment, as unworthy of what God has given him, in the same way as Saul was deprived of his kingdom, as St Maximos explains.[1] But he who devotes himself to spiritual knowledge and struggles to attain it, St Maximos states, should call upon God at all times, as did David, saying: 'Create in me a pure heart, O God, and renew an upright Spirit within me' (Ps. 51 : 10). In this way he may become worthy of God's indwelling, like the apostles who received grace 'at the third hour' (Acts 2 : 15). For the Spirit came down on the apostles, as St Luke declares, at the third hour of the day, a Sunday, since Pentecost is the seventh Sunday after the Sunday on which 'Pascha' is celebrated.

This Hebrew word, 'Pascha', when translated, means 'passing over' or 'freedom'; and the Sunday that follows fifty days later is therefore called 'Pentecost' or 'Fiftieth', for in the Law it marks the completion of the fifty days that follow Pascha. As St John the Theologian says in his Gospel, 'On that last, that great day of the feast' (John 7 : 37), because Pentecost constitutes the conclusion of the feast of Pascha. 'The third hour received this grace', says St John of Damaskos.[2] At the same time, the grace was given on 'day one', the Lord's day. This signifies that we worship three persons with but a single power, that is, a single Godhead. For Sunday is called 'day one' and not the first day of the week, says St John Chrysostom; such is the way in which it is singled out and described prophetically in the Old Testament. It is not simply enumerated with the other days of the week, such as the second day and the rest. Had it not been singled out, it would have been called the 'first day', but as it is it is called 'day one' of the week (cf. Gen. 1 : 5. LXX). In the new dispensation of grace, however, this 'holy' and 'chosen day' (Lev. 23 : 35. LXX) is called 'the Lord's day' (Rev. 1 : 10), because on it the more lordly and masterful events in Christ's life took place, the Annunciation, the Nativity, the Resurrection; and on this day the general resurrection of the dead will also take place. For it was on

---

[1] *On Theology* II, 53 (*The Philokalia*, vol. ii, p. 150).
[2] *Pentikostarion*: Feast of Pentecost, Mattins, Second Canon, Canticle 7, troparion.

this day that God created the visible light, says St John of Damaskos,[1] and it will also be the day of Christ's second coming. Thus it will last for limitless ages: it is both day one and the eighth day, as being outside the other seven ages that have days and nights in them.

It has been granted to us to learn about the meaning of these things from the saints. Let us then also learn thoroughly the meaning of each topic of this present work, from beginning to end. We should recite straight through the names of the biblical books and of the saints, so that we may continually remember their words and zealously imitate their lives, as St Basil the Great says; and we should make these things known to those who are ignorant of them. The person who already knows them will recollect them, while the person who does not know them may thus be encouraged to search out the books in question. We mention the name of a saint or a particular book from time to time so that we may call them to mind more frequently, and by means of this brief mention may remember the acts and words of each. This also helps us to grasp the implications of scriptural passages, and to understand the discrimination and counsel of the teacher in question. It also makes clear that what is said here, in this work, is not mine, but comes from Holy Scripture. Moreover, it increases our wonder at and comprehension of God's ineffable love: how by means of pen and ink He has provided for the salvation of our souls, and has given us so many writings and teachers of the Orthodox faith.

I myself marvel how I, untutored and lazy though I am, have been privileged to go through so many texts, although I have not one book of my own nor any other possession, but am always a stranger and poor; and yet I pass my time in complete ease and security, with much bodily enjoyment. If any books are left unnamed, it is because of my carelessness or so that my work should not grow too long. The questions and solutions I propose here with regard to our common problems are put forward to help our understanding. They are also a way of expressing gratitude to Him who has granted spiritual knowledge and discrimination to His saints, our holy fathers, and through them to us, unworthy though we are. They likewise help us to condemn our own weakness and ignorance.

I have said something about the righteous men of old who were saved in the midst of great wealth and among sinners and unbelievers,

---

[1] *Exposition of the Faith* II, 7 (ed. Kotter, §21, p. 54).

although they were by nature the same as us. But we lack the will to attain perfection, even though we can draw upon greater experience and knowledge of good and evil, since we have learned from them and so have been granted fuller grace and knowledge of the Scriptures. I have also mentioned details from the lives of us monks, so that we may know that we can be saved in any situation, provided we renounce our own will. Indeed, unless we do this, we cannot find rest, nor can we gain either knowledge of God's will or practice in fulfilling it. For our own will is a dividing wall, separating us from God;[1] and if it is not torn down, we cannot learn and do what accords with God's will, but are estranged from Him and tyrannized by our enemies against our will.

We must remember, too, that stillness is the highest gift of all, and that without it we cannot be purified and come to know our weakness and the trickery of the demons; neither will we be able to understand the power of God and His providence from the divine words that we read and sing. For we all need this devotion and stillness, total or partial, if we are to attain the humility and spiritual knowledge necessary for the understanding of the mysteries hidden in the divine Scriptures and in all creation. We must also remember that we should not use any object or any word, or engage in any activity or thought, that is not necessary for the life and salvation of soul and body; and that, unless we exercise discrimination, not even what appears to be good is acceptable to God, and that unless they are rightly motivated even good works are of no use to anyone.

The troparia to be found in the liturgical books are intended to assist us in understanding these books as well as other texts. In addition, as St John Klimakos says, they stimulate compunction in people whose intellect is still weak. For the melody, says St Basil the Great, draws the mind where it will, whether to grief or longing, to remorse or joy. Moreover, we should search the Scriptures in accordance with the Lord's commandment, so that we may find eternal life in them (cf. John 5 : 39); and we should pay attention to the meaning of the psalms and troparia, becoming in this way totally aware of our ignorance. For if one does not taste of knowledge, says St Basil the Great, one does not know how much one lacks. To promote this experience and knowledge I have described the origins

---

[1] *Apophthegmata*, Poimin 54; E.T., p. 174.

of the virtues and the passions; for thereby others may come to recognize them, and so struggle to acquire what engenders the virtues and to expel by retaliatory action that which produces the passions. We should also and at all times keep a watch over our bodily activities as if they were plants, and should always give attention to the virtues of the soul and study how we can acquire each virtue. We should learn about this from the divine Scriptures and from saintly men; and what we learn we should through our actions zealously and in labour of soul guard as a treasure, until we have firmly established the virtue in question. Then we should diligently begin to acquire another virtue, as St Basil the Great says, so as not to exhaust ourselves through trying to acquire them all at once.

We should begin by patiently enduring what befalls us and should then press on eagerly and forcefully to tackle the other virtues, our purpose being to conform to God's will. For we should all, as Christians, keep the commandments, since in order to acquire the virtues of the soul we need, not bodily effort, but simply probity of intention and the desire to receive what is given, as St Basil the Great, St Gregory the Theologian and many others say. Yet bodily asceticism does help in the acquisition of the virtues, especially in the case of those who lead a life of stillness and are completely undistracted and detached. For a man cannot see his own habits and correct them unless he is free from worry about worldly things. Hence we ought first to acquire dispassion by withdrawing from worldly affairs and human society; for only then can we begin, when the time is ripe, to look after others and administer things without going wrong and without causing harm. This is possible only because, our detachment having become a habit, we have attained total dispassion; and above all, as St John of Damaskos says, because we have received a call from God, as happened in the case of Moses (cf. Exod. 3 : 4), Samuel (cf. 1 Sam. 3 : 10) and the other prophets (cf. Isa. 6 : 8; Jer. 1 : 5), as well as the holy apostles (cf. Matt. 4 : 19), for the salvation of many others. St John of Damaskos also says that one should at first refuse to accept the call, as did Moses (cf. Exod. 3 : 11; 4 : 10), Habakkuk (cf. Bel and Dragon, verse 35), St Gregory the Theologian[1] and others.

St Prochoros says of St John the Evangelist that he did not wish to leave his beloved stillness, even though as an apostle he was under

---

[1] Cf. *Oration* 2 (*P.G.* xxxv, 408–513).

obligation to renounce the stillness and to proclaim the Gospel.[1] It was not in the least because he was subject to the passions that St John took refuge in stillness, for he of all men was most free of them. He did so because he did not want ever to be cut off from the contemplation of God or to be deprived of the great sweetness of stillness. But others, although dispassionate, fled into the farthest deserts out of humility, fearing confusion. St Sisois the Great is an example of this: when his disciple told him to rest, he refused to do so and said, 'Let us go where no one is to be found'; and yet he had reached such a high state of dispassion that he had become a captive of his love for God and was no longer aware whether he ate or not.[2]

In short, by withdrawing into complete stillness all of these men cut off their own wills. Then some of them, as disciples, were appointed by their Teacher to instruct others, accepting the confession of their thoughts and ruling over them, either as bishops or as abbots. They received through their spiritual senses confirmation of this from the Holy Spirit Himself, when He came to dwell in them. This was what happened to the holy apostles (cf. Acts 2 : 3) and to those who went before them, such as Aaron (cf. Exod. 28 : 1; Heb. 5 : 4), Melchisedec (cf. Gen. 14 : 18; Ps. 110 : 4) and others. But St John of Damaskos says that he who brazenly tries to assume this status of his own accord is condemned. For if those who shamelessly assume high office without royal authorization are severely punished, how much more so are those who audaciously take charge of what is God's without receiving His call? This is especially so if out of ignorance or pride they think that such an awesome task involves no danger of condemnation, imagining that it will bring them honour or ease, and not realizing that they will rather be required, when the moment comes, to enter into an abyss of humility and death for the sake of their spiritual children and their enemies. For this is what was done by the holy apostles – who were to the highest degree compassionate and wise – when they taught others.

If we do not even know that we are weak and insufficient for the task, what is to be said? For pride and ignorance blind those who, refusing to devote themselves to God in stillness, fail to recognize their own weakness and ignorance. As the *Gerontikon* puts it, the cell of a monk is like the furnace of Babylon in which the three holy

---

[1] Cf. *Acts of John*, ed. Zahn, pp. 5–6.
[2] *Apophthegmata*, Sisois 3–4; E.T., p. 213.

children found the Son of God (cf. Dan. 3 : 23).[1] Again it says, 'Sit in your cell and it will teach you all things.'[2] And the Lord Himself says: 'Where two or three are gathered together in My name, I am in the midst of them' (Matt. 18 : 20). St John Klimakos exhorts us: 'Do not turn to the right or to the left, as Solomon puts it (cf. Prov. 4 : 27), but rather travel the royal road, living in stillness with one or two others, neither alone in the desert nor in great company; for the mean between these two is suited to most men.'[3] Again he says: 'Fasting humbles the body, vigils illumine the intellect, stillness induces inward grief, and grief baptizes a man, washes his soul and frees it from sin.'

On account of this the names of almost all the virtues and the passions are listed at the end of this discourse, so that we may know how many virtues we have to acquire and how many sinful acts we have to grieve for. For without grief there is no purification, and there can be no grief in the midst of continuous distraction. Without purification of the soul there is no assurance; and without assurance the separation of soul and body is full of dangers. For, as St John Klimakos has said, 'We cannot trust what still remains unknown.'[4]

The eight stages of contemplation previously mentioned are not achieved by our own labours, but are the reward granted in return for our efforts to acquire the virtues. We should not try to attain these stages of contemplation simply by reading, or by striving for them with an eagerness full of pride, as St John Klimakos says with reference to the four highest and more perfect stages; for these stages are celestial, and an unpurified intellect is incapable of embracing them. Instead, we should devote all our efforts to acquiring the virtues of soul and body, and in this way the first commandment will be born in us, that is, the fear of God. And if we persevere in this, grief will be born as well. For as soon as we are established in one stage of contemplation, then the grace of God, the common mother of us all, as St Isaac calls it,[5] will grant to us what lies beyond. This will continue until we have established the seven stages of spiritual knowledge in ourselves; and then the eighth, which

---

[1] *Apophthegmata*, anonymous collection, §206 (74); E.T., p. 24.
[2] *Apophthegmata*, Moses 6; E.T., p. 139.
[3] *Ladder*, Step 1 (641D; E.T., p. 56).
[4] *Ladder*, Step 5 (780A; E.T., p. 108).
[5] *Mystic Treatises*, E.T., p. 85; Greek, p. 54.

is the work of the age to come, will be granted to those who labour diligently at the virtues with the genuine intention of fulfilling God's will.

Each time that a godlike thought comes to us spontaneously, suddenly and without our knowing how, whether it belongs to the first stage or whatever it may be, we should always at once abandon every worldly concern and even our rule of prayer. We should do this in order to guard, as the apple of our eye, whatever spiritual knowledge or compunction it may bring, until through God's providence it withdraws from us. Then, after such an experience and before resuming our rule, we should always meditate on what has been written about fear and grief. Weak as we still are, and inclined towards sleep and laziness, at whatever time of the night or day we have a free moment, whether we are involved in some handiwork, or are without occupation and so able to give ourselves entirely over to grief, we should surrender ourselves to what is said in these writings and to the tears that they induce. For they have been written so that even those – especially myself – who have no experience of the things they describe may rouse their sluggish intellects through studying them attentively. Those who possess the purpose and the experience that comes from the habitual practice of the virtues know and can speak about much more than we have said in this work. This is the case particularly at the moment when they feel spontaneous contrition; for that moment possesses great power, far beyond our capacity.

Yet let no one think that he himself brings about these gifts of grace. Rather, he has received much more than he deserves, and he should be deeply grateful, and should go in fear lest he incur greater condemnation because of what has been given to him; for without labouring he has been granted the fruits for which the angels strive. Knowledge is given to anoint the intellect, to strengthen us in the keeping of the commandments, and to help us in the practice of the virtues. It is also given so that we may know how and why we practise the virtues, and what we should do and what we should not do, so as to avoid condemnation. For thus, borne on the wings of knowledge, we strive joyfully and receive yet greater knowledge, strength and gladness through our striving; and, when this happens, we are enabled by grace to give thanks to Him who has bestowed these great blessings on us, knowing whence we have received them. For when

God is thanked, He gives us still further blessings, while we, by receiving His gifts, love Him all the more and through this love attain that divine wisdom whose beginning is the fear of God (cf. Prov. 1 : 7). Fear brings about repentance, says St Isaac,[1] and through repentance comes the revelation of hidden things.

This is how we should meditate on the fear of God. After the service of Compline each of us should recite the Creed and the Lord's Prayer, and then repeat 'Lord, have mercy' many times. We should sit facing east, like someone mourning for the dead, moving our heads backward and forward with pain in our souls and with a grieving heart, and saying the words appropriate to our particular stage of knowledge, beginning with the first stage, until we attain the state of prayer. Then we should fall upon our face before God with inexpressible awe and should begin to pray. First our prayer should be thanksgiving, then confession of our sins, and then the other words of prayer as given previously. St Athanasios the Great says that we should confess the sins we have committed in ignorance, as well as those that we would have committed had we not been saved from them by God's grace, so that these may not be counted against us in the hour of our death. We should also pray for each other, according to the commandment of the Lord (cf. Luke 22 : 32) and of the Apostle James (cf. Jas. 5 : 16).

The purpose of what we say in our prayers is as follows. The thanksgiving is in recognition of our incapacity to offer thanksgiving as we should at this present moment, of our negligence in doing so at other times, and of the fact that the present moment is a gift of God's grace. Our confession of sins proclaims that God's gifts are measureless and that we are unable to understand them all or even to recognize them: we have only known of them from hearsay, and then not of them all. It also proclaims that we are constantly being benefited, visibly and invisibly, and that God's restraint in the face of our many sins cannot be put into words. We confess that, like the publican, we are unworthy even to raise our eyes to heaven (cf. Luke 18 : 13) and that, relying solely on His ineffable love, we fall down before Him, as Daniel, the Apostle John and the other fathers fell down before the holy angel (cf. Dan. 8 : 17; Rev. 1 : 17). We fall down with all our soul, and indeed with a certain temerity, since we

[1] *Mystic Treatises*, E.T., p. 211; Greek, p. 282.

are unworthy to do even this. And we should briefly confess all the various types of sin into which we fall, so as to recall them and to grieve for them, acknowledging our own weakness so that the power of Christ may come upon us, as St Paul says (cf. 2 Cor. 12 : 9), and so that our many evil actions may be forgiven. We do not dare to entreat on behalf of all, but only for our own sins. We ask that our every vice and every evil habit may be curbed, since we cannot control them, and we call upon the Almighty to restrain the impulses of our passions and not to permit us to sin against Him or against any man, so that we may in this way find salvation through His grace.

We also pray that through the recollection of our sins we may acquire tribulation of soul and the ability to pray for others, thereby fulfilling the commandment of St James (cf. Jas. 5 : 16), as well as expressing our love for all men. By listing the forms of passion that tyrannize us, we are led to take refuge in our Master and brought to a state of contrition. We pray for those whom we have distressed, and for those who have distressed us, or who will distress us, because we do not want to harbour the least trace of rancour, and because we fear that on account of our own weakness we will not be able to endure with forbearance when the time comes or to pray for those who mistreat us, as the Lord commands (cf. Luke 6 : 28). For this reason we anticipate that time and, as St Isaac says, we seek a doctor before becoming ill and pray before we are faced by temptation. We then pray for the departed, that they may receive salvation and so as to remind ourselves of our own death. It is a sign of love to pray for all men, even when we need the prayers of all. We also pray to be directed by God and to become what He wishes us to be; and to be united with others, so that through their prayers we may receive mercy, all the while regarding them as superior to ourselves.

We do not yet dare to seek forgiveness for all our sins, lest by minimizing our own faults we come to regard others as unworthy of forgiveness. Ignorant, incapable of doing anything, we take refuge in Christ; and fearing His righteousness because we are sinners, we ask Him to order all things as He judges best in His compassionate love. We also ask that we may not be deprived of a place at His right hand, even though we are the least of all those who are saved and are unworthy of being numbered with them. We pray as well for the whole world, as we have been taught to do by the Church, and that though sinful we may be found worthy to partake of holy communion as we should, and that by praying before taking it we may find Him ready to help us when the moment for communion comes. We pray that we may remember the holy Passion of our Saviour and may cleave with love to this remembrance. We pray that through the sacrament we may enter into communion with the Holy Spirit; for in this world and in the next the Paraclete Himself solaces those who are filled with godlike grief (cf. Matt. 5 : 4), and who with all their soul and with many tears call upon Him for help and say, 'O heavenly King, Paraclete, the Spirit of truth...'. We pray that our participation in the undefiled mysteries may be a pledge of eternal life in Christ, through the intercessions of His Mother and of all the saints. Then we fall down before the saints, calling upon them to make intercession for us, since they are able to bring their petitions before the Master. Then we say as usual the prayer of St Basil the Great, so wonderfully charged with theology, asking that we may seek only the divine will and may ever bless God. After this, watching over our thoughts with full attentiveness, at once we say three times, 'O come, let us worship and fall down before God our King', in the way already described, so that by means of prayer of the heart and meditation on the divine Scripture the intellect may be purified and begin to see the mysteries hidden in Scripture.

The soul must be free from all evil, especially rancour, at the time of prayer, as the Lord Himself has told us (cf. Mark 11 : 25). For this reason St Basil the Great, castigating contentiousness as the source of rancour, says that the abbot should submit anyone who argues with him to as many as a thousand prostrations. He said, when giving this high figure, 'either a thousand or one'; that is, the person who answers back ought to make either a thousand prostrations before God, or one before the abbot himself, saying simply, 'Forgive me, father.' In this way he will be absolved with one prostration only, but it has to be a genuine prostration, one that eradicates the passion of contentiousness. Contentiousness is alien to the Christian way of life, states St Isaac, appealing to the words of St Paul who said, 'But if anyone wants to argue, we have no such custom among us'; and so that he would not seem to be expelling the contentious person merely on the basis of his own personal opinions, St Paul adds, 'nor in the churches of God' (1 Cor. 11 : 16). In this way everyone may know that when he argues he is outside all the churches and estranged from

God. He has need of that one marvellous act of repentance, and if he fails to make that genuinely, and so remains unrepentant, not even a thousand prostrations will help him.

For repentance, properly speaking, is the eradication of evil, says St John Chrysostom;[1] while what are called acts of repentance or prostrations are a bending of the knees, which expresses the fact that the person who bows sincerely before God and man after having offended someone assumes the attitude of a servant. By doing this he can claim in self-defence that he has not answered back at all or attempted to justify himself, as did the Pharisee, but is more like the publican in considering himself the least of all men and unworthy to lift his eyes to heaven (cf. Luke 18 : 11–13). For if he thinks he is repentant and nevertheless attempts to refute the person who – rightly or wrongly – is judging him, he is not worthy of the grace of forgiveness, since he acts as if he seeks a hearing in court and the opportunity to justify himself, hoping to achieve what he wants through a due process of law. Such behaviour is entirely at odds with the Lord's commandments. And naturally so; for if one attempts to justify oneself, then one is appealing to lawful rights, not to love for one's fellow-men. In such a case grace is no longer our guiding principle – the grace that justifies the ungodly without the works of righteousness (cf. Rom. 4 : 5), but only on condition that we are grateful for rebukes and endure them with forbearance, giving thanks to those who rebuke us and remaining patient and unresentful before our accusers. In this way our prayer will be pure and our repentance effective. For the more we pray for those who slander and accuse us, the more God pacifies those who bear enmity towards us and also gives us peace through our pure and persistent prayer.

When we make specific requests in our prayers, this is not so as to inform God, for He already knows our hearts; we make them so that we may be brought to contrition. We also do it because we desire to remain longer in His presence, attentively addressing yet more words to Him, giving thanks to Him, acknowledging the many blessings we have received from Him, for as long as we can, as St John Chrysostom says of the Prophet David. For to repeat the same or similar things again and again is not to talk garrulously or haphazardly, since, as in the case of the prophet, it is done out of longing and so that the word

[1] *On Repentance* VII, 3 (*P.G.* xlix, 327–8).

of divine Scripture should be imprinted in the intellect of whoever is reading or praying. For God knows all things before they occur and does not need to be told about them. We, however, have need of hearing things, so that we may know what we ask for and why we are praying, and may be filled with gratitude and cleave to God through our entreaties. It is through such repetition that we avoid being overcome by our enemies when we are troubled in thought, for then they will not find us unmindful of Him; and it is also through it that, helped by prayer and the study of divine Scripture, we may come to acquire the virtues about which the holy fathers have written in their various works, through the grace of the Holy Spirit. It is from the fathers that I myself have learned about the virtues, and I will give a list of them, so far as I can, even though it is not complete because of my lack of knowledge.

A LIST OF THE VIRTUES

The virtues are: moral judgment, self-restraint, courage, justice, faith, hope, love, fear, religious devotion, spiritual knowledge, resolution, strength, understanding, wisdom, contrition, grief, gentleness, searching the Scriptures, acts of charity, purity of heart, peace, patient endurance, self-control, perseverance, probity of intention, purposiveness, sensitivity, heedfulness, godlike stability, warmth, alertness, the fervour of the Spirit, meditation, diligence, watchfulness, mindfulness, reflection, reverence, shame, respect, penitence, refraining from evil, repentance, return to God, allegiance to Christ, rejection of the devil, keeping of the commandments, guarding of the soul, purity of conscience, remembrance of death, tribulation of soul, the doing of good actions, effort, toil, an austere life, fasting, vigils, hunger, thirst, frugality, self-sufficiency, orderliness, gracefulness, modesty, reserve, disdain of money, unacquisitiveness, renunciation of worldly things, submissiveness, obedience, compliance, poverty, possessionlessness, withdrawal from the world, eradication of self-will, denial of self, counsel, magnanimity, devotion to God, stillness, discipline, sleeping on a hard bed, abstinence from washing oneself, service, struggle, attentiveness, the eating of uncooked food, nakedness, the wasting of one's body, solitude, quietude, calmness, cheerfulness, fortitude, boldness, godlike zeal, fervency, progress, folly for Christ, watchfulness over the intellect, moral integrity, holiness, virginity, sanctification, purity of body, chasteness of soul, reading for Christ's sake, concern for God, comprehension, friendliness, truthfulness, uninquisitiveness, uncensoriousness, forgiveness of debts, good management, skilfulness, acuity, fairness, the right use of things, cognitive insight, good-naturedness, experience, psalmody, prayer, thanksgiving, acknowledgment, entreaty, kneeling, supplication, intercession, petition, appeal, hymnody, doxology, confession, solicitude, mourning, affliction, pain, distress, lamentation, sighs of sorrow, weeping, heart-rending tears, compunction, silence, the search for God, cries of anguish, lack of anxiety about all things, forbearance, lack of self-esteem, disinterest in glory, simplicity of soul, sympathy, self-retirement, goodness of disposition, activities that accord with nature, activities exceeding one's natural capacity, brotherly love, concord, communion in God, sweetness, a spiritual disposition, mildness, rectitude, innocence, kindliness, guilelessness, simplicity, good repute, speaking well of others, good works, preference of one's neighbour, godlike tenderness, a virtuous character, consistency, nobility, gratitude, humility, detachment, dignity, forbearance, long-suffering, kindness, goodness, discrimination, accessibility, courtesy, tranquility, contemplation, guidance, reliability, clearsightedness, dispassion, spiritual joy, sureness, tears of understanding, tears of soul, a loving desire for God, pity, mercy, compassion, purity of soul, purity of intellect, prescience, pure prayer, passion-free thoughts, steadfastness, fitness of soul and body, illumination, the recovery of one's soul, hatred of life, proper teaching, a healthy longing for death, childlikeness in Christ, rootedness, admonition and encouragement, both moderate and forcible, a praiseworthy ability to change, ecstasy towards God, perfection in Christ, true enlightenment, an intense longing for God, rapture of intellect, the indwelling of God, love of God, love of inner wisdom, theology, a true confession of faith, disdain of death, saintliness, successful accomplishment, perfect health of soul, virtue, praise from God, grace, kingship, adoption to sonship – altogether 228 virtues. To acquire all of them is possible only through the grace of Him who grants us victory over the passions.

A LIST OF THE PASSIONS

The passions are: harshness, trickery, malice, perversity, mindlessness, licentiousness, enticement, dullness, lack of understanding, idleness, sluggishness, stupidity, flattery, silliness, idiocy, madness, derangement, coarseness, rashness, cowardice, lethargy, dearth of good actions, moral errors, greed, over-frugality, ignorance, folly, spurious knowledge, forgetfulness, lack of discrimination, obduracy, injustice, evil intention, a conscienceless soul, slothfulness, idle chatter, breaking of faith, wrongdoing, sinfulness, lawlessness, criminality, passion, seduction, assent to evil, mindless coupling, demonic provocation, dallying, bodily comfort beyond what is required, vice, stumbling, sickness of soul, enervation, weakness of intellect, negligence, laziness, a reprehensible despondency, disdain of God, aberration, transgression, unbelief, lack of faith, wrong belief, poverty of faith, heresy, fellowship in heresy, polytheism, idolatry, ignorance of God, impiety, magic, astrology, divination, sorcery, denial of God, the love of idols, dissipation, profligacy, loquacity, indolence, self-love, inattentiveness, lack of progress, deceit, delusion, audacity, witchcraft, defilement, the eating of unclean food, soft living, dissoluteness, voracity, unchastity, avarice, anger, dejection, listlessness, self-esteem, pride, presumption, self-elation, boastfulness, infatuation, foulness, satiety, doltishness, torpor, sensuality, overeating, gluttony, insatiability, secret eating, hoggishness, solitary eating, indifference, fickleness, self-will, thoughtlessness, self-satisfaction, love of popularity, ignorance of beauty, uncouthness, gaucherie, lightmindedness, boorishness, rudeness, contentiousness, quarrelsomeness, abusiveness, shouting, brawling, fighting, rage, mindless desire, gall, exasperation, giving offence, enmity, meddlesomeness, chicanery, asperity, slander, censure, calumny, condemnation, accusation, hatred, railing, insolence, dishonour, ferocity, frenzy, severity, aggressiveness, forswearing oneself, oathtaking, lack of compassion, hatred of one's brothers, partiality, patricide, matricide, breaking fasts, laxity, acceptance of bribes, theft, rapine, jealousy, strife, envy, indecency, jesting, vilification, mockery, derision, exploitation, oppression, disdain of one's neighbour, flogging, making sport of others, hanging, throttling, heartlessness, implacability, covenant-

breaking, bewitchment, harshness, shamelessness, impudence, obfuscation of thoughts, obtuseness, mental blindness, attraction to what is
fleeting, impassionedness, frivolity, disobedience, dullwittedness,
drowsiness of soul, excessive sleep, fantasy, heavy drinking, drunkenness, uselessness, slackness, mindless enjoyment, self-indulgence,
venery, using foul language, effeminacy, unbridled desire, burning lust,
masturbation, pimping, adultery, sodomy, bestiality, defilement,
wantonness, a stained soul, incest, uncleanliness, pollution, sordidness,
feigned affection, laughter, jokes, immodest dancing, clapping,
improper songs, revelry, fluteplaying, licence of tongue, excessive love
of order, insubordination, disorderliness, reprehensible collusion,
conspiracy, warfare, killing, brigandry, sacrilege, illicit gains, usury,
wiliness, grave-robbing, hardness of heart, obloquy, complaining,
blasphemy, fault-finding, ingratitude, malevolence, contemptuousness,
pettiness, confusion, lying, verbosity, empty words, mindless joy, day-
dreaming, mindless friendship, bad habits, nonsensicality, silly talk,
garrulity, niggardliness, depravity, intolerance, irritability, affluence,
rancour, misuse, ill-temper, clinging to life, ostentation, affectation,
love of power, dissimulation, irony, treachery, frivolous talk,
pusillanimity, satanic love, curiosity, contumely, lack of the fear of God,
unteachability, senselessness, haughtiness, self- vaunting, self- inflation,
scorn for one's neighbour, mercilessness, insensitivity, hopelessness,
spiritual paralysis, hatred of God, despair, suicide, a falling away from
God in all things, utter destruction – altogether 298 passions.

These, then, are the passions which I have found named in the
Holy Scriptures. I have set them down in a single list, as I did at the
beginning of my discourse with the various books I have used. I have
not tried, nor would I have been able, to arrange them all in order;
this would have been beyond my powers, for the reason given by St
John Klimakos: 'If you seek understanding in wicked men, you will
not find it.'[1] For all that the demons produce is disorderly. In
common with the godless and the unjust, the demons have but one
purpose: to destroy the souls of those who accept their evil counsel.
Yet sometimes they actually help men to attain holiness. In such
instances they are conquered by the patience and faith of those who
put their trust in the Lord, and who through their good actions and
resistance to evil thoughts counteract the demons and bring down
curses upon them.

[1] *Ladder*, Step 15 (897D; E.T., p. 159).

THE DIFFERENCE BETWEEN THOUGHTS
AND PROVOCATIONS

Our thoughts differ greatly one from the other.[1] Some are altogether free from sin. Others do not initially involve sin: this is the case with what are called provocations, in other words, conceptions of either good or evil, which in themselves are neither commendable nor reprehensible. What follows on these is known as 'coupling'; that is to say, we begin to entertain a particular thought and parley with it, so to speak; and this leads us either to give assent to it or to reject it. Our reaction to the thought, if in accordance with God's will, is praiseworthy, though not highly so; but if it accords with evil, then it deserves censure. After this comes the stage at which our intellect wrestles with the thought, and either conquers it or is conquered by it; and this brings the intellect either credit or punishment when the thought is put into action. The same is true with what is called assent: this is a pleasurable inclination of the soul towards what it sees; and it leads to the state of seduction, or captivity, in which the heart is induced forcibly and unwillingly to put the thought into effect.

When the soul dallies for a long time with an impassioned thought there arises what we call a passion. This in its turn, through its intercourse with the soul, becomes a settled disposition within us, compelling the soul to move of its own accord towards the corresponding action. Where passion is concerned, unquestionably and invariably we must either repent proportionately or else undergo punishment in the age to come, as St John Klimakos states.[2] We are punished for our lack of repentance, and not because we had to struggle against temptation; otherwise most of us could not receive forgiveness until we had attained total dispassion. But as St John Klimakos again observes, 'It is not possible for all to achieve dispassion, yet all can be saved and reconciled with God.'[3]

An intelligent person, aware of all this, will thus reject the initial malicious provocation, mother of all evil, so that he may cut off at one stroke all its pernicious consequences. But he is always ready to put

[1] Peter follows here the teaching of Mark the Ascetic and John Klimakos: see Glossary, 'Temptation'.

[2] *Ladder*, Step 15 (897B; E.T., p. 158).

[3] *Ladder*, Step 26 (1029D; E.T., p. 213).

the good provocation into effect, so that his soul and body may grow firmly disposed to virtue and be delivered from the passions through the grace of Christ. For we have nothing that we have not received from Him (cf. 1 Cor. 4 : 7), nor can we offer Him anything except our faculty of free choice. If we lacked this, we would not possess the knowledge or the strength to do what is good. Yet even this faculty of free choice is given to us by God in His love, so that we may not be condemned as incapable of doing anything. For idleness is the source of all evil.

Moreover, according to the *Gerontikon*, even the doing of what is good requires discrimination. For the virgin who fasted for six days in each week, and constantly studied the Old and New Testaments, did not look with detachment on what is pleasant and what is unpleasant.[1] After such labours she ought to have attained the state of dispassion, but this did not happen; for the good is not good unless its purpose is conformed to God's will. On many occasions in divine Scripture God is grieved with someone who is doing something that appears to all to be good, and He looks favourably on someone who appears to be doing evil. A case in point is that of the prophet who asked someone to strike him; when the man refused he was eaten by a wild beast, although he had acted in a way that was ostensibly good (cf. 1 Kgs. 20 : 35–36). St Peter, too, thought he was acting rightly when he refused to have his feet washed, but he was rebuked for this (cf. John 13 : 8). Hence we should do all we can to discern the will of God and to do it, whether it corresponds to what we think good or not. Thus the doing of good is not to be accomplished without effort on our part; for in this way we are deprived neither of our freedom of choice nor of the praise we earn for exerting pressure on ourselves. In short, all that God arranges is admirable, beyond the grasp of intellect and thought.

We must admire not only the inner meaning of all the things that are celebrated in the Church of the Orthodox Christians, but also the sacramental actions through which this meaning is expressed: how through divine baptism we become sons of God by grace, though we have done nothing before this, and do nothing after except keep the commandments; and how these awesome mysteries – I refer to holy baptism and holy communion – cannot take place without the

---

[1] Paul Evergetinos, *Collection* III, xxix, 3, §4.

priesthood, as St John Chrysostom says.[1] Here, too, we see the significance of the power given to St Peter, chief of the apostles; for if the gates of the kingdom of heaven are not opened by priestly action, no one can enter (cf. Matt. 16 : 19). As the Lord says: 'Unless a man is born of water and the Spirit . . .' (John 3 : 5); and again: 'Unless you eat the flesh of the Son of man and drink His blood, you have no life in you' (John 6 : 53).

In the same way we must reflect with wonder how the outer part of the temple of the Old Covenant, where the priests performed sacrifices, was an image of the cosmos (cf. 1 Kgs. 8 : 64), while within there was the Holy of Holies (cf. Exod. 30 : 10; Heb. 9 : 3), in which was offered the incense made of four components, fragrant gum, myrrh, balsam and cassia, which represent the four universal virtues.[2] The ceremonies performed in the outer part were a concession accorded by God, so that the Jews, with their childlike mentality, might not be led astray by songs and revelling to the worship of idols. But the Church of the New Covenant is the image of the blessings held in store, and for this reason what is accomplished within it is spiritual and heavenly. For just as there are nine orders in heaven, so there are nine orders in the Church; patriarchs, metropolitans, bishops, priests, deacons, subdeacons, readers, singers and monks.

Then we should also marvel how demons and various diseases are dispelled by the sign of the precious and life-giving Cross, which all can make without cost or effort. Who can number the panegyrics composed in its honour? The holy fathers have handed down to us the inner significance of this sign, so that we can refute heretics and unbelievers. The two fingers[3] and single hand with which it is made represent the Lord Jesus Christ crucified, and He is thereby acknowledged to exist in two natures and one hypostasis or person. The use of the right hand betokens His infinite power and the fact that He sits at the right hand of the Father. That the sign begins with a downward movement from above signifies His descent to us from heaven. Again, the movement of the hand from the right side to the left drives away our enemies and declares that by His invincible

---

[1] *On Priesthood* III, 5 (*P.G.* xlviii, 643).

[2] Cf. Evagrios, *On Prayer* 1 (*The Philokalia*, vol. i, p. 57).

[3] In the time of Peter of Damaskos, the sign of the Cross was evidently made with two fingers – as is still done by the Old Ritualists ('Old Believers') in Russia – and not with three fingers (i.e., two fingers and the thumb), as in modern Orthodox practice.

power the Lord overcame the devil, who is on the left side, dark and lacking strength.

Again, we must marvel how through little strokes of colour paintings show us so many wonderful things performed over so many years by our Lord and all His saints, making them look as if they had only just been performed. This comes about through God's providence, so that by becoming eyewitnesses, as it were, of these things, our longing for God may grow even greater, as St Peter, chief of the apostles, says in the account of the martyrdom of his disciple Pankratios.[1]

All that has been said from the beginning of this discourse is of no benefit to anyone without the true faith; nor can it be put into practice without faith, just as there is no faith without works (cf. Jas. 2 : 20). Many of the holy fathers have written concerning faith and works. As a concluding reminder I shall say briefly that, to whatever order we belong, we ought all of us to undertake the works I have written about, as well as holding fast to the Orthodox faith we have received from the saints I have cited, so that with them we may attain eternal blessings through the grace and love of our Lord Jesus Christ, to whom rightly belong honour and worship, together with His unoriginate Father and His all-holy, blessed and life-giving Spirit, now and always and through all the ages. Amen.

Having completed this I said: 'Christ, glory is rightly Thine.'

[1] Ed. P. F. de'Cavalieri, *Studi e Testi* 19 (Rome, 1908), pp. 109–12; but there is no reference here to the Apostle Peter.

BOOK II

Twenty-Four Discourses

I
SPIRITUAL WISDOM[1]

In all languages the first letter of the alphabet is A, though some people are unaware of this. Similarly, the first of all the virtues is spiritual wisdom, though it is also their consummation. For if the intellect is not imbued with spiritual wisdom, no one can accomplish anything of value, for he will not even have learnt what is of value. But if he has been enabled by grace to learn something about this, he will to that extent possess wisdom. Yet although learning the alphabet is something elementary, unless we learn it we cannot proceed to any more advanced study. In the same way, although our first steps in spiritual knowledge may be very slight, unless we make them we will not acquire any virtue at all. Because of this I am afraid to write anything about wisdom, since I am entirely lacking in it.

It seems to me that there are four things which make the intellect articulate: first, supranatural grace and blessedness; second, the purity that comes from the practice of the virtues and that restores the soul to its pristine beauty; third, experience of the lower forms of teaching, through human education and secular learning; fourth, the accursed and satanic delusion that works in us through pride and demonic cunning, and distorts our nature. I have no share in any of these things. So how can I write? Perhaps the faith of you who in your devotion to God urge me to write will bring grace to my pen; for my intellect and my hand are unworthy and impure. I know from experience that this can happen. For, fathers, whenever I have wanted to write something I have not been able to formulate it in my intellect

---

[1] Each of the *Twenty-Four Discourses* begins with four or more lines of verse. Since these add nothing to the substance of the text that follows, and are probably not the work of Peter himself but of some later scribe, they have been omitted from our translation; but we have assigned short titles to each *Discourse*.

until I have actually picked up my pen. Frequently it was some small thought suggested by Scripture, or something I had heard or seen in this world, that set my mind to work; but as soon as I took up my pen and began to write, at once I discovered what I needed to say. It is as if someone is forcing me to write the thing down; and when this happens I begin to write freely and without anxiety for as long as my hand holds out. If God puts something into my darkened heart, I write it down without thinking. This prevents me from imagining that I am the source of what I have received through the prayers of another, as St John Klimakos puts it,[1] basing himself on St Paul's words: 'What do you have which you did not receive? Now if you received it, why do you boast, as if you had not received it?' (1 Cor. 4 : 7) – as if, that is to say, you were yourself the author of it.

According to St Isaac the ideas that arise spontaneously in the intellect of those who have attained a state of stillness, free from discursive thought, are to be accepted.[2] But what comes from discursive thought is a purely subjective and individual notion. St Antony says that every word or act ought to be supported by divine Scripture.[3] It is in this spirit that I begin to write, just as the ass of Balaam began to talk (cf. Num. 22 : 28–30). I do this not in order to teach others – God forbid! – but in order to reprove my unhappy soul, so that, shamed by my own words, as St John Klimakos says, I who have done nothing but speak may begin to act. Who knows whether I shall live and have the strength to write? Or whether you will be able to carry out what I say? But let us both begin to do both things, each to the extent of his own ability. For we do not know when we will die and when our end will come. But God who foreknows all things knows about us as well. To Him be glory through all the ages. Amen.

[1] *Ladder*, Step 15 (900B; E.T., p. 159).
[2] Cf. *Mystic Treatises*, E.T., pp. 3, 14, 351; Greek, pp. 4, 313–14.
[3] *Apophthegmata*, Antony 3; E.T., p. 2.

II
THE TWO KINDS OF FAITH

St Paul said that faith was the basis of all actions that conform to
God's will, and that we have received it through holy baptism by the
grace of Christ and not through works (cf. Col. 1 : 23; Rom. 11 : 6).
According to St Isaac, this is the first kind of faith, and it engenders
the fear that is inherent in it.[1] Such fear leads us to keep the
commandments and patiently to endure trials and temptations, as St
Maximos has explained.[2] Then, after we have begun to act in this
way, a second kind of faith is born in us, the great faith of
contemplation, to which the Lord was referring when He said: 'If you
have faith as a mustard seed . . . nothing will be impossible for you'
(Matt. 17 : 20). Thus there is, first, the ordinary faith of all Orthodox
Christians, that is to say, correct doctrinal belief concerning God and
His creation, both visible and invisible, as the Holy Catholic Church,
by God's grace, has received it; and there is, second, the faith of
contemplation or spiritual knowledge, which is not in any way
opposed to the first kind of faith; on the contrary, the first gives birth
to the second, while the second strengthens the first.

We acquire the first kind of faith through hearing about it,
inheriting it from devout parents and teachers of the Orthodox faith;
but the second is engendered in us by our true belief and by our fear
of the Lord in whom we have come to believe. For because of this
fear we have chosen to keep the commandments and so have resolved
to practise the virtues that pertain to the body – stillness, fasting,
moderate vigils, psalmody, prayer, spiritual reading, and the
questioning of those with experience about all our thoughts, words,
or undertakings. We practise these virtues so that the body may be
purified of the worst passions – gluttony, unchastity and superfluous
possessions – and so that we may be content with what we have, as
the apostle puts it (cf. Heb. 13 : 5).

It is in this way that a man finds the strength to devote himself
undistractedly to God. He learns from the Scriptures and from people
of experience about divine doctrines and commandments, and he

---

[1] *Mystic Treatises*, E.T., p. 213; Greek, p. 65.
[2] *On Love* I, 81 (*The Philokalia*, vol. ii, p. 62).

begins to reject the rest of the eight leading passions. Perceiving the punishments that threaten man, he is not merely afraid of God: he fears Him as God, in the words of St Neilos. As a consequence of this fear he begins to keep the commandments with true knowledge of why he does so. And the more he endures voluntary death for the sake of each commandment, the more he enters into greater knowledge and contemplates what is taking place in himself through the grace of Christ. As a result he comes to believe that the Orthodox faith is truly glorious, and he begins to long to do God's will. He no longer has any doubts about God's help, but 'casts his burden upon the Lord' (Ps. 55 : 22). As St Basil the Great says, he who wishes to acquire the higher kind of faith should not worry about his own life or death: even if faced by a wild beast or attacked by demons or evil men, he should not be at all afraid, since he knows that they are all the creatures of a single Creator and are co-servants with him, and would have no power against him if God did not allow it. He should fear God alone, for He alone has power.

This is made clear by the Lord Himself when He says: 'I will warn you whom to fear', continuing: 'Fear Him who has the power to cast both soul and body into hell'; and in order to confirm His words, He says: 'Yes, I tell you, fear Him' (cf. Luke 12 : 5). He has good reason to say this; for if someone else apart from God had power, we ought to fear him; but since God alone is the Creator and Master of things above and things below, who can do anything without Him? If someone says that there are creatures that possess free will, I too agree that angels and men, as well as the demons, do indeed possess it. But the angelic orders and good men cannot bear to inflict any harm at all on one of their fellow-servants, even though he is very evil; instead, they feel compassion for him and entreat God on his behalf, as St Athanasios the Great says. As for evil men and their teachers in evil, the demons, they would certainly like to harm others, but are utterly unable to do so, unless the person in question has himself caused God to abandon him through his own sinful actions. Yet even this occurs for the sake of his instruction and salvation at the hands of the all-bountiful God, provided, that is to say, he is willing to accept God's correction of his sinfulness with thankful endurance. If he refuses to do this, then God's action proves of benefit to someone else, since God desires the salvation of everyone.

The trials and temptations of righteous and holy men take place with God's consent and contribute both to the perfecting of their souls and to the shaming of their enemies, the demons. Thus when the person who carries out Christ's commandments becomes aware of these things, he does not believe simply that Christ is God and that He has power; for even the demons realize this because of His actions and they shudder (cf. Jas. 2 : 19). On the contrary, he believes that all things are possible for Christ, that His every will is good, and that without Him nothing good can happen. It is for this reason that such a person does not want to do anything contrary to the divine will, even if it is a question of saving his life; though, of course, it is impossible to save one's life unless one does perform God's will, for this divine will is eternal life (cf. John 12 : 50), the greatest of blessings, even if the effort needed to attain it appears to some to be arduous.

Because of this I in my wretchedness am worse than the infidel, for I am unwilling to make efforts to find that greater faith and through it to come to the fear of God, the beginning of the wisdom of the Spirit (cf. Prov. 1 : 7). At times I deliberately close my soul's eyes and transgress the law; at other times I am blinded by forgetfulness and enter a state of total ignorance: unaware of what profits my soul I fall into bad habits and become an inveterate sinner. As a result, even if I want to return whence I fell, I cannot do so, since my own will has become a dividing wall between myself and God, as the holy fathers say, and I have no wish to exert myself in order to destroy it.[1] Had I the faith that comes from performing works of repentance, I would be able to say, 'With the help of my God I will leap over the wall' (Ps. 18 : 29. LXX). I would not hesitate out of cowardice, asking myself what will happen to me if I rush over this wall, and whether there may not be a pit on the other side, and what I will do if I cannot get over, and fall headlong backwards again after my efforts, and many other questions of this kind. Such questions never even occur to someone who has faith that God is close at hand and not far off (cf. Jer. 23 : 23), and who in his determination to attain his end advances directly towards God, source of all strength, power, goodness and love, acting not like one who 'beats the air' (cf. 1 Cor. 9 : 26), but like a swimmer. He aspires to the realm above and, leaving all self-will

---

[1] *Apophthegmata*, Poimin 54; E.T., p. 174.

behind, journeys towards the divine will until he hears 'new tongues' and even perhaps speaks with them (cf. Mark 16 : 17), perceiving the mysteries. So he gains, or rather he is given, the power to ascend from the practice of the virtues to the state of contemplation, through the grace and love of our Lord Jesus Christ, to whom belong all glory, honour and dominion throughout the ages. Amen.

III
THE TWO KINDS OF FEAR

Gluttony is the first of the eight champions of evil. But fear of God, which is the first commandment, defeats all eight of them, while without this fear one cannot possess any blessing. For how can the person who feels no fear keep the commandment, unless indeed he has already attained the state of love? Even he who has attained the state of love began with fear, though he may not know how this initial fear passed from him. Should someone say that he has reached the state of love by some other path, he has been taken captive either by spiritual joy or by his own obduracy, so that he is like someone crossing a river while asleep, as St Ephrem puts it. The man seized by spiritual joy is astounded by the many blessings that God in his grace has bestowed on him, and he loves his Benefactor. But he who obdurately indulges in luxury and splendour, like the rich man (cf. Luke 16 : 19), thinks that those consumed by fear and facing trials and temptation suffer in this way because of their sins, and in his comfort and complacency he despises them. He imagines that he deserves his easy life, although in fact he does not deserve it at all; for, blinded by his inane love for the ephemeral, he has made himself unworthy of the life held in store. He may even think that he has attained the state of love and on account of this has received greater benefits than others have. This shows that he is totally unaware of God's forbearance towards him. For this reason he will find himself defenceless on the day of judgment and deservedly will hear the words, 'You received your good things during your lifetime' (Luke 16 : 25). All this is obvious from the fact that there are many non-believers of this type, who are benefited by God without deserving it;

yet no one with any sense would call them blessed or say that they are
worthy of being loved by God, or that they love God and perhaps on
this account live comfortably in the present life.

But to return to the question of the fear of God. Like faith, fear is
of two kinds: the first is introductory, while the second, which grows
out of the first, is perfect. He who is afraid of God's punishment has a
slave-like fear of God, and it is this that makes him refrain from evil:
'Out of fear of the Lord men shun evil' (Prov. 16 : 6. LXX); 'I will
teach you the fear of the Lord' (Ps. 34 : 11). According to St
Dorotheos, these and similar things are said with regard to the
introductory fear, so that through fear of what threatens us we
sinners may be led to repent and may seek to find deliverance from
our sins.[1] Moreover, when it is active within us, this introductory fear
teaches us the way that leads to life, for it is said: 'Shun evil, and do
good' (Ps. 34 : 14).

The more a man struggles to do good, the more fear grows in him,
until it shows him his slightest faults, those which he thought of as
nothing while he was still in the darkness of ignorance. When fear in
this way has become perfect, he himself becomes perfect through
inward grief: he no longer desires to sin but, fearing the return of the
passions, he remains in this pure fear invulnerable. As the psalm puts
it, 'The fear of the Lord is pure, and endures for ever' (Ps. 19 : 9.
LXX). The first kind of fear is not pure, for it arises in us because of
our sins. But, independent of sin, the person who has been purified
continues to feel fear, not because he sins, but because, being human,
he is changeable and prone to evil. In his humility, the further he
advances through the acquisition of the virtues, the more he fears.
This is natural; for everyone who possesses wealth greatly fears loss,
punishment, dishonour, and the consequent fall from his high estate.
The poor man, on the contrary, is on the whole without fear: he is
only afraid of being beaten.

What has just been said applies to those who are entirely perfect
and pure in soul and body. But if someone is still stumbling, even
though his sins are of the slightest and most insignificant kind, let him
not mislead himself by thinking that his fear is pure. For if he does
think this, he is deceived, as St John Klimakos states: his fear is not
pure, nor is it humility. It is but servile prudence and fear of

---

[1] *Instructions* IV, 47 (ed. Regnault, p. 220).

punishments threatened. Thus such a person's thoughts need to be corrected, so that he may learn what kind of fear he is subject to, and through the deepest grief and by patiently enduring affliction may purify himself of sins, and in this way through Christ's grace may attain perfect fear. The sign of the first kind of fear is hatred of sin and anger towards it, like someone wounded by a wild beast. The sign of perfect fear is the love of virtue and the fear of relapsing, since no one is unalterable.

Thus in every situation throughout this present life we ought always to be afraid of falling; for we see the great king and prophet David mourning for his two sins (cf. Ps. 51; 2 Sam. 11 : 1–17), and Solomon himself giving way to grievous evil (cf. 1 Kgs. 11 : 1–10). As St Paul said: 'Let anyone who thinks he stands firm take care lest he fall' (1 Cor. 10 : 12). If someone says that, according to St John, 'love casts out fear' (1 John 4 : 18), he is right; but this refers to the first, the introductory fear. Concerning perfect fear David has said: 'Blessed is the man who fears the Lord and who greatly delights in His commandments' (Ps. 112 : 1), that is, who greatly cherishes virtue. Such a person has the status of a son, for he cherishes virtue not out of fear of punishment, but because of the love that 'casts out fear'. This is why he 'greatly delights', unlike the slave who carries out orders under constraint because of his fear of punishment. From this punishment may we all be saved, through the grace and love of our Lord Jesus Christ, to whom belong all glory, honour and worship throughout the ages. Amen.

IV

TRUE PIETY AND SELF-CONTROL

It is clear that true piety embraces a great variety of things, as does secular philosophy. For philosophy presupposes the completion of ten different branches of learning, embracing not just one or two of these branches but all ten together. Similarly, true piety consists not in the possession of a single virtue alone, but in the keeping of all the commandments. In its Greek form, the term 'true piety' comes from a word meaning 'to serve well'. If some people say that 'to serve well' is the same thing as faith, let them explain how it is possible to fear the Lord before believing in Him. Does one not first believe in the Lord and then fear Him? Hence faith gives rise to fear, and from fear comes true piety. The prophet Isaiah indicates that this is the correct sequence: starting with wisdom, he proceeds in a descending order, referring to 'the spirit of knowledge and true piety', and last of all to 'the spirit of the fear of God' (Isa. 11 : 2–3. LXX). The Lord Himself starts with fear and then guides the man who possesses this fear to a state of inward grief.

This is not the moment to speak systematically about every form of true piety or spiritual activity. Leaving to one side the ascetic practices pertaining to the body that precede the acquisition both of the higher kind of faith and of pure fear – for everyone knows what these practices are – I will speak of the trees of the spiritual paradise, that is, with the help of God's grace I will speak briefly about the virtues of the soul. Of these, the most all-embracing is self-control, by which I mean abstinence from all the passions. There is also another, more partial form of self-control, that applies to bodily actions and teaches us the proper use of food and drink. Here, however, I am referring to the self-control that applies, as I said, to the passions and that restrains every thought and every movement of the limbs that is not in harmony with God's will. The person who possesses this virtue does not tolerate any thought or word, any movement of hand or foot or of any other member of the body, unless it is essential to the life of the body or to the soul's salvation.

It is after the acquisition of this virtue that the trials and temptations incited by the demons multiply, for they see before them an embodied angel, wholeheartedly committed to doing what is right and good. This is what is meant by the command given to man in paradise, 'to cultivate and to keep it' (Gen. 2 : 15); for self-control needs to be cultivated and guarded ceaselessly, so as to prevent any of the passions that are outside the garden from stealthily creeping in. As I have said, the two forms of self-control or self-restraint are not identical, for while the first curbs unchastity and the other shameful passions, the second controls even the slightest thought, bringing it under surveillance before it can lead to sin, and then conducting it to God.

No one can speak or learn about this with precision merely through hearsay; it is only through experience that one can come to understand and counteract all these things that so disturb the intellect. How, indeed, is it possible merely by giving things a name to resurrect the dust and to make the material immaterial? Names are one thing, and secular learning, on the basis of etymology, can provide one with knowledge about them. But the experience and acquisition of the virtues require God's help; and they are achieved only through much effort and over a long period of time. This is especially true of the virtues of the soul, for these are the more inward and essential virtues. The virtues that pertain to the body – which are better described as the tools of the virtues – are easier to acquire, even though they do demand bodily effort. But the virtues of the soul, although they demand the control of thought alone, are much more difficult to achieve. Because of this the Law says first: 'Watch yourself attentively' (Exod. 23 : 21. LXX). St Basil the Great has written an excellent treatise on this phrase.[1]

But what shall we say, we who are not attentive at all? We are like the Pharisees. Some of us may fast and keep vigil and perform other such things, and we may often do this with partial understanding. But we lack discrimination because we do not pay attention to ourselves and do not know what it is that is being asked of us. Nor are we willing to give persistent and patient attention to our thoughts, so as to gain experience from our many trials and battles, and thus become for others at least an experienced sailor, if not a captain. Although we are all of us blind, we claim that we ourselves see, as the Pharisees claimed. That is why it is said that they will be judged more severely (cf. John 9 : 41). For if we acknowledged our blindness, we should not be condemned; it would be enough for us to be grateful and to admit our failure and ignorance. But, alas, we shall receive the greater condemnation, as did the pagan Greeks; for, according to Solomon, they aspired after so many things and yet failed to attain what they sought. Should we therefore keep silence, as though there was nothing for us to do? That would be even worse. Let us rather rebuke ourselves, for it is shameful even to mention the things that we do in secret (cf. Eph. 5 : 12). Hence I will say nothing about such things, but will speak about the virtues that so deserve our esteem. For the recollection of their sweetness fills my darkened heart with pleasure, and I forget my limitations and am no longer troubled about the condemnation that awaits me if I speak and do not act.

Self-control, then, and self-restraint have the same power and are

---

[1] See above, p. 104.

twofold, as has been said. But now I want to say something further about their more perfect form. He who by God's grace enjoys the great faith of contemplation together with pure and divine fear, and who wishes on the basis of these to keep possession of self-control and self-restraint, should first master himself both outwardly and inwardly, acting as if he were already dead in soul and body as regards this world and all other men. In every circumstance he should say to himself: 'Who am I? What is my existence? Nothing but abomination. For I start as earth and I end as putrefaction, and in between I am filled with all manner of insolence and worse. What is my life? And how long? A single hour and then death comes. Why do I bother about this and that? Already I am dying. For Christ controls both life and death. Why do I worry and strive in vain? All one needs is a bit of bread: why seek more? If I have this, there is nothing to worry about. If I don't, it may be that in my ignorance I do worry about it; yet it is God who provides.'

For these reasons every man should make it his whole concern to guard his senses and his thoughts, so as not to devise or do anything that does not seem to be in accordance with God's will. Let him prepare himself to accept patiently the things that befall him at the hands of men and demons, whether these things are pleasant or unpleasant. Neither the one nor the other should excite him or make him give way either to senseless joy and presumption, or to dejection and despair. He should entertain no over-confident thought until the Lord comes. To Him be glory throughout the ages. Amen.

V

PATIENT ENDURANCE

The Lord said: 'He who endures patiently to the end will be saved' (Matt. 10 : 22). Patient endurance is the consolidation of all the virtues, because without it not one of them can subsist. For whoever turns back is not 'fit for the kingdom of heaven' (Luke 9 : 62). Indeed, even though someone thinks that he is in possession of all the virtues, he is still not fit for the kingdom until he has first endured to the end and escaped from the snares of the devil; for only thus can he attain it. Even those who have received a foretaste of the kingdom stand in need of patient endurance if they are to gain their final reward in the age to be. Indeed, in every form of learning and knowledge persistence is needed. This is natural, since even sensible things cannot be produced without it: when any such thing is born, there has to be a period of patient waiting if it is to continue to live.

In short, patient endurance is required before anything can come about; and, once something has come about, it can be sustained and brought to perfection only through such endurance. If it is something good, this virtue assists and guards it; if something evil, it confers relief and strength of soul and does not permit the person being tempted to grow faint-hearted, thus experiencing a foretaste of hell. Patient endurance kills the despair that kills the soul; it teaches the soul to take comfort and not to grow listless in the face of its many battles and afflictions.

Judas lacked this virtue, and because of his inexperience in spiritual warfare suffered a double death (cf. Matt. 27 : 5). Peter, chief of the apostles, possessed it, being an experienced warrior; and when he fell, he defeated the devil who had overthrown him (cf. Matt. 26 : 75; John 21 : 15–17). The monk who once lapsed into unchastity acquired it, and conquered his conqueror by not yielding to the counsel of despair that urged him to abandon his cell and his solitude.[1] Patiently he said to the thoughts that tempted him: 'I have not sinned; and again I say to you, I have not sinned.' What divine understanding and patience in that noble man! This blessed virtue brought the righteous Job and his initial good works to fulfilment; for had he lacked it even slightly, he would have obliterated all the good he had previously done. But God who knew his patience allowed the plague to strike him for his own perfecting and for the benefit of many others.

He, then, who knows what is to his benefit should struggle to acquire this virtue before anything else, according to St Basil the Great. For St Basil advises us not to fight against all the passions at once, since if we are unsuccessful we might turn back and no longer be fit for the kingdom of heaven. Rather we should fight the passions one at a time, and start by patiently enduring whatever befalls us. This is right; for the person who lacks patient endurance will never be able

---

[1] Cf. John Cassian, *Conferences* II, 13; *The Philokalia*, vol. i, p. 105.

to stand fast even in an ordinary battle, but will bring only flight and destruction upon himself and others by retreating. This is why God told Moses not to allow anyone who was cowardly to go out with the army (cf. Deut. 20 : 8). In an ordinary war it may be possible for someone to remain inside in his house and not go out to fight; and though by doing this he loses gifts and honours, he may live on in poverty and dishonour. But in spiritual warfare it is impossible to find a place anywhere in creation in which a battle is not being waged. In the desert there are wild beasts and demons and other malefic and terrifying things; in places of solitude and stillness there are demons, trials and temptations; in the midst of human company there are demons and men who try one and tempt one. There is no place anywhere where one is unmolested; and, because of this, without patient endurance it is impossible to find peace.

Such endurance is born of fear and faith, though it originates in understanding. He who is sensible tests things in the light of his intellect and, when he finds that he is 'hemmed in on every side' – to use Susanna's words – he chooses what is better, as she did. For she said to God: 'I am hemmed in on every side. If I do the will of the lawless priests, my soul will perish because of my adultery; but if I disobey them, they will accuse me of adultery and as judges of the people will condemn me to death. It is better for me to take refuge in the Almighty, even if death awaits me' (cf. Sus., verses 22–23). How great was the wisdom of that blessed woman! For as soon as the people had gathered together and the lawless judges had sat down to accuse her, blameless as she was, and to condemn her to death as an adulteress, then Daniel, though only twelve years old, was shown by God to be a prophet and saved her from death, transferring the death sentence from her to the priests who were about to judge her unjustly (cf. Sus., verses 44–62).

Through Susanna God has shown how close He is to those who are willing to endure trials for His sake, and who will not abandon virtue out of cowardice because of the suffering involved, but cleave to the law of God by patiently enduring what befalls them, rejoicing in the hope of salvation. And they have good cause to do this; for when confronted by two perils, one with temporary and the other with eternal consequences, is it not better to choose the first? For this reason St Isaac says that it is better to endure dangers out of love for God, and to cleave to Him in the hope of eternal life, than through fear of trials to fall away from God into the hands of the devil and to be condemned with him to punishment. If we love God, then like the saints we should rejoice in our own trials. But even if we are not like them, let us at least choose the better path simply out of constraint; for we are in fact constrained either to run bodily risks in this present life, thereby attaining the state of dispassion, and so coming to reign with Christ spiritually in this age and in the age to be; or else, as I have said, to fall away through fear of trials and be committed to agelong punishment.

May God save us from punishment by giving us the strength patiently to endure whatever terrible things befall us. Endurance is like an unshakeable rock in the winds and waves of life. However the tempest batters him, the patient man remains steadfast and does not turn back; and when he finds relief and joy, he is not carried away by self-glory: he is always the same, whether things are hard or easy, and for this reason he is proof against the snares of the enemy. When storms beset him, he endures them with joy, awaiting their end; and when the heavens smile on him, he expects temptation – until his last breath, as St Antony has said.[1] Such a person knows that nothing in life is unchangeable, and that all things pass. Thus he is not troubled or anxious about any of them, but leaves all things in the hands of God, for He has us in His care (cf. 1 Pet. 5 : 7); and to Him belong all glory, honour and dominion throughout the ages. Amen.

VI
HOPE

Life is hope free from all anxiety, wealth hidden from the senses but attested by the understanding and by the true nature of things. Farmers work laboriously, sowing and planting, sailors endure many dangers, and children learn reading and writing and other branches of knowledge. They all look forward with hope, labouring with joy. Outwardly they sacrifice immediate advantages, but in reality, even if they forfeit what they sacrifice, through their patient endurance they

---

[1] *Apophthegmata*, Antony 4; E.T., p. 2.

gain what is of far greater value. But in such instances, it might be said, they do this because they know from experience that they stand to gain something, while in the realm of the spiritual no one has risen from the dead so that we can know what rewards to expect. It is, however, only because we have no experience of spiritual gifts and spiritual knowledge that we think like this. Nor is it surprising that we should do so. For even farmers and sailors are full of apprehension so long as they have not acquired experience. And children, ignorant of the value of writing and the other subjects, seek to avoid learning them; but their parents, aware of what is to be gained, in their love compel them to study; then, when the time is ripe, the children themselves acquire experience and not only begin to love their lessons and those who force them to study, but even to accept with joy the ordeals of learning. Thus we, too, setting out in faith should strive patiently to advance, and not lose heart because of our tribulations; and then, when the time is ripe, we like them will come to know the value of what is happening to us and so will work tirelessly and with joy and gladness. 'We walk by faith,' as St Paul says, 'not by sight' (2 Cor. 5 : 7).

Yet just as it is impossible for someone engaged in business to make a profit on the basis of faith alone, so it is impossible for anyone to attain spiritual knowledge and repose before he has laboured in thought and action to acquire the virtues. And just as business men always fear loss and hope for gain, so should we, until our final breath; and as they exert themselves not only when they make a profit, but also after suffering loss and taking risks, so should we as well, knowing that the idle man will not eat from the fruit of his own labours and so will become a pauper, perhaps even falling heavily into debt. It is because of this that the prophet says, 'Thou hast made me to dwell in hope' (Ps. 4 : 8. LXX); and the apostle writes, 'Through hope were they made perfect' (cf. Heb. 11 : 39–40).

Such in brief is what we can learn from nature and from Holy Scripture. But if someone wishes to know these things through experience, let him do all that he can to practise assiduously, as though he were at school, the seven forms of bodily discipline, and let him pay attention to the moral virtues as well, that is, to the virtues that pertain to the soul. Then, after attaining hope and persisting in it, he will obtain precise knowledge of what has been said. He will realize that from the very outset of his repentance, when he began to practise the first of the seven forms of bodily discipline – namely, stillness – the reward of hope and the blessings it confers were granted to him even before he began to practise the other six, that is to say, fasting, vigils, and so on. As soon as he had begun to practise the first of them – stillness, the beginning of the soul's purification – at once the blessings to which he aspired were bestowed on him. But being an inexperienced student he did not recognize the grace of his Master, just as a child does not recognize the bounty of his parents, though before he was born it was already their desire to help him, for they prayed that he would be born and would live. The child even fails to realize that he will be their heir and will have all they already possess as well as what their labours may still accumulate. In his ignorance he pays no attention whatsoever to such things, but thinks of obedience to his parents as a trial. Indeed, were he not in need of food and other natural necessities he would not be grateful towards them at all.

He who wishes to inherit the kingdom of heaven, yet does not patiently endure what befalls him, shows himself even more ungrateful than such a child. For he was created by God's grace, has received all things in this world, awaits what is to come, and has been called to reign eternally with Christ, who has honoured him, in spite of his nothingness, with such great gifts, visible and invisible, to the extent even of shedding His most precious blood for him, not asking anything from him at all except that he should choose to receive His blessings. For this is Christ's only request, and whoever can understand that will be astonished. 'What does God require of you?' we are asked (cf. Mic. 6 : 8. LXX). How stupid we are! How is it that we look and fail to see His awesome mysteries? For precisely that which He seems to demand from us is in fact another, a greater gift. How do we not understand that he who cultivates the virtues is the greatest of men, superior to all, even if he is a pauper and of humble birth? How can we recognize the prophets, apostles and martyrs in this present life, and yet be doubtful about the blessings held in store? Let us consider their lives and what they have done, and whence it is they say they have received grace and strength. Do they not perform miracles even after their death? Have we not remarked how kings and rich people venerate their holy ikons? We have seen how virtuous men live even in this present life full of thankfulness and virtue and spiritual joy, while the rich are troubled and experience greater trials and temptations than ascetics and those who possess nothing. All this gives us grounds for hoping that virtue is truly greater than everything else. But if it is not enough, then we should note how unbelievers, although they may not know God, still praise virtue, despite the fact that the virtuous man seems to have a faith other than their own. For even an enemy is capable of respecting virtue in his opponent.

If we believe that virtue is good, then of necessity God, who created virtue and gave it to men, is also good; and if He is good, then of necessity He is likewise righteous, for righteousness is a virtue and thus is good. If God is both good and righteous, then He has certainly done all that He has done and is doing out of goodness, even if this does not seem to be so to the wicked. For nothing darkens a man's mind so much as evil, while God reveals Himself to simplicity and humility, not to toil and weariness. But He reveals Himself, not in the way that some in their inexperience think, but through the contemplation of created beings and through the revelation of the mysteries hidden in the divine Scriptures. Such is the reward, in this present life, of stillness and of the other virtues. As for the age to be, 'the eye has not seen, and the ear has not heard, and man's heart has not grasped the things that God has prepared for those who love Him' (1 Cor. 2 : 9), and who renounce their own will in patient endurance and in the hope of the blessings held in store. We pray that we too may attain these blessings through the grace and love of our Lord Jesus Christ, to whom belong all glory, honour and dominion throughout the ages. Amen.

VII
DETACHMENT

Detachment has its origin in hope, for he who hopes to acquire elsewhere eternal wealth readily despises that which is material and transient, even if it offers him every kind of comfort. For although his life may be harsh and full of pain, who could persuade a man of intelligence to value material wealth above love for God, who gives both forms of wealth to those who love Him? This could only happen to someone blind and unable to see at all because of his lack of faith or because of his evil disposition and habits. Had he possessed faith, he would have been enlightened; and had he through his firm faith received but a small measure of the enlightenment that comes from spiritual knowledge, he would have struggled to destroy those evil habits. And if he had resolved to do this, God's grace would have worked and struggled with him. But the Lord has said that few are saved (cf. Luke 13 : 23–24); for the things we see appear to be sweet, even when they are actually bitter. The dog that licks his wound with his tongue is not aware of the pain because of the sweetness, and does not realize that he is drinking his own blood; and the glutton who eats what harms him in both soul and body is not aware of the damage he does himself. All those who are the slaves of passion suffer likewise because of their lack of awareness; and even if they resist for a while they are again overcome by habit.

For this reason the Lord says, 'The kingdom of heaven is subjected to violence' (Matt. 11 : 12). Such violence is due, not to our nature, but to our intimacy with the passions. Had it been due to our nature, no one would enter the kingdom. For those who have chosen the kingdom, however, the yoke of the Lord is easy to bear and His burden is light (cf. Matt. 11 : 30), while for those who have not made this choice, 'strait is the gate, and narrow is the way' (Matt. 7 : 14) and 'the kingdom is subjected to violence' (Matt. 11 : 12). In the case of those who choose it, the kingdom is within and close to them, because they wish for it, and desire to attain here and now the state of dispassion. For what helps or hinders our salvation is the will, and nothing else. If you want to do something good, do it; and if you cannot do it, then resolve to do it, and you will have achieved the resolution even if you do not fulfil the action itself. Thus a habit, whether good or bad, can gradually and spontaneously be overcome. If this were not the case, no criminals would ever be saved, whereas in fact not only have they been saved, but many have become conspicuous for their excellence. Think what a great gulf separates the criminal from the saint; yet resolution finally overcame habit. If by Christ's grace someone is religious, or a monk, what prevents him from achieving sanctity, as criminals have achieved it? They were far from sanctity, he is near it; he has already completed the greater part of the journey, helped by grace, or by nature, or by the devotion and reverence he has inherited from his parents. Is it not strange, then, that when brigands and grave-robbers become saints, monks are condemned? But, alas, 'the shame of my face has covered me' (Ps. 44 : 15).

Kings renounce their riches, as Joasaph did and others like him;[1] but often a poor man is unable to continue in his original state, and so to enter without struggle into the kingdom of heaven simply by remaining detached from things which he has not acquired by inheritance from his parents. For although at baptism he renounced even what did not belong to him – since another possesses the world and the things in it, he merely has the power to desire them – and although he renounced this world-ruler as well, yet even so he may afterwards try to acquire possessions. He may say, 'I am not able to live without possessions or to endure the things that befall me.' 'What things?' it may be asked. The prison cells and chains which he endured previously, and might have had to endure, even if he had been a ruler? For even those who are in positions of authority and who possess wealth are subject to these things. What, then? The deprivation of life's necessities, the nakedness and the other things that he has to endure? But in order not to prolong this discussion by going into details and so heaping further disgrace on those who are already full of shame, I will add only the following. If we crave but one of the visible things, the desire for which we have renounced, then like Gehazi and Judas (cf. 2 Kgs. 5 : 25–27; Matt. 27 : 3–5) we will reap shame and disgrace in the age to come. For Gehazi desired what he did not have and so both contracted leprosy and fell away from God; while Judas desired to repossess what he had renounced and so was punished not only with hanging but also with perdition.

In what way is the monk exceptional if he does not persevere in virginity and a state of total dispossession? All men are under an obligation to keep the other commandments, because they pertain to our nature; that is to say, we are all required to love God and our neighbour, to endure patiently what befalls us, to make use of things according to their true nature, and to refrain from committing evil. We should keep these commandments even if we do not want to. Indeed, unless we keep them, we will not find peace even in this world, since the laws punish those who offend against them, and our rulers compel us to live virtuously. As St Paul says, the ruler 'does not

---

[1] John of Damaskos (attributed to), *Barlaam and Joasaph* XXXVII, 337; E.T. G. R. Woodward (Loeb Classical Library 34: new ed., London, 1967), p. 561.

bear the sword to no purpose' (Rom. 13 : 4); and again: 'You wish to
have no fear of the authorities? Do what is right and you will have
their approval' (Rom. 13 : 3). Everyone does and wants to do these
things because they accord with nature – indeed, we insist that they
should be done. But the lot of the monk as a soldier of Christ is to do
that which is beyond nature; for this reason he should taste Christ's
sufferings, so that he may also attain His glory.

Indeed, this too is a law of nature, verified by what happens in this
world. Are not the soldiers of the king honoured because they suffer
with him? And does not each of them receive praise in proportion to
his suffering? And to the extent that he shows himself incapable of
suffering in this way, is he not dishonoured? Is it not obvious that the
more regal the garments a person wears, the closer he is to the king?
And the less regal, the farther away? The same things apply in
connection with our own King. The more we suffer with Christ and
imitate His poverty, tasting His sufferings and the ill-treatment to
which He was subjected before He was crucified for our sake and
buried, the more intimate we become with Him and the more we
share in His glory. It is as St Paul says: if we suffer with Him, we will
also be glorified with Him (cf. Rom. 8 : 17).

Why, as we know, soldiers and thieves suffer simply trying to get
food, travellers and sailors are absent from home for long periods, and
people endure great trials quite apart from any hope of the kingdom
of heaven, often indeed failing to achieve whatever it is they struggle
for. But we are unwilling to endure even slight hardship for the sake
of the kingdom of heaven and eternal blessings. Yet these might not
prove so difficult to attain if our resolution abetted us and if we
regarded the acquisition of the virtues not as a laborious and
intolerable task, but rather as a joy and a relaxation, because of the
hope, freedom from anxiety and unsolicited honour that come
through virtue; for even its enemy respects it and admires it. Finally,
virtue brings us happiness and exultation. Indeed, detachment is full
of joy, just as material existence and its shameful passions are full of
sorrow. May we be redeemed from this material existence and may
we attain eternal, immaterial life through the detachment that leads
to the mortification of the body, in Jesus Christ our Lord, to whom
belong all glory, honour and worship throughout the ages. Amen.

VIII
MORTIFICATION OF THE PASSIONS

He who has achieved detachment has his attention fixed always on God through contemplation. For detachment from material things gives rise to the contemplation of spiritual realities – contemplation not of created beings in this present life, but of the awesome things that take place before and after death. For the detached person is taught about these things by grace, so that through inward grief he may mortify the passions and, when the time is ripe, attain peace and gentleness in his thoughts.

From faith comes fear, and from fear comes true piety, or self-control, the endurance of grief, and the other things of which the Lord's Beatitudes speak (cf. Matt. 5 : 3–12) – gentleness, hunger and thirst for righteousness, that is, for all the virtues, acts of mercy – and also detachment. From detachment comes the mortification of the body, realized through compunctive sorrow and bitter tears of repentance and distress. By means of these the soul in its anguish renounces the joys of this world and even the food we eat, for it begins to see that its faults are countless as the sand of the sea. This is the start of the soul's enlightenment and the sign of its health. The tears that may occur before this, and the apparently divine thoughts, compunction and the like, are all deceits and ruses of the demons, especially in the case of those living among men or subject to distraction, even though it be but slight.

For no one still attracted by any sensible object can overcome the passions. And if it is said that the saints of old not only lived among men but also possessed material things, the answer is that, though this is certainly true, they never used any of these objects under the influence of the passions. This is clear from the fact that, as is recorded in the genealogies of the Old Testament, they married wives and yet knew them only after many years, thus showing that they were in a sense both married and unmarried. The same is true of Job and other righteous men. Indeed, David was both king and prophet, and Solomon likewise up to a certain point in his life. He himself describes how God has sent subtle temptations to the sons of men, so that they might be distracted by vain things (cf. Eccles. 1 : 13) and thus prevented from turning towards what is even worse. All this is clear from the very nature of things. For if, when there are thousands of distractions, some still find opportunity to commit sins, how much more would this be the case if our lives were without distraction? In such circumstances, it is better for us to be superficially distracted, and so prevented from devoting ourselves to holy things and holy thoughts, rather than for us to do many other things which are in fact worse.

But he who by God's grace has achieved a certain degree of spiritual knowledge and can understand the awesome things that occur before and after death as a result of man's primal disobedience, should continue in all stillness and detachment to occupy himself with such thoughts as well as with the actions that induce them, and should not let himself be distracted by vain things. 'Vanity of vanities, all is vanity' (Eccles. 1 : 2); and on the basis of this text St John of Damaskos said, 'Truly all things are vanity, and life is but a shadow and a dream.'[1] For everyone worries in vain, as the Scripture rightly says (cf. Ps. 39 : 6): for what can be more vain than a life whose end is putrefaction and dust? Thus detachment is mortification, not of the intellect, but of the body's initial impulses towards pleasure and comfort. For the desire for comfort, however slight, is a non-spiritual desire. And when the soul recognizes in itself some altogether spiritual activity or knowledge, it feels still greater distress at the presence of this non-spiritual desire; for if the soul is non-spiritual, the Spirit of God will not abide in it (cf. Gen. 6 : 3). When this happens, the soul will not be interested in any good work, but will struggle to fulfil the desires of the body and of its own indwelling passions, piling darkness upon darkness, and gladly accepting to live always in utter ignorance.

When a man has been sufficiently illumined, however, to perceive his own faults, he never ceases mourning for himself and for all men, seeing God's great forbearance and what sins we in our wretchedness have committed and still persist in committing. As a result of this he becomes full of gratitude, not daring to condemn anyone, shamed by the profusion of God's blessings and the multitude of our sins. Thereupon he joyfully renounces everything in his own will that is counter to God, and he watches over his own senses, so as to prevent them from doing anything beyond what is unavoidably needed.

[1] From the Funeral Service: Hapgood, *Service Book*, p. 381.

In this way he emulates the psalmist, who wrote: 'Lord, my heart is not haughty, nor are my eyes presumptuous' (Ps. 131 : 1). But after having reached such heights he must be careful lest through negligence or self-inflation he suffers what David suffered, without perhaps being able to repent as David did. For to sin, even in the case of those who are most righteous, is easy, while repentance is not easy for everyone because death is near; and even before death comes there is despair. It is good, then, not to fall; or, if we fall, to rise again. And should we fall, we should not despair and so estrange ourselves from the Lord's love. For if He so chooses, He can deal mercifully with our weakness. Only we should not cut ourselves off from Him or feel oppressed when constrained by His commandments, nor should we lose heart when we fall short of our goal. Rather, let us learn that a thousand years in the sight of the Lord are but a single day, and a single day is as a thousand years (cf. Ps. 90 : 4). Let us be neither hasty nor tardy, and let us be always ready to make a new start. If you fall, rise up. If you fall again, rise up again. Only do not abandon your Physician, lest you be condemned as worse than a suicide because of your despair. Wait on Him, and He will be merciful, either reforming you, or sending you trials, or through some other provision of which you are ignorant.

For the devil is in the habit of promoting in the soul whatever he sees is in accordance with the soul's own disposition, whether this be joy or self-conceit, distress or despair, excessive toil or utter indolence, or thoughts and actions that are untimely and profitless, or blindness and unreflecting hatred of all that exists. Quite simply, he inflames in the soul whatever material he finds there already, so as to do it as much harm as he can, even though in itself the thing may be good and acceptable to God, provided that it is used with due restraint by one who is able to judge things and to discern the intention of God hidden in the six passions that surround him – those, that is, above him and below, to his right and to his left, within him and without. Whether it relates to the practice of the virtues or to spiritual knowledge, there is some good purpose lying within the six passions that oppose him.

Thus, as St Antony says,[1] we should always seek counsel about everything; and we should consult not just anyone, but those who

---

[1] *Apophthegmata*, Antony 37–8; E.T., pp. 8–9.

have the grace of discrimination; for if the person we consult lacks experience, we may both fall into the ditch, as in the example given in the Gospel (cf. Matt. 15 : 12–14). For without discrimination nothing good is ever done, even though to the ignorant it appears to be altogether good; for what is done without discrimination will be either untimely, or profitless, or disproportionate, or beyond the strength or knowledge of the person doing it, or faulty in some other way. He who has the gift of discrimination has received it on account of his humility. Through it he knows all things by grace and, when the time is ripe, he attains spiritual insight.

From inward grief, then, and patient endurance come hope and detachment; and through hope and detachment we die to the world. We may also die to the world by enduring patiently and by not despairing when we see everywhere dismay and death, knowing that this is both a trial and an illumination; or by not being over-confident about having reached our goal. Shedding many tears of distress, we begin to see clearly before us the holy sufferings of the Lord, and we are greatly solaced by them. And we truly regard ourselves as inferior to all other men, perceiving how many blessings are bestowed on us through the grace of God, to whom be glory and dominion through all the ages. Amen.

IX
THE REMEMBRANCE OF CHRIST'S SUFFERINGS

So that we will not think that we are doing something great through our ascetic efforts and our many sighs and tears, we are given knowledge of the sufferings of Christ and His saints. Meditating on these we are astonished, and in our amazement we exhaust ourselves through our ascetic labours. For by contemplating the numberless trials that the saints joyfully accepted and the many sufferings that the Lord endured on our behalf, we become aware of our own feebleness. At the same time we are illumined by the knowledge of what the Lord did and said. And by understanding what is stated in the Gospel, we begin sometimes to mourn bitterly in sorrow, sometimes to rejoice spiritually in thanksgiving. Not because we think that we have done anything good, for that would be self-conceit; but because, in spite of being such sinners, we have been granted the contemplation of these things.

In this way we become all the more humble in action and thought, practising the seven forms of bodily discipline of which we have spoken, as well as the moral virtues, that is to say, the virtues of the soul; and we guard the five senses and keep the Lord's commandments. We do not regard these as good works deserving reward; rather we view them as a debt to be paid. Nor do we hope in any way to be released from the debt, for we recognize how enormous are the gifts of knowledge that we have received. We become, as it were, captive to the meaning of what we read and the message of what we chant; and in our delight we often unconsciously forget our sins, and in our joy we begin to shed tears that are sweet as honey. But then, fearful of being deluded in case this is all premature, we restrain ourselves; and recalling our former way of life, we again weep bitterly. In this manner we oscillate between these two kinds of tears, the sweet and the bitter.

So we go forward, provided we are attentive and always consult someone of experience, and provided we come before God with the pure prayer that is appropriate for one practising the virtues, while at the same time we withdraw our intellect from all that it has known or heard, and concentrate it on the remembrance of God, asking only that God's will may be done in all our thoughts and undertakings. But if we fail to do this, then we are liable to be deluded, thinking that we will see an apparition of one of the holy angels, or of Christ. We fail to realize that he who seeks to see Christ should look not outside himself, but within himself, emulating Christ's life in this world, and becoming sinless in body and soul, as Christ was. His intellect should apprehend everything through Christ.

To have in mind any form, colour or thought during the time of prayer is not good – in fact it may be extremely dangerous. Evagrios has explained what is meant by the intellect being in the realm or dwelling-place of God.[1] He took the expression from the Psalter: 'In peace is His dwelling-place' (Ps. 76 : 2. LXX). To be 'in peace' means to have no thoughts, whether bad or good, because, as Evagrios says, if the intellect perceives something, it is not in God alone, but also in

---

[1] *Gnostic Centuries* V, 39; cf. *On Prayer* 58 (*The Philokalia*, vol. i, p. 62).

itself. This is true; for since God is undetermined and indeterminable, without form or colour, the intellect that is with God alone should itself be without form or colour, free from all figuration and undistracted.[1] Otherwise it will be subject to demonic illusion. That is why we must be careful and, unless we have taken advice from someone of experience, we should not entertain any thought, whether good or bad, for we do not know which it is. For the demons take whatever shape they want and appear in this way to us, just as the human intellect is shaped by what it wants and is coloured by the forms of the things that it perceives. The demons do this in order to deceive us, and under their influence our intellect wanders senselessly in its efforts to reach perfection.

Thus one ought to constrain the intellect as much as possible within the bounds of some meditation acceptable to God. For as there are seven forms of bodily discipline, so there are eight types of contemplation, or types of spiritual knowledge, that pertain to the intellect. Three of these, which have already been mentioned, are connected with the holy sufferings of the Lord and we should always of our own accord meditate on them, so as to grieve over our own soul and over those of our fellow men. But in addition to these, we should also think about the terrible things that happened at the very beginning because of man's transgression; about how our nature succumbed to so many passions; about our own faults and the trials that occur for the sake of our correction and recovery. Finally we should think both of death and of the fearful punishments that await sinners after death. In this way the soul may be strengthened and devote itself to grief. At the same time it will be solaced and humbled, neither despairing because of these terrible thoughts nor imagining that it has attained the level of spiritual work; and it will continue in fear and hope, a state equivalent to gentleness of thought and one that is always the same. It is this that leads the intellect to spiritual knowledge and discrimination. The psalmist confirms this when he writes: 'He will lead the gentle to judgment' (Ps. 25 : 9), or rather, to discrimination, or what the prophet describes as spiritual knowledge and holiness (cf. Isa. 11 : 2. LXX).

Yet as true piety, although a single term, takes many outward forms, so spiritual knowledge, also a single term, includes many forms of

---

[1] Cf. *On Prayer* 67, 114, 117, 120 (*The Philokalia*, vol. i, pp. 63, 68).

knowledge and contemplation. For even the first step in the practice of bodily discipline is a form of knowledge; in fact, without knowledge no one does anything good. Until we attain our goal – by which I mean until we are adopted as sons and our intellect ascends into the heavens in Christ – each state is a form of knowledge and contemplation. The knowledge that we have before we begin to practise a spiritual discipline helps to make this practice effective, serving thus as a kind of tool; while the knowledge that follows on faith protects our faith with fear as with a wall.

The knowledge and the practice of the soul's virtues have as their goal the preparation and planting of the trees of paradise. These trees are the knowledge of a man's intellect and his spiritual labour; in other words, the attentiveness of his intellect and the moral state of his soul. By practising the commandments he 'cultivates and keeps' the trees (cf. Gen. 2 : 15) with understanding and insight. At the same time he is helped by divine providence, that acts like sun, rain, wind and growth, without which all the effort of the gardener is in vain, even if everything has been done in due order. For nothing good can come about without help from above; yet help from above and grace are only granted to those who have resolved to act, as St John Chrysostom says.[1]

In this life, all things go in pairs: practice and spiritual knowledge, free will and grace, fear and hope, struggle and reward. The second does not come until the first has been actualized; and if it seems as if it does, this is illusion. Just as someone who lacks horticultural knowledge, on seeing the flower and thinking that it is the fruit, rushes forward to pick it, not realizing that by picking the flower he destroys the fruit, so it is here: for, as St Maximos puts it, 'To think that one knows prevents one from advancing in knowledge.'[2] Hence we ought to cleave to God and to do all things with discrimination.

Discrimination comes from seeking advice with humility and from criticizing oneself and what one thinks and does. There is nothing astonishing in the fact that the devil assumes the form of 'an angel of light' (2 Cor. 11 : 14), for the thoughts that he sows in us also appear to be righteous when we lack experience. Humility is the gateway to

---

[1] *Homilies on Matthew* 82, 4 (*P.G.* lviii, 742).

[2] *On Love* III, 81 (*The Philokalia*, vol. ii, p. 96). Peter here attributes the saying to Neilos; cf. above, p. 101, where it is attributed correctly to Maximos.

dispassion, said St John Klimakos;[1] and, according to St Basil the Great, the fuel of humility is gentleness.[2] It is this that gives man constancy, so that he is always the same whether circumstances and thoughts are pleasant or unpleasant. He is indifferent to both honour and dishonour, joyfully accepting things sweet and painful, and remaining unperturbed.

In this he is unlike the virgin about whom St Antony the Great speaks.[3] One day, while St Antony was sitting with a certain Abba, a virgin came up and said to the Elder: 'Abba, I fast six days of the week and I repeat by heart portions of the Old and New Testaments daily.' To which the Elder replied: 'Does poverty mean the same to you as abundance?' 'No', she answered. 'Or dishonour the same as praise?' 'No, Abba.' Are your enemies the same for you as your friends?' 'No'. she replied. At that the wise Elder said to her: 'Go, get to work, you have accomplished nothing.' And he was justified in speaking like this. For if she fasted so strictly as to eat only once a week, and then very little, should she not have regarded poverty in the same way as abundance? And if she repeated passages from the Old and New Testaments daily, should she not also have learnt humility? And since she had surrendered everything worldly, should she not have considered all people to be her friends? And if she did still have enemies, could she not learn to treat them as friends after so much ascetic effort? The Elder was quite right when he said, 'You have accomplished nothing.'

Indeed, I would add that such a person deserves severe condemnation. It is as St John Chrysostom said with regard to the five foolish virgins:[4] they had the strength to practise the more difficult form of asceticism – the virginity which is beyond nature – but not to perform what is less difficult – acts of mercy – though pagans and non-believers perform such acts as something natural. So with this virgin: because she did not know what was really needed, she laboured in vain. As the Lord said: 'All this you should have done, without neglecting the rest' (Matt. 23 : 23). Ascetic practice is a good thing, but only when done with the right goal in mind. We ought to think of it not as the real task, but as a preparation for the real task;

[1] *Ladder*, Step 4 (709D; E.T., p. 87).
[2] Cf. *Sermon on the Renunciation of the World* 10 (*P.G.* xxxi, 648B).
[3] Paul Evergetinos, *Collection* III, xxix, 3, §4; cf. above, p. 208.
[4] *Homilies on Matthew* 78, 1 (*P.G.* lviii, 711).

not as the fruit, but as the earth that can, with time, labour and the help of God, bear trees from which the fruit will come – the fruit that is purity of intellect and union with God. To Him be glory throughout the ages. Amen.

X
HUMILITY

The truly humble man never ceases to reproach himself, even when the whole world attacks and insults him. He acts in this way, not simply in order to attain salvation as it were passively by enduring with patience whatever befalls him, but in order to press forward actively and deliberately to embrace the sufferings of Christ. From these sufferings he learns the greatest of all the virtues, humility: the dwelling-place of the Holy Spirit, the gateway to the kingdom of heaven, that is to say, to dispassion. He who passes through this gateway comes to God; but without humility his road is full of pain and his effort useless. Humility bestows complete repose upon whoever possesses it in his heart, because he has Christ dwelling within him. Through it grace remains with him and God's gifts are preserved. It is the offspring of many different virtues: of obedience, patient endurance, shedding of possessions, poverty, fear of God, spiritual knowledge and others as well. But above all it is the offspring of discrimination, the virtue that illumines the farthest reaches of the intellect. Yet let no one think that it is a simple, casual matter to become humble. It is something beyond our natural powers; and it is almost true to say that the more a person is gifted, the harder it is for him to attain humility. It presupposes great judgment and endurance in the face of the trials and evil spirits that oppose us. For humility slips through all their snares.

Humility is also the offspring of spiritual knowledge, and such knowledge is born of trials and temptations. To the man who knows himself is given the knowledge of all things; and to the man who submits to God, all things will be subject when humility reigns in his members. For it is precisely through undergoing many trials and temptations, and through patiently enduring them, that a man acquires experience; and as a result he comes to know both his own weakness and the power of God. In becoming aware of his own weakness and ignorance, he recognizes that he has now learned what once he did not know; and this allows him to see that just as he used not to know these things, and was unaware that he did not know, so there are many other things which he may later be able to learn. St Basil the Great observes in this connection that unless one tastes something one is unaware of what one is missing. But he who has tasted spiritual knowledge knows at least to some extent that he is ignorant, and so his knowledge becomes for him a source of humility. Again, he who knows that he is a mutable creature will never maintain a high opinion of himself; he will recognize that anything he may have belongs to his Creator. You do not praise a pot on the grounds that it has made itself useful; you praise its maker. And when it is broken, you blame whoever broke it, not its maker.

Yet if the vessel of which we are speaking is endowed with intelligence, then necessarily it will possess free will. Whatever is good in it comes from its Creator, and He is also the cause of its being made; but its fall or deviation will depend upon how it exercises its own free will. If you do not deviate, God in His grace will grant you the seal of His approval; but if you give ear to the serpent's evil counsel, disapprobation will be your lot. Approval and gratitude, however, are due not to the man who receives the gifts but to Him who bestows them. Yet by grace he who receives a gift may deserve approval because by his own choice he accepted what he did not have or, rather, because he is grateful to his Benefactor. And if he is not grateful, not only does he forfeit all approval, but he is self-condemned for his ingratitude as well. Yet no one, I trust, is so shameless as to claim that the gift was not freely bestowed on him and to pretend in his iniquity that he deserves praise, calmly puffing himself up and condemning those who are apparently not like him, on the grounds that he himself has conferred on himself the wealth he thinks he possesses, and has not received it by God's grace. Should such a person thank the Giver, he does so in the same way as the Pharisee in the Gospel, and says to himself, 'I thank Thee, O God, that I am not like other men' (Luke 18 : 11). The Evangelist – or, rather, God, who knows men's hearts – was right to say that he spoke 'to himself', for the Pharisee was not speaking to God. Even though orally he did seem to be speaking to God, yet God who knew his self-applauding soul says that he stood and prayed not to God but to himself.

The fact that the Scriptures often make use of identical or very similar phrases is due, says St John Chrysostom, not to repetitiveness or prolixity, but to the desire to imprint what is said on the heart of the reader. In the ardour of his writing the psalmist did not want to stop, as do those who have not tasted the sweetness of his words and who in their listlessness trample them underfoot so as to be freed from the weight of them. Will such a person ever reap any profit from Holy Scripture? Does he not simply earn condemnation and a darkening of his intellect by opening the door to the demons who are attacking him?

As the Lord has said: 'If they do these things when the wood is green, what will happen when it is dry?' (Luke 23 : 31); and again: 'If the righteous man is only just saved, where will the ungodly and the sinner appear?' (1 Pet. 4 : 18). The demons attack even those whose intellect, immaterial and formless, is concentrated entirely on the remembrance of God; and, unless God assisted them on account of their humility, their prayer would not mount to heaven but would fall back empty. What then will be our lot, abject as we are? We do not even open our lips and speak into the air, so that at the last God may have mercy on us, descending to the level of our ignorance and weakness because we have shown gratitude to Him.

As for whether or not the demons attack even the perfect in this world, let us hear what St Makarios says:[1] 'No one becomes perfect in this present age; for if they did, then what is given here would not be simply a pledge of the blessings held in store but their full realization.' He adduces in testimony one of the brethren who was praying with several others and who was suddenly snatched up mentally to heaven and saw the heavenly Jerusalem and the tabernacles of the saints.[2] When he returned to his habitual state, however, he fell from virtue and ended up by being completely destroyed; for he thought he had achieved something and did not realize that, being unworthy and only dust by nature, he was that much the more in debt for having been privileged to ascend to such a height. St Makarios also says that he had known many men, and from his experience had come to

---

[1] *Homilies* (collection II), VIII, 5; cf. below, pp. 327–8.
[2] Cf. pp. 175, 321.

recognize without any doubt that no one in this world is perfect: even if he becomes altogether immaterial and is almost one with God, yet sin pursues him and will not disappear completely before his death.

Evagrios the Solitary has recounted how a certain monk was praying when, for his benefit and for that of many others, God allowed the demons to take him by his hands and feet and throw him in the air; and so that his body would not be hurt when he fell to the earth, they caught him in a rush-mat. This they did for a long time, but were unable to distract his intellect from heaven.[1] How would such a man even perceive what he was eating? When would he have need of psalmody or reading? But we have need of them because of the weakness of our intellect, though even in this way we fail to concentrate. Alas, such a holy man suffered attacks from the demons, yet we do not worry at all about their assaults. The saints are protected by their humility from the snares of the devil, while we in our ignorance are puffed up. It is indeed a sign of great ignorance for someone to be self-elated about what is not his. For 'what do you have which you did not receive', either freely from God or through the prayers of others? 'Now if you received it, why do you boast as if you had not received it' (1 Cor. 4 : 7), but had achieved it yourself? So Abba Cassian puts it.[2]

Humility, then, is born from spiritual knowledge, and itself gives birth to discrimination; while from discrimination comes the spiritual insight which the prophet calls 'counsel' (Isa. 11 : 2). By means of such insight we see things according to their true nature, and the intellect dies to the world because it now contemplates the creations of God. To Him be glory throughout the ages. Amen.

XI
DISCRIMINATION

It is excellent to seek advice about everything, but only from those with experience. It is dangerous to ask questions of the inexperienced, because they do not possess discrimination. Discrimination

---

[1] *On Prayer* 111 (*The Philokalia*, vol. i, p. 68).
[2] John Cassian, *Institutes* XII, 10; *The Philokalia*, vol. i, p. 93.

knows when the time is ripe, what means to employ, the inner state
of the questioner, what level he has reached, his strength, his degree
of spiritual knowledge and his intention, as well as God's purpose and
the meaning of each verse of Holy Scripture, and much else besides.
Hence he who lacks discrimination may exert himself enormously,
but he cannot achieve anything; while the person who possesses it is a
guide to the blind and a light to those in darkness (cf. Rom. 2 : 19).
We should refer everything to such a person and accept whatever he
says, even if because of our inexperience we do not see its import as
well as we would like. Indeed, he who has discrimination is to be
recognized in particular from the fact that he is able to communicate
the sense of what he says even to those who do not want to know it.
For the Spirit searches things out; and God's presence has the power
to persuade even an unwilling intellect to believe. This is what
happened in the case of Jonah (cf. Jonah 1 : 3), Zacharias (cf. Luke
1 : 18) and the monk David, once a brigand, whom the angel
prevented from saying anything except the psalms that he recited
according to his rule of prayer.

If in this present generation no one possesses discrimination, it is
because no one has the humility that engenders it. We should
therefore pray fervently about everything we do, as St James counsels
(cf. Jas. 5 : 16). For even if we lack holy hands, that is, if we lack
purity of soul and body, we should at least strive to be without
rancour and evil thoughts. For St Paul tells us to 'lift up holy hands
without anger and without quarrelling' (1 Tim. 2 : 8). If we think
that something is in accordance with God's will, we should do it
dispassionately; and even if it is not such a very good thing, what we
do will be counted to our credit by God's grace, because of our
perplexity and the fact that we do it with God in mind. Even if we do
God's will when passion is still present, the consequences will be as
stated. This is inevitably so, simply because of God's goodness. But
where our own will is involved, and not God's, there self-inflation is
present as well, and God does not approve; nor does He reveal His
will to us then, lest we should know what it is and still not do it, and
thereby incur greater condemnation. For whether God gives us
something or withholds it from us, He acts for our good, even if we,
like children, are naware of this. He does not send down His Holy
Spirit to someone who has not purified himself from the passions
through the practice of the virtues that pertain both to body and to

soul, lest this person should out of habit succumb to his passions and so become guilty of abusing the presence of the Holy Spirit within him.

A person must first spend a long time in ascetic practice. He must begin by purifying his body from the actual committing of sin, whether great or small, and then purge his soul of every form of desire or anger. His moral impulses need to be disciplined by good habit, so that he does not do anything whatsoever through his five senses that is contrary to the purpose of his intellect, nor does his inner self consent to any such thing. It is then, when finally he becomes subject to himself, that God makes all things subject to him through dispassion and by the grace of the Holy Spirit. For a man must first submit to the law of God, and then he will rule as an intelligent being over all around him. His intellect will reign as it was originally created to reign, with judgment and self-restraint, with courage and justice. Now he will calm his wrath with the gentleness of his desire, now quieten his desire with the austerity of his wrath; and he will know that he is a king. All the limbs of his body, no longer abducted by ignorance and forgetfulness, will act in accordance with God's commandment. Then through his devotion to God he will achieve spiritual insight and will begin to anticipate the snares prepared by the devil and his secret and stealthy attacks.

He will not, however, foresee the future as did the prophets. For this ability is a supranatural gift granted for the good of the community. Insight, however, is intrinsic to man's nature; and, once the intellect is purified, it emerges from the tyranny of the passions under which it has been concealed, as it were, in the dark. Then, through humility, comes grace and opens the soul's eye, blinded by the devil, and immediately man begins to see things according to their true nature. He is no longer seduced by the outward appearance of things as he was before. He looks dispassionately on gold, silver and precious stones and is not led astray, nor does he assess them falsely because of his passions: he knows that these and other such material things come from the earth, as the holy fathers point out. He looks at a man, and knows that he too is from the earth and is going to return to it (cf. Gen. 3 : 19). And he does not simply think about this in an abstract way, for we all know from experience that this is the case; yet because we are tyrannized by the passions we still have a craving for material things.

Should someone in his presumption think that even without the prerequisite struggles and virtues he is able to see things according to their true nature, there is nothing strange in this. For presumption can make even the blind think that they can see and foolish men boast when they have nothing to boast about. Yet if it were easy to see things according to their true nature merely by thinking about them in an abstract way, then inward grief and the purification that comes from it would be superfluous; and so would the many forms of ascetic labour, as well as humility, supranatural grace, and dispassion. But this is not the case at all. For often this capacity to see things according to their true nature comes more readily to simple people, to those whose intellects are free from the hustle and wiliness of this world, once they have submitted themselves to an experienced spiritual father. It may also be granted through the special dispensation of God's grace, as it was to people in ancient times, before they knew either their left hand or right hand (cf. Jonah 4 : 11). But the fact that we have served the passions from our youth up, and have practised virtually every form of malice and fraud with complete willingness and zeal, means that it is impossible for us to be freed from such evils and to see things as they truly are without effort, time, and God's help. It is indeed impossible, unless we devote ourselves to the acquisition of the virtues as once we devoted ourselves to the passions, and unless we cultivate these virtues diligently in thought and action.

If in spite of this our efforts are often of no avail, this is either because we do not endure our trials to the end, or because we do not know the road or the goal, or because of slothfulness or lack of faith, or for one of the numberless other reasons. But if this is the case, and we strike very wide of the mark, how can we dare claim that we have attained the ancient beauty, unless we have been deluded by self-satisfaction and unperceived self-destruction? For just as self-criticism is a form of invisible progress – since it carries us along the right path even though we are unaware of it – so both presumption and self-satisfaction are forms of unseen destruction, since we have turned back without realizing it. This is inevitably so; for the passions expelled by grace return to an arrogant soul, as the Lord told us when He spoke of the unclean spirit that, after being expelled from a man, later returned, bringing with it seven other spirits more wicked than itself (cf. Matt. 12 : 43–45). Why does this happen? Because the place from which the unclean spirit departed is not filled with spiritual activity, or with humility; and therefore the unclean spirit comes out of bondage and again takes up its dwelling in this place, along with many other evils.

Let him who understands take note. For the Logos wishes to transmit things to us in a way that is neither too clear nor too obscure, but is in our best interests. St John Chrysostom says that it is a great blessing from God that some parts of the Scriptures are clear while others are not. By means of the first we acquire faith and ardour and do not fall into disbelief and laziness because of our utter inability to grasp what is said. By means of the second we are roused to enquiry and effort, thus both strengthening our understanding and learning humility from the fact that everything is not intelligible to us. Hence, if we take stock of the gifts conferred on us, we will reap humility and longing for God from both what we understand and what we do not. Thus the gauge of the fifth stage of contemplation, about which we are now speaking, is this: that we are enabled to look with discrimination at sensible creation and at our own thoughts, not blinded by any delusion, or doing anything contrary to God's purpose because of our subjection to the passions, or submitting to any of our evil thoughts. Even if threatened with death, we would not deviate from God's purpose in thought or action.

What has just been said applies to the final stages of spiritual knowledge. Where the initial stage is concerned, we will unavoidably fall short of our goal because we are learners. Indeed, defeated by our bad habits, we may achieve nothing as a result of our labour. Sometimes, however, God in His providence allows us to go slightly astray, and then at once to return with great humility; at other times He permits us in our presumption to think too much of ourselves. When this happens we should realize that God's grace is disciplining us, teaching us to be humble and to recognize whence we receive our strength and knowledge, 'so that we should rely not on ourselves but on God who raises the dead' (2 Cor. 1 : 9), something which happens even in this world. For if we endure with patience, and do not grow presumptuous or lapse from virtue, we will be raised from the deathlike state of the body and of material things to the spiritual knowledge of created realities. Indeed, according to St Paul (cf. Rom. 6 : 4–6), we are crucified with Christ bodily through the practice of bodily discipline, and in soul through the practice of the virtues that pertain to the soul. We are then buried through the mortification of the senses and of natural knowledge. Finally, through attaining the state of dispassion we are resurrected spiritually in Christ Jesus our Lord,[1] to whom be glory and honour through all the ages. Amen.

XII
CONTEMPLATION OF THE SENSIBLE WORLD

Until our intellect has died to the passions, it should not attempt to embark on the contemplation of sensible realities. For if it is still subject to distraction and is unable to devote itself to meditation on the divine Scriptures in stillness and spiritual knowledge, then by turning prematurely to such contemplation we tend to sink more deeply into forgetfulness and gradually to approach a state of ignorance, even though our intellect may have already attained some degree of spiritual knowledge. This happens especially if, unknown to ourselves, our knowledge has not come to us through God's grace, but we are still learning about such mysteries through reading and from people who have experienced them.

Just as the earth – and especially good earth – becomes cloddish if the farmer does not work it, so our intellect becomes coarse and obtuse if we do not devote ourselves to prayer and reading, making this our chief task. And just as the earth, even when moistened by rain and warmed by the sun, yields nothing unless the farmer sows and cultivates it, so our intellect cannot keep possession of spiritual knowledge, even if this knowledge has been bestowed on it by grace, unless we practise the moral virtues, those, that is to say, of the soul. For as soon as the intellect grows negligent and turns even slightly towards the passions, it at once goes astray; while if presumption seduces it, it is abandoned by grace.

Because of this, even though the fathers often reduced their practice of bodily discipline because of age or lack of physical strength, they never relaxed their practice of the moral virtues at all. For in the place of bodily asceticism they had bodily weakness, which

[1] Cf. Maximos the Confessor, *On Theology* I, 67 (*The Philokalia*, vol. ii, p. 127).

is able to constrain the flesh. But we cannot keep the soul sinless so that the intellect may be illumined unless we practise the virtues of the soul. The farmer frequently changes his implements, and may even reduce their number, but he never leaves the ground unworked, unsown or unplanted, nor does he ever leave the fruit unprotected if he wishes to gather it.

If, however, a thief or robber tries to enter, not by the proper door, but by 'climbing up some other way', as the Lord puts it (John 10 : 1), then the sheep – that is, according to St Maximos, divine thoughts [1] – pay no attention to him. For the thief enters only so that he can deceive by hearsay, and kill the Scriptures by turning them into allegory, since he is unable to interpret them spiritually. Thus through his presumption and his pseudo-knowledge he destroys both himself and the divine thoughts contained in the Scriptures. But the shepherd, as a good soldier of Christ, feels compassion for these thoughts; and by keeping the divine commandments he enters in through the narrow gate (cf. Matt. 7 : 13), the gate of humility and dispassion. Before receiving divine grace he devotes himself to studying and to learning about everything by listening to others; and whenever the wolf approaches in the guise of a sheep (cf. Matt. 7 : 15), he chases him off by means of self-criticism, saying, 'I do not know who you are: God knows.' And should a thought approach shamelessly and ask to be received, saying to him, 'If you do not watch over thoughts and discriminate between things, you are ignorant and lacking in faith', then he replies, 'If you call me a fool, I accept the title; for like St John Chrysostom[2] I know that whoever is foolish in this world becomes wise, as St Paul puts it' (cf. 1. Cor. 3 : 18).

The Lord Himself said that the children of this world are more astute in dealing with their own kind than are the children of the kingdom of heaven (cf. Luke 16 : 8). And He was quite right: for the children of this world long to make good and to grow rich, to be clever and to win praise, to gain power and so on; and even though they are likely to fail in their aspirations and their effort will prove vain, they still exert more than human strength to attain these things. But the children of the kingdom aspire to things that are completely

---

[1] On Love II, 55 (The Philokalia, vol. ii, p. 75).
[2] Cf. Homilies on 1 Corinthians 10, 1 (P.G. lxi, 82).

different, and because of this they often receive in this world a foretaste of the blessings held in store. Like the children of this world they exert themselves, but they do this so that by grace their intellect may be liberated and may thereby become unforgettingly mindful of God. In this way it comes to know the divine thoughts to which the Holy Scriptures and those with experience in spiritual knowledge bear witness; or else in its perplexity it realizes that in spite of its great knowledge it is still ignorant of them. Then it understands that its former thoughts were trials intended to test its free will.

Thus he who is humble will turn away from his own thoughts and purposes, having no faith in them; indeed, he will be afraid, and seek advice with many tears, taking refuge in humility and self-criticism, and regarding spiritual knowledge and gifts of grace as great liabilities. But the arrogant man will promptly insist upon his own thoughts, ignoring the warning of St John Klimakos that we should not search prematurely for things that have their appointed time.[1] He also ignores St Isaac's counsel that we should not enter in recklessly, but should give thanks in silence.[2] Nor does he listen to St John Chrysostom when he says, 'I do not know', having learned to say this from St Paul (cf. 2 Cor. 12 : 2–3); or to St John of Damaskos when he says of Adam that he embarked prematurely on the contemplation of sensible realities.[3] For the stomachs of infants are too tender for solid food and need milk, as St Paul says (cf. 1 Cor. 3 : 2; Heb. 5 : 12–14). That is why we should not attempt to embark on contemplation when it is not yet time for contemplation. Let us first acquire in ourselves the mothers of the virtues, and then spiritual knowledge will come spontaneously through the grace of Christ: to whom be glory through all the ages. Amen.

[1] *Ladder* Step 26 (1032C; E.T., p. 214).
[2] *Mystic Treatises*, E.T., p. 36; Greek, p. 97.
[3] *Exposition of the Faith* II, 11 (ed. Kotter, §25, p. 74).

XIII
KNOWLEDGE OF THE ANGELIC ORDERS

Knowledge becomes spiritual after we are firmly established in the contemplation of sensible realities. Yet the gnostic cannot by his own power see an angel; for how can man, who cannot see even his own soul, see something that is non-material and known only to its Creator? For the common good, however, angels by God's providence often appeared to our fathers in visible form. But such a thing does not happen to us, because it is our presumption that makes us want it to happen, and we do not think of the common good or suffer in order to fulfil God's will. Thus should we want to see a thing of this kind we are really asking to see a demon. Indeed, St Paul speaks of Satan himself being 'transformed into an angel of light' (2 Cor. 11 : 14). Rather, it is when we do not think about such things at all, and perhaps do not even believe that they occur, that they do in fact happen, if received for the common good. We can gauge our attitude by asking ourselves whether we have any desire to experience such a thing, even in a dream, or would attach great importance to it if it were to happen, or would behave as if we did not know anything about the state in which we found ourselves. For the true angel has power from God to reassure even the intellect that repudiates it and to make it receptive. The demons cannot do this; but when they see an intellect disposed to receive them, only then with God's consent they appear to it. If the intellect is not thus disposed, however, the demons depart, chased away by the guardian angel given us at holy baptism, since the intellect has not surrendered its free will to the enemy.

So much for these matters. Now I will say something about the contemplation of the angelic orders. According to St Dionysios the Areopagite[1] and as we find confirmed in Holy Scripture (cf. Isa. 6 : 2; Ezek. 1 : 5; Rom. 8 : 38; Eph. 1 : 21; Col. 1 : 16; 1 Thess. 4 : 16), there are nine such orders. These nine orders have been named according to their natures and activities. They are called 'bodiless' because they are non-material, 'spiritual' because they are intellects, and 'hosts' because they are the ministering spirits of the King of all

---

[1] *The Celestial Hierarchy* VI, 2 (*P.G.* iii, 200D).

(cf. Luke 2 : 13; Heb. 1 : 14). They also have other names and titles, both specific and general; thus they are called 'powers' (cf. Eph. 1 : 21; 1 Pet. 3 : 22) and 'angels', that is to say, 'messengers' (cf. Matt. 1 : 20). 'Powers' is the name of a single order but it applies also to all nine orders with regard to their activities, for all have been empowered to fulfil God's will. Again, one particular order – that which is closest to us and ninth from God's inaccessible throne – is called the order of 'angels'; yet with regard to their activities all are called 'angels', or 'messengers', because all announce the divine ordinances to men.

The book of Job speaks several times of 'another messenger' (cf. Job 1 : 14–19); but this was not a holy angel, since, as St John Chrysostom points out, in each case he was the only one of Job's servants to escape, and he then came to give Job the news. The Holy Scriptures even call the Lord an 'angel' in several places, as when it is said that Abraham 'entertained angels' (Heb. 13 : 2; cf. Gen. 18 : 1–2). Indeed, the Lord Himself was 'fleshless', as St John of Damaskos says in a hymn to the Mother of God: 'In the tent Abraham saw the mystery that is in you, O Mother of God; for he received your Son fleshless.'[1] The Lord was also together with the three holy children in the fiery furnace (cf. Dan. 3 : 25); and because of His activity He is also called 'angel' or 'messenger' by the prophet Isaiah, who uses the expression 'the angel of great counsel' (Isa. 9 : 6. LXX). As the Lord Himself said, 'I will announce to you those things that I have heard from My Father' (cf. John 8 : 26). To Him be glory throughout the ages. Amen.

XIV
DISPASSION

Dispassion is a strange and paradoxical thing: once someone has consolidated his victory over the passions, it is able to make him an imitator of God, so far as this is possible for man. For though the person who has attained the state of dispassion continues to suffer

---

[1] *Paraklitiki*, Tone 4, Sunday Mattins, Canon to the Theotokos, Canticle 8, troparion.

attacks from demons and vicious men, he experiences this as if it were happening to someone else, as was the case with the holy apostles and martyrs. When he is praised he is not filled with self-elation, nor when he is insulted is he afflicted. For he considers that what is pleasant comes to him by the grace of God and as an act of divine concession of which he is unworthy, while what is unpleasant comes as a trial: the former is given us by grace to encourage us in this world, while the latter is given us to increase our humility and our hope in the world to be. Such a person is impassible, and yet because of his power of discrimination is acutely aware of what gives pain.

Dispassion is not a single virtue, but is a name for all the virtues. A man is not merely one limb, for it is the many limbs of the body that constitute a man; and not merely the limbs, but the limbs together with the soul. Similarly, dispassion is the union of many virtues, while the place of the soul is taken by the Holy Spirit. For all activities described as 'spiritual' are soul-less without the Holy Spirit, and it is by virtue of the presence of the Holy Spirit that a 'spiritual father' is given this title. Yet if the soul does not reject the passions, the Holy Spirit will not come to it; nor, on the other hand, unless the Holy Spirit is present can one properly speak of the all-embracing virtue of dispassion. And if someone were to become dispassionate without the Holy Spirit, he would really be, not dispassionate, but in a state of insensitivity. For this reason even the pagan Greeks, who do not understand these things fully, counsel us not to become dispassionate as though without soul, or impassioned as though without mind. When they say 'dispassionate as though without soul', they are speaking in terms of their own knowledge, for they lack the knowledge bestowed by the Holy Spirit. But when they call the impassioned man mindless, we agree with them. Not that we have learnt it from them, for they had neither true knowledge nor true experience; we have learnt it because we have ourselves experienced the tyranny of the passions and so have come to understand why we suffer from them.

Again, what we write about the acquisition of the virtues we have learnt from the fathers who were enabled by grace to attain the state of dispassion. For they say that because of his amity with the passions the highly impassioned person becomes like a prisoner and as one who is insensate. Sometimes because of his desire for something he rushes forward thoughtlessly like some mindless thing; at other times, when anger champions desire, he gnashes his teeth like a wild beast at his fellow-men. The man who has attained dispassion becomes impassible out of his perfect love for God. At times he meditates on God, at times on the spectacle of some of God's marvellous works or on a passage from the divine Scriptures, as St Neilos explains. Even if he is in the market place among crowds of people, his intellect acts as if it were alone. This state comes through keeping the divine commandments of Christ: to whom be glory and power throughout the ages. Amen.

XV
LOVE

To speak of love is to dare to speak of God; for, according to St John the Theologian, 'God is love; and he who dwells in love dwells in God' (1 John 4 : 16). And the astonishing thing is that this chief of all the virtues is a natural virtue. Thus, in the Law, it is given pride of place: 'You shall love the Lord your God with all your heart, and with all your soul, and with all your might' (Deut. 6 : 5). When I heard the words 'with all your soul' I was astounded, and no longer needed to hear the rest. For 'with all your soul' means with the intelligent, incensive and desiring powers of the soul, because it is of these three powers that the soul is composed. Thus the intellect should think at all times about divine matters, while desire should long constantly and entirely, as the Law says, for God alone and never for anything else; and the incensive power should actively oppose only what obstructs this longing, and nothing else. St John, consequently, was right in saying that God is love. If God sees that, as He commanded, these three powers of the soul aspire to Him alone, then, since He is good, He will necessarily not only love that soul, but through the inspiration of the Spirit will dwell and move within it (cf. 2 Cor. 6 : 16; Lev. 26 : 12); and the body, though reluctant and unwilling – for it lacks intelligence – will end by submitting to the intelligence, while the flesh will no longer rise in protest against the Spirit, as St Paul puts it (cf. Gal. 5 : 17).

Just as the sun and moon, at the command of God, travel through the heavens in order to light the world, even though they are soul-less, so the body, at the behest of the soul, will perform works of light. As the sun journeys each day from east to west, thus making one day, while when it disappears night comes, so each virtue that a man practises illumines the soul, and when it disappears passion and darkness come until he again acquires that virtue, and light in this way returns to him. As the sun rises in the furthest east and slowly shifts its rays until it reaches the other extreme, thus forming time, so a man slowly grows from the moment he first begins to practise the virtues until he attains the state of dispassion. And just as the moon waxes and wanes every month, so with respect to each particular virtue a man waxes and wanes daily, until this virtue becomes established in him. At times, in accordance with God's will, he is afflicted, at times he rejoices and gives thanks to God, unworthy as he is to acquire the virtues; and sometimes he is illumined, sometimes filled with darkness, until his course is finished.

All this happens to him by God's providence: some things are sent to keep him from self-elation, and others to keep him from despair. Just as in this present age the sun creates the solstices and the moon waxes and wanes, whereas in the age to come there will always be light for the righteous and darkness for those who, like me, alas, are sinners, so, before the attainment of perfect love and of vision in God, the soul in the present world has its solstices, and the intellect experiences darkness as well as virtue and spiritual knowledge; and this continues until, through the acquisition of that perfect love to which all our effort is directed, we are found worthy of performing the works that pertain to the world to be. For it is for love's sake that he who is in a state of obedience obeys what is commanded; and it is for love's sake that he who is rich and free sheds his possessions and becomes a servant, surrendering both what he has and himself to whoever wishes to possess them. He who fasts likewise does so for love's sake, so that others may eat what he would otherwise have eaten. In short, every work rightly done is done out of love for God or for one's neighbour. The things we have spoken of, and others like them, are done out of love for one's neighbour, while vigils, psalmody and the like are done out of love for God. To Him be glory, honour and dominion through all the ages. Amen.

XVI
KNOWLEDGE OF GOD

All things that God has created have an origin and, if He wishes, an end, since they were brought into existence out of non-existence. God, however, has neither origin nor end. The same is true of His virtues, since He was not at any time without them: He is always beyond goodness, righteous, all-wise, all-powerful, unconquerable, dispassionate, uncircumscribed, infinite, unsearchable, incomprehensible, unending, eternal, uncreated, invariable, unchanging, true, incomposite, invisible, untouchable, ungraspable, perfect, beyond being, inexpressible, inexplicable, full of mercy, full of compassion and sympathy, all-ruling, all-seeing. But, as St Dionysios the Areopagite has said, the fact that God possesses these virtues does not mean that He is compelled to exercise each one of them, as holy men are: He acts virtuously because He chooses to, and uses the virtues as tools with complete freedom and power over them.

It is from God that, along with their being, angels and holy men have by grace received the virtues, and it is through emulating Him that they become righteous, good and wise. Because they are creatures, they have need of God's assistance and inspiration, for without this they can possess neither virtue nor wisdom. All creatures are susceptible to change, and because they are composed of various elements they are called composite. But God is bodiless, simple, unoriginate, one God, worshipped and glorified by all creation in the Father, the Son and the Holy Spirit. He who becomes like God has but one will and not many composite wills. His intellect is simple and – so far as this is possible – is always concentrated on what is formless; but by divine providence it descends reluctantly from the realm of the formless to the contemplation of some verse of Scripture or aspect of creation. Yet in order not to be condemned, such a person makes provision for his body, not because in his love for it he wishes to keep it alive, but so as not to make it utterly useless and on this account to incur condemnation.

For just as the intellect does not reject the passions that surround it, but uses them in accordance with their true nature, so the soul does not reject the body, but uses it for every good work. And as the intellect, controlling the mindless impulses of the passions, directs each of them according to the divine will, so man, controlling the members of his body, makes them subject so a single will and not to many. For he does not allow the four constituent elements of the body, or its many members, to do what they wish, nor does he allow the three faculties of the soul to act, or impel the body to act, thoughtlessly and licentiously; but, guided by spiritual wisdom, he makes the will of the three faculties one and indivisible. Four principles constitute this wisdom: moral judgment, self-restraint, courage and justice. St Gregory the Theologian[1] has written about these most excellently under the inspiration of Jesus Christ our Lord: to whom be glory and dominion throughout the ages. Amen.

XVII
MORAL JUDGMENT

Although it is easy for everyone who so wishes to learn from St Gregory about the four principal virtues mentioned above, yet I will speak briefly about each of them here. Every other virtue has need of them, and every undertaking has need of the first – moral judgment – for without it nothing can be brought to a successful conclusion. How can anything be accomplished without moral judgment? It is born of the intelligence and constitutes the mean between craftiness – that is, excessive astuteness – and thoughtlessness. Craftiness pulls moral judgment towards cunning and guile, and injures the soul of its possessor and as many other people as it can; lack of thought makes one obtuse and trivial, and does not allow the intellect to concentrate on divine matters or on something of profit to one's soul or to one's neighbour. The first is like a high mountain, the second like a ravine.

The man of moral judgment, then, is he who travels along the plain that lies between these two. But he who strays from this path either falls into the ravine or attempts to climb up into the heights and, not finding a way through, plunges in spite of himself headlong into the ravine; nor is he able to climb out of it, for he refuses to renounce the

---

[1] *Poems* I, ii, 34, lines 54–61 (*P.G.* xxxvii, 949–50).

mountain tops and through repentance to turn back to the path of moral judgment. But the person who has fallen into the ravine calls with humility upon the One who can lead him out again onto the royal road of virtue. The man of moral judgment, however, neither climbs arrogantly upward seeking to harm others, nor descends foolishly only to be harmed by someone else. Choosing the middle way, he keeps to this with the help of Christ our Lord; to whom be glory and dominion throughout the ages. Amen.

XVIII
SELF-RESTRAINT

Self-restraint is a sure and unfailing sense of discretion. It does not permit its possessor to lapse into either licentiousness or obduracy, but safely preserves the blessings reaped through moral judgment while rejecting all that is bad. At the same time it unites to itself the intelligence and through itself leads the intelligence up toward God. Like a good shepherd it folds the sheep – the divine thoughts – and through refraining from what is harmful it slays licentiousness as if it were a mad dog. It expels stupidity as though it were a fierce wolf, and prevents it from devouring the sheep one by one; but it constantly keeps an eye on such stupidity and reveals it to the intelligence, so that it cannot lie hidden in the moonless dark and infiltrate among our thoughts.

Self-restraint is born of the desiring power of the soul. Without it, should any good thing come to pass, it cannot be preserved; for without self-restraint the soul's three powers are carried either upward towards licentiousness or downwards towards stupidity. And I do not mean only the licentiousness involved in gluttony and unchastity, but that involved in every passion and thought not deliberately nurtured in a manner that accords with God's will. For self-restraint disciplines all things and bridles the mindless impulses of soul and body, directing them towards God: to whom be glory throughout the ages. Amen.

XIX
COURAGE

Courage does not consist in defeating and oppressing one's neighbour; for this is overbearingness, which oversteps the bounds of courage. Nor again does it consist in fleeing terrified from the trials that come as a result of practising the virtues; for this is cowardice and falls short of courage. Courage itself consists in persisting in every good work and in overcoming the passions of soul and body. For our struggle is not against flesh and blood, that is, against men, as was the case with the Jews of old, where to conquer other nations was to do the work of God; it is against principalities and powers, that is, against the unseen demons (cf. Eph. 6 : 12). He who is victorious conquers spiritually; otherwise he is conquered by the passions. The warfare described in the Old Testament prefigures our spiritual warfare.

These two passions of overbearingness and cowardice, though they appear to be opposites, are both caused by weakness. Overbearingness pulls one upwards and is outwardly something startling and frightening, like some powerless bear, while cowardice flees like a chased dog. No one who suffers from either of these two passions puts his trust in the Lord, and therefore he cannot stand firm in battle, whether he is overbearing or cowardly. But the righteous man is as bold as a lion (cf. Prov. 28 : 1) in Christ Jesus our Lord, to whom be glory and dominion throughout the ages. Amen.

XX
JUSTICE

St Dionysios the Areopagite says that God is praised through justice.[1] This is true; for without justice all things are unjust and cannot endure. Justice is sometimes called discrimination: it establishes the just mean in every undertaking, so that there will be no falling short due to over-frugality, or excess on account of greed. For even if

---

[1] *The Divine Names* VIII, 7 (*P.G.* iii, 893D).

over-frugality and greed appear to be opposites, the one below and the other above justice, yet they both push us in some way towards injustice. Whether a line is convex or concave, it still deviates from what is straight; and to whichever side the balance tilts, that side gets the better of the other side. But the person able to hold fast to justice is neither dragged down through thoughtlessness, licentiousness, cowardice or greed, like the serpent that goes on its belly eating dust (cf. Gen. 3 : 14), a slave to the shameless passions; nor does he fall victim to craftiness and overbearingness, to stupidity and over-frugality, to excessive astuteness and cunning. Rather, he 'judges with self-restraint' (Rom. 12 : 3) and endures with patient humility, fully acknowledging that whatever he possesses he has received by grace, as St Paul puts it (cf. 1 Cor. 4 : 7). For he does an injustice to himself and to his neighbour – or, rather, to God – when he ascribes his own achievements to himself. If he thinks that any good thing he possesses is due to himself, then what he thinks that he has will be taken away from him, to use the words of our Lord (cf. Matt. 13 : 12): to whom be glory and dominion throughout the ages. Amen.

XXI
PEACE

When the Lord said to the apostles, 'My peace I give unto you', He added 'not as the world gives' (John 14 : 27). He did not, that is to say, give peace in a simple, conventional manner, as people do when they greet one another with the words 'Peace to you', or as the Shunammite woman did when she said 'Peace be with you' (cf. 2 Kgs. 4 : 23. LXX). Nor did Christ mean the peace that Elisha had in mind when he told Gehazi to say to the Shunammite, 'Is there peace with you?' (cf. 2 Kgs. 4 : 26. LXX) – in other words, is there peace with your husband, is there peace with your son? No, Christ's peace is the peace which transcends every intellect (cf. Phil. 4 : 7), and which God gives to those who love Him with all their soul, because of the dangers and battles they have been through. In the same spirit the Lord also said, 'In Me you have peace', and added, 'In the world you will experience affliction; but have courage, for I have overcome the world' (John 16 : 33). By this He meant that though a person may experience many afflictions and dangers at the hands of demons and other men, these will be as nothing if he possesses the Lord's peace. Again He said, 'Be at peace with one another' (Mark 9 : 50). The Lord said all these things to them in advance because they were going to fight and suffer for His sake.

In a similar way each of us faithful is attacked and led astray by the passions; but if he is at peace with God and with his neighbour he overcomes them all. These passions are the 'world' which St John the Theologian told us to hate (cf. 1 John 2 : 15), meaning that we are to hate, not God's creatures, but worldly desires. The soul is at peace with God when it is at peace with itself and has become wholly deiform. It is also at peace with God when it is at peace with all men, even if it suffers terrible things at their hands. Because of its forbearance it is not perturbed, but bears all things (cf. 1 Cor. 13 : 7), wishes good to all, loves all, both for God's sake and for the sake of their own nature. It grieves for unbelievers because they are destroying themselves, as our Lord and the apostles grieved for them. It prays for the faithful and labours on their behalf, and in this way its own thoughts are filled with peace and it lives in a state of noetic contemplation and pure prayer to God. To Him be glory through all the ages. Amen.

XXII
JOY

'Rejoice in the Lord', said St Paul (Phil. 3 : 1). And he was right to say, 'in the Lord'. For if our joy is not in the Lord, not only do we not rejoice, but in all probability we never shall. Job, as he described the life of men, found it full of every kind of affliction (cf. Job 7 : 1–21), and so also did St Basil the Great. St Gregory of Nyssa said that birds and other animals rejoice because of their lack of awareness, while man, being endowed with intelligence, is never happy because of his grief. For, he says, we have not been found worthy even to have knowledge of the blessings we have lost. For this reason nature teaches us rather to grieve, since life is full of pain and effort, like a state of exile dominated by sin. But if a person is constantly mindful of God, he will rejoice: as the psalmist says, 'I remembered God, and I rejoiced' (Ps. 77 : 3. LXX). For when the intellect is gladdened by the remembrance of God, then it forgets the afflictions of this world, places its hope in Him, and is no longer troubled or anxious. Freedom from anxiety makes it rejoice and give thanks; and the grateful offering of thanks augments the gifts of grace it has received. And as the blessings increase, so does the thankfulness, and so does the pure prayer offered with tears of joy.

Slowly the man emerges from the tears of distress and from the passions, and enters fully into the state of spiritual joy. Through the things that bring him pleasure, he is made humble and grateful; through trials and temptations his hope in the world to come is consolidated; in both he rejoices, and naturally and spontaneously he loves God and all men as his benefactors. He finds nothing in the whole of creation that can harm him. Illumined by the knowledge of God he rejoices in the Lord on account of all the things that He has created, marvelling at the care He shows for His creatures. The person who has attained spiritual knowledge not only marvels at visible things, but also is astounded by his perception of many essential things invisible to those who lack experience of this knowledge.

Thus he looks with wonder not only on the light of day, but also at the night. For the night is a benediction to all: to those practising the virtues that pertain to the body it offers stillness and leisure; it encourages the remembrance of death and hell in those who grieve; those engaged in practising the moral virtues it spurs to study and examine more closely the blessings they have received and the moral state of their soul. In the words of the psalmist, 'As you lie in bed, repent of what you say in your heart' (Ps. 4 : 4. LXX), that is, repent in the stillness of the night, remembering the lapses that occurred in the confusion of the day and disciplining yourself in hymns and spiritual songs (cf. Col. 3 : 16) – in other words, teaching yourself to persist in prayer and psalmody through attentive medita-tion on what you read. For the practice of the moral virtues is effectuated by meditating on what has happened during the day, so that during the stillness of the night we can become aware of the sins we have committed and can grieve over them.

When in this way through God's grace we make some progress,

and discover that in truth and not just in fantasy we have realized in
either action or thought some moral virtue of soul or body according
to Christ's commandment, then we give thanks with fear and
humility; and we struggle to preserve that moral virtue by means of
prayer and many tears offered to God, disciplining ourselves to
remember it lest we lose it again because of forgetfulness. For it takes
much time to make a moral virtue effective in ourselves, while what
has been achieved with so much time and effort can be lost in a single
instant.

All this applies to those practising the virtues. Where the
contemplative life is concerned, the night supplies us with many
themes for contemplation, as St Basil the Great has said.[1] First of all,
it reminds us daily of the creation of the world, since all creation
becomes invisible because of the darkness, as it was before it came
into existence. This in its turn prompts us to reflect how the sky was
empty then and without stars, as happens now when they become
invisible because of the clouds. When we enter our cell and see only
darkness, we are reminded of the darkness that was over the abyss (cf.
Gen. 1 : 2); and when suddenly the sky becomes clear again, and we
stand outside our cell, we are struck by wonder at the world above,
and offer praise to God, just as the angels are said in the Book of Job
to have praised God when they saw the stars (cf. Job 38 : 7). We see
in the mind's eye the earth as it was originally, invisible and without
form (cf. Gen. 1 : 2), and men held fast by sleep as if they did not
exist. We feel ourselves alone in the world like Adam and, united
with the angels, in full knowledge we praise the Maker and Creator of
the universe.

In thunder and lightning we see the day of judgment; in the call of
cocks we hear the trumpet that will sound on that day (cf. 1 Thess.
4 : 16); in the rising of the morning star and the light of dawn we
perceive the appearance of the precious and life-giving Cross (cf.
Matt. 24 : 30); in men's rising from sleep we see a sign of the
resurrection of the dead, and in the rising of the sun a token of the
second advent of Christ. Some, like the saints caught up in clouds on
the last day (cf. 1 Thess. 4 : 17), we see go forth to greet Him with
song, while others, like those who will then be judged, are indifferent
and remain asleep. Some we see rejoicing throughout the day in the

---

[1] *Sermon on the Martyr Julitta* 3 (*P.G.* xxxi, 244C).

offering of praise, in contemplation and prayer, and in the other virtues, living in the light of spiritual knowledge, as will the righteous at the second coming; while others we see persisting in the passions and in the darkness of ignorance, as will sinners on that day.

In short, the man of spiritual knowledge finds that everything contributes to his soul's salvation and to God's glory: indeed, it was because of this glory that all things were brought into existence by the Lord and God of knowledge, as Hannah the mother of the prophet Samuel calls Him (cf. 1 Sam. 2 : 3). 'Therefore let the wise man not vaunt himself because of his wisdom,' she said, 'or the strong man because of his strength, or the rich man because of his wealth; but let him who boasts do so because of his understanding and knowledge of the Lord' (1 Sam. 2 : 10. LXX). That is to say, let him boast because he knows the Lord with full understanding from His works, and because he imitates Him, so far as is possible, through the keeping of His divine commandments. For it is through them that he knows God and can 'work judgment and righteousness in the midst of the earth' (1 Sam. 2 : 10. LXX), as God does. Hannah spoke these words prophetically concerning the crucifixion and resurrection of the Lord. The gnostic's aspiration, too, is to suffer with the Lord through the acquisition of the virtues and to be glorified with Him through dispassion and spiritual knowledge, and to boast because of Him, in that, unworthy though he is, he has been enabled by grace to be a servant of such a master and an imitator of His humility. Then 'praise will come from God' (cf. 1 Cor. 4 : 5). But when will that happen? When He says to those on His right hand, 'Come, you blessed, inherit the kingdom' (Matt. 25 : 34). May we all be found worthy to inherit that kingdom through His grace and love: to Him be glory and dominion throughout the ages. Amen.

XXIII
HOLY SCRIPTURE

'Sing the psalms with understanding', says the psalmist (Ps. 47 : 7); and the Lord says, 'Search the Scriptures' (John 5 : 39). He who pays attention to them is illumined, while he who pays no attention is filled with darkness. For unless a person attends to what is said in divine Scripture, he will gather but little fruit, even though he sings or reads them frequently. 'Devote yourself to stillness and know', it is written (Ps. 46 : 10), because such devotion concentrates the intellect: even if it is attentive for only a short time, none the less it knows 'in part', as St Paul puts it (1 Cor. 13 : 12). This is especially true of the person who has made some progress in the practice of the moral virtues, for this teaches the intellect many things related to its association with the passions. Nevertheless, he does not know all the mysteries hidden by God in each verse of Scripture, but only as much as the purity of his intellect is able to comprehend through God's grace. This is clear from the fact that we often understand a certain passage in the course of our contemplation, grasping one or two of the senses in which it was written; then after a while our intellect may increase in purity and be allowed to perceive other meanings, superior to the first. As a result, in bewilderment and wonder at God's grace and His ineffable wisdom, we are overcome with awe before 'the God of knowledge', as the prophetess Hannah calls Him (cf. 1 Sam. 2 : 3).

I am not speaking here about the mere act of listening to a passage of Scripture or to some other person; for this does not by itself involve purity of intellect or divine revelation. I am speaking about the person who possesses knowledge but distrusts himself until he finds another passage from Scripture or from one of the saints that confirms his spontaneous knowledge of the scriptural passage or of some sensible or intelligible reality. And if instead of one meaning he should find many as a result of giving attention to either the divine Scriptures or the holy fathers, he should not lose faith and think that there is a contradiction. For one text or object can signify many things. Take clothing, for example: one person may say that it warms, another that it adorns, and another that it protects; yet all three are correct, since clothing is useful alike for warmth, for adornment and for protection. All three have grasped the purpose assigned by God to clothing; and Holy Scripture and the very nature of things themselves confirm it. But if someone whose intention is to rob and pilfer should say that clothing exists in order to be stolen, he would be an utter liar, for neither the Scriptures nor the nature of things suggest that it exists for this purpose; and even the laws punish those who do steal it.

The same applies to everything, whether visible or invisible, and to every word of the divine Scriptures. For the saints neither know the whole of God's purpose with regard to every object or scriptural text, nor on the other hand do they write down once and for all everything that they do know. This is because in the first place God is beyond comprehension, and His wisdom is not limited in such a way that an angel or man can grasp it in its entirety. As St John Chrysostom says with regard to a certain point of spiritual exegesis, we say about it as much as should be said at the moment, but God, in addition to what we say, knows other unfathomable meanings as well. And, in the second place, because of men's incapacity and weakness it is not good for even the saints themselves to say all that they know; for they might speak at too great a length, thus making themselves offensive or unintelligible because of the confusion in their reader's mind. As St Gregory the Theologian observes, what is said should be commensurate to the capacity of those to whom it is addressed.

For this reason the same saint may say one thing about a certain matter today, and another tomorrow; and yet there is no contradiction, provided the hearer has knowledge and experience of the matter under discussion. Again, one saint may say one thing and another say something different about the same passage of the Holy Scriptures, since divine grace often gives varying interpretations suited to the particular person or moment in question. The only thing required is that everything said or done should be said or done in accordance with God's intention, and that it should be attested by the words of Scripture. For should anyone preach anything contrary to God's intention or contrary to the nature of things, then even if he is an angel St Paul's words, 'Let him be accursed' (Gal. 1 : 8), will apply to him. This is what St Dionysios the Areopagite, St Antony and St Maximos the Confessor affirm. For this reason St John Chrysostom says: 'It was not the Greeks but the Holy Scriptures that transmitted these things to us. There is no contradiction when Scripture says about a certain person both that he did not see Babylon as a captive and, elsewhere, that they took him to Babylon with the rest. For one who reads attentively will find it said about this same man in another part of Scripture that they blinded him and in this condition took him off as a captive (cf. 2 Kgs. 25 : 7; Jer. 52 : 11). Thus he went to Babylon, as the one writer says, but did not see it, as the other says.'[1]

---

[1] *Homilies on the Statues* XIX, 3 (*P.G.* xlix, 195).

Again, some say in their lack of experience that the Epistle to the Hebrews was not written by St Paul, or that St Dionysios the Areopagite did not write one of the treatises ascribed to him. But if a man will pay attention to these same works, he will discover the truth. If the matter pertains to nature, the saints gain their knowledge of it from spiritual insight, that is, from the spiritual knowledge of nature and from the contemplation of created beings that is attained through the intellect's purity; and so they expound God's purpose in these things with complete accuracy, searching the Scriptures, as St John Chrysostom says, like gold-miners who seek out the finest veins. In this way they ensure that 'not the smallest letter or most insignificant accent is lost', as the Lord put it (Matt. 5 : 18).

Such is the situation with regard to things that pertain to nature. When the matter in question is something that lies beyond nature, whether it be sensible or intelligible, or even a written phrase, the saints know about it through the gift of prophecy and through revelation, provided that such knowledge is given them by the Holy Spirit. But if this knowledge is not given them, and if for their own good the matter remains beyond their understanding, they are not ashamed to speak the truth and to confess their human weakness, saying with St Paul, 'I do not know; God knows' (2 Cor. 12 : 2). As Solomon said, 'There are three things of which I am ignorant and a fourth which I do not know' (Prov. 30 : 18. LXX). Again, St John Chrysostom says, 'I do not know; and if the heretics call me an unbeliever, let them call me a fool as well.'

In short, the saints possessed both spiritual and secular knowledge but preferred the first; they made use, however, of their worldly education wisely and for a limited purpose, guided by St Paul's rule not to boast beyond limits (cf. 2 Cor. 10 : 13), as did those Egyptians who, according to the Clementine writings,[1] mocked the prosaic diction of the Apostle Barnabas, not realizing that his preaching contained words of life (cf. John 6 : 68). Many of us are guilty of doing the same: when we hear someone speaking with a strange accent we laugh, though he may perhaps be a wise man in his own tongue and be speaking of awe-inspiring mysteries. This happens because of our inexperience. But the fathers themselves often deliberately wrote in a very simple manner, depending on the

---

[1] *Recognitions* I, 7, 14; 8, 1; 9, 1 (ed. Rehm, pp. 10–11).

particular circumstances and the people for whom they were writing. St Gregory of Nyssa remarks on this when praising St Ephrem: though he was wise, says Gregory, he wrote simply. Gregory also marvels at the way in which, being deeply versed in theological doctrine, Ephrem refuted with great learning the accursed books of a childish heretic, and how the latter, because of his pride, was unable to bear the shame of this and died.[1]

Saintly humility is something that transcends nature, and an unbeliever cannot achieve it, but thinks that it is contrary to nature. St Dionysios the Areopagite speaks of this when writing to St Timothy about such men: he says that to the ancients the resurrection of the dead appeared contrary to nature, whereas to himself and to St Timothy – and in the eyes of the truth itself – it is not contrary to nature but it transcends nature.[2] This at least is how it looks to us; in God's eyes, however, it does not transcend nature, but is quite natural; for God's commandment *is* His nature. The fathers had a special love for humility in action and thought, as did the compiler of the *Gerontikon*, though he was a bishop and in exile for Christ's sake; for he says with regard to the tattered garment of some virgin that he took it in order to receive a blessing. And the holy fathers St Dorotheos and St Cassian, though wise, wrote simply. I say this lest anyone should think that some fathers wrote in a learned manner out of pride, while others wrote in a simple style because of their lack of intelligence. Both alike wrote through the same power of the intellect, conferred by the one Holy Spirit, and their purpose was to be of service to everyone. Had they all written simply, no learned person would ever benefit, for he would regard what was written as worthless because of its pedestrian style; nor on the other hand would a simpler type of person ever benefit had all of them written in a learned style, since he would not have understood the meaning of what was said.

Whoever is experienced in the spiritual interpretation of Scripture knows that the simplest passage is of a significance equal to that of the most abstruse passage, and that both are directed to the salvation of man. Whoever lacks such experience, however, is often at a loss, being unaware that secular learning is of great help when it acts as a

---

[1] Cf. Gregory of Nyssa, *Encomium on our Holy Father Ephrem* (P.G. xlvi, 825D).
[2] Cf. *The Ecclesiastical Hierarchy* VII, 1 (P.G. iii, 553A).

vehicle for the higher wisdom of the Spirit. For the wisdom of the Spirit bestows inspired thoughts, while secular learning provides power of expression, so long as it is accompanied by moral judgment and by the humility that teaches us to fear both thoughtlessness and craftiness and to 'judge with self-restraint', as St Paul puts it (Rom. 12 : 3).

Just as the term 'amen', which St Luke translates as 'truly' (cf. Luke 9 : 27), is a stable and decisive word endorsing what comes before it, so moral judgment is a stable and decisive form of intellection enabling us to cleave to the truth. The word 'amen' affirms the permanence of the new grace conferred by Christ; hence it is not found in the Old Testament at all,[1] since the Old Testament is but a prefiguration. In the New Testament, however, it is used everywhere because this testament will endure for ever and through all the ages.

XXIV
CONSCIOUS AWARENESS IN THE HEART

How many tears would I like to shed whenever I gain even a partial glimpse of myself! If I do not sin, I become elated with pride; while if I sin and am able to realize it, in my dismay I lose heart and begin to despair. If I take refuge in hope, again I become arrogant. If I weep, it feeds my presumption; if I do not weep, the passions visit me again. My life is death, yet death seems even worse because of my fear of punishment. My prayer proves a source of temptation to me, and my inattention a cause of disaster. 'He that increases knowledge increases sorrow,' says Solomon (Eccles. 1 : 18). I am at a loss, beside myself, and do not know what to do. And should I know, and then not do it, my knowledge would contribute to my condemnation. Alas, what shall I choose? In my ignorance all things seem contradictory and I cannot reconcile them. I do not find the virtue and wisdom hidden in my trials, since I do not endure these trials with patience. I flee from stillness because of my evil thoughts, and so I find myself beset by the

---

[1] The author is mistaken here.

passions that tempt me through the senses. I want to fast and to keep vigil, but am impeded by presumption and laxity. I eat and sleep lavishly, and sin without knowing it. I withdraw myself from everything and flee out of fear of sin, but listlessness is again my undoing.

Yet I realize that many, because they had a firm faith, received crowns of victory after going through battles and trials like these. It was because of their faith that they were granted fear of God; and through this fear they were enabled to practise the other virtues. Had I faith as they had, I would have found this fear through which, according to the prophet, I would have received true piety and spiritual knowledge; and from this knowledge would have come strength, counsel, understanding and the wisdom of the Holy Spirit (cf. Isa. 11 : 2). These are the gifts conferred on those who, free from anxiety, wait on God and devote themselves to the Holy Scriptures with the patience that makes it possible to view all things, whether from above or from below, with an equal mind.

Time and experience make it clear when a particular passion has been transformed into virtue. When, on the other hand, a virtue veers towards passion, time and experience permit us to set them apart through patient endurance. For if such endurance is not born in the soul out of faith, the soul cannot possess any virtue at all. 'You will gain possession of your souls through your patient endurance', said the Lord (Luke 21 : 19), who alone has fashioned the hearts of men, as the psalmist puts it (cf. Ps. 33 : 15). From this it is clear that the heart, that is, the intellect, comes into possession of itself through the patient endurance of what befalls it. For if we believe that someone else is invisibly guiding our life, how can we ever obey our own thoughts when they say 'I want this' or 'I do not want it', 'This is good' or 'This is bad'? If we had some visible guide, we would ask him about everything, would hear the reply and carry into effect what was said. But even when we do not have a visible guide, we do have Christ, as the bishop of Evchaïta remarks.[1] We should therefore put questions to Him through prayer from the heart, in faith hoping His answer will manifest itself in our thoughts and actions. Otherwise Satan, not being able to affect us in our actions, may answer us in our

[1] This may refer to John Mavropous, Metropolitan of Evchaïta (eleventh century); or, more probably, to Symeon, Metropolitan of Evchaïta (date uncertain: ? eleventh or twelfth century).

thoughts, pretending that he is the guide and in this way dragging us to perdition because we lack patient endurance.

It is those lacking such endurance who in their ignorance impetuously hurry on to seize what they have not yet been given, failing to realize that one day in the eyes of the Lord is as a thousand years, and a thousand years as a single day (cf. Ps. 90 : 4). But he who by enduring patiently has gained experience of the devil's machinations will fight and strive forward with patience so as to reach the goal, as St Paul puts it (cf. 1 Cor. 9 : 26; Phil. 3 : 12). He will be able to say, 'We are not ignorant of Satan's devices' (2 Cor. 2 : 11), that is, of the devil's invisible ploys, unknown to most men. For St Paul says, 'Satan himself is transformed into an angel of light' (2 Cor. 11 : 14); and there is nothing surprising in this, since the thoughts that he causes to appear in our heart seem to be righteous thoughts to those who lack experience.

For this reason it is good to say 'I do not know', so that we neither disbelieve what is said by an angel nor place credence in what occurs through the deceitfulness of the enemy. By thus accepting patiently whatever comes we may avoid both pitfalls. We may wait for many years until the answer is given us, unsolicited and unperceived, in the form of some concrete action – as someone has put it with reference to the contemplation of created beings. In this way we reach the haven of active spiritual knowledge. When we see this knowledge persisting in us over many years, then we will understand that truly we have been heard and have invisibly received the answer.

Someone prays, for example, for victory over those who fight against him. He hears nothing and sees no deceitful sign; or even if he does hear or see something, either in sleep or when awake, he gives it absolutely no credence. But after a certain length of time he observes that the battle is being won by God's grace and that certain thoughts are drawing his intellect towards humility and the knowledge of his own weakness. Yet he still does not put his trust in this, fearing that it might be deception, but waits for many years. It was such an attitude, according to St John Chrysostom,[1] that Christ wanted to induce in the apostles: that is why He warned them of coming tribulations, adding, 'He who endures to the end will be saved' (Matt. 10 : 22), so that they would not grow careless or over-confident, but would

---

[1] Cf. *Homilies on Matthew* 46, 1 (*P.G.* lviii, 476).

struggle on out of fear. For a person derives no benefit from the other virtues, even though he dwells in heaven, if he is in the grip of the presumption that led to the fall of the devil, Adam and many others.

Hence we should never abandon fear until we have reached the haven of perfect love and are no longer in the world or the body. Even the person who has reached that haven will not abandon such fear of his own accord. Rather, by virtue of his great faith his intellect is freed from all anxiety about the life and death of the body, and he attains the pure fear that is inspired by love. St Athanasios the Great was referring to this fear when he told the perfect not to fear God as a tyrant, but to fear Him because of His love; that is, they should fear Him not simply because they sin, but because they are loved without themselves showing love, thus receiving His blessings unworthily. It is through fear in the face of such blessings that God leads the soul towards love, so that through its gratitude to Him it may become worthy of the good things that have been and will be bestowed on it. Then by means of the pure fear inspired by love the soul attains the humility that transcends nature.

For no matter how many blessings a person in the state of pure fear receives, or how many appalling things he suffers, he never for a moment thinks that it is due to his own strength and understanding that he is able to endure or prosper in soul and body. On the contrary, in his humility he has received the discrimination by means of which he realizes that he is a creature of God, and that of himself he can do nothing good and cannot even preserve what has been given him by grace; and that he can neither remove temptation nor endure it through his own courage and judgment. By means of discrimination he thus attains a certain degree of spiritual knowledge and begins to see all things with the eye of the intellect. But, ignorant of the inner principles of these things, he longs for the Teacher; yet he fails to find Him, because He is invisible. At the same time he is unwilling to accept anyone else because his discrimination tells him – although there is no clear evidence for this – that anyone else may be an impostor; so he is at a loss, and as a result regards all that he has done and all that he has been taught as nothing.

For he sees how many men, beginning with Adam, have fallen in spite of their efforts and their knowledge; and he realizes as well that, though he hears, yet he does not understand what is said in the Holy Scriptures. This knowledge – the knowledge that in fact he does not know as he should know – brings him to tears. It is indeed truly astonishing that, if a man thinks he knows, he knows nothing yet (cf. 1 Cor. 8 : 2); and that what he thinks he has will be taken from him, as the Lord says (cf. Matt. 13 : 12) – that is, will be taken away because he thinks he has it while he does not have it. Thus the man who acknowledges that he is stupid and witless, ignorant and weak, weeps and laments because he thought he had received what he now realizes that he does not have.

Humility is born of many virtues, and in its turn gives birth to things more perfect still. It is the same with spiritual knowledge, thanksgiving, prayer and love, since these virtues are always capable of increase. For example, a person becomes humble and grieves because he is a sinner. In consequence of this he begins to practise self-control and patient endurance in the face of afflictions sought and unsought. What comes from the demons he endures through ascetic discipline, and what comes from men he endures as a test of his faith. In this way it becomes clear whether he puts his trust in God, or in man, or in his own strength and judgment. And when his worthiness has been proved by his patient endurance and by his entrusting all things to God, he receives that great faith to which Christ referred when He said, 'When the Son of man comes, will He find faith on the earth?' (Luke 18 : 8). Through such faith he gains victory over his enemies; and when he has achieved this, then through the power of God and through the wisdom granted him he becomes aware of his own weakness and ignorance.

As a result of this he begins to give thanks with a humble soul, and he trembles with fear lest he should relapse into disobedience. Because of this pure fear – fear which is not due to the fact that he has sinned – and because of the thankfulness, patient endurance and humility which have been bestowed on him as a result of his knowledge, he begins to have hope that by God's grace he will obtain mercy. In the light of his experience of the blessings he has received, he watches and fears lest he should be found unworthy of such gifts from God. Hence he receives greater humility and more intense prayer from the heart; and the more these increase, together with thankfulness, the greater the knowledge he receives. Thus he advances from knowledge to fear, and from fear to thankfulness, and so he attains the knowledge that transcends all these. As a consequence, he comes truly to love his Benefactor and longs to serve Him with joy, indebted as he is to God for the knowledge bestowed upon him.

At once he receives a still further increase of knowledge, and he contemplates not just the blessings he personally has been granted, but also those that are universal. Not being able to give thanks adequately for these, he grieves; and then, again marvelling at the grace of God, he is consoled. At times he weeps painfully; at times, because of his love, his tears are made sweeter than honey by the spiritual joy that comes from ineffable humility. When in truth he longs for God's will to be done in everything and abhors every honour and comfort; when he regards himself as lower than all other men and does not even think that he is anybody at all, but holds himself indebted to God and to all men as much as to God, then he will consider trials and afflictions to be great blessings, and enjoyment and comfort to be extremely harmful. For trials and afflictions he longs with all his soul, wherever they may come from; enjoyment and comfort he fears, even though they may be sent by God to test him.

While he is experiencing the tears of which we have spoken, his intellect begins to attain purity and to return to its pristine state, that is, to the state of natural spiritual knowledge which it lost through its amity with the passions. By some this is called moral judgment, since the intellect then sees things as they are by nature; by others it is called spiritual insight, since he who possesses it knows something at least of the hidden mysteries – that is, of God's purpose – in the Holy Scriptures and in every created thing. Such natural knowledge springs from discrimination, and enables us to perceive the inner principles of things sensible and intelligible. On account of this it is known as the contemplation of created beings, that is, of God's creation. It is natural and comes from purity of intellect. But if for the common good a person receives the gift of prophecy, he has attained something that transcends nature; for only God foreknows all things, as well as the purpose for which He created each thing and inspired each word of Holy Scripture; and it is by grace that He grants such knowledge to the saints.

Thus, the contemplation of sensible and intelligible creation, sometimes called moral judgment, is also a form of spiritual insight and of natural spiritual knowledge – 'natural' since it pre-exists in nature. But when the passions darken the intellect, it is lost; and unless God removes the passions through our practice of the virtues, the intellect remains blinded. The gift of prophecy, however, is of a different order, for it transcends nature and is granted only by grace. Yet even natural spiritual knowledge cannot be attained without God, though it is natural; for the pagan Greeks perceived many things but, as St Basil the Great has said, they were unable to discern God's purpose in created beings, or even God Himself, since they lacked the humility and the faith of Abraham.

A person is said to have faith when, on the basis of what he can see, he believes in what he cannot see. But to believe in what we can see of God's works is not the same as to believe in Him who teaches and proclaims the truth to us. Hence the trials sent to test our faith are visible, while God's assistance comes to us invisibly. In this way, the person who in faith endures these trials patiently will discover, once they have passed, that he has acquired spiritual knowledge, through which he knows things previously unknown to him, and that blessings have been bestowed on him. As a result he gains humility together with love both towards God, as his benefactor, and towards his fellow-men for the healing wrought by God through them. He regards this as something natural, and yet as a debt, which fills him with the desire to keep God's commandments. He hates the passions as his enemies and pays scant attention to the body, considering it an obstacle to his attainment of dispassion and of the knowledge of God, that is, of 'hidden wisdom' (1 Cor. 2 : 7).

This wisdom is rightly called 'hidden'. If someone seeks for success and pleasure, comfort and glory in this world, then he loves the wisdom of this world. But if someone struggles for what is contrary to these things – if he suffers, practises self-control, and endures all kinds of affliction and disgrace for the sake of the kingdom of heaven – then he loves the wisdom of God. The first longs to attain material benefits, secular learning and secular power, and often suffers on this account; but the second shares the sufferings of Christ. Thus the first places all his hopes in the things of this world, desiring to possess them even though they are transitory and hard to come by; while the second is hidden from 'the eyes of the foolish', as Holy Scripture puts it (Wisd. 3 : 2), but is clearly revealed in the world to come, when everything hidden is disclosed. Moreover, according to St John Chrysostom the knowledge of what is hidden – that is, the contemplation of the divine Scriptures and of created beings – is given as an encouragement to those who grieve in this world. For from faith is born fear, and from fear comes inward grief. This in turn produces humility, which gives rise to discrimination. Discrimination, finally, gives birth to spiritual insight and, by God's grace, to the gift of prophecy.

The gnostic ought not to rely in any way on his own thoughts, but should always seek to confirm them in the light of divine Scripture or of the nature of things themselves. Without such confirmation, there can be no true spiritual knowledge, but only wickedness and delusion, as St Basil the Great says when speaking about the stars.[1] Divine Scripture names only a few stars, while the pagan Greeks in their delusion give names to many. For the intention of divine Scripture is to speak of things that can save the soul, and to reveal to us the mysteries it contains in itself, as well as the inner principles of created beings, that is, the purpose for which each thing was created. In this way it aims to illumine our intellect with the love of God, and to enable it to perceive His greatness and His inexpressible wisdom and providence, as they are revealed in His care for His creation. Such knowledge makes us afraid of breaking His commandments and conscious of our own weakness and ignorance. This in its turn makes us humble and teaches us to love God and not to despise His commandments, as do those who lack effective knowledge of Him. Moreover, God withholds some of the mysteries from us, so that we may long for them and not be quickly sated, as was Adam, whom the enemy caught off his guard and led into his own base ways.

This, then, is the position of those who have acquired the virtues. Those who lack knowledge, on the other hand, God alarms with trials and temptations so that they will refrain from sin; at the same time He encourages them by bestowing on them bodily blessings so as to keep them from despair. God in His unbounded goodness does this at all times so that He may save all men and free them from the snares of the devil, either by conferring on them or else by withholding from them His favours and knowledge. According to the gratitude of each He bestows His gifts and divine thoughts. Similarly, in accordance with the propensity of each reader and with what is to his profit, God

---

[1] Cf. *On the Six Days of Creation* VI, 4–5 (P.G. xxix, 125A–128A).

either conceals the meaning of Holy Scripture or allows it to be known.

The aim of the teachers of secular wisdom was different, for each was eager to defeat the other and to appear wiser; hence they did not discover Christ, nor do those who emulate them, in spite of all their efforts. For, as St John Klimakos says,[1] God reveals Himself, not in response to our exertions, but in response to the humility and simplicity that come through faith, that is, through the contemplation of the Scriptures and of created beings. On this account the Lord said, 'How can you have faith when you receive honour from one another, and do not seek the honour that comes from the only God?' (John 5 : 44). This is that great faith which makes it possible for us to put all our cares into the hands of God. The apostle calls it the foundation (cf. Heb. 6 : 1), St John Klimakos, the mother of stillness,[2] and St Isaac, the faith of contemplation and the gateway of the mysteries.[3] He who possesses this faith is completely free from worry and anxiety, as were all the saints.

The saints, like the righteous men of old, even had names to suit them. Peter's name, that comes from the Greek word for 'rock', indicates his firmness; Paul's name, that comes from the Greek word for 'rest', refers to the 'rest' he found in Christ; James is called the 'tripper up', because he tripped up the devil; and Stephen – from the Greek word for 'crown' – is named from the unfading crown he won; Athanasios means 'deathless' in Greek; Basil means 'kingdom'; Gregory signifies 'vigilance', for he was vigilant in wisdom and theology; Chrysostom, meaning 'golden-mouthed' in Greek, is so named from his rich style and admirable grace in speaking; and Isaac means forgiveness.

In short, in both the Old and the New Testament, the names given are appropriate. Thus Adam was named from the four cardinal points; for the four letters of his name are the initial letters of the Greek words for East, West, North and South. Man, in the Syrian language, was denoted by the word for 'fire', because of the similitude of his nature to that of fire. For the whole of humanity is descended from one man, just as from a single lamp one can light as many others as one wishes without the first suffering any loss. But, after the

---

[1] *Ladder*, Step 26 (1024C; E.T., p. 209).
[2] *Ladder*, Step 27 (1113B; E.T., p. 247).
[3] *Mystic Treatises*, E.T., pp. 210, 214; Greek, pp. 281, 65.

confusion of the tongues (cf. Gen. 11 : 1–9), in one language the name 'man' is derived from the forgetfulness which man incurred, in another from his other characteristics. The Greek language derives its word for 'man' from the fact that he looks upward, yet his chief natural quality is his intelligence: it is for this reason that he is called an intelligent being, since he alone has this quality. As regards the other qualities from which he is named, there are many other created beings with which he shares them.

Hence we ought to abandon all other things and as intelligent beings cleave to the intelligence, offering with the intelligence intelligible worship to the divine Intelligence. Then we will be found worthy to receive from Him in this present age, in return for human words, the divine words of the Holy Spirit. For it is said of God that He 'gives prayer to him who prays' (1 Sam. 2 : 9. LXX); and indeed to one who truly prays the prayer of the body God gives the prayer of the intellect; and to one who diligently cultivates the prayer of the intellect, God gives the imageless and formless prayer that comes from the pure fear of Him. Again, to one who practises this prayer effectively, God grants the contemplation of created beings. Once this is attained – once the intellect has freed itself from all things and, not content with hearing about God at second hand, devotes itself to Him in action and thought – God permits it to be seized in rapture, conferring on it the gift of true theology and the blessings of the age to be.

Thus spiritual knowledge is good if it fills its possessor with shame and so leads him involuntarily towards humility, making him think that he possesses such knowledge unworthily; indeed, according to St John Klimakos,[1] in his humility he even rejects it as harmful, God-given though it may be. Yet how disastrous if it affects him as it affected that monk who was torn apart by the triple-teethed prongs of the demons! He was so greatly respected and loved that all mourned his death and thought it a great loss. Yet he was a victim of hidden pride; and the person who has told us about him heard from on high the words, 'Allow him no rest, for never for a single moment did he give rest to Me.' Alas, someone whom everyone called a saint, and through whose prayers many hoped to be saved from a host of trials and temptations, came to such an end because he thought so

---

[1] *Ladder*, Step 25 (996D; E.T., p. 196).

highly of himself. And it is obvious that the reason was his pride. For had it been some other sin, he would not have been able to take everyone in or to commit it continuously. It is true that, had it been heresy, he would have continually angered God through his wilful blasphemy; but heresy does not remain concealed for ever. Through God's providence it is revealed, so that he who holds it may recant, provided he is willing to; if he is not, then it is revealed in order to safeguard other people.

Thus it is self-satisfied haughtiness alone that can escape the notice of everyone. It all but escapes the notice even of its victim, unless he is permitted to fall into temptations which put his soul to the test and allow him to recognize his own weakness and ignorance. Thus not even for a single moment was the Holy Spirit given rest in the hapless soul of that monk, since he was always preoccupied with the thought of his own excellence and rejoiced in this thought as though it were some lofty achievement. For this reason he was filled with darkness, as are the demons. Moreover, in order to conceal his fault, he nourished this single passion instead of all the others. And this was sufficient for the demons since, as St John Klimakos says, this single passion is capable of taking the place of the other vices.[1]

I am not here recording something that I discovered with my own understanding and discrimination, but I write what I have learnt from the saint who was my spiritual father. He also told me of an occasion on which St Antony the Great ordered St Paul the Simple to cast the demon out of a certain girl.[2] St Paul did not at once prostrate himself and obey, but made objections, asking St Antony why he did not cast the demon out himself. It was only after St Antony told him that he was otherwise occupied that St Paul finally obeyed. On account of Paul's procrastination, said my spiritual father, the demon did not obey at once, but only went out of the girl after Paul had struggled for a long time. That things are in fact like this can be believed not only on the testimony of the holy elder, but also from the washing of the disciples' feet in the Bible (cf. John 13 : 6–8), as well as from the account of Moses' argument with the Lord (cf. Exod. 4 : 10), and from the story of the prophet who asked someone to strike him (cf. 1 Kgs. 20 : 35–42).

---

[1] *Ladder*, Step 23 (965D; E.T., p. 180).
[2] Palladios, *Lausiac History* 22.

Because this latter story is capable of a spiritual interpretation which has not been given elsewhere, I will recount it here. A certain king ruled his kingdom so tyrannically that God, in His love for mankind, could not endure this tyranny and commanded his prophet to go and rebuke that king. The prophet, however, knew the king's cruelty and did not wish simply to go to him, lest seeing him from afar and surmising the reason for which he had come, the king would drive him away and thus prevent him from carrying out his task; or lest, if he was given audience and began by saying, 'My God has sent me here because of your cruelty', the king would not pay attention to what was said. Instead he devised a plan whereby he would be struck by somebody and then go, covered with blood, as if he were lodging a complaint; in this way he would deceive the king and force him to listen to what he had to say.

As the prophet was going along he came upon someone at the roadside who had an axe, and he said to him, 'Thus says the Lord, take your axe and strike my head.' But the other, being a devout man, said, 'Certainly not; I am a man of God and will not lay a hand on the Lord's anointed.' Then the prophet said, 'Thus says the Lord: as you did not obey the voice of the Lord, let a lion come from the desert and devour you.' This was not done in anger – God forbid! It happened for the benefit of all. This righteous man deserved not to die in an ordinary fashion like other men, but to be devoured by a wild beast in accordance with God's word and so to receive a crown of glory because of his bitter death. The *Gerontikon* records a similar story.[1] Four priests made a pact and prayed that, when they had fallen asleep in Christ, their servant should be eaten by a lion because of his unchastity. But the Lord did not hear them, and chose rather to listen to the hesychast who was praying for the servant so that the lion would not touch him.

To return to the prophet. He then found another man, who was obedient, and he said to him, 'Thus says the Lord: lift your axe and strike my head.' This man, when he heard the words, 'Thus says the Lord', without hesitation struck the head of the prophet with his axe, and the prophet said to him, in words similar to those used by Moses when he spoke to the children of Levi, 'The blessing of the Lord be upon you, for you have listened to the voice of the Lord' (cf. Exod.

[1] Paul Evergetinos, *Collection* III, xxxviii, 1, §§10–14.

32 : 29). Thus the first man, in his great devoutness, respected the prophet and did not obey him, like Peter at the washing of the feet (cf. John 13 : 8); while the other obeyed without further thought, as the sons of Levi were obedient to Moses when they slew their brethren (cf. Exod. 32 : 26–29).

Judging by outward appearances, he who obeys the will of God does the better thing, for he obeys the supranatural command of the Lord of nature, which he regards as wiser and more righteous than natural knowledge; whereas he who disobeys does a lesser thing, in that he regards his own opinion about what is right as more righteous than the word of God. But if we look deeper, things turn out to be different. What matters is the motive behind the obedience or disobedience; and so he whose motive is to do God's will has chosen the better path. In the present case, to all appearances God seems to be angry with the man who is disobedient and to bless the man who is obedient. But in reality it is not so, as has been said already: from the viewpoint of natural contemplation both were equally good, since the motive of both was to do God's will.

Then the prophet went to the king and standing before him said, 'Give me justice, O king! For as I was coming someone met me on the road and struck my head.' And the king, seeing the wound and the blood, became angry in his usual way, but not with the prophet; and, thinking that he was condemning someone else, and not himself, he denounced with extreme severity the man who had wounded the prophet. Then the prophet, having achieved what he wanted, said, 'You have spoken well, O king, for thus says the Lord: I shall surely tear this kingdom from your hands and from your seed, for it is you that have done these things.' Thus the prophet delivered his message as he wished, skilfully compelling the king to pay attention to what he said. He then departed, praising God.

Such, then, were the souls of the prophets. They loved God and, because of their knowledge of God, they were eager to suffer for the sake of His will. This is natural; for he who is familiar with a certain path or a certain skill pursues it readily and easily, with assurance explaining to others the direction of the path or the secrets and finer points of the craft; and he often does this even though he is young in years and lacks formal training, while those to whom he is explaining things may be advanced in years and wise in other matters. For the prophets, apostles and martyrs did not gain their knowledge of God and their wisdom at second hand, as we have gained ours. On the contrary, they poured out their blood and received the Spirit, exemplifying the words of the fathers: 'Spill your blood and receive the Spirit.'[1] Thus the fathers suffered martyrdom, not in an outward sense, but in their conscience: instead of undergoing physical death they showed themselves willing to die, and in this way their intellect proved victorious over all earthly desires and reigns in Christ Jesus our Lord. To Him þe glory and dominion, honour and worship, now and always and throughout the ages. Amen.

[1] *Apophthegmata*, Longinus 5; E.T., p. 123.

ST SYMEON METAPHRASTIS
PARAPHRASE OF THE HOMILIES
OF
ST MAKARIOS OF EGYPT

Introductory Note

The Makarian Homilies were attributed in the past to St Makarios the Great of Egypt (*c.* 300–*c.* 390). A Coptic monk, priest and spiritual father in the desert of Sketis, he figures prominently in the *Lausiac History* of Palladios[1] and in the *Sayings of the Desert Fathers*,[2] and is commemorated in the Church's calendar on 19 January. But this ascription is open to doubt for many reasons: in particular, the early sources say nothing whatever about any writings by Makarios of Egypt, while the background presupposed by the Homilies is not Egyptian but Syrian. All that can be said with any confidence is that the Homilies are the work of an unknown author, writing probably in Syria or Mesopotamia during the late fourth or the early fifth century.

There are similarities in language and symbolism, and sometimes also in thought, between the Homilies and Messalianism, an ascetic movement that originated in Syria in the late fourth century and spread rapidly to other parts of the Christian East. Some scholars have even concluded that the Homilies are in reality the 'Ascetic Book' of the Messalians, and on somewhat slender evidence they attribute them to Symeon of Mesopotamia, one of the leading Messalians. Other specialists, without denying the points of resemblance, argue that they should not be exaggerated. The heretical teachings characteristic of extreme Messalianism are not in fact to be found in the Homilies; when language and symbols associated with the Messalians are employed, they are used in a fundamentally Orthodox way.

---

[1] See chapter 17.

[2] See *Apophthegmata*, alphabetical collection, *P.G.* lxv, 257–81; E.T., pp. 124–38. Cf. also *The Philokalia*, vol. i, p. 29.

Indeed, the Homilies may continue to be regarded, today as in the past, as an authentic expression of Eastern Christian spirituality at its best.[1]

St Nikodimos and St Makarios included in the *Philokalia*, not the original text of the Homilies – which, while lively, is also repetitive and diffuse – but an eleventh-century adaptation attributed to St Symeon Metaphrastis ('the Translator': not to be confused with St Symeon the New Theologian). Symeon Metaphrastis followed an administrative career in the civil service, rising to the high rank of logothete or chancellor, which he held under the Emperors Nikiphoros II Phokas (963–9), John I Tzimiskis (969–76) and Basil II (976–1025). It is thought that he became a monk at the end of his life, and he is commemorated on 9 November. Probably he is to be identified with the chronicler Symeon Magistros. A voluminous writer, he is chiefly remembered for his edition of the *Menologion* or *Lives of the Saints*. He is also probably the author of the prayers for use before and after communion, often ascribed to his namesake Symeon the New Theologian. The Greek title in the *Philokalia* states that Symeon has paraphrased the main group of Fifty Homilies (known as collection II),[2] but in reality most of the material comes from another group of Twenty-Six Homilies (collection IV).[3]

In his selection[4] St Symeon Metaphrastis has embodied the master-themes that dominate the Makarian Homilies: the constant conflict or 'unseen warfare' (§146) in the depths of the human heart between grace and Satan, between the Holy Spirit and the spirit of evil; the 'co-operation' or *synergeia* (§41) between divine grace and human free will; the need for direct personal experience, for a 'full and conscious assurance' (§106) of the indwelling presence of the

[1] For a thorough discussion of the whole subject, see the works of H. Dörries, especially *Symeon von Mesopotamien. Die Überlieferung der messalianischen 'Makarios'-Schriften (Texte und Untersuchungen 55, 1: Leipzig, 1941); Die Theologie des Makarios/Symeon (Abhandlungen der Akademie der Wissenschaften in Göttingen, Philologisch-Historische Klasse, Dritte Folge, Nr 103: Göttingen, 1978).* A brief summary of the evidence, with further bibliography, is provided by V. Desprez and M. Canévet, in *Dictionnaire de Spiritualité* x (1977), col. 20–43. For an Orthodox viewpoint, see J. Meyendorff, 'Messalianism or Anti-Messalianism? A Fresh Look at the "Macarian" Problem', in *Kyriakon. Festschrift Johannes Quasten*, vol. ii (Münster, 1971), pp. 585–90; reprinted in *Byzantine Hesychasm: historical, theological and social problems* (Variorum Reprints: London, 1974), chapter xv.

[2] *Die 50 Geistlichen Homilien des Makarios*, ed. H. Dörries, E. Klostermann and M. Kroeger (*Patristiche Texte und Studien* 4: Berlin, 1964).

[3] See *Dictionnaire de Spiritualité* x, col. 21.

[4] In *P.G.* xxxiv, 821–41, there is a further treatise 'On the Guarding of the Heart', immediately preceding the other six treatises; this is absent from the *Philokalia*.

Holy Spirit – a theme taken up and developed by St Symeon the New Theologian. Much is said about the resurrection glory of the human body at the last day (§§61–3, 140–1), but it is also insisted that the saints experience here and now a genuine foretaste of the glory of the age to come: the final resurrection is simply the outward and bodily manifestation of what is already hidden during this present life in the souls of the righteous. The passages on the vision of divine light (§§137–9) anticipate the teaching of St Gregory Palamas and the fourteenth-century Hesychasts.

While the Makarian Homilies do not underestimate the need for 'labour and sweat of the brow' (§51), what chiefly distinguishes them is their sense of communion with the Holy Spirit, and of the love and joy that He imparts. With their message of encouragement, their vigorous style and simple illustrations, it is not surprising that they should often be given as reading to novices at their first entry to the monastery.

I

Spiritual Perfection

1. We receive salvation by grace and as a divine gift of the Spirit. But to attain the full measure of virtue we need also to possess faith and love, and to struggle to exercise our free will with integrity. In this manner we inherit eternal life as a consequence of both grace and justice. We do not reach the final stage of spiritual maturity through divine power and grace alone, without ourselves making any effort; but neither on the other hand do we attain the final measure of freedom and purity as a result of our own diligence and strength alone, apart from any divine assistance. If the Lord does not build the house, it is said, and protect the city, in vain does the watchman keep awake, and in vain do the labourer and the builder work (cf. Ps. 127 : 1–4).

2. What is the will of God that St Paul urges and invites each of us to attain (cf. 1 Thess. 4 : 3)? It is total cleansing from sin, freedom from the shameful passions and the acquisition of the highest virtue. In other words, it is the purification and sanctification of the heart that comes about through fully experienced and conscious participation in the perfect and divine Spirit. 'Blessed are the pure in heart,' it is said, 'for they shall see God' (Matt. 5 : 8); and again: 'Become perfect, as your heavenly Father is perfect' (Matt. 5 : 48). And the psalmist says: 'Let my heart be unerring in Thy statutes, so that I am not ashamed' (Ps. 119 : 80); and again: 'When I pay attention to all Thy commandments, then I will not be ashamed' (Ps. 119 : 6). And to the person that asked, 'Who will ascend the Lord's hill, or who will stand in His holy place?', the psalmist replied: 'He that has clean hands and a pure heart' (Ps. 24 : 3–4), that is to say, he who has completely destroyed sin in act and thought.

3. The Holy Spirit, knowing that the unseen and secret passions are hard to get rid of – for they are as it were rooted in the soul – shows us through the psalmist how we can purify ourselves from

them. 'Cleanse me from my secret faults', writes the psalmist (Ps. 19 : 12), as though to say that through much prayer and faith, and by turning completely to God, we are able, with the help of the Spirit, to conquer them. But this is on condition that we too strive against them and keep strict watch over our heart (cf. Prov. 4 : 23).

4. Moses indicates figuratively that the soul should not be divided in will between good and evil, but should pursue the good alone; and that it must cultivate not the dual fruits of virtue and vice but those of virtue only. For he says: 'Do not yoke together on your threshing floor animals of a different species, such as ox and ass; but yoke together animals of the same species and so thresh your corn' (cf. Deut. 22 : 10). This is to say, do not let virtue and vice work together on the threshing floor of your heart, but let virtue alone work there. Again he says: 'Do not weave flax into a woollen garment, or wool into a linen garment' (cf. Deut. 22 : 11); and: 'Do not cultivate two kinds of fruit together on the same patch of your land' (cf. Deut. 22 : 9). Similarly, you are not to mate an animal of one species with an animal of another species, but to mate like with like. All this is a concealed way of saying that you must not cultivate virtue and vice together in yourself, but you must devote yourself singlemindedly to producing the fruits of virtue; and you must not share your soul with two spirits – the Spirit of God and the spirit of the world – but you must give it solely to the Spirit of God and must reap only the fruits of the Spirit. It is for this reason that the psalmist writes: 'I have prospered in all Thy commandments; I hate every false way' (Ps. 119 : 128).

5. The virgin soul that desires to be united to God must keep itself pure not only from overt sins like unchastity, murder, theft, gluttony, backbiting, falsity, avarice, greed and so on; but to an even greater degree it must keep itself pure from sins that are hidden, such as desire, self-esteem, love of popularity, hypocrisy, love of power, wiliness, malice, hatred, unbelief, envy, self-love, affectation and other things of this kind. According to Scripture, these concealed sins of the soul are just as pernicious as the overt sins. 'The Lord has scattered the bones of those who seek to please men', it says (Ps. 53 : 5. LXX); and: 'The Lord will abhor the bloody and deceitful man' (Ps. 5 : 6), thus making it clear that deceitfulness is just as abhorrent to God as murder. Again, it numbers among the 'workers of iniquity' those who 'speak peace to their neighbour but have evil in their hearts' (Ps.

28 : 3), and elsewhere it speaks of those who commit lawless acts in their hearts (cf. Ps. 58 : 2). It also says: 'Woe to you, when men speak well of you' (Luke 6 : 26) – that is to say, when you want to hear people say good things about you and when you hang upon their glory and praise. It is true that those who do good cannot escape notice altogether. Indeed, the Lord Himself says: 'Let your light shine before men' (Matt. 5 : 16), though here it is understood that we do good for the glory of God and not for our own glory or because we desire men's praise. If this is not the case, then we are lacking in faith, as the Lord makes clear when He says: 'How can you have faith when you receive honour from one another, and do not seek the honour that comes from the only God?' (John 5 : 44). St Paul bids us to do everything, even to eat and to drink, for the glory of God; 'for,' he says, 'whether you eat or drink, or do anything else, do it for the glory of God' (1 Cor. 10 : 31). And St John equates hatred with murder when he says: 'Whoever hates his brother is a murderer' (1 John 3 : 15).

6. 'Love bears with all things, patiently accepts all things; love never fails' (1 Cor. 13 : 7–8). This phrase 'never fails' makes it clear that, unless they have been granted total deliverance from the passions through the most complete and active love of the Spirit, even those who have received spiritual gifts are still liable to falter: they are still in danger, and must struggle in fear against the attacks launched on them by the spirits of evil. St Paul shows that not to be in danger of falling or liable to passion is such a lofty state that the tongues of angels, prophecy, all knowledge and gifts of healing are as nothing compared to it (cf. 1 Cor. 13 : 1–8).

7. St Paul has here indicated the goal of perfection so that everyone, realizing his poverty in the face of such richness, may long for it intensely and may strive forward along the spiritual path until he attains it. As has been said: 'Run, that you may reach your goal' (1 Cor. 9 : 24).

8. To deny oneself (cf. Matt. 16 : 24) is to be ready to give up everything for the brethren's sake and not to follow one's own will in anything, or to possess anything except one's own clothes. He who attains this state, and is thus freed from all things, joyfully does only what he is asked to do. He regards all the brethren, and especially the superiors and those appointed to bear the burdens of the monastery, as lords and masters for Christ's sake. In this way he obeys Christ who

said: 'He among you who wants to be first and pre-eminent, let him be the last of all and the servant and slave of all' (cf. Mark 9 : 35), not inviting any glory, honour or praise from the brethren for his service and conduct. He serves the brethren with complete goodwill, with love and simplicity, not with outward show and with an eye to gaining popularity, but regarding himself as a debtor in everything.

9. The superiors of the community, who shoulder a great burden, must fight the crafty designs of evil with the weapon of humility, lest because of the authority they exercise over their subordinate brethren they grow proud and so act to their own detriment rather than to their profit. They should be like compassionate fathers, in the name of God giving themselves bodily and spiritually to the service of the community, keeping watch over the brethren and constantly looking after them as children of God. Outwardly they should not disown the rank of superior, as for instance in giving orders or advice to the more experienced monks, or in punishing or rebuking someone when necessary, and in encouraging where it is appropriate; otherwise, on the grounds that they are being humble or gentle, they will introduce confusion into the monastery through not preserving the due order of superiors and subordinates. But inwardly, in their own minds, they should regard themselves as unworthy servants of all their brethren, and as teachers entrusted with the Lord's children; and with unreserved goodwill and fear of God they should do all they can to make each of the brethren apt for every good work, knowing that the reward they will receive from God for such labour will be great and inalienable.

10. There are times when servants whose task it is to instruct the young do not hesitate in all charity to beat them for the sake of discipline or good behaviour, even if those they punish are the children of their own masters. Similarly, superiors should punish those of the brethren in need of discipline, yet not in anger or haughtiness, or for personal revenge, but with compassion and with a view to their reform and spiritual profit.

11. He who wants to be stamped with the virtues should pursue before everything else and at all times fear of God and holy love, the first and greatest of the commandments (cf. Matt. 22 : 38). Let him continually beseech the Lord to send this love into his heart, and thus let him advance and grow, augmenting it by grace day by day through the ceaseless and unbroken remembrance of God. Through diligence

and effort, concern and struggle he becomes capable of acquiring love for God, given form within him by the grace and bounty of Christ. Through such love the second commandment, love for one's neighbour (cf. Matt. 22 : 39), can easily be attained. Let these two primary commandments take precedence over the others and let him pursue them more than the others. In this way the secondary commandments will follow naturally on the primary. But should he neglect this first and great commandment, the love for God that is formed with divine help from our inner disposition, our clear conscience and our life-giving remembrance of God, then in consequence of this neglect he cannot soundly and purely accomplish the second commandment, that requires simply the outward diligence of service. For the guile of evil, finding the intellect void of the remembrance of God, and of love and longing for Him, will make the divine commandments appear harsh and laborious, kindling in his soul grumbling, resentment and complaints about having to serve the brethren; or else it will deceive him with the presumption of self-righteousness, filling him with arrogance and making him think that he is of great importance and worthy of esteem, and that he has entirely fulfilled the commandments.

12. When a man thinks that he is keeping the commandments perfectly, it is obvious that he is mistaken and that he is breaking one of them, since he judges himself and does not submit to the true judge. But when, in St Paul's words (cf. Rom. 8 : 16), the Spirit of God testifies along with our spirit, then indeed we are worthy of Christ and are children of God. This is not the case, however, when we justify ourselves merely on the basis of what we ourselves think. It is not the man who commends himself that is to be trusted, but he whom Christ commends (cf. 2 Cor. 10 : 18). When a man lacks the remembrance and fear of God, it is inevitable that he will long for glory and will seek for praise from those whom he serves. As has already been explained, such a person is called an unbeliever by Christ; for He says: 'How can you have faith when you receive honour from one another, and do not seek the honour that comes from the only God?' (John 5 : 44).

13. As has been said, love for God can be attained through the intellect's great struggles and labours in holy meditation and in unremitting attention to all that is good. The devil, on the contrary, impedes our intellect, not letting it devote itself to divine love

through the remembrance of what is good, but enticing the senses with earthly desires. For the intellect that dwells undistractedly in the love and remembrance of God is the devil's death and, so to say, his noose. Hence it is only through the first commandment, love for God, that genuine love for one's brother can be established, and that true simplicity, gentleness, humility, integrity, goodness, prayer and the whole beautiful crown of the virtues can be perfected. Much struggle is needed, therefore, and much inward and unseen travail, much scrutiny of our thoughts and training of our soul's enfeebled organs of perception, before we can discriminate between good and evil, and strengthen and give fresh life to the afflicted powers of our soul through the diligent striving of our intellect towards God. For by always cleaving to God in this way our intellect will become one spirit with the Lord, as St Paul puts it (cf. 1 Cor. 6 : 17).

14. Those aspiring to the state of virtue must strive to fulfil the commandments by sustaining this inward struggle, travail and meditation unceasingly night and day, whether praying or serving, eating or drinking, or doing anything else. In this way, if any good comes about it will be to God's glory and not to their own. The fulfilment of the commandments presents no difficulty or trouble to us when it is facilitated by the love of God and when this love relieves it of all that is burdensome. As has been said, the whole effort of the enemy is directed towards distracting the intellect from the remembrance, fear and love of God, and to turning it by means of earthly forms and seductions away from what is truly good towards what appears to be good.

15. The patriarch Abraham, when he was receiving Melchisedec, the priest of God, made him an offering from the firstfruits of the earth and so obtained his blessing (cf. Gen. 14 : 19–20). Through this incident the Spirit indicates that the first and highest elements of our constitution – the intellect, the conscience, the loving power of the soul – must initially be offered to God as a holy sacrifice. The firstfruits and the highest of our true thoughts must be continually devoted to remembrance of Him, engrossed in His love and in unutterable and boundless longing for Him. In this way we can grow and move forward day by day, assisted by divine grace. Then the burden of fulfilling the commandments will appear light to us, and we will carry them out faultlessly and irreproachably, helped by the Lord Himself on account of our faith in Him.

16. Where outward ascetic practice is concerned, which virtue is the most important? The answer to this is that the virtues are linked one to the other, and follow as it were a sacred sequence, one depending on the other. For instance, prayer is linked to love, love to joy, joy to gentleness, gentleness to humility, humility to service, service to hope, hope to faith, faith to obedience, and obedience to simplicity. Similarly, the vices are linked one to another: hatred to anger, anger to pride, pride to self-esteem, self-esteem to unbelief, unbelief to hardheartedness, hardheartedness to negligence, negligence to sluggishness, sluggishness to apathy, apathy to listlessness, listlessness to lack of endurance, lack of endurance to self-indulgence, and so on with all the other vices.

17. The devil tries to soil and defile every good thing a man would do by intermingling with it his own seeds in the form of self-esteem, presumption, complaint, and other things of this kind, so that what we do is not done for God alone, or with a glad heart. Abel offered a sacrifice to God of the fat and firstlings of his flock, while Cain offered gifts of the fruits of the earth, but not of the firstfruits; and that is why God looked with favour on Abel's sacrifices, but paid no attention to Cain's gifts (cf. Gen. 4 : 3–5). This shows us that it is possible to do something good in the wrong way – that is to say, to do it negligently, or scornfully, or else not for God's sake but for some other purpose; and for this reason it is unacceptable to God.

II
Prayer

18. The crown of every good endeavour and the highest of achievements is diligence in prayer. Through it, God guiding us and lending a helping hand, we come to acquire the other virtues. It is in prayer that the saints experience communion in the hidden energy of God's holiness and inner union with it, and their intellect itself is brought through unutterable love into the presence of the Lord. 'Thou hast given gladness to my heart', wrote the psalmist (Ps. 4 : 7); and the Lord Himself said that 'the kingdom of heaven is within you' (cf. Luke 17 : 21). And what does the kingdom being within mean except that the heavenly gladness of the Spirit is clearly stamped on the virtuous soul? For already in this life, through active communion in the Spirit, the virtuous soul receives a foretaste and a prelude of the delight, joy and spiritual gladness which the saints will enjoy in the eternal light of Christ's kingdom. This is something that St Paul also affirms: 'He consoles us in our afflictions, so that we can console others in every affliction through the consolation with which we ourselves have been consoled by God' (2 Cor. 1 : 4). And passages in the Psalms likewise hint at this active gladness and consolation of the Spirit, such as: 'My heart and my flesh have rejoiced in the living God' (Ps. 84 : 2. LXX); and: 'My soul will be filled with marrow and fatness' (Ps. 63 : 5).

19. Just as the work of prayer is greater than other work, so it demands greater effort and attention from the person ardently devoted to it, lest without him being aware the devil deprives him of it. The greater the good a person has in his care, the greater the attacks the devil launches on him; hence he must keep strict watch, so that fruits of love and humility, simplicity and goodness – and, along with them, fruits of discrimination – may grow daily from the constancy of his prayer. These will make evident his progress and increase in holiness, thus encouraging others to make similar efforts.

20. Not only does St Paul instruct us to pray without ceasing and to persist in prayer (cf. 1 Thess. 5 : 17; Rom. 12 : 12), but so also does the Lord when He says that God will vindicate those who cry out to Him day and night (cf. Luke 18 : 7) and counsels us to 'watch and pray' (Matt. 26 : 41). We must therefore pray always and not lose heart (cf. Luke 18 : 1). To put things more succinctly: he who persists in prayer has to struggle greatly and exert himself relentlessly if he is to overcome the many obstacles with which the devil tries to impede his diligence – obstacles such as sleep, listlessness, physical torpor, distraction of thought, confusion of intellect, debility, and so on, not to mention afflictions, and also the attacks of the evil spirits that violently fight against us, opposing us and trying to prevent the soul from approaching God when it truly and ceaselessly seeks Him.

21. He who cultivates prayer has to fight with all diligence and watchfulness, all endurance, all struggle of soul and toil of body, so that he does not become sluggish and surrender himself to distraction of thought, to excessive sleep, to listlessness, debility and confusion, or defile himself with turbulent and indecent suggestions, yielding his mind to things of this kind, satisfied merely with standing or kneeling for a long time, while his intellect wanders far away. For unless a person has been trained in strict vigilance, so that when attacked by a flood of useless thoughts he tests and sifts them all, yearning always for the Lord, he is readily seduced in many unseen ways by the devil. Moreover, those not yet capable of persisting in prayer can easily grow arrogant, thus allowing the machinations of evil to destroy the good work in which they are engaged and making a present of it to the devil.

22. Unless humility and love, simplicity and goodness regulate our prayer, this prayer – or, rather, this pretence of prayer – cannot profit us at all. And this applies not only to prayer, but to every labour and hardship undertaken for the sake of virtue, whether this be virginity, fasting, vigil, psalmody, service or any other work. If we do not see in ourselves the fruits of love, peace, joy, simplicity, humility, gentleness, guilelessness, faith, forbearance and kindliness, then we endure our hardship to no purpose. We accept the hardships in order to reap the fruits. If the fruits of love are not in us, our labour is useless. In such a case we differ in nothing from the five foolish virgins: because their hearts were not filled here and now, in this present life, with spiritual oil – that is to say, with the energy of the

Spirit active in the virtues of which we have spoken – they were called fools and were abjectly excluded from the royal bridechamber, not enjoying any reward for their efforts to preserve their virginity (cf. Matt. 25 : 1–13). When we cultivate a vineyard, the whole of our attention and labour is given in the expectation of the vintage; if there is no vintage, all our work is to no purpose. Similarly, if through the activity of the Spirit we do not perceive within ourselves the fruits of love, peace, joy and the other qualities mentioned by St Paul (cf. Gal. 5 : 22), and cannot affirm this with all assurance and spiritual awareness, then our labour for the sake of virginity, prayer, psalmody, fasting and vigil is useless. For, as we said, our labours and hardships of soul and body should be undertaken in expectation of the spiritual harvest; and where the virtues are concerned, the harvest consists of spiritual enjoyment and incorruptible pleasure secretly made active by the Spirit in faithful and humble hearts. Thus the labours and hardships must be regarded as labours and hardships and the fruits as fruits. Should someone through lack of spiritual knowledge think that his work and hardship are fruits of the Spirit, he should realize that he is deluding himself, and in this way depriving himself of the truly great fruits of the Spirit.

23. The person who has surrendered himself entirely to sin indulges with enjoyment and pleasure in unnatural and shameful passions – licentiousness, unchastity, greed, hatred, guile and other forms of vice – as though they were natural. The genuine and perfected Christian, on the other hand, with great enjoyment and spiritual pleasure participates effortlessly and without impediment in all the virtues and all the supranatural fruits of the Spirit – love, peace, patient endurance, faith, humility and the entire truly golden galaxy of virtue – as though they were natural. He does not fight any longer against the passions of evil, for he has been totally set free of them by the Lord; while from the blessed Spirit he has received Christ's perfect peace and joy in his heart. Of such a man it may be said that he cleaves to the Lord and has become one spirit with Him (cf. 1 Cor. 6 : 17).

24. Those who because of their spiritual immaturity cannot yet commit themselves entirely to the work of prayer should undertake to serve the brethren with reverence, faith and devout fear. They should do this because they regard such service as a divine commandment and a spiritual task; they should not expect reward,

honour or thanks from men, and they should shun all complaint, haughtiness, negligence or sluggishness. In this way they will not soil and corrupt this blessed work, but through their reverence, fear and joy will make it acceptable to God.

25. The Lord descended to the human level with such love, goodness and divine compassion for us, that He took it upon Himself not to overlook the reward of any good work, but to lead us step by step from the small to the great virtues, so that not even a cup of cold water should go unrequited. For He said: 'If anyone gives even a cup of cold water to someone simply in the name of a disciple, I tell you truly that he will not go unrewarded' (cf. Matt. 10 : 42); and elsewhere: 'Whatever you did to one of these, you did to Me' (cf. Matt. 25 : 40). Only the action must be done in the name of God, not for the sake of receiving honour from men: the Lord said, 'simply in the name of a disciple', that is to say, in the fear and love of Christ. Those who do good with ostentation are rebuked categorically by the Lord: 'I tell you truly, they have received their reward' (Matt. 6 : 2).

26. Simplicity before others, guilelessness, mutual love, joy and humility of every kind, must be laid down as the foundation of the community. Otherwise, disparaging others or grumbling about them, we make our labour profitless. He who persists ceaselessly in prayer must not disparage the man incapable of doing this, nor must the man who devotes himself to serving the needs of the community complain about those who are dedicated to prayer. For if both the prayers and the service are offered in a spirit of simplicity and love for others, the superabundance of those dedicated to prayer will make up for the insufficiency of those who serve, and *vice versa*. In this way the equality that St Paul commends is maintained (cf. 2 Cor. 8 : 14): he who has much does not have to excess and he who has little has no lack (cf. Exod. 16 : 18).

27. God's will is done on earth as in heaven when, in the way indicated, we do not disparage one another, and when not only are we without jealousy but we are united one to another in simplicity and in mutual love, peace and joy, and regard our brother's progress as our own and his failure as our loss.

28. He who is sluggish in prayer, and slothful and negligent in serving his brethren and in performing other holy tasks, is explicitly called an idler by the apostle, and condemned as unworthy even of his bread. For St Paul writes that the idler is not to have any food (cf. 2

Thess. 3 : 10); and elsewhere it is said that God hates idlers, that the idle man cannot be trusted, and that idleness has taught great evil (cf. Ecclus. 33 : 27). Thus each of us should bear the fruit of some action performed in God's name, even if he has employed himself diligently in but one good work. Otherwise he will be totally barren, and without any share in eternal blessings.

29. When people say that it is impossible to attain perfection, to be once and for all free from the passions, or to participate fully in the Holy Spirit, we should cite Holy Scripture against them, showing them that they are ignorant and speak falsely and dangerously. For the Lord said: 'Become perfect, as your heavenly Father is perfect' (Matt. 5 : 48), perfection denoting total purity; and: 'I desire these men to be with Me wherever I am, so that they may see My glory' (John 17 : 24). He also said: 'Heaven and earth will pass away, but My words will not pass away' (Matt. 24 : 35). And St Paul is saying the same as Christ when he writes: '. . . so that we may present every man perfect in Christ' (Col. 1 : 28); and: '. . . until we all attain to the unity of the faith and of the knowledge of the Son of God, to a perfect man, to the measure of the stature of the fulness of Christ' (Eph. 4 : 13). Thus by aspiring to perfection two of the best things come about, provided we struggle diligently and unceasingly: we seek to attain this perfect measure and growth; and we are not conquered by vanity, but look upon ourselves as petty and mean because we have not yet reached our goal.

30. Those who deny the possibility of perfection inflict the greatest damage on the soul in three ways. First, they manifestly disbelieve the inspired Scriptures. Then, because they do not make the greatest and fullest goal of Christianity their own, and so do not aspire to attain it, they can have no longing and diligence, no hunger and thirst for righteousness (cf. Matt. 5 : 6); on the contrary, content with outward show and behaviour and with minor accomplishments of this kind, they abandon that blessed expectation together with the pursuit of perfection and of the total purification of the passions. Third, thinking they have reached the goal when they have acquired a few virtues, and not pressing on to the true goal, not only are they incapable of having any humility, poverty and contrition of heart but, justifying themselves on the grounds that they have already arrived, they make no efforts to progress and grow day by day.

31. People who think it is impossible to attain through the Spirit

the 'new creation' of the pure heart (cf. 2 Cor. 5 : 17) are rightly and explicitly likened by the apostle to those who, because of their unbelief, were found unworthy of entering the promised land and whose bodies on that account 'were left lying in the desert' (Heb. 3 : 17). What is here outwardly described as the promised land signifies inwardly that deliverance from the passions which the apostle regards as the goal of every commandment. This is the true promised land, and for its sake these figurative teachings have been handed down. In order to protect his disciples from yielding to unbelief the apostle says to them: 'Make sure, my brethren, that no one among you has an evil heart of unbelief, turning away from the living God' (Heb. 3 : 12). By 'turning away' he means not the denial of God but disbelief in His promises. Interpreting the events of Jewish history allegorically and indicating their true meaning, he says: 'For some, when they heard, were rebellious, though not all of those who were brought out of Egypt by Moses. And with whom was God angry for forty years? Was it not with those who had sinned, whose bodies were left lying in the desert? And to whom did He vow that they would not enter into His rest unless it was to those who refused to believe? We see, then, that it was because of their unbelief that they could not enter' (Heb. 3 : 16–19). And he continues: 'Let us be fearful, then: although the promise of entering into His rest still holds good, some of you may be excluded from it. For we have heard the divine message, as they did; but the message that they heard did not profit them, since it was not accompanied by faith on their part. We, however, who have faith do enter into God's rest' (Heb. 4 : 1–3). Shortly after this he draws the same conclusion: 'Let us strive therefore to enter into that rest, so that no one may fall through copying this example of unbelief' (Heb. 4 : 11). For Christians what true rest is there other than deliverance from the sinful passions and the fullest active indwelling of the Holy Spirit in the purified heart? And the apostle again impels his readers towards this by referring to faith: 'Let us then draw near with a true heart and in the full assurance of faith, our hearts cleansed of an evil conscience' (Heb. 10 : 22). And again: 'How much more will the blood of Jesus purge our conscience of dead works, so that we may serve the living and true God' (cf. Heb. 9 : 14). Because of the measureless blessings promised by God to men in these words, we should dedicate ourselves as grateful servants and regard what is promised as true and certain. In this way, even if through sluggishness or debility of resolution we do not give ourselves once for all to our Maker, or if we do not strive to achieve the greatest and most perfect measure of virtue, none the less through an upright and undistorted will and a sound faith we may attain some degree of mercy.

32. Prayer rightly combined with understanding is superior to every virtue and commandment. The Lord Himself testifies to this. For in the house of Martha and Mary He contrasted Martha, who was engaged in looking after Him, with Mary, who sat at His feet joyfully drinking the ambrosia of His divine words. When Martha complained and appealed to Christ, He made clear to her what takes precedence, saying: 'Martha, Martha, you are anxious and troubled about many things; one thing alone is needful: Mary has chosen what is best, and it cannot be taken away from her' (Luke 10 : 41–42). He said this not in order to disparage acts of service, but so as to distinguish clearly what is higher from what is lower. For how could He not give His sanction to service when He Himself performed such service in washing His disciples' feet, and was so far from discountenancing it that He bade His disciples to behave in the same way towards each other (cf. John 13 : 4–16)? Moreover, the apostles themselves, when they were oppressed by serving at table, also singled out prayer and under-standing as the higher form of work. 'It is not right', they said, 'for us to abandon the word of God in order to serve at table. Let us appoint chosen men, full of the Holy Spirit, for this service; we will devote ourselves to the ministry of the Logos and to prayer' (cf. Acts 6 : 2–4). In this way they put first things before secondary things, although they recognized that both spring from the same blessed root.

III

Patient Endurance and Discrimination

33. The signs that accompany those who wish to submit to the Logos of God and who bring forth good fruit are: sighing, weeping, sorrow, stillness, shaking of the head, prayer, silence, persistence, bitter grief, tribulation of heart arising from religious devotion. In addition, their actions manifest vigilance, fasting, self-control, gentleness, forbearance, unceasing prayer, study of the divine Scriptures, faith, humility, brotherly affection, submission, rigorous toil, hardship, love, kindliness, courtesy and – the sum of all – light, which is the Lord. The signs that accompany those who are not producing the fruit of life are listlessness, day-dreaming, curiosity, lack of attention, grumbling, instability; and in their actions they manifest gluttony, anger, wrath, back-biting, conceit, untimely talk, unbelief, disorderliness, forgetfulness, unrest, sordid greed, avarice, envy, factiousness, contempt, garrulity, senseless laughter, wilfulness and – the sum of all – darkness, which is Satan.

34. In accordance with divine providence, the devil was not sent at once to the Gehenna assigned to him, but his sentence was postponed in order to let him test and try men's free will. In this way, he unintentionally fosters greater maturity and righteousness in the saints by promoting their patient endurance, and so is the cause of their greater glory; and, at the same time, through his malevolence and his scheming against the saints he justifies more fully his own punishment. In this way, too, sin becomes more utterly sinful, as St Paul puts it (cf. Rom. 7 : 13).

35. By deceiving Adam and in this way gaining mastery over him, the devil deprived him of his authority and proclaimed himself lord of this world. For in the beginning God appointed man to be the lord of this world and the master of visible things (cf. Gen. 1 : 26). On this account, fire had no power over him, water did not drown him, no animal injured him, poisonous snakes had no effect on him. But once he

had been deceived, he surrendered his lordship to his deceiver. For this reason sorcerers and magicians, through the use of diabolic energy, become with God's permission miracle-workers: they have power over poisonous snakes and they challenge fire and water, as was exemplified by the followers of Jannes and Jambres who opposed Moses (cf. Exod. chs. 7–8; 2 Tim. 3 : 8), and by the Simon who resisted the chief apostle, Peter (cf. Acts 8 : 18–24).

36. When the devil beheld Adam's original glory shining from the face of Moses (cf. Exod. 34 : 30–31), he was cut to the quick since he saw in this a sign of the coming destruction of his kingdom. St Paul's words, 'Death held sway from Adam to Moses, even over those who had not sinned' (Rom. 5 : 14), may be taken to refer to this. In my opinion the glorified face of Moses preserved the type and example of the first man created by the hands of God. It is for this reason that when death – that is to say, the devil, who is the cause of death – saw it, he then guessed that his kingdom would fall, as in fact happened with the advent of the Lord. Genuine Christians are therefore encompassed by this glory even in this present life; and inwardly they have annulled death, that is to say, the shameful passions, which cannot operate within them, since the glory of the Holy Spirit shines fully and consciously in their souls. In the resurrection, moreover, death is totally abolished.

37. When, using the woman as his accomplice, the devil deceived Adam, he divested him of the glory that enveloped him. Thus Adam found himself naked and perceived his disfigurement, of which he had been unaware until that moment since he had delighted his mind with celestial beauty. After his transgression, on the other hand, his thoughts became base and material, and the simplicity and goodness of his mind were intertwined with evil worldly concerns. The closing of paradise, and the placing of the cherubim with the burning sword to prevent his entrance (cf. Gen. 3 : 24), must be regarded as actual events; but they are also realities encountered inwardly by each soul. A veil of darkness – the fire of the worldly spirit – surrounds the heart, preventing the intellect from communing with God, and the soul from praying, believing and loving the Lord as it desires to do. All these things may be learnt from experience by those who truly entrust themselves to the Lord, persist in prayer, and fight zealously against the enemy.

38. The lord of this world is a rod of chastisement and a scourge to

beginners in the spiritual life. Yet, as has been said, he brings them great glory and added honour because of the afflictions and trials they endure. In this way he helps them to attain the state of perfection, while he prepares even greater and harsher punishment for himself. In short, something most beneficial is broght about through him: as has been said, evil, while intending what is not good, contributes to the good. For, in souls whose intention is sound, even that which appears harmful results in something good. As St Paul says: 'All things work together for good to them that love God' (Rom. 8 : 28).

39. It is on this account that the rod of chastisement was permitted, so that through it, as in a furnace, the vessels might be more rigorously fired; but those unequal to the test, being easily broken, are rejected as faulty, since they cannot endure the heat of the fire. Being a servant and the Lord's creation, the devil tests and afflicts people, not as he thinks fit or desires, but to the extent that his Master allows him. Knowing the exact nature of everything, God permits each person to be tested according to his strength. As St Paul puts it: 'God is to be trusted not to let you be tried beyond your strength, but with the trial He will provide a way out, so that you are able to bear it' (1 Cor. 10 : 13).

40. As the Lord affirms, the person who seeks and knocks and who never gives up asking will attain what he asks for (cf. Matt. 7 : 8). Only he must have the courage to entreat continually with intellect and tongue, and to cleave to God relentlessly with bodily worship; and he must not entangle himself in worldly things or indulge in evil passions. He who said, 'Whatever you ask for in prayer, believing, you will receive' (Matt. 21 : 22), is not a liar. Those who say that even if you fulfil all the commandments in the hope of attaining grace in this present life, you will gain nothing, are ignorant and what they say is wrong and contrary to divine Scripture. There is no injustice in God that would make Him fail to fulfil His obligations if we fulfil ours. Only you must see to it that when the time comes for your soul to leave your hapless body you are still engaged in spiritual struggle, pressing on, awaiting the promise, persevering, trusting, seeking with discrimination. Do not disbelieve me when I say that you will go forth joyfully, with confidence, and you will be found worthy to see the kingdom of God. Indeed, if your soul is refined through your faith and ardour, you are already in communion with God. The person who looks lustfully at a woman has already committed adultery with her in his heart (cf. Matt. 5 : 28), and even if he has not sullied his body is regarded as already

guilty of adultery. Similarly, the person who expels evil from his heart and who cleaves to God with longing, supplication, diligence and love, already enjoys communion with God, and has even now received from God this great gift, that he can persist in prayer diligently and devotedly. If the giving of a cup of cold water does not go unrewarded (cf. Matt. 10 : 42), how much more will God give what He has promised to those who devote themselves to Him night and day?

41. Those who are troubled by what will happen to them if one day they find themselves full of hatred for their brother, or realize that involuntarily they are in the grip of some other evil passion, should be told that they need to struggle without intermission against the devil and evil thoughts. For where the darkness of the passions and death – that is to say, the will of the flesh – hold sway, it is impossible for some evil fruit not to manifest itself, visibly or invisibly. A bodily wound, even if it only discharges slightly, exudes moisture and festers or is puffy and swells up, until it is totally healed. This is so even when it is being treated and when no remedy is wittingly omitted. But if the festering is neglected it can lead to the corruption of the whole body. In a similar way the soul's passions, even if they receive great attention, will go on smouldering within the soul until with steadfast diligence they are finally cured through the grace and co-operation of Christ. For there is a certain hidden pollution and a strange darkness of the passions that, in spite of man's pure nature, have insinuated themselves into the whole of humanity as a result of Adam's transgression; and they obscure and defile both body and soul. But just as iron when fired and struck is purified, or gold mixed with copper or iron is separated out by fire, so through the most pure Passion of the Saviour the soul, fired and struck by the Holy Spirit, is cleansed of every passion and of every sin.

42. Just as many lamps may be lit from the same oil and from a single light, and yet often do not give out an equal radiance, so the gifts that come from different virtues reflect the light of the Holy Spirit in different ways. Or as the many inhabitants of a single city all use bread and water, though some of them are men, some infants, some children, some old people, and there is a great variety and difference among them; or as wheat sown in the same field may bear dissimilar ears of corn, though they are all brought to the same threshing-floor and stored in the same barn: so it seems to me that in the resurrection of the dead different degrees of glory will be distinguished and recognized among those who are resurrected, depending on the level of virtue they

have attained and the extent of their participation during this present life in the Holy Spirit that already dwells within them. This is the significance of the phrase, 'Star differs from star in glory' (1 Cor. 15 : 41).

43. Even if some stars are smaller than others, they all shine with a single light. The image is quite clear; but let us give attention to one thing only: after being born in the Holy Spirit, to wash away our indwelling sin. Once this birth through the Holy Spirit has taken place, it means that an image of perfection is active within us in an initial form, though it is not yet expressed in terms of power, intellect or courage. Whoever has attained the full measure of mature manhood naturally lays aside childish things (cf. 1 Cor. 13 : 11). That is why St Paul says that speaking in tongues and prophecies will come to an end (cf. 1 Cor. 13 : 8). Just as an adult does not eat foods or use words fitting for a child, but scorns them as unworthy of him, since he has entered another stage of life, so the person who approaches perfection in the evangelic virtues ceases to be an infant with respect to that perfection. To quote St Paul again, 'When I grew up I finished with childish things' (1 Cor. 13 : 11).

44. The person who is born in the Spirit is in a certain manner perfect, just as we call an infant perfect when all his limbs are sound. But the Lord has not bestowed the grace of the Spirit so that one may fall into sin. Men are themselves the cause of the evils into which they fall: not living in accordance with grace they are taken captive by evil. Man can lapse through his own natural thoughts if he is negligent or inattentive or presumptuous. St Paul himself says: 'To stop me from growing unduly elated I was given a thorn in the flesh, the messenger of Satan' (2 Cor. 12 : 7). You see how even those who have attained such great heights as St Paul stand in need of protection. Yet if man did not give the devil the opportunity he would not be forcibly dominated by him. Because of this, his actions are not to be imputed either to Christ or to the devil. But if finally he submits to the grace of the Spirit, he is on the side of Christ. If this is not the case, even though he is born in the Spirit – that is to say, even though he participates in the Holy Spirit – yet because of his actions he follows the will of Satan. For if it were the Lord or Satan who had forcibly seized hold of him, then he himself would not be the cause of his falling into hell or of his attaining God's kingdom.

45. He who follows the spiritual path must pay great attention to

discrimination, since the ability to distinguish between good and evil, and to scrutinize and understand the various tricks through which the devil by means of plausible fantasies leads most people astray, keeps us safe and helps us in every way. If a man wanting to test his wife's virtue comes to her at night disguised as someone else, and she repels him, he will rejoice at this and welcome the assurance it gives. It is exactly the same with us in relation to the attacks of the evil spirits. Even if you repel the heavenly spirits, they will be gladdened by this, and will help you to participate still further in grace: because of this proof of your love for the Lord they will fill you brim-full with spiritual delight. So do not from light-mindedness speedily surrender yourself to the visitations of spirits, even if they are heavenly angels, but be wary, submitting them to the most careful scrutiny. Thus you will welcome the good and repel the evil. In this way you will increase in yourself the workings of grace, which sin, however much it may assume the appearance of the good, cannot altogether simulate. According to St Paul, Satan can even change himself into an angel of light in order to practise his deceptions (cf. 2 Cor. 11. : 14); yet though he may manifest himself in such a glorious manner, he cannot, as we said, produce within us the effects of grace, and so it becomes quite clear that the vision is counterfeit. For the devil cannot bring about love either for God or for one's neighbour, or gentleness, or humility, or joy, or peace, or equilibrium in one's thoughts, or hatred of the world, or spiritual repose, or desire for celestial things; nor can he quell passions and sensual pleasure. These things are clearly the workings of grace. For the fruits of the Spirit are love, joy, peace, and so on (cf. Gal. 5 : 22), while the devil is most apt and powerful in promoting vanity and haughtiness. You may know from its effect whether the intellectual light shining in your soul is from God or from Satan. Indeed, once it has developed its powers of discrimination, the distinction is immediately clear to the soul itself through intellectual perception. Just as the throat through its sense of taste distinguishes the difference between vinegar and wine, although they look alike, so the soul through its intellectual sense and energy can distinguish the gifts of the Spirit from the fantasies of the devil.

46. The soul must watch and anticipate carefully so that it is not even for the twinkling of an eye taken captive by the devil's power. Even if only one part of an animal is caught in a trap, the whole animal is held fast and falls into the hands of the hunters; and the same thing is

liable to happen to the soul at the hands of its enemies. The psalmist makes this quite clear when he says: 'They prepared a trap for my feet and bowed down my soul' (Ps. 57 : 6. LXX).

47. He who wants to enter the strong man's house through the narrow gate and to make off with his goods (cf. Matt. 7 : 14; 12 : 29) must not surrender to luxury and obesity, but must strengthen himself in the Holy Spirit, having in mind the phrase, 'Flesh and blood cannot inherit the kingdom of God' (1 Cor. 15 : 50). But how should he strengthen himself in the Spirit? Here he should heed the words of St Paul, that God's wisdom is regarded as foolishness by men (cf. 1 Cor. 1 : 23), as well as those of Isaiah, that he had seen the son of man, and His form was despised, and He was forsaken by all the sons of men (cf. Isa. 53 : 3). Thus he who wants to be a son of God must first humble himself in the same way and be regarded as foolish and despicable, not turning his face aside when spat upon (cf. Isa. 50 : 6), not pursuing the glory and beauty of this world or anything of this kind, not having anywhere to lay his head (cf. Matt. 8 : 20), vilified, mocked, downtrodden, regarded by all as an object of contempt, attacked invisibly and visibly, yet resisting in his mind. It is then that the Son of God, who said, 'I will dwell and walk among you' (cf. Lev. 26 : 12), will become manifest in his heart, and he will receive power and strength so that he can tie the strong man up and make off with his goods (cf. Matt. 12 : 29), and tread upon asp and basilisk (cf. Ps. 91 : 13. LXX), snakes and scorpions (cf. Luke 10 : 19).

48. No little struggle is required of us to break through death. Christ says: 'The kingdom of God is within you' (Luke 17 : 21); but he who fights against us and takes us captive also finds some way of being within us. The soul, therefore, must not rest until it has killed him who takes it prisoner. Then all pain, sorrow and sighing will flee away (cf. Isa. 35 : 10), because water has sprung up in thirsty earth (cf. Isa. 43 : 20) and the desert has become full of waters (cf. Isa. 41 : 18). For He has promised to fill the barren heart with living water, speaking first through the prophet Isaiah, saying: 'I will give water to those who are thirsty and who walk through dry land' (Isa. 44 : 3. LXX); and then through Himself, with the words: 'Whoever drinks of the water that I will give him will never thirst again' (John 4 : 14).

49. The soul overcome by listlessness is manifestly also possessed by lack of faith. It is on account of this that it lets day after day go by without heeding the Gospels. Not paying attention to the inner

warfare, it is taken captive by conceit and frequently elated by dreams. Conceit blinds the soul, not letting it perceive its own weakness.

50. As the new-born child is the image of the full-grown man, so the soul is in a certain sense the image of God who created it. The child, on growing up, begins gradually to recognize its father, and when it reaches maturity, they dispose things mutually and equally, father with son and son with father, and the father's wealth is disclosed to the son. Something similar should have happened to the soul. Before the fall, the soul was to have progressed and so to have attained full manhood (cf. Eph. 4 : 13). But through the fall it was plunged into a sea of forgetfulness, into an abyss of delusion, and dwelt within the gates of hell. As if separated from God by a great distance, it could not draw near to its Creator and recognize Him properly. But first through the prophets God called it back, and drew it to knowledge of Himself. Finally, through His own advent on earth, He dispelled the forgetfulness, the delusion; then, breaking through the gates of hell, He entered the deluded soul, giving Himself to it as a model. By means of this model the soul can grow to maturity and attain the perfection of the Spirit. It is therefore for our sakes that the Logos of God is by divine permission tempted by the devil, and then endures vilifications, mockeries, beatings at the hands of savage men, and finally death on the Cross, showing us, as we said, what attitude we must take up towards those who vilify and mock us and bring us to our death. Thus we become as though deaf and dumb before them, not opening our mouth, so that clearly perceiving the subtlety and energy of evil, and as though nailed to the cross, we may call loudly to Him who can deliver us from death (cf. Heb. 5 : 7) and cleanse us from our secret faults (cf. Ps. 19 : 12); for 'if they do not have dominion over me, then I shall be faultless' (Ps. 19 : 13). When we are faultless we find Him 'who has brought all things into subjection' (Ps. 8 : 6), and we reign and enjoy repose with Christ. Overpowered through the fall by material and unclean thoughts, the soul became as though witless. As a result, no small effort is needed for it to rise out of materiality and to grasp the subtlety of evil, so that it can commingle with unoriginate Intellect.

51. If you want to return to yourself and to recover your original glory, which you lost through your disobedience, heedlessly paying more attention to the orders and counsel of the devil than to the commandments of God, then you must now have done with him whom you obeyed and turn towards the Lord. But you must know that only

after much labour and sweat of the brow will you recover your richness. Nor is it to your advantage to attain this blessed state without suffering and great effort, for if you do you will lose what you have received and betray your inheritance to the enemy. Let us each realize, then, what we have lost and repeat the lamentation of the prophet: 'Our inheritance is despoiled by strangers and our house by aliens' (Lam. 5 : 2), because we disobeyed the commandment and surrendered ourselves to our own desires, delighting in sordid and worldly thoughts. Then our soul was far away from God and we were like fatherless orphans. Thus, if we are concerned for our own soul we must make every effort to purge away evil thoughts and 'all the self-esteem that exalts itself against the knowledge of God' (2 Cor. 10 : 5). And when we have forcibly applied ourselves to keeping God's temple spotless, then He who promised to make His dwelling in it will come to us. Then the soul recovers its inheritance and is privileged to become a temple of God. For, after thus Himself expelling the devil and his army, from henceforth He reigns within us.

52. What the Creator outwardly said to Cain, that he would wander over the earth lamenting and trembling (cf. Gen. 4 : 12. LXX), is in its inner meaning a figure and image of all sinners. For the race of Adam, having broken the commandment and become guilty of sin, is shaken by restless thoughts, full of fear, cowardice and turmoil. Every soul not reborn in God is tossed hither and thither by the desires and multifarious pleasures of the enemy, and whirled about like corn in a sieve. To show that those who act in accordance with the desires of the devil bear in themselves the image of Cain's iniquity, the Lord Himself said: 'You seek to carry out the desires of your father, the murderer. He was a murderer from the first and is not rooted in the truth' (cf. John 8 : 44).

53. It is significant how deeply attracted men are by the spectacle of an earthly king and how eagerly they seek after it; and how everyone who lives in a city where the king has his residence longs to catch a glimpse simply of the extravagance and ostentation of his *entourage*. Only under the influence of spiritual things will they disregard all this and look down on it, wounded by another beauty and desiring a different kind of glory. If the sight of a mortal king is so important to worldly people, how much more desirable must the sight of the immortal king be to those into whom some drops of the Holy Spirit have fallen and whose hearts have been smitten by divine love? For this

they will relinquish all amity with the world, so that they may keep that longing continually in their hearts, preferring nothing to it. But few indeed there are who add to a good beginning an equivalent end and who endure without stumbling until they reach it. Many are moved to repentance and many become partakers of heavenly grace and are wounded by divine love; but, unable to bear the ensuing tribulations and the wily and versatile assaults of the devil, they submit to the world and are submerged in its depths through the flabbiness and debility of their will, or are taken captive by some attachment to worldly things. Those who wish to pursue the way with assurance to the end will not permit any other longing or love to intermingle with their divine love.

54. Just as the blessings promised by God are unutterably great, so their acquisition requires much hardship and toil undertaken with hope and faith. This is clear from Christ's words: 'If any man will come after Me, let him deny himself, take up his cross, and follow Me' (Matt. 16 : 24); and: 'He who does not hate father and mother, brothers and sisters, wife and children, and even his own soul, cannot be a disciple of Mine' (Luke 14 : 26). Most people are so lacking in intelligence as to want to attain the great and inconceivable blessing of the kingdom of God, and to inherit eternal life and reign for ever with Christ, while living according to their own desires – or rather, according to him who sows within them these clearly noxious vanities.

55. Those who reach the goal without falling do so through hating themselves and all worldly desires, distractions, pleasures and pre-occupations, for this is what 'denying oneself' amounts to. Hence everyone expels himself from the kingdom by his own choice, through not embracing suffering and denying himself for the sake of the truth, but wanting to enjoy something of this world in addition to that divine longing, and not surrendering the whole inclination of his will to God. This may be understood from a single example. On examining himself a man realizes that what he is so eager to do is wicked. At first he feels doubt about it in his heart. Next, the measure and balance in his conscience make it clear inwardly whether the bias inclines to love for God or love for the world; and after that he proceeds to outward action. If for instance someone happens to have fallen out with his brother, then he examines himself, as we have said. At first he finds himself hesitant about whether to speak or not to speak, whether to return the insults hurled at him or to keep silent. At this point the man still remembers God's commandments, but he also thinks about his

own reputation and has not fully chosen to deny himself. If a bias in favour of the world tips his heart's balance even slightly, an evil word will at once be on the tip of his tongue. When this happens, with the intellect stretched inwardly like a bow he attacks his neighbour with his tongue and even with his hands – indeed, the evil can proceed so far that wounds result, or even murder. Thus it is possible to compare the starting-point of the slight movement in his soul with the terrible consequences to which it led. In this way every sin and malpractice, whether adultery, theft, greed, self-esteem or anything else, occurs when the will of the soul is beguiled and coaxed to evil by worldly desires and pleasures of the flesh.

56. Even good actions are frequently carried out for the sake of empty glory, and on this account they will be judged by God in the same way as theft, injustice and other major sins. 'God has scattered the bones of those who seek to please men', it is said (Ps. 53 : 5. LXX). The devil, being wily, versatile, tortuous and inventive, seeks to gain our allegiance and service even through our good actions.

57. Whenever anyone loves something belonging to this world, it will burden his mind, dragging it down and not allowing it to rise up. In such people the weight, bias and balance of the will, that is, of the heart, are inclined to what is evil. It is in this way that torment and trial afflict the whole human race, whether they are Christians living in cities or on mountains, in monasteries, in the country or the desert. For if one is willingly enticed by what one loves it is clear that one has not yet dedicated all one's love to God. Whether one likes possessions, or gold, or serving one's stomach, or indulging in fleshly desires, or wordy wisdom designed to gain men's praise, or authority, or honours from men, or anger and wrath, or useless speeches, or merely day-dreaming and listening to idle words, or acting as a teacher for the sake of men's esteem – in each and every case to give oneself to a passion is manifestly to love it. One person surrenders himself to sluggishness and negligence, another delights in extravagant clothes, another in sleep, another in silly jokes: whatever the worldly thing, big or small, by which one is bound and held fast, it prevents one from raising oneself up. Clearly, we indulge ourselves in whatever passion we do not resist and fight against bravely: like some shackle it binds us and drags us down, degrading the mind so that it does not dedicate itself to God and worship Him alone. The soul that truly directs its desire towards the

Lord focuses all its longing on Him, denying itself and not following the desires of its own intellect.

58. Example makes it clear that man is destroyed by his own free choice: for out of love for some worldly thing he throws himself into fire, is drowned in the sea and gives himself into captivity. Let us suppose that someone's house or field has caught fire. The person who wanted to save himself fled without anything as soon as he noticed the fire, leaving everything in it and concerned only with his own life. But someone else thought he would take some of the goods with him, so he stayed behind to collect them; and as he was taking them the fire, which had already overwhelmed the house, caught him as well and burnt him. In this way, through his attachment to some transient thing, he was destroyed in the fire by his own free choice. Again, two men were shipwrecked. One of them, wanting to save himself, stripped off his clothes and threw himself into the water; and in this way he was able to save his life. The other, wanting to save his clothes as well, was drowned, destroying himself for the sake of a slight gain. Or again, let us suppose that news of an attack by an enemy was announced. One man, as soon as he heard the news, fled as fast as his feet would carry him, without a thought for his possessions. Another, either because he distrusted the news, or because he wanted to take with him some of his goods, waited until later, and when the enemy arrived he was caught. Thus, through his lack of alertness and his attachment to worldly things, he lost body and soul by his own free choice.

59. Few are those who really acquire perfect love for God, looking upon all worldly pleasures and desires as nothing and patiently enduring the devil's trials. But one must not despair on this account, or give up hope. Even if many ships suffer shipwreck there are always those that come safely through to port. For this reason we need great faith, endurance, attentiveness, struggle, hunger and thirst for what is right, as well as great understanding and discrimination, together with clear-sightedness and lack of shame in making our requests. As we have said, most men want to attain the kingdom without toil and sweat; and although they praise the saints and desire their dignity and gifts, they are not willing to share with them in the same afflictions, hardships and sufferings. Everyone – prostitutes, tax-collectors and everyone else – wants this. For this reason, trials and temptations are set before us, so as to make it clear who in truth loves their Lord and deserves to attain the kingdom of heaven.

60. In afflictions and sufferings, endurance and faith, are concealed the promised glory and the recovery of celestial blessings. Even the grain of corn sown in the earth, or the graft on a tree, has to go through a kind of putrefaction and, so to say, humiliation before it clothes itself in its full glory and produces a rich crop. But for this putrefaction and, as it were, dishonouring, neither would attain its final glory and beauty. This is confirmed by the apostles when they say that to enter the kingdom of God we have to pass through many afflictions (cf. Acts 14 : 22). And the Lord Himself says: 'You will gain possession of your souls through your patient endurance' (Luke 21 : 19); and: 'In the world you will experience affliction' (John 16 : 33).

61. If through faith and effort we are enabled to become partakers of the Holy Spirit, then to a corresponding degree our bodies also will be glorified on the last day. For what is now treasured up within the soul will then be revealed outwardly in the body. Trees provide an illustration of this: once winter is past and the sun shines more brightly and fully and the winds blow benignly, they put forth buds from within and clothe themselves in leaves, flowers and fruits. Similarly, in springtime flowering plants shoot up from the breast of the earth so that the ground is covered with them, wearing them as though they were a beautiful dress; as Christ says: 'Even Solomon in all his glory was not arrayed like one of these' (Matt. 6 : 29). All these are types and examples and images of the reward that the redeemed will receive at the resurrection; for to all devout souls – that is to say, to all true Christians – it is in the first month, which is April, that the power of the resurrection is revealed. In the words of Holy Scripture, 'This month . . . will be to you the first among the months of the year' (Exod. 12 : 2). This month will clothe the naked trees with the glory previously hidden within them. And so, too, will the bodies of the righteous be glorified through the ineffable light – the power of the Spirit – that is already present within them; and this will be to them clothing, food, drink, exultation, joy, peace and, crowning all, life eternal.

IV
The Raising of the Intellect

62. Through the glory of the Spirit that shone from his face in such a way that no one could look at it (cf. Exod. 34 : 30–31), Moses showed how in the resurrection of the righteous their bodies will be glorified with the glory that their souls already possess inwardly during this present life. For, as St Paul says, 'with unveiled face' – that is to say, inwardly – 'we reflect as in a mirror the glory of the Lord, and are transfigured into the same image from glory to glory' (2 Cor. 3 : 18). In this connection, too, it is said that Moses did not eat or drink for forty days and forty nights (cf. Exod. 34 : 28), something that human nature cannot accomplish unless nourished by spiritual food. Such is the food that the souls of the saints already during this present life receive from the Spirit.

63. The glory that in the present life enriches the souls of the saints will cover and enfold their naked bodies at the resurrection and will carry them to heaven. Then with body and soul the saints will rest with God in the kingdom for ever. For God, when He created Adam, did not give him bodily wings, as He gave to the birds: His purpose was to confer the wings of the Spirit on him at the resurrection, so that he might be lifted up by them and carried wherever the Spirit desired. Such spiritual wings are given to the souls of the saints in this present life, so that their understanding may be raised by them to the spiritual realm. For the world of the Christians is a different world, with different garments, different food and a different form of enjoyment. We know that when Christ comes from heaven to resurrect all those who have died during the present age, He will divide them into two groups (cf. Matt. 25 : 31–33). Those who bear His sign, which is the seal of the Holy Spirit, He will set at His right hand, saying: 'My sheep, when they hear My voice, recognize Me' (cf. John 10 : 14). Then He will envelop their bodies with the divine glory that, through their good works and the Spirit,

their souls have already received in the present life. Thus glorified by the divine light and caught up into the heavens to meet the Lord, they will always be with Him (cf. 1 Thess. 4 : 17–18).

64. Those who intend to fulfil the Christian way of life to the best of their ability must first devote all their attention to the rational, discriminative and directing aspect of the soul. Perfecting in this way their discrimination between good and evil, and defending the purity of their nature against the attacks of the passions that are contrary to nature, they go forward without stumbling, guided by the eye of discrimination and not embroiled with the impulses of evil. For the soul's will is able to preserve the body free from the vitiation of the senses, to keep the soul away from worldly distraction, and to guard the heart from scattering its thoughts into the world, completely walling them in and holding them back from base concerns and pleasures. Whenever the Lord sees someone acting in this manner, perfecting and guarding himself, disposed to serve Him with fear and trembling, He extends to him the assistance of His grace. But what will God do for the person who willingly gives himself up to the world and pursues its pleasures?

65. The five watchful virgins who bore in the vessels of their hearts the oil that was not inherent in their nature – for it is the grace of the Holy Spirit – were able to enter with the bridegroom into the bridal-chamber. But the other foolish and sinful virgins, who remained fixed in their own nature, did not practise watchfulness, nor did they think it important to receive this oil of joyfulness in their hearts, for they still walked according to the flesh. On the contrary, in their negligence, slothfulness and self-righteousness, they were as though asleep, and for this reason they were shut out from the bridal-chamber of the kingdom (cf. Matt. 25 : 1–13). It is clear that they were held back by some kind of bond and amity with the world, inasmuch as they could not offer all their love and longing to the celestial bridegroom. For souls aspiring to acquire the sanctifying power of the Spirit that is not intrinsic to human nature direct all their love towards Christ: they walk, pray, think and meditate in Christ, and they turn away from everything else. And if the soul's five senses – understanding, spiritual knowledge, discrimination, patient endurance and compassion – receive the grace and sanctification of the Spirit, they will in truth be wise virgins; but if they are left imprisoned in their own nature then they are indeed foolish virgins, children of the world and subject to the wrath of God.

66. Evil is foreign to our nature; but, given admittance by us through the transgression of the first man, it has with time become as though natural to us. Yet through the celestial gift of the Spirit, that is also foreign to our nature, this nature can once more be completely purged of evil and we can be restored to our original purity. But unless this comes about as the result of great supplication, faith and attentiveness, and by our turning away from the things of the world; and unless our nature, defiled as it is by evil, is sanctified by the love that is the Lord, and we continue unfailingly to apply ourselves to His divine commandments, we cannot attain the kingdom of Heaven.

67. I wish to elucidate, so far as I can, a subject that is as subtle as it is profound. The infinite and bodiless Lord, who is beyond being, in His infinite bounty embodies and, so to say, reduces Himself so that He can commingle with the intelligible beings that He has created – with, that is, the souls of saints and of angels – thereby making it possible for them to participate in the immortal life of His own divinity. Now each thing – whether angel, soul or demon – is, in conformity with its own nature, a body. No matter how subtle it may be, each thing possesses a body whose subtlety in substance, form and image corresponds to the subtlety of its own nature. In the case of human beings the soul, which is a subtle body, has enveloped and clothed itself in the members of our visible body, which is gross in substance. It has clothed itself in the eye, through which it sees; in the ear, through which it hears; in the hand, the nose. In short, the soul has clothed itself in the whole visible body and all its members, becoming commingled with them, and through them accomplishing everything it does in this life. In the same way, in His unutterable and inconceivable bounty Christ reduces and embodies Himself, commingling with and embracing the soul that aspires to Him with faith and love and, as St Paul puts it (cf. 1 Cor. 6 : 17), becoming one spirit with it, His soul united with our soul and His Person with our person. Thus such a soul lives and has its being in His divinity, attaining immortal life and delighting in incorruptible pleasure and inexpressible glory.

68. In a soul of this kind the Lord when He wills is fire, consuming every sinful and alien thing in it, in accordance with the words, 'Our God is a consuming fire' (Deut. 4 : 24); at other times He is repose, wondrous and indescribable; or else joy and peace, cherishing and embracing it. Only it must aspire to Him with love and devote itself

to holy ways of life, and then through direct experience, with its own perception, it will see itself partaking of unutterable blessings that 'the eye has not seen, and the ear has not heard, and man's heart has not grasped' (1 Cor. 2 : 9). For to the soul that proves itself worthy of Him the Spirit of the Lord is now repose, now intense joy, now delight and life. Just as He embodies Himself in spiritual food, so He embodies Himself in indescribable raiment and beauty, so that He fills the soul with spiritual gladness. As He Himself said: 'I am the bread of life' (John 6 : 35); and: 'If anyone drinks of the water that I give him . . . it will be in him a spring of water welling up for eternal life' (John 4 : 14).

69. Hence God was seen by each priest and saint as He willed and as was most profitable to the beholder. Thus He was seen in one way by Abraham, in another by Isaac, in another by Jacob, in another by Noah, by Daniel, by Moses, by David and by each of the prophets. He reduced and embodied Himself, giving Himself a different form and appearing to those who loved Him, not as He is in Himself – for He is beyond man's grasp – but according to their capacity and strength; and He did this because of the great, incomprehensible love that He had for them.

70. The soul found worthy to be the dwelling-place of supernal power, and whose members are commingled with that divine fire and with the celestial love of the Holy Spirit, is set free completely from all worldly love. Iron or lead, or gold and silver, melts when put into fire, and its natural solidity is softened, so that it is malleable and pliant so long as it is in the fire. Similarly, once the soul has received the celestial fire of the love of the Spirit, it renounces every attachment to the spirit of this world, breaks free from the bonds of evil, loses the natural obduracy of sin, and regards all worldly things as of no account. So much is this the case that should a soul, conquered by such love, find that certain brothers who are very dear to it impede its dedication to that love, then it will withdraw its affection from them. Nuptial love separates one from the love of father and mother, sister and brother, and any love one may bear them will be slight, since one's whole heart and desire are directed towards one's spouse. If earthly love dissolves all other worldly affection in this way, those wounded by that dispassion-ate longing will not be held back in the least by the love of anything worldly.

71. Being bountiful and full of love, God awaits with great patience the repentance of every sinner, and He celebrates the return of the sinner with celestial rejoicing; as He Himself says, 'There is joy in

heaven over one sinner who repents' (cf. Luke 15 : 7,10). But when someone sees this generosity and patience, and how God awaits repentance and so does not punish sins one by one, he may neglect the commandment and make such generosity an excuse for indifference, adding sin to sin, offence to offence, laziness to laziness. In this way he will reach the furthest limits of sin, and fall into such transgression that he is not able to recover himself. On the contrary, sinking into the lowest depths and finally committing himself to the devil, he destroys himself. That is what happened to the people of Sodom: reaching and even going beyond the furthest limits of sin – for not a single spark of repentance was to be found among them – they were consumed by the fire of divine justice (cf. Gen. 19 : 1–28). It also happened in the time of Noah: people had surrendered so unrestrainedly to the impulses to evil, piling up such a load of sin on themselves and showing not the least sign of repentance, that the whole earth became corrupt (cf. Gen. 6 : 5). Similarly, God was bountiful to the Egyptians, although they had sinned greatly and had maltreated His people: He did not hand them over to total destruction, but through gradual chastisement He induced them to repent. Yet when they lapsed and returned enthusiastically to their evil ways and to their original disbelief, finally even pursuing the Lord's people as they departed from Egypt, divine justice destroyed them completely (cf. Exod. 14 : 23–28). God also showed His habitual forbearance towards the people of Israel, although they too had sinned greatly and had killed His prophets. Yet when they became so committed to evil that they did not respect even the royal dignity of His Son, but laid murderous hands upon Him, they were utterly rejected and cast aside: prophecy, priesthood and service were taken from them and were entrusted to the Gentiles who believed (cf. Matt. 21 : 33–43).

72. Let us draw near eagerly to Christ who summons us, surrendering our hearts to Him, and let us not despair of our salvation, deliberately giving ourselves over to evil. For it is a trick of the devil to lead us to despair by reminding us of our past sins. We must realize that if Christ when on earth healed and restored the blind, the paralysed and the dumb, and raised the dead that were already in a state of decomposition, how much more will He heal blindness of mind, paralysis of soul, and dumbness of the dissolute heart. For He who created the body also created the soul. And if He

was so bounteous and merciful to what is mortal and disintegrates, how much more compassionate and healing will He not be to the immortal soul, overpowered by the sickness of evil and ignorance, when it turns to Him and asks Him for help? For it is He who said: 'Will not My heavenly Father vindicate those who call to Him night and day? Yes, I assure you, He will vindicate them swiftly' (cf. Luke 18 : 7–8); and: 'Ask and it will be given to you, seek and you will find, knock and it will be opened to you' (Matt. 7 : 7); and again: 'If he will not give to him out of friendship, yet on account of his persistence he will get up and give him what he needs' (cf. Luke 11 : 8). Moreover, He came so that sinners should turn back to Him (cf. Matt. 9 : 13). Only let us devote ourselves to the Lord, rejecting in so far as we can our evil prepossessions; and He will not overlook us, but will be ready to offer us His help.

73. When a person is so sick and weak that his body cannot accept food and drink, he is reduced to despair and becomes a living image of death, and his friends and relatives mourn over him. Similarly, God and the angels mourn and are full of sorrow for souls incapable of absorbing celestial nourishment. But if you become God's throne and He Himself takes His seat on it; if your whole soul is a spiritual eye, all light; if you nourish yourself on the sustenance of the Spirit and drink living water and the spiritual wine that rejoices the heart (cf. Ps. 104 : 15); if you clothe your soul in ineffable light – if inwardly you attain experience and full assurance of all these things, then you will live the truly eternal life, reposing in Christ while still in this present world. If you have not yet attained this state or have not started to acquire it, you should weep bitterly and lament because you still do not as yet possess such riches; and you should constantly be mindful of your poverty and should pray because of it. But even the man who has attained this state should still be aware of his dearth lest, as though sated with divine riches, he becomes negligent. As the Lord says, he who seeks will find and to him who knocks it will be opened (cf. Matt. 7 : 8).

74. If the oil formed from different spices (cf. Exod. 30 : 23–25) had such power that those anointed with it attained a royal status (cf. 1 Sam. 10 : 1; 16 : 13), will not those whose intellect and inner being are anointed with the sanctifying oil of gladness (cf. Ps. 45 : 7), and who have received the pledge of the Holy Spirit, even more surely attain the realm of perfection – that is to say, Christ's kingdom and

adoption by Him – and become the King's companions, entering and leaving the Father's presence as they wish? Even if they have not yet entered totally into their inheritance, being still burdened with the weight of the flesh, yet through the pledge of the Spirit they will be fully assured of the things for which they hope, and will not have any doubt that they will reign with Christ and will enjoy the supra-abundant fulness of the Spirit: though still clothed in the flesh, they have had direct experience of that power and that pleasure. For grace, once it has been conferred as a result of the purification of the intellect and the inner being, completely removes the veil in which man was wrapped by Satan after the fall, expelling every defilement and every sordid thought from the soul. Its aim is to cleanse the soul, so enabling it to recover its original nature and to contemplate the glory of the true light with clear, unimpeded eyes. Once this is achieved, man is here and now raised to the eternal world and perceives its beauty and its wonder. Just as the physical eye, as long as it is sound and healthy, gazes confidently at the sun's rays, so such a man, his intellect illumined and purified, always contemplates the never-setting light of the Lord.

75. It is not easy for men to reach this level. It requires much toil, struggle and suffering. In many, although grace is active, evil is still present together with it, lying hidden: the two spirits, that of light and that of darkness, are at work in the same heart. Naturally, you will ask what communion light can have with darkness, or what concord can God's temple have with idols (cf. 2 Cor. 6 : 14,16). I will answer you with the same words: what communion can light have with darkness? Pure and unsullied as it is, in what way is the divine light darkened, obscured or sullied? 'The light shines in the darkness and the darkness did not grasp it' (John 1 : 5). Thus things must not be interpreted in isolation or in a single way. Some repose in God's grace only for as long as they can keep a hold over themselves and can avoid being vanquished by the sinfulness dwelling within them: for a time they can pray diligently and are at rest, but then unclean thoughts become active within them and they are taken captive by sin, which in their case clearly coexists with grace. Those who are superficial, and who have not yet grasped the precise degree to which divine energy is active in them, think they have been delivered once and for all from sin; but those who are intelligent and possess discrimination would not deny that, though God's grace dwells

within them, they may also be harassed by shameful and unnatural thoughts.

76. We have often known brethren who have enjoyed such richness of grace that all sinful desire has completely dried up and been extinguished in them for five or six years. Then, just when they thought they had reached a haven and found peace, evil has leapt upon them as though from an ambush so savagely and with such hostility that they have been thrown into confusion and doubt. No one, therefore, who possesses understanding would dare to say that once grace dwells in him he is thereafter free from sin. As we said, both grace and sin may be active in the same intellect, even if the gullible and ignorant, after having had some slight spiritual experience, claim that they have already won the battle. This, in my opinion, is how things are: dark air or mist suddenly rising may obscure the sun's light even when it is shining brightly; in a similar manner those who, although enjoying God's grace, have not yet been completely purified and in their depths are still under the sway of sin, may also be suddenly overcome by darkness. Truly, it needs great discrimination to perceive these things in one's actual experience in a foolproof way.

77. Just as it is impossible for a person without eyes, tongue, ears and feet, to see, talk, hear or walk, so also it is impossible to commune in the divine mysteries, know God's wisdom or be enriched by the Spirit, without God's help and the energy He gives. The Greek sages were trained in the use of words and engaged spiritedly in verbal battles. The servants of God, even if they lack skill in argument, are familiar in every way with divine knowledge and God's grace.

78. I am convinced that not even the apostles, although filled with the Holy Spirit, were therefore completely free from anxiety. In addition to exultation and inexpressible joy they also felt a certain fear, prompted, to be sure, not from the side of evil but by grace itself; for grace was so securely established within them that they could not in fact deviate at all from the right path. And just as a child by throwing a small pebble does no real harm to a wall, or as a feeble arrow can damage a strong breastplate only very slightly, so even if some evil thing assailed them, the attack proved to be utterly ineffectual and vain, since they were well protected by the power of Christ. Yet even though they were perfect they still possessed their free will; contrary to the stupid view expressed by some, the advent

of grace does not mean immediate deliverance from anxiety. The Lord asks even from the perfect that the soul's will should serve the Spirit, so that the two come together. 'Do not quench the Spirit', says St Paul (1 Thess. 5 : 19).

79. To explain things in superficial terms is not difficult or troublesome. For example, it is easy for anyone to say that this loaf is made from wheat; yet to expound stage by stage how bread is made lies within the competence not of everyone but only of those with experience. Similarly, it is easy to speak superficially about dispassion and perfection; but the stages by which they are achieved can be truly understood only by those who have attained them in their actual experience.

80. Those who hold forth about spiritual realities without having tasted and experienced them are like a man traversing an empty and arid plain at high noon on a summer's day: in his great and burning thirst he imagines that there is a cool spring close at hand, full of sweet clear water, and that there is nothing to prevent him from drinking it to his heart's content. Or they are like a man who, without having tasted a drop of honey, tries to explain to others what its sweetness is like. Such indeed are those who try to introduce others to perfection, sanctity and dispassion without having learnt about these things through their own efforts and direct experience. And had God given them even a slight awareness of the things about which they speak, they would at all events see that the truth about them differs greatly from the explanation that they give. Christianity is liable to be misconstrued little by little in this way, and so turned into atheism. But in reality Christianity is like food and drink: the more a man tastes it, the more he longs for it, until his intellect becomes insatiable and uncontrollable. It is as if one were to offer to a thirsty person a sweet drink such that he would want, not simply to slake his thirst, but to go on drinking more and more because of the pleasure it gave him. These things are not to be understood merely in a theoretical way; they must be achieved within the intellect in a mysterious manner through the activity of the Holy Spirit, and only then can they be spoken about.

81. The Gospel commands everyone categorically to do this or not to do that, thus enabling us to become friends of the loving King. 'Do not be angry', it says (cf. Matt. 5 : 22), and, 'Do not lust' (cf. Matt. 5 : 28); and, 'If someone strikes you on the right cheek, turn to him the other cheek as well' (Matt. 5 : 39). St Paul, following closely in

the steps of these commandments, teaches how the actual work of purification should take place stage by stage, patiently and with long-suffering: first he nourishes the uninstructed with milk (cf. 1 Cor. 3 : 1–2), next he brings them to maturity (cf. Eph. 4 : 14–15), and then to perfection (cf. Heb. 5 : 12–14). In this way the Gospel forms as it were a complete woollen garment, while St Paul explains clearly how the wool for this garment is to be carded, woven and made up.

82. There are some who have desisted from outward unchastity, fraud, greed and similar iniquity and who on this account regard themselves as saints, when in fact they are far from being true saints. For evil frequently dwells in the intellects of such people, thriving there and creeping around; and after it has destroyed them it leaves them and goes on its way. The saint is he who is sanctified and totally purified in his inner being. One of the brethren was praying with others when he was seized and taken captive by the divine power, and he saw the heavenly Jerusalem and the resplendent dwelling-places there and the boundless and ineffable light. Then he heard a voice saying that this was the place of repose for the righteous. After this he became very conceited and full of presumption, and fell deeply into sin and was overcome by many evils. If such a man fell, how can anyone say that because he fasts, lives in voluntary exile, gives away all his property and desists from all outward sins, there is nothing wanting for him to be a saint? For perfection consists not in abstention from outward sins but in the total cleansing of the mind.

83. Understanding these things, enter within yourself by keeping watch over your thoughts, and scrutinize closely your intellect, captive and slave to sin as it is. Then discover, still more deeply within you than this, the serpent that nestles in the inner chambers of your soul and destroys you by attacking the most sensitive aspects of your soul. For truly the heart is an immeasurable abyss. If you have destroyed that serpent, have cleansed yourself of all inner lawlessness, and have expelled sin, you may boast in God of your purity; but if not, you should humble yourself because you are still a sinner and in need, and ask Christ to come to you on account of your secret sins. The whole Old and New Testament speaks of purity, and everyone, whether Jew or Greek, should long for purity even though not all can attain it. Purity of heart can be brought about only by Jesus; for He is authentic and absolute Truth, and without this Truth it is impossible to know the truth or to achieve salvation.

V
Love

84. Having outwardly renounced visible things and given away your goods, you must in the same way also renounce your inner prepossessions and attitudes. If you have acquired worldly wisdom or material knowledge, you must reject it. If you have put your trust in earthly privileges, give them up, humbling and belittling yourself. In this way you can discover what St Paul meant by the 'folly' of the Gospel; for in this folly you will find true wisdom, which resides not in fine words but in the power of the Cross that is active as an actual reality in those found worthy to achieve such wisdom. As St Paul says, Christ's Cross is 'a stumbling-block to the Jews and folly to the Greeks, but to those who are saved it is God's power and wisdom' (cf. 1 Cor. 1 : 21–24).

85. Even if you have tasted things celestial and partaken of divine wisdom, and your soul is at rest, do not exalt yourself or grow over-confident, thinking that you have already reached your goal and understand all truth, lest St Paul's words also apply to you: 'You are sated already, you are already rich, you have reigned as kings without us. Would that you did reign, so that we could reign with you' (1 Cor. 4 : 8). Even if you have been given some taste, regard yourself as still not yet a Christian; and do not just think this superficially, but let it be as though planted and established permanently in your mind.

86. A lover of riches is never satisfied, no matter how many possessions he accumulates, but the more he acquires daily, the more his appetite increases; and a person forcibly pulled away from a stream of pure water before he has quenched his thirst feels even more thirsty. In a similar way, once one has experienced the taste of God, one can never be satisfied or have enough of it, but however much one is enriched by this wealth one still feels oneself to be poor. Christians do not set great store by their own lives, but regard themselves rather as rightly set at nought by God and as everyone's

servants. God rejoices greatly at this, and takes His repose in the soul because of its humility. If therefore you attain something or are enriched, do not on this account presume you are something or have something. Presumption is an abomination to the Lord, and it was this that originally expelled man from paradise when he heard the serpent say, 'You will be like gods' (Gen. 3 : 5), and put his trust in this vain hope. Have you not learnt how your God and King, and the very Son of God, emptied Himself and took on the form of a slave (cf. Phil. 2 : 7)? How He became poor, was ranked among criminals, and suffered? If this is what happened to God, do you think that man, formed of flesh and blood, who is but earth and ashes, totally without goodness and wholly depraved, has reason to be proud and boastful? If you have understanding you will recognize that even what you have received from God is not your own, since you were given it by another; and should He think fit, it will certainly be taken away from you again. Attribute, therefore, every blessing to God and every evil to your own weakness.

87. That treasure which St Paul said we hold in pots of clay (cf. 2 Cor. 4 : 7) is the sanctifying power of the Spirit which while still in the flesh he was enabled to receive. Again St Paul says: '. . . who has been made by God our wisdom, righteousness, sanctification and redemption' (1 Cor. 1 : 30). He who finds and possesses this supernal treasure of the Spirit can accomplish all righteous acts and works prescribed by the commandments, not only in purity and faultlessly, but also without any suffering or exertion, whereas before he was far from accomplishing them in such a painless way. For no one, however he tries, can truly cultivate spiritual fruits before participating in the Holy Spirit. But everyone should put pressure on himself, striving to advance with endurance and faith, and fervently beseeching Christ that he may acquire this heavenly treasure; for in it and through it he can accomplish, as was said, every righteous act in purity and perfectly, without toil or distress.

88. Whenever those who possess in themselves the divine riches of the Spirit take part in spiritual discussion, they draw as it were on their inner treasure-house and share their wealth with their hearers. Those, however, who do not have stored in the sanctuary of their heart the treasure from which springs forth the bounty of divine thoughts, mysteries and inspired words, but who cull what they say from the Scriptures, speak merely from the tip of the tongue; or if

they have listened to spiritual men, they preen themselves with what others have said, putting it forward as though it were their own and claiming interest on someone else's capital. Their listeners can enjoy what they say without great effort, but they themselves, when they have finished speaking, prove to be like paupers. For they have simply repeated what they have taken from others, without acquiring treasures of their own from which they could first derive pleasure themselves and which they could then communicate profitably to others. For this reason we must first ask God that these true riches may dwell within us, and then we can readily benefit others and speak to them of spiritual matters and divine mysteries. For God's goodness delights to dwell in every believer. As Christ said: 'He who loves Me will be loved by My Father; and I will love him and disclose Myself to him' (John 14 : 21); and again: 'I and My Father will come to him, and take up Our abode with him' (John 14 : 23).

89. Those who are privileged to become children of God and to have Christ shining forth within them are guided by varied and differing qualities of the Spirit, and are cherished by grace in the secret places of the heart. The seeming joys of the world are not to be compared with the experience of divine grace in the soul. Those who share in this grace are sometimes filled with an inexpressible and nameless joy and exultation, as if they were at some royal banquet; sometimes they feel like bride and bridegroom delighting together spiritually; and sometimes like bodiless angels, since the body has become so weightless and light that it seems that they are not clothed with it. Sometimes it seems that they are in some realm greatly rejoicing and drunk with the inexpressible drunkenness of the mysteries of the Spirit; and then at other times they are full of grief, weeping and lamenting as they intercede for man's salvation. For, burning with the divine love of the Spirit for all men, they take into themselves the grief of all Adam; and sometimes they are kindled by the Spirit with such untold love and delight that, were it at all possible, they would clasp everyone to their breast, not making any distinction between who is good and who is bad; and sometimes they so disparage themselves that they regard themselves as the least of all men. Now they are consumed with unutterable spiritual joy; and now, like some mighty warrior donning royal armour, marching to war and putting the enemy to flight, they arm themselves with the weapons of the Spirit, attack their invisible enemies and tread them

underfoot. Now they are embraced by great tranquillity and stillness, peace nourishes them and they experience great delight; and now they acquire understanding, divine wisdom and unsearchable spiritual knowledge. In short, it is impossible to describe the grace of Christ by which they are illumined. At other times they can appear to be like any ordinary person. Divine grace, taking in them many different forms, teaches and disciplines the soul so as to present it perfect, pure and spotless to the heavenly Father.

90. All these workings of the Spirit are characteristic of those at a high level and very close to perfection. For these manifold blessings of grace are variously but unceasingly made active in such people by the Spirit, one spiritual energy succeeding another. When the soul attains spiritual perfection, totally purged of all the passions and wholly united and commingled with the Holy Spirit, the Intercessor, in ineffable communion, then through this commingling with the Spirit the soul is itself enabled to become spirit: it becomes all light, all spirit, all joy, repose, exultation, all love, all tenderness, all goodness and kindness. It is as though it had been swallowed up in the virtues belonging to the power of the Holy Spirit as a stone in the depths of the sea is surrounded by water. Totally united in this way to the Holy Spirit, such people are assimilated to Christ Himself, maintaining the virtues of the Spirit immutable in themselves and revealing their fruits to all. Since through the Spirit they have been made inwardly spotless and pure in heart, it is impossible for them to produce outwardly the fruits of evil: always and through all things the fruits of the Spirit will be manifest in them. Such is the state of spiritual perfection, such the fulness of Christ that St Paul exhorts us to attain when he says: '. . . so that you may be filled with the whole fulness of Christ' (cf. Eph. 3 : 19); and again: '. . . until we all attain to a perfect man, to the measure of the stature of the fulness of Christ' (Eph. 4 : 13).

91. There are times when, simply after kneeling down, we find our heart filled with divine energy and our soul delights in the Lord as a bride with the bridegroom: in Isaiah's words, 'As the bridegroom delights in the bride, so will the Lord delight in you' (Isa. 62 : 5. LXX). A man may be occupied throughout the day, and devote himself for but a single hour to prayer, and still be carried away inwardly by it, entering into the infinite depths of the other world. He experiences then an ineffable and measureless delight; his intellect, wholly suspended and ravished, is overwhelmed, and during the time

he is in this state he is mindless of every worldly concern. For his thoughts are filled, as we said, with numberless incomprehensible realities and are taken captive by them. In that hour his soul through prayer becomes one with his prayer and is carried away with it.

92. If it is asked whether it is possible for such a person always to be in this state, it should be said that he is never without grace; it is rooted and established in him as though it were part of his nature. Although single, it adapts itself in many ways, according to what is most profitable for him. Sometimes its fire burns in him strongly, sometimes faintly; and its light sometimes shines brightly and sometimes diminishes and wanes, always as God wills, even though the lamp itself burns inextinguishably. When it shines more vividly, then the man himself appears even more intoxicated with God's love. Sometimes the fire that burns unceasingly in the heart manifests itself with a more inward and deeper light, so that the whole man, swallowed up by this sweetness and vision, is no longer in himself, but seems to the world like an uncouth fool because of the overpowering love and delight that floods his soul, and because of the deep mysteries which he has been privileged to share. It often happens at such a time that he attains the measure of perfection and is free and secure from all sinfulness. Afterwards, grace contracts in a certain manner, and the veil of the contrary power spreads itself over him.

93. Grace operates in the following way. Suppose that a person attains perfection on ascending to the twelfth step. You reach this level and remain there for a time; but grace again withdraws, so you go down one step, and stand on the eleventh. The wonders of the higher step have been revealed to you, and you have had experience of them. But if you had remained on that step for ever, it would not have been possible for you to submit to the charge and burden of teaching; you would not have been able to hear or speak anything, or to concern yourself with the least thing, but could only have lain in some corner, enraptured and intoxicated. You were not allowed to remain on that final step so that you would have time to devote to the care and instruction of the brethren.

94. If on hearing about the kingdom of heaven we are brought to tears, do not let us be content with these tears, or think that we hear well with our ears or see well with our eyes, and that we need nothing further. For there are other ears, other eyes, other tears, just as there is another mind and another soul. I am referring to the divine

and heavenly Spirit, that hears and weeps, prays and knows, and that truly carries out God's will. When the Lord promised the great gift of the Spirit to the apostles, He said: 'I am going; but the Intercessor, the Holy Spirit whom the Father will send in My name, will teach you everything' (John 14 : 26); and: 'I still have much to tell you, but its burden is more than you can bear now. When, however, He who is the Spirit of truth comes, He will guide you into all the truth' (John 16 : 12–13). He, therefore, will pray, and He will weep. For, as St Paul says, 'we do not know what to pray for as we should; but the Spirit Himself makes intercession for us with cries that cannot be uttered' (Rom. 8 : 26). God's will is clear only to the Spirit. Again, as St Paul says: 'No one but the Spirit of God knows about the things of God' (1 Cor. 2 : 11). When, as promised, on the day of Pentecost the Paraclete made Himself present and the power of the Holy Spirit came to dwell in the souls of the apostles, the veil of sinfulness was once and for all removed from them, their passions were annulled and the eyes of their heart were opened. Henceforth they were filled with wisdom and made perfect by the Spirit: through Him they knew how to carry out God's will, and through Him they were initiated into all truth, for He directed and reigned in their souls. Thus, when we are brought to tears on hearing God's word, let us entreat Christ with unwavering faith and in the expectation that the Spirit, who truly hears and prays according to God's will and purpose, will indeed come to us.

95. There is a certain cloud-like power, fine as air, that lightly covers the intellect; and even though the lamp of grace always burns and shines in a man, as we said, yet this power covers its light like a veil in such a way that he is forced to confess that he is not perfect or wholly free from sin, but is, so to speak, both free and not free. This, certainly, does not happen without God's assent but is, on the contrary, in accordance with divine providence. Sometimes the dividing wall (cf. Eph. 2 : 14) is loosened and shattered, sometimes it is not entirely broken down. Nor is prayer always equally effective: sometimes grace is kindled more brightly, confers greater blessings, and refreshes more fully, and sometimes it is duller and less strong, as grace itself ordains according to what is of most profit to the person concerned. At certain times I have attained the level of perfection and have tasted and experienced the age to be; but never yet have I known any Christian who is perfect or absolutely free. Even if one

finds refreshment in grace and is enabled to share in mysteries and
revelations, and experiences the great sweetness of grace, sin still
dwells within one. Those who because of surpassing grace and the
light that shines within them think that they are perfect and free do
so from lack of experience. As I have said, I have never yet
encountered anyone who was absolutely free; but, having at certain
times partially attained that level of which I have spoken, I know from
experience what the perfected man is.

96. Whenever you hear about the communion of bridegroom and
bride, about dancing, music and feasting, do not take these things in a
material or worldly manner: they are spoken of simply by way of
illustration, as a condescension to our understanding. For the things
they denote are spiritual and inexpressible, indiscernible to corporeal
eyes, and these illustrations help holy and faithful souls to perceive
what is meant. The communion itself of the Holy Spirit, celestial
treasures, the dances and festivals of the angels – these things are clear
only to those who have experience of them; to the uninitiated they
are totally beyond comprehension. Thus you must listen with
reverence to what is said about them, until through faith you are
enabled to attain them; then you will know, with the actual
experience of the soul's eyes, in what blessings and mysteries the souls
of Christians can share even during this present life. When in the
resurrection their body becomes spiritual, it too is enabled to attain,
behold and, so to speak, grasp these things.

97. When our soul's own intrinsic qualities and fruits – prayer,
love, faith, vigilance, fasting and the other expressions of the
virtues – mingle and commune in the fellowship of the Spirit,
they effuse a rich perfume, like burning incense. At the same time
it then becomes easy for us to live in accordance with God's will,
whereas without the Holy Spirit this is impossible, as we have
already said. Before a woman is married she acts in accordance with
her own will and desires; but once married she lives under the
direction of her husband, abandoning her self-will. Similarly the soul
has its own will, and its own laws and activities; but when it
becomes worthy of uniting with Christ the heavenly bridegroom, it
submits to His law and is obedient no longer to its own will but to
that of Christ.

98. The wedding garment about which Christ speaks (cf. Matt.
22 : 11–12) signifies the grace of the Holy Spirit: the man who is not

worthy of wearing it has no part in the celestial marriage and in the spiritual wedding-feast.

99. We should eagerly drink spiritual wine and become drunk with a sober-minded drunkenness so that, just as those glutted with ordinary wine become more talkative, we too, brim-full with this spiritual wine, may speak of the divine mysteries. 'Thy cup has made me drunk as with the strongest wine', says the psalmist (Ps. 23 : 5. LXX).

100. The soul that is 'poor in spirit' (Matt. 5 : 3) is aware of its own wounds, perceives the encompassing darkness of the passions, and always calls upon the Lord for deliverance. It endures suffering, and does not delight in any of the good things of this world, but seeks out only the good doctor and entrusts itself to His treatment. How can the wounded soul become fair and seemly, and fit to live with Christ, except by truly recognizing its wounds and poverty and by recovering the state in which it was originally created? If it does not take pleasure in the wounds and weals of the passions, or defend its faults, the Lord will not call it to account for these things, but will come and heal it, restoring its dispassion and its incorruptible beauty. Only it must not deliberately associate with past acts of passion or give its consent to the passions that are still active within it; but with all its strength it must call upon the Lord, so that through His Holy Spirit it may be granted liberation from all the passions. Such is the soul that is called blessed; but alas for the soul that is unaware of its wounds and that in its endless sinfulness and obduracy does not think that it has anything evil within it: the good doctor will not visit it or heal it, since it does not seek Him out or have any concern for its wounds, because it thinks it is well and in good health. As the Lord said: 'It is not the healthy that need a doctor, but the sick' (Matt. 9 : 12).

101. Truly blessed and zealous for life and for surpassing joy are those who through fervent faith and virtuous conduct receive consciously and experientially the knowledge of the celestial mysteries of the Spirit and whose citizenship is in heaven (cf. Phil. 3 : 20). Clearly they excel all other men; for who among the powerful or the wise or the prudent could ascend to heaven while still on earth, and perform spiritual works there and have sight of the beauty of the Spirit? Such a person may appear poor, utterly poor, may be regarded as nothing and be totally unrecognized by his neighbours; but falling on his face before the Lord he rises to heaven under the guidance of

the Spirit and with assurance of soul, delighting in his mind with its wonders, occupying himself there, living there, having his citizenship there, as St Paul puts it. For he says: 'Our citizenship is in heaven' (Phil. 3 : 20); and he also says: 'The eye has not seen, and the ear has not heard, and man's heart has not grasped the things that God has prepared for those who love Him. But God has revealed them to us through His Spirit' (1 Cor. 2 : 9–10). These are the truly wise and powerful, these are the noble and the prudent.

102. Even apart from these celestial gifts distinguishing the saints from other living people, there are further ways of recognizing their superiority. For instance, Nebuchadnezzar, king of Babylon, summoned to him all the peoples to worship the image that he had set up (cf. Dan. 3 : 1–30). But God in His wisdom so disposed things that the virtue of three children should be made known to everyone and should teach everyone that there is one true God, who dwells in the heavens. Three children, captive and deprived of their liberty, spoke out boldly before him; and while everyone else, in great fear, worshipped the image, and even if not convinced did not dare to say anything, but was virtually speechless, like beasts dragged along by the nose, these children behaved very differently. They did not want their refusal to worship the image to go unrecognized or to escape notice, but they declared in the hearing of all: 'We do not worship your gods, O king, nor will we bow down before the golden image that you have set up.' Yet the terrible furnace into which they were cast as punishment was not a furnace for them and did not manifest its normal function; but as if reverencing the children it kept them free from harm. And everyone, including the king himself, through them recognized the true God. Not only those on earth, but the angelic choirs themselves were amazed at these children. For the angels are not absent when the saints perform their acts of courage, but keep them company, as St Paul confirms when he says: 'We have become a spectacle ... to angels and men' (1 Cor. 4 : 9). Another example of how saints are to be distinguished is that of Elijah who, though but a single man, prevailed over a great number of false prophets when the fire came down from heaven (cf. 1 Kgs. 18 : 38). And Moses prevailed over all Egypt and Pharaoh the tyrant (cf. Exod. chs. 5–13). Similarly Lot (cf. Gen. ch. 19) and Noah (cf. Gen. chs. 6–7) and many others, despite their apparent weakness, overcame many powerful and notable people.

103. Unless something of a different nature comes to its help, every phenomenon retains its inherent imperfection and deficiency. Thus God's inexpressible wisdom has shown forth in symbols and images through visible things that human nature in itself cannot manifest the full glory of the virtues and the spiritual beauty of holiness unless it has the assistance of God's helping hand. If the earth abides by itself, not receiving the farmer's attention and the assistance of rain and sun, it is unfit and incapable of bearing fruit; and every house would be filled with darkness but for the light of the sun, which is not of its own nature; and other things are in a similar state. In the same way, human nature, which in itself is powerless to produce the fruits of the virtues in their full perfection, needs the spiritual husbandman of our souls; in other words, it needs the Spirit of Christ, and this Spirit is of a totally different nature from our own, for we are created while He is uncreated. Skilfully tilling the hearts of the faithful so that they surrender their whole will to Him, He enables them to produce perfect spiritual fruits, while He makes His light shine in the soul's dwelling-place that has been darkened by the passions.

104. The warfare and struggle in which Christians are engaged is twofold. First, it is against visible things, for these excite, titillate and entice the soul to become attached to them and to take pleasure in them. And, second, it is against the principalities and powers of the terrible lord of this world (cf. Eph. 6 : 12).

105. The glory that shone from the face of Moses (cf. Exod. 34 : 29–30) was a prefiguring of the true glory of the Holy Spirit. Just as it was impossible then for anyone to gaze at it, so now the darkness of the passions cannot bear the same glory shining in the souls of Christians, but is put to flight, repulsed by its brilliance.

106. The truly sincere and devout Christian who has tasted the sweetness of divine things, whose soul is infused and mingled with grace, and who has entrusted his whole being to the purposes of grace, hates every worldly thing. Whether it is gold or silver, honour or glory, esteem or praise, or anything else, he is superior to it, and none of these things is able to captivate him; for he has experienced other riches and another honour and glory, his soul is nourished by an incorruptible delight, and through the fellowship of the Spirit he has full and conscious assurance.

107. In understanding, spiritual knowledge and discrimination, such a person differs as much from other men as an intelligent

herdsman differs from witless cattle; for he partakes of another Spirit and another intellect, of another understanding, and of a wisdom that is not the wisdom of this world. As St Paul says: 'We proclaim wisdom to those who are perfect; not the wisdom of this world, or of the doomed rulers of this world; but we proclaim the secret wisdom of God' (cf. 1 Cor. 2 : 6–7). For this reason, such a person differs in everything from those who are dominated by the spirit of the world, however intelligent or wise they are. Again as St Paul says (cf. 1 Cor. 2 : 15), he judges all men, he knows from what source he speaks and where he stands and among whom he is. Those dominated by the spirit of the world, on the other hand, have no power to know and judge him; this is possible only for one who possesses as he does the Spirit of divinity. As St Paul puts it: 'We interpret spiritual things to those who possess the Spirit. The worldly man does not accept spiritual things: they are folly to him. . . . But the spiritual man judges all things, while he is himself judged by no one' (1 Cor. 2 : 13–15).

108. It is altogether impossible to attain the Holy Spirit unless you alienate yourself from all the things of this world and dedicate yourself to the pursuit of Christ's love. The intellect must divest itself of every material concern and give its attention solely to achieving this one goal, thus becoming worthy of uniting in one spirit with Christ. As St Paul writes: 'He who cleaves to the Lord becomes one spirit with Him' (1 Cor. 6 : 17). The soul that is wholly attached to some worldly thing like riches or glory or natural affection is not able to escape and transcend the darkness of the powers of evil.

109. Truly sincere and devout souls cannot endure even a slight slackening of their longing for the Lord but, with their attention riveted entirely to His Cross, they seek to grow ever more fully conscious of their spiritual progress. Wounded by their longing and, so to speak, hungering for the righteousness of the virtues and the illumination of the Holy Spirit, they place no reliance on themselves and do not think they are anything even though they have been vouchsafed divine mysteries and partake of celestial felicity and grace. But the more they are enabled by grace to receive spiritual gifts, the more insatiable and diligent becomes their pursuit of heavenly realities; and the more they are aware of their spiritual progress, the more fervent grows their desire to participate in these realities. Spiritually enriched, they feel themselves to be poor. As Scripture

puts it: 'Those who eat Me will still be hungry and those who drink
Me will still be thirsty' (Ecclus. 24 : 21).

110. Such souls are not only granted complete freedom from the
passions but also perfectly acquire the illumination and communion of
the Holy Spirit in the fulness of grace. But souls that are sluggish and
indolent and do not seek in this life, and while still in the flesh, to
achieve through patient endurance and long-suffering the heart's
sanctification not just partially but totally, cannot hope to commune
in the Holy Spirit with full consciousness and assurance, or to be
delivered from the passions of evil through the Spirit. Such sluggish
and indolent souls, even though granted divine grace, are deceived by
evil and cease to trouble themselves further: because they have
received grace and enjoy the solace and spiritual sweetness that it
confers, they grow complacent, not mortifying their heart or
humbling their thought, and not thirsting and aspiring after the full
measure of dispassion. Content with this slight solace of grace, they
progress not in humility but in self-inflation, and are sometimes
stripped even of the gift they have been given. With the truly devout
soul it is different: even if it practises a thousand works of
righteousness, crushes the body with extreme fasting and the most
demanding vigils, and is vouchsafed various gifts, revelations and
mysteries of the Spirit, it is so modest that it feels it has not yet even
embarked on the spiritual path or acquired any of the virtues; and it
craves insatiably for divine love.

111. No one can attain such a state as this swiftly or easily: it can
only be reached by way of many hardships and struggles, after much
time and diligence, testing and temptation, thus bringing one to the
full measure of dispassion. It is he who has thus been sifted by every
kind of suffering and tribulation, and who has courageously endured
all the trials of evil, that is finally found worthy to receive the great
blessings, gifts and riches of the Spirit and to inherit the kingdom of
heaven.

112. The soul that has not yet acquired this citizenship in heaven
and is not yet conscious of the heart's sanctification should be full of
sorrow and should implore Christ fervently, that it may attain this
blessing as well as the energy of the Spirit that is manifest in the
intellect in the form of inexpressible visions. According to
ecclesiastical law, those who are conquered by bodily sins are initially
excluded from communion by the priest; then, when they have

shown the appropriate repentance, they are allowed to communicate once more. Those, however, who have not stumbled but have lived in purity may advance to priesthood and take their place within the sanctuary, officiating before the Lord at the Liturgy. We can apply the same distinction to inner communion in the Holy Spirit. Speaking of this, St Paul says: 'The grace of our Lord Jesus Christ, and the love of God the Father, and communion in the Holy Spirit . . .' (2 Cor. 13 : 14). Thus the Holy Trinity dwells in the pure soul, divine grace assisting. It dwells in the soul, not as it is in itself, for the Trinity is infinite and cannot be embraced by any created thing, but according to man's capacity and receptivity. Whenever the intellect turns aside from the pursuit of God's will and purpose, and grieves the Spirit, it is cast out and excommunicated from spiritual felicity: God's grace and love, and all the energy of the Holy Spirit, withdraw, and the intellect is delivered up to afflictions, trials and evil powers until the soul again walks in the path of the Spirit. When through confession and self-abasement it has shown that it is repentant, then it is again enabled to receive the visitation of grace and celestial felicity, even more than before. But should the soul not grieve the Spirit in any way, but live acceptably, rejecting every evil thought and cleaving continually to the Lord, rightly and fittingly will it go forward, receiving unutterable gifts and advancing from glory to glory and from peace to greater peace. Finally, when it has attained the full measure of the Christian life, it will be ranged among the perfect liturgists and faultless ministers of Christ in His eternal kingdom.

113. Visible things are figures and reflections of invisible things. Thus the visible church figures and reflects the church of the heart, the visible priest the true priest of Christ's grace; and so on. In the visible church, if the readings, psalms and other parts of the appointed rite do not succeed one another in the proper sequence, then it is not possible for the priest to proceed with the celebration of the divine sacrament of Christ's body and blood; and even if the rest of the order of the service is properly carried out, but the mystical thanksgiving of the sacrifice is not offered by the priest and there is no communion in the body of Christ, then the ecclesiastical rite has not been fulfilled and again the celebration of the sacrament is deficient. One must look on the life of the Christian in a similar way. He may have fasted, kept vigils, chanted the psalms, carried out every ascetic practice and acquired every virtue; but if the mystic working of the

Spirit has not been consummated by grace with full consciousness and spiritual peace on the altar of his heart, all his ascetic practice is ineffectual and virtually fruitless, for the joy of the Spirit is not mystically active in his heart.

114. Fasting is good and so are vigils, ascetic practice and voluntary exile. But all these things are but the start, the prelude to the citizenship of heaven, so that it is altogether senseless to put one's trust merely in them. It sometimes happens that we attain a certain state of grace but that evil, as we said above, lying in ambush within us, plays a trick on us: it deliberately withdraws and remains inactive, thus making us think that our intellect has been cleansed. In this way it produces in us the self-conceit of perfection, whereupon it stealthily attacks us and carries us down to the lowest depths of the earth. It often happens that young soldiers or brigands resort to tricks against the enemy: they set up ambushes and, catching their opponents unexpectedly from behind and surrounding them, they slaughter them. If that is what they do, then how much more skilled must evil be, that has dedicated itself for thousands of years to the crucial task of destroying souls. It knows exactly how to devise such ambushes in the secret places of the heart, sometimes keeping quiet and inactive deliberately in order to entice the soul into the self-conceit of perfection. Indeed, the cardinal rule of the Christian life is not to put one's trust in acts of righteousness even if one practises all of them, or to imagine that one has done anything great; and even if one participates in grace, one must not think that one has achieved anything or reached the goal. On the contrary, one should then hunger and thirst, grieve and weep even more, and be totally contrite in heart.

115. The spiritual state is like some royal palace that possesses many exterior courts, vestibules and outer residences; then there are various inner buildings, usually housing the royal robes and the treasure; and then, yet further within, are the king's living quarters. Someone still in the outer courts and apartments may think he has reached the inner chambers, but he would be wrong. The same is true where the spiritual life is concerned. Those struggling against greed and sleep, and continually occupied with psalms and prayers, should not think that they have already attained the final place of rest: they are still in the exterior courts and vestibules, and have not even reached the place where the royal robes and treasure are kept. Even if

they are found worthy of some spiritual grace, again this should not deceive them into thinking that they have attained their goal. They must examine to see whether they have found the treasure in the pot of clay (cf. 2 Cor. 4 : 7),[1] whether they have put on the purple robe of the Spirit, whether they have seen the king and are at peace.

Again, our soul has depths and many faculties. When sin insinuates itself, it lays hold of all these faculties and all the heart's thoughts. Then we ask for the grace of the Spirit: it is granted and perhaps embraces two of the soul's faculties. If we lack experience we fancy that this grace we have invoked has laid hold of all the soul's faculties and that sin has been completely uprooted: we do not realize that most of our soul is still subject to sin. For, as has been shown many times, it is possible for grace to be ceaselessly active, as the eye is in the body, and yet for the evil that despoils the mind to coexist with it. Hence, if we do not know how to discriminate, we fancy that we have attained something great and begin to think highly of ourselves, deluding ourselves that we have reached the final stage of purification, though this is very far from the truth. As has been said, one of the devil's ploys is to withdraw deliberately for a certain time and to remain inactive, thus promoting the conceit of perfection in those pursuing the spiritual way. But does the man who plants a vineyard immediately gather grapes? Or does he who sows seeds in the earth at once reap the harvest? Does the new-born child attain maturity straight away? Think how Jesus Christ, the Son of God and God Himself, descended from the heights of glory to suffering, dishonour, crucifixion and death; and how because of this self-abasement He was taken up again and set at the right hand of the Father. But the evil serpent, that first sowed in Adam the desire for divinity (cf. Gen. 3 : 5), dragged him down into disgrace through this presumption. Think about these things and try to protect yourself as much as you can, keeping your heart always in a state of humility and contrition.

[1] See §87 above.

VI
The Freedom of the Intellect

116. When you hear that Christ descended into hell in order to deliver the souls dwelling there, do not think that what happens now is very different. The heart is a tomb and there our thoughts and our intellect are buried, imprisoned in heavy darkness. And so Christ comes to the souls in hell that call upon Him, descending, that is to say, into the depths of the heart; and there He commands death to release the imprisoned souls that call upon Him, for He has power to deliver us. Then, lifting up the heavy stone that oppresses the soul, and opening the tomb, He resurrects us – for we were truly dead – and releases our imprisoned soul from its lightless prison.

117. It often happens that Satan will insidiously commune with you in your heart and say: 'Think of the evil you have done; your soul is full of lawlessness, you are weighed down by many grievous sins.' Do not let him deceive you when he does this and do not be led to despair on the pretext that you are being humble. After gaining admission through the fall evil has the power to commune at all times with the soul, as man to man, and so to suggest sinful actions to it. You should answer it: 'I have God's written assurance, for He says: "I desire, not the sinner's death, but that he should return through repentance and live"' (cf. Ezek. 33 : 11). What was the purpose of His descent to earth except to save sinners, to bring light to those in darkness and life to the dead?'

118. Just as the power of evil works by persuasion, not by compulsion, so does divine grace. In this way our liberty and free will are preserved. If a man commits sins when he is subject to the devil, he himself pays the penalty, not the devil, since he was impelled to evil not by force but by his own will. It is the same where a good action is concerned: grace does not ascribe this action to itself but to the man, giving him the credit for it, since he is the cause of the goodness that befalls him. Grace does not make a man incapable of sin

by forcibly and compulsorily laying hold of his will but, though present, allows him freedom of choice, so as to make it clear whether the man's own will inclines to virtue or to evil. For the law looks not to man's nature but to his free power of choice, which is capable of turning towards either good or evil.

119. One must guard the soul and not allow it to commune with impure pernicious thoughts. Just as the body is defiled through intercourse with another body, so the soul is corrupted through coupling with evil and polluted thoughts, assenting to them and uniting with them. Not simply thoughts of cunning and unchastity, but of every vice: unbelief, guile, self-esteem, anger, envy, contentiousness and so on. That is what St Paul means when he says: 'Let us cleanse ourselves from all pollution of the flesh and spirit' (2 Cor. 7 : 1). For corruption and unchastity work also through shameless thoughts in the hidden places of the soul; and just as God will destroy the person who destroys His temple, which is the body (cf. 1 Cor. 3 : 17), so the person who corrupts his soul and intellect by assenting to shameless thoughts and uniting with them is liable to punishment. Just as one should guard the body against visible sins, so one should guard the soul, which is the bride of Christ, against shameless thoughts. 'I betrothed you to Christ, hoping to present you to Him as a pure virgin to her sole husband', writes St Paul (2 Cor. 11 : 2). 'Guard your heart with all diligence, for on this depends the outcome of life', says Scripture (Prov. 4 : 23); and: 'Crooked thoughts separate us from God' (Wisd. 1 : 3).

120. Let everyone call his own soul to account, examining it and testing it to see to what it is attached; and should he find that his heart does not conform to God's laws, let him try with all his strength to keep not only the body but also the intellect free from corruption and involvement with evil thoughts – if, that is to say, he wishes God in His purity to take up His dwelling within him according to His promise. For God has promised to dwell within souls that are pure and devoted to what is beautiful and good (cf. 2 Cor. 6 : 16).

121. The prudent farmer first clears his land of brambles before sowing it with seed. Similarly, the man who aspires to receive from God the seed of grace must first clear the earth of his heart, so that when the seed of the Spirit falls it may yield a good and abundant harvest. If he does not first cleanse himself from 'all pollution of the flesh and spirit' (2 Cor. 7 : 1), he remains flesh and blood and is far from the realm of life (cf. 1 Cor. 15 : 50).

122. One must watch very carefully and in every direction for the enemy's trickery, guile and malice. Speaking through St Paul, the Holy Spirit says: 'I became all things to all men so as to save everyone' (cf. 1 Cor. 9 : 22); and in the same way the enemy tries to become all things so as to bring everyone to destruction. He pretends to pray with those who pray, so as to cheat them into self-conceit by making them think they have attained the state of prayer. He fasts with those who fast, with the purpose again of filling them with self-conceit because they have succeeded in fasting. With those who understand the Scriptures he tries to do the same, hoping to lead them astray by making them claim to possess spiritual knowledge. To those who have been granted a vision of the light, he pretends to offer the same kind of vision, transforming himself into 'an angel of light' (2 Cor. 11 : 14), so that through this simulation of the true light he may seduce them to him. In short, he uses every kind of deceit and adapts himself to every kind of appearance, so that by assuming the likeness of what is good he becomes a plausible agent of destruction. 'We destroy evil thoughts and all the self-esteem that exalts itself against the knowledge of God', says St Paul (2 Cor. 10 : 5). You see to what limits the impostor carries his defiance, wanting to cast down even those who have already attained a divine knowledge of the truth. Hence we must guard the heart with all diligence and beseech God for much understanding, so that He enables us to discern the devil's wiliness, to cultivate and train the intellect in understanding, to attend continually to our thoughts, and to conform ourselves to His will. There is no work greater than this. 'Praise and magnificence are His works', as the psalmist writes (Ps. 111 : 3. LXX).

123. The devout soul, even if it practises all the virtues, ascribes everything to God and nothing to itself. God, on the other hand, when He sees its sound and healthy understanding and knowledge, attributes everything to the soul, and rewards it as though it had achieved everything through its own efforts. He does this in spite of the fact that, if He were to bring us to judgment, no true righteousness would be found in us. For material possessions and everything that man regards as valuable and through which he is able to do good, the earth and whatever is in it, all belong to God. Man's body and soul, and even his very being, are his only by grace. What, then, is left to him that he can call his own, by virtue of which he can pride himself or vindicate himself? Yet when the soul recognizes – what is

indeed the truth – that all its good actions for God's sake, together with all its understanding and knowledge, are to be ascribed to God alone and that everything should be attributed to Him, then God accepts this as the greatest gift that man can make, as the offering that is most precious in His eyes.

124. When a woman comes to live and share her life with a man, all that each has is held in common. They share one house, a single being and existence. And the woman is mistress not only of the man's possessions but also of his very body: as St Paul says, 'The man does not have power over his own body, but the woman does' (1 Cor. 7 : 4). Similarly the soul, in its true and ineffable communion with Christ, becomes one spirit with Him (cf. 1 Cor. 6 : 17). It necessarily follows that, since the soul has become His bride, it is as it were mistress of all His untold treasures. For there is no doubt that, when God joins Himself to the soul, all that He has belongs also to the soul, whether it be world, life, death, angels, principalities, things present or things to come (cf. Rom. 8 : 38).

125. While the Israelites were well pleasing to the Lord – though they were never as they should have been, but at least while they seemed to have some faith in Him – the Lord went before them in a pillar of fire and in a pillar of cloud (cf. Exod. 13 : 21), He made the sea go back (cf. Exod. 14 : 21), and conferred on them a thousand other wonders. But when they lost their love for God, then they were handed over to their enemies and were sold into bitter slavery. Something similar happens in the case of the soul. When through grace it has come to know God and has been cleansed of its many past stains, then it is granted gifts of grace; but when it does not ceaselessly maintain befitting love for the celestial bridegroom, it falls away from the life in which it shared; for the enemy can attack even those who have attained a high level of grace. Let us struggle, therefore, as much as we can, and guard our life with fear and trembling. In particular, those who have come to share in the Spirit of Christ should be careful not to grieve the Spirit by acting negligently in any way, great or small. Just as there is joy in heaven over one sinner who repents (cf. Luke 15 : 7), so there is grief over one soul that falls away from eternal life.

126. When a soul has become worthy of grace, then God will give it spiritual knowledge, understanding and discrimination to the degree that is profitable for it. God will give these things when the

soul asks for them, so that it may be enabled acceptably to serve the Spirit that it has received, and not be seduced by evil, or led into error through ignorance, or perverted by negligence and lack of fear into doing something contrary to His will.

127. The energy of the passions – which is the worldly spirit of delusion, darkness and sin – fills the man in whom it dwells with concern for things of the flesh. The energy and power of the Spirit of light, on the other hand, dwell in the saintly man, as St Paul indicates when he says: 'Do you seek a proof that Christ is speaking through me?' (2 Cor. 13 : 3); and: 'I no longer live, but Christ lives in me' (Gal. 2 : 20); and: 'Those of you who have been baptized in Christ have clothed yourselves in Christ' (Gal. 3 : 27). And Christ affirms the same when He says: 'I and My Father will come and make Our dwelling with him' (cf. John 14 : 23). To those who are found worthy of them these things happen, not unperceived or without manifesting their activity, but with power and truth. The Law with its implacable sentence first brought men to repentance, placing them under an unbearably heavy yoke without being able to hold out the least help. But what the Law cannot offer, the power of the Spirit can provide: 'For what the Law could not do because it was enfeebled through our fleshliness, God has done', says St Paul (Rom. 8 : 3). Since Christ's coming the door of grace has been opened to those who truly believe, and they have been given the power of God and the energy of the Holy Spirit.

128. Christ first sent the gift of the natural goodness of the Holy Spirit to His disciples (cf. Acts 2 : 3). Thereafter the divine power, overshadowing all the faithful and dwelling in their souls, healed the passions of sin and delivered them from darkness and spiritual death. For until then the soul was wounded and captive, held fast in the obscurity of sin. Indeed, even now the soul is still in darkness if Christ has not yet come to dwell in it, and if the power of the Holy Spirit is not active in it, filling it with all strength and assurance. But to those on whom the grace of the divine Spirit has descended, coming to dwell in the deepest levels of their intellect, Christ is as the soul. As St Paul says: 'He who cleaves to the Lord becomes one spirit with Him' (1 Cor. 6 : 17). And as the Lord Himself says: 'As I and Thou are one, so may they be one in Us' (cf. John 17 : 21). What blessing and goodness has human nature received, abased as it was by the power of evil! But when the soul is entangled in the depravity of the passions, it becomes as though one with it, and even though it possesses its own

will it cannot do what it wants to do. As St Paul says: 'What I do is
not what I want to do' (Rom. 7 : 15). On the other hand, how much
closer is the union it enjoys when one with God's will, when His
power is conjoined with it, sanctifying it and making it worthy of
Him. For then in truth the soul becomes as the soul of the Lord,
submitting willingly and consciously to the power of the Holy Spirit
and no longer acting in accordance with its own will. 'What can
separate us from the love of Christ' (Rom. 8 : 35), when the soul is
united to the Holy Spirit?

129. He who wants to be an imitator of Christ, so that he too may
be called a son of God, born of the Spirit, must above all bear
courageously and patiently the afflictions he encounters, whether
these be bodily illnesses, slander and vilification from men, or attacks
from the unseen spirits. God in His providence allows souls to be
tested by various afflictions of this kind, so that it may be revealed
which of them truly loves Him. All the patriarchs, prophets, apostles
and martyrs from the beginning of time traversed none other than
this narrow road of trial and affliction, and it was by doing this that
they fulfilled God's will. 'My son,' says Scripture, 'if you come to
serve the Lord, prepare your soul for trial, set your heart straight, and
patiently endure' (Ecclus. 2 : 1–2). And elsewhere it is said: 'Accept
everything that comes as good, knowing that nothing occurs without
God willing it.'[1] Thus the soul that wishes to do God's will must
strive above all to acquire patient endurance and hope. For one of the
tricks of the devil is to make us listless at times of affliction, so that
we give up our hope in the Lord. God never allows a soul that hopes
in Him to be so oppressed by trials that it is put to utter confusion. As
St Paul writes: 'God is to be trusted not to let us be tried beyond our
strength, but with the trial He will provide a way out, so that we are
able to bear it' (1 Cor. 10 : 13). The devil harasses the soul not as
much as he wants but as much as God allows him to. Men know what
burden may be placed on a mule, what on a donkey, and what on a
camel, and load each beast accordingly; and the potter knows how
long he must leave the pots in the fire, so that they are not cracked by
staying in it too long or rendered useless by being taken out of it
before they are properly fired. If human understanding extends this
far, must not God be much more aware, infinitely more aware, of the

[1] *Didache* iii, 10.

degree of trial it is right to impose on each soul, so that it becomes tried and true, fit for the kingdom of heaven?

130. Hemp, unless it is well beaten, cannot be worked into fine yarn, while the more it is beaten and carded the finer and more serviceable it becomes. And a freshly moulded pot that has not been fired is of no use to man. And a child not yet proficient in worldly skills cannot build, plant, sow seed or perform any other worldly task. In a similar manner it often happens through the Lord's goodness that souls, on account of their childlike innocence, participate in divine grace and are filled with the sweetness and repose of the Spirit; but because they have not yet been tested, and have not been tried by the various afflictions of the evil spirits, they are still immature and not yet fit for the kingdom of heaven. As the apostle says: 'If you have not been disciplined you are bastards and not sons' (Heb. 12 : 8). Thus trials and afflictions are laid upon a man in the way that is best for him, so as to make his soul stronger and more mature; and if the soul endures them to the end with hope in the Lord it cannot fail to attain the promised reward of the Spirit and deliverance from the evil passions.

131. It was by experiencing many torments and enduring even to the point of death that the martyrs earned their crowns of glory; and the greater and more grievous the suffering, the greater their glory and the more intimate their communion with God. In the same way, when our souls are undergoing afflictions – whether they come in a visible form from men, or in an intellectual form by means of evil thoughts, or derive from bodily illnesses – if we endure them to the end, we will gain the same crowns as the martyrs and will enjoy the same intimacy with God. For we will have sustained the martyrdom of afflictions produced by the evil spirits, as the martyrs sustained those that came through men; and the greater the diabolic afflictions we have endured, the greater the glory we receive from God, not only in the future but also in this present life through the grace of the Holy Spirit.

132. Since the road leading to immortal life is extremely narrow and full of affliction, and on account of this there are few who traverse it (cf. Matt. 7 : 14), we must staunchly endure every trial of the devil, awaiting with hope our heavenly reward. For, however great the afflictions we suffer, what are they compared with the promised future reward, or with the grace of the Holy Spirit that

visits souls even in this present life, or with the deliverance that we have received from the obscurity of evil passions, or with the enormous debts we owe because of our sins? As St Paul says: 'The sufferings of this present life are not worthy to be compared with the glory which shall be revealed in us' (Rom. 8 : 18). Hence we must patiently endure everything for the Lord's sake, like brave soldiers dying for our King. Yet why is it that when we gave our attention to the world and to worldly things we did not fall into such distress, but now that we have come to serve God we suffer these manifold trials? It is because the devil, jealous of the blessings stored up for us, tries to make our souls sluggish and lazy, lest by enduring these afflictions for Christ's sake in the way that He wishes we should be granted our reward. No matter how much the devil arms himself against us, if we endure his attacks courageously, with Christ's help all his designs against us will be brought to nothing. For we have Jesus as our defender and ally: let us keep in mind that He too passed through this present life vilified, persecuted and reviled, and that finally He was made perfect by a shameful death on the Cross (cf. Heb. 2 : 10).

133. If we want to endure every affliction and trial readily, let us long to die for Christ and let us keep this death continually before our eyes. For we have been commanded to take up the cross and to follow Him (cf. Matt. 16 : 24); and this means that we must be prepared and ready for death. If we have this disposition we will endure every affliction, visible and invisible, much more easily. How can he who is anxious to die for Christ's sake have any difficulty in putting up with suffering and distress? Yet we think afflictions are hard to bear, for we do not keep death for Christ's sake before us or rivet our mind always on Christ. But if we want to share His inheritance we must be willing to share His sufferings with an equal zeal. Those who love the Lord may be recognized by the fact that because of their hope in Him they bear every affliction that comes, not simply courageously but also wholeheartedly.

134. If we want to draw close to Christ we must first drag ourselves forcibly towards the good, even though our heart may not wish it. 'The kingdom of heaven is subjected to violence, and the violent take it by force', said the Lord (Matt. 11 : 12). And He also said: 'Strive to enter through the narrow gate' (Luke 13 : 24). We must, then, force ourselves even against our will towards virtue, towards love when we lack love, towards gentleness when we have

need of it, towards sympathy of heart and compassion, towards patience in the face of insult and contempt, and steadfastness in the face of mockery, if we have not yet acquired the habit of these things, and towards prayer if we still have not attained spiritual prayer. If God sees us struggling in this way and forcibly dragging ourselves towards the good even when our heart seems to oppose it, He will bestow true prayer on us, will give us compassion, patience, forbearance, and in general will fill us with all the fruits of the Spirit. Indeed, if a person lacking the other virtues forces himself towards, say, prayer alone, so that he may possess the grace of prayer, but at the same time is not apathetic or indifferent with regard to gentleness, humility, love and all the other virtues that ennoble our soul, including firmness of faith and trust in Christ, then sometimes the Holy Spirit gives him, at least in part, the grace of prayer for which he has asked, and fills him with gladness and repose. But he is still bereft of all the other virtues, because he has not forced himself to acquire them, nor has he besought Christ for them. Moreover, we should force ourselves, even unwillingly, not only towards the virtues mentioned, asking to receive them from God, but also towards the power to judge useless and wholly idle words, unworthy of being spoken; for we should assiduously meditate upon God's words both when we speak and in our heart. And we must also force ourselves not to get angry or to shout – 'Rid yourselves of all bitterness, anger and shouting', the apostle says (Eph. 4 : 31); not to defame or to judge anyone, not to become puffed up. When the Lord sees us putting pressure on ourselves and dragging ourselves along forcibly, He will assuredly give us the strength to do painlessly and easily what it was impossible for us to do before, even with force, because of the evil dwelling within us. And then the whole practice of the virtues becomes as it were part of our nature, since henceforward the Lord, as He promised, comes and dwells in us, as we equally dwell in Him; and in Him we fulfil the commandments with great ease.

135. When someone forces himself only towards prayer, while he does not exert or force himself with regard to humility, love, gentleness and all the other interdependent virtues, the result is much as follows. Sometimes in response to his entreaty divine grace visits him, because God in His goodness and love does respond to the petitions of those who call upon Him; but because he has not habituated and trained himself in the practice of the other virtues,

either he lapses from the grace he has received, falling through self-conceit, or else he does not dedicate himself to this grace and grow in it. The abode and resting-place of the Holy Spirit is humility, love, gentleness and the other holy commandments of Christ. If, therefore, a person desires to grow and to attain perfection by acquiring all these virtues, he must initially force himself to acquire and must establish himself in the first – that is to say, in prayer – wrestling and striving with his heart to make it receptive and obedient to God. If he first forces himself in this way, completely subduing the resistance of his soul, through good habit making it obedient to him so that it joins with him in his prayer and supplication, then the grace of prayer that he has been given by the Spirit grows and flourishes, reposing upon him together with the humility, love and blessed gentleness which he has also sought to acquire. So, then, the Spirit grants him these virtues as well, teaching him the true humility, genuine love and gentleness that he has previously impelled himself to ask for. Thus he grows and is made perfect in the Lord, and is found worthy of the kingdom of heaven. For the humble man never falls: where, indeed, can he fall to if he regards himself as lower than all things? While lofty-mindedness leads to great humiliation, humble-mindedness on the contrary is a great and highly exalted glory.

136. Those who truly love God do not serve Him in order to obtain the kingdom, as though they were engaged in commerce for the sake of gain, nor yet to avoid the punishment that is in store for sinners. They love Him because He is their sole God and Creator, since they know the proper hierarchy of things and that it is the duty of servants to please their lord and maker; and they submit to Him with great understanding in the face of all the afflictions that befall them. Many are the obstacles that stand in the way of pleasing God; for not merely poverty and obscurity but also riches and honour are trials for the soul. Indeed, to some extent even the solace and ease which grace bestows on the soul can easily become a temptation and a hindrance if the soul is not properly conscious of these effects of grace and does not enjoy them with great circumspection and understanding: for the spirit of evil tries to persuade the soul to relax now it possesses grace, and so contrives to implant in it sluggishness and apathy. Thus even participation in grace requires caution and discretion on the soul's part, so that the soul shows proper respect for grace and produces fruit worthy of it. There is a danger, then, that

not only affliction but also relaxation may prove a temptation for the soul, since through both it is tested by the Creator, so as to make it quite clear that it loves Him not for the sake of some gain but for Himself alone, who is truly worthy of love and honour. For the inattentive, who are deficient in faith and immature in mind, there are many obstacles to eternal life – not only distressing and painful things such as sickness, poverty and obscurity, but equally their opposites like riches, honour and praise from others, as well as the unseen warfare of the devil. For those with faith, understanding and courage, on the other hand, such things aid and abet progress towards the kingdom of God: as St Paul says, 'All things work together for good to them that love God' (Rom. 8 : 28). The devout man, therefore, breaking through, overcoming and transcending those things re-garded by the world as obstacles, cleaves to divine love alone. 'The cords of sinners have entangled me,' writes the psalmist, 'but I have not forgotten Thy law' (Ps. 119 : 61. LXX).

137. St Paul most accurately and lucidly revealed to every believing soul the perfect mystery of the Christian faith, showing to all how to attain experience of it through divine grace. This mystery is the effulgence of celestial light in the vision and power of the Spirit. He did not want anyone to think that the illumination of the Spirit consists simply in enlightening us through conceptual knowledge, and so to risk falling short of the perfect mystery of grace through ignorance and laziness. To indicate the true character of spiritual knowledge St Paul therefore gives as an example the glory of the Holy Spirit that shone from the face of Moses. 'If the ministry of death,' he says, 'engraved in letters on stone, was accompanied by such glory that the sons of Israel could not bear to gaze at the face of Moses because of the glory, transitory though it was, that shone from it, then how much greater must the glory be that accompanies the ministry of the Spirit? If the ministry of condemnation is glorious, the ministry of righteousness must greatly excel it in glory. Indeed, what once seemed full of glory now seems to have no glory at all, because it is outshone by a glory that is so much greater. If what was transitory came with glory, what endures will be far more glorious' (2 Cor. 3 : 7–11). He says 'transitory' because it was Moses' mortal body that shone with the glory of light. And he continues: 'Having such hope as this, we can proceed with great confidence' (2 Cor. 3 : 12). A little later he affirms that this everlasting and immortal glory of the Spirit

shines even now with immortal and indestructible power in the immortal inner being of the saints: 'With unveiled face we all' – all, that is to say, who through perfect faith are born in the Spirit – 'reflect as in a mirror the glory of the Lord, and are transfigured into the same image from glory to glory through the Lord who is the Spirit' (2 Cor. 3 : 18). The words 'with unveiled face' indicate the soul; he adds that when one turns back to the Lord the veil is taken off, and that the Lord is the Spirit (cf. 2 Cor. 3 : 16–17). By this he clearly shows that from the time of Adam's transgression a veil of darkness has encroached upon mankind and has covered the soul. But we believe that through the illumination of the Spirit this veil is now removed from truly faithful and saintly souls. It was for this reason that Christ came; and to those who truly believe in Him God has given the grace to attain this measure of holiness.

138. As we said, the effulgence of the Holy Spirit is not merely some kind of revelation on the level of conceptual images, or merely an illumination of grace. It is the true and unceasing effulgence of God's own light in the soul: 'The God who said, "Out of darkness let light shine", has made His light shine in our hearts, to give us the illumination of the knowledge of Christ's glory' (2 Cor. 4 : 6). And the psalmist says: 'Give light to my eyes, lest I sleep unto death' (Ps. 13 : 3) – that is to say, lest when my flesh is dissolved my soul is darkened by the veil of the death that is the result of sin. And other passages in the psalms speak in the same way: 'Open my eyes and I will perceive the wonders of Thy law' (Ps. 119 : 18); and: 'Send Thy light and Thy truth, and they will guide and lead me to Thy holy mountain and into Thy tabernacles' (Ps. 43 : 3); and: 'We have been marked by the light of Thy countenance, O Lord' (Ps. 4 : 6. LXX), and so on.

139. Again, the light that illumined St Paul on the road to Damaskos (cf. Acts 9 : 3), the light through which he was raised to the third heaven where he heard unutterable mysteries (cf. 2 Cor. 12 : 4), was not merely the enlightenment of conceptual images or of spiritual knowledge. It was the effulgence of the power of the Holy Spirit shining in His own person in the soul. Such was its brilliance that corporeal eyes were not able to bear it and were blinded (cf. Acts 9 : 8); and through it all spiritual knowledge is revealed and God is truly known by the worthy and loving soul.

140. Every soul that through its own effort and faith is privileged

in this present life to put on Christ completely in the power and full assurance of grace, and to unite with the heavenly light of the incorruptible image, is initiated here and now substantively into the knowledge of all the heavenly mysteries. Moreover, in the great day of the resurrection the body also will be glorified with the same heavenly image of glory; it will be caught up by the Spirit to the heavens (cf. 1 Thess. 4 : 17), will be given a form like the body of Christ's glory (cf. Phil. 3 : 21), and with Him will coinherit the eternal kingdom.

141. In so far as a man through his own effort and faith has partaken of the heavenly glory of the Holy Spirit, and has beautified his soul with good works, to the same degree will his body, too, be glorified on the day of the resurrection. What he has now stored up inwardly will then manifest itself outwardly, just as the fruit hidden during winter inside the tree comes out when it is spring. The deiform image of the Spirit imprinted even now on the inner being of the saints will make their body, too, outwardly deiform and heavenly. But impure sinners who enwrap the soul in the tenebrous veil of the spirit of this world, and who darken and disfigure the intellect with the ugliness of the passions, will outwardly manifest a body that is also tenebrous and full of every vileness.

142. When God in His love condemned Adam to death after his transgression, he first experienced this death in his soul (cf. Gen. 3 : 19): his spiritual and deathless organs of perception, deprived of their celestial and spiritual enjoyment, were quenched and became as though dead. Later, after 930 years (cf. Gen. 5 : 5), came the death of the body. Similarly, now that God has reconciled mankind through the Cross and death of the Saviour, He restores to the truly believing soul its enjoyment of spiritual light and mystery while it is still in the flesh, and once more enlightens its spiritual organs of perception with the divine light of grace. Later He will invest the body also with deathless and incorruptible glory.

143. Those who have withdrawn from the world and lead a godly and devout life are still in many cases subject to the veil of the passions to which we all became liable through Adam's transgression: I refer to the carnal will, fittingly called death by St Paul when he said that 'the will of the flesh is death' (Rom. 8 : 6). Such people may be likened to men walking at night, their way lighted by the stars that are God's holy commandments; but since they have not yet completely escaped from the darkness, they cannot see everything

clearly. Thus, cultivating virtue with tribulation and great faith, they should beseech Christ, the sun of righteousness, to shine in their hearts, so that they can see everything lucidly. For to those who have reached the heights of virtue, and whose hearts have been actively illumined by spiritual light, the manifold attacks of the demons are clearly evident, as are also the inexpressible vision and the hidden delight and beauty of the incorruptible world. As St Paul says: 'The perfect, whose organs of perception have been trained by practice to discriminate between good and evil, take solid food' (Heb. 5 : 14). And St Peter also says: 'We have the assurance of the message of the prophets; and until the day breaks and the morning star rises in your hearts you do well to give attention to it, for it is like a lamp shining in a dark place' (2 Pet. 1 : 19). Most people, however, are exactly like men walking at night wholly without light and not enjoying the slightest illumination in their souls from the divine Logos, so that they scarcely differ from the blind. They are totally caught up in material entanglements and the chains of temporal life, neither restrained by divine awe nor performing any virtuous acts. On the other hand, those who live in the world and are illumined by the holy commandments as by the stars, and who do cleave to God with faith and awe, are not utterly shrouded in darkness and for this reason can hope to attain salvation.

144. Worldly riches come to men from different sources and pursuits, from high-ranking office, trade, industry, farming and so on. Something similar is the case where spiritual riches are concerned: some derive them from various gifts of grace, as St Paul makes clear when he says, 'Having then gifts different according to the grace given to us . . .' (Rom. 12 : 6); and some from various ascetic labours and acts of righteousness and virtue carried out for God alone, when through grace they refrain from judging, mocking or censuring their fellow-men. But some can be likened to people who dig for gold, and they are quite unmistakable: they are those who strive forward with forbearance and patience, gradually enriching the blessed hope that sustains them. Unmistakable, too, are those who are like hirelings, who are stupid and sluggish, who consume at once whatever they can lay hands on, and never patiently bring to conclusion what they have undertaken but are always threadbare and indigent. Even if they are anxious and ready to receive grace, they are lazy, indolent and fickle when it comes to putting it into practice or developing it. They have

no sooner started than they have had enough, and lose all impetus for spiritual labour. For this reason whatever grace they may have received is taken away from them. The dull, slothful, lifeless and negligent disposition, always at variance with grace, barren of good works, worthless and ignoble in the sight of God, is recognizable both now and in the age to come.

145. When man broke God's commandment and was expelled from paradise he was bound in consequence as by two chains. The first is that of temporal things and worldly pleasures – riches, glory, affection, wife, children, relations, country, possessions and, in short, all visible things from which God has summoned us to liberate ourselves through our own free choice. The second is hidden and invisible; for the soul is bound by a certain chain of darkness to the spirits of evil, and because of this darkness it cannot love God, or believe or pray as it wishes. In consequence of the transgression of the first man, we each of us find that all things visible and invisible are opposed to us. Thus, whenever someone listens obediently to the word of God, he must first begin by cutting his attachment to temporal things and renouncing all worldly pleasures. Then, if he waits attentively upon God and enters into constant communion with Him, he will receive the power to learn that there is another struggle and another battle of thoughts hidden in the depths of his heart. Persevering in this way and beseeching Christ's mercy, combining great faith in Him with endurance, he can with God's help escape from these inner bonds and fetters and from the darkness of the spirits of evil, which are the energies of the hidden passions. Through Christ's grace and power we can bring this war to a successful conclusion. But by ourselves and without divine aid it is altogether impossible for us to free ourselves from the struggle against evil thoughts: we can merely rebut them and not take pleasure in them.

146. If a man is entangled in the things of this world, caught by their many shackles, and seduced by the evil passions, it is very hard for him to recognize that there is another invisible struggle and another inner warfare. But, after detaching himself from all visible things and worldly pleasures, and beginning to serve God, he then becomes capable of recognizing the nature of this inner struggle and unseen warfare against the passions. Yet, as we said, unless he first achieves outward detachment by aspiring to serve God totally with his whole soul, he will not recognize the secret passions of evil and his

inner fetters. On the contrary, he will be in danger of thinking that he is healthy and not ailing, when in fact he is full of wounds and nourishes unseen passions. But if he has despised desire and glory, he may first become aware of these inner passions and then fight against them, calling on Christ with faith and receiving from heaven the weapons of the Spirit: the breastplate of righteousness, the helmet of salvation, the shield of faith, and the sword of the Spirit (cf. Eph. 6 : 14,17).

147. The devil tries to disrupt our hope in Christ and our love for Him in a thousand ways. Inwardly he brings afflictions on the soul by means of the evil spirits, or he fills it with foul and immoral thoughts by stirring up its memory of former sins, so as to make it grow sluggish and to despair of ever attaining salvation. His aim is to cheat the soul into thinking that it generates these thoughts of its own accord and that they are not sown in it maliciously by an alien spirit. Or else he inflicts bodily suffering and brings on us vilification and tribulation through the agency of other people. But the more he shoots his fiery arrows at us, the more we must enkindle our hope in God, knowing with certainty that He deliberately permits souls that long for Him to suffer these things, so as to discover if they truly love Him.

148. Compared with the incorruptible and eternal world, a thousand years of this world are like a grain of sand. I look at things in this way. Suppose it is within your power to be sole king of the entire world and to possess all its treasures; and suppose that your rule had begun with the first creation of mankind, and was to continue until the final transformation of the whole visible world. Would you, then, given the choice, exchange the true and unchanging kingdom, that contains nothing fleeting or perishable, for this temporal kingdom? Not, it seems to me, if your judgment is sound and you have a proper regard for yourself. 'What good will it do a man if he gains the whole world but loses his soul?' Christ asks His disciples (Matt. 16 : 26); and He says that there is nothing equal in value to the soul. Since the soul by itself is far more valuable than the whole world and any worldly kingdom, is not the kingdom of heaven also more valuable? That the soul is more valuable is shown by the fact that God did not see fit to bestow on any other created thing the union and fellowship with His own coessential Spirit. Not sky, sun, moon, stars, sea, earth or any other visible thing did He bless in this way, but man alone, whom of

all His creatures He especially loved. If, therefore, no one with sound judgment would exchange the eternal kingdom for all the great wealth of the world and for the kingdom of the whole earth, how great is the folly of those who exchange it for accidental and casual things such as desire for something, meagre glory, mediocre gain, and so on? For whenever we love something worldly and are attached to it, we are certainly choosing it instead of the kingdom of heaven. Worst of all, we regard this thing as God: as it has been said, 'A man is the slave to whatever has mastered him' (2 Pet. 2 : 19). We should, therefore, commit ourselves entirely to God, making ourselves dependent on Him and crucifying ourselves in soul and body as we advance in the practice of all His holy commandments.

149. Would you think it right if this perishable glory, ephemeral kingdom and other such temporal things were gained only after great toil and sweat by those who hanker after them, while to reign endlessly with Christ and to enjoy inexpressible blessings was something to be gained cheaply and easily, and could be attained without labour and effort by anyone who wished?

150. What is the purpose of Christ's advent? The restoration and reintegration of human nature in Him. For He restored to human nature the original dignity of Adam, and in addition bestowed on it the unutterable grace of the heavenly inheritance of the Holy Spirit. Leading it out of the prison of darkness, He showed it the way and the door to life. By traversing this way and knocking on this door we can enter the kingdom of heaven. As He said: 'Ask and it will be given to you . . . knock and it will be opened to you' (Matt. 7 : 7). By passing through this door it is possible for everyone to attain the freedom of his soul, to cut off his evil thoughts, and to become Christ's bride and consort through the communion of the Holy Spirit. Such is the ineffable love of the Lord towards man, whom he has created in His own image.

GLOSSARY

AGE (αἰών – aeon): the ensemble of cosmic duration. It includes the angelic orders, and is an attribute of God as the principle and consummation of all the centuries created by Him. The term is used more particularly in two ways:

(i) Frequently a distinction is made between the 'present age' and the 'age to come' or the 'new age'. The first corresponds to our present sense of time, the second to time as it exists in God, that is, to eternity understood, not as endless time, but as the simultaneous presence of all time. Our present sense of time, according to which we experience time as sundered from God, is the consequence of the loss of vision and spiritual perception occasioned by the fall and is on this account more or less illusory. In reality time is not and never can be sundered from God, the 'present age' from the 'age to come'. Because of this the 'age to come' and its realities must be thought of, not as non-existent or as coming into existence in the future, but as actualities that by grace we can experience here and now. To indicate this, the Greek phrase for these realities (τὰ μέλλοντα – ta mellonta) is often translated as 'the blessings held in store'.

(ii) Certain texts, especially in St Maximos the Confessor, also use the term aeon in a connected but more specific way, to denote a level intermediate between eternity in the full sense (ἀϊδιότης – aïdiotis) and time as known to us in our present experience (χρόνος – chronos). Where this is the case we normally employ the rendering 'aeon' instead of 'age'. There are thus three levels:

(a) eternity, the *totum simul* or simultaneous presence of all time and reality as known to God, who alone has neither origin nor end, and who therefore is alone eternal in the full sense;

(b) the aeon, the *totum simul* as known to the angels, and also to human persons who possess experience of the 'age to come':

although having no end, these angelic or human beings, since they are created, are not self-originating and therefore are not eternal in the sense that God is eternal;

(c) time, that is, temporal succession as known to us in the 'present age'.

APPETITIVE ASPECT OF THE SOUL, or the soul's desiring power (τὸ ἐπιθυμητικόν – to epithymitikon): one of the three aspects or powers of the soul according to the tripartite division formulated by Plato (see his *Republic*, Book iv, 434D–441C) and on the whole accepted by the Greek Christian Fathers. The other two are, first, the intelligent aspect or power (τὸ λογιστικόν – to logistikon: *see* Intelligent); and, second, the incensive aspect or power (τὸ θυμικόν – to thymikon), which often manifests itself as wrath or anger, but which can be more generally defined as the force provoking vehement feelings. The three aspects or powers can be used positively, that is, in accordance with nature and as created by God, or negatively, that is, in a way contrary to nature and leading to sin (q.v.). For instance, the incensive power can be used positively to repel demonic attacks or to intensify desire for God; but it can also, when not controlled, lead to self-indulgent, disruptive thought and action.

The appetitive and incensive aspects, in particular the former, are sometimes termed the soul's passible aspect (τὸ παθητικόν – to pathitikon), that is to say, the aspect which is more especially vulnerable to *pathos* or passion (q.v.), and which, when not transformed by positive spiritual influences, is susceptive to the influence of negative and self-destructive forces. The intelligent aspect, although also susceptible to passion, is not normally regarded as part of the soul's passible aspect.

ASSENT (συγκατάθεσις – synkatathesis): *see* Temptation.

ATTENTIVENESS (προσοχή – prosochi): *see* Watchfulness.

COMPUNCTION (κατάνυξις – katanyxis): in our version sometimes also translated 'deep penitence'. The state of one who is 'pricked to the heart', becoming conscious both of his own sinfulness and of the forgiveness extended to him by God; a mingled feeling of sorrow, tenderness and joy, springing from sincere repentance (q.v.).

CONCEPTUAL IMAGE (νόημα – noïma): *see* Thought.

CONTEMPLATION (θεωρία – theoria): the perception or vision of the intellect (q.v.) through which one attains spiritual knowledge (q.v.). It may be contrasted with the practice of the virtues (πρακτική – praktiki) which designates the more external aspect of the ascetic life – purification and the keeping of the commandments – but which is an indispensable prerequisite of contemplation. Depending on the level of personal spiritual growth, contemplation has two main stages: it may be either of the inner essences or principles (q.v.) of created beings or, at a higher stage, of God Himself.

COUPLING (συνδυασμός – syndyasmos): see Temptation.

DELUSION (πλάνη – plani): see Illusion.

DESIRE, Desiring power of the soul: see Appetitive aspect of the soul.

DISCRIMINATION (διάκρισις – diakrisis): a spiritual gift permitting one to discriminate between the types of thought that enter into one's mind, to assess them accurately and to treat them accordingly. Through this gift one gains 'discernment of spirits' – that is, the ability to distinguish between the thoughts or visions inspired by God and the suggestions or fantasies coming from the devil. It is a kind of eye or lantern of the soul by which man finds his way along the spiritual path without falling into extremes; thus it includes the idea of discretion.

DISPASSION (ἀπάθεια – apatheia): among the writers of the texts here translated, some regard passion (q.v.) as evil and the consequence of sin (q.v.), and for them dispassion signifies passionlessness, the uprooting of the passions; others, such as St Isaiah the Solitary, regard the passions as fundamentally good, and for them dispassion signifies a state in which the passions are exercised in accordance with their original purity and so without committing sin in act or thought. Dispassion is a state of reintegration and spiritual freedom; when translating the term into Latin, Cassian rendered it 'purity of heart'. Such a state may imply impartiality and detachment, but not indifference, for if a dispassionate man does not suffer on his own account, he suffers for his fellow creatures. It consists, not in ceasing to feel the attacks of the demons, but in no longer yielding to them. It is positive, not negative: Evagrios links it closely with the quality of love (agapi) and Diadochos speaks of the 'fire of dispassion' (§ 17: in our translation, vol. i, p. 258). Dispassion is among the gifts of God.

ECSTASY (ἔκστασις – ekstasis): a 'going out' from oneself and from all created things towards God, under the influence of *eros* or intense longing (q.v.). A man does not attain ecstasy by his own efforts, but is drawn out of himself by the power of God's love. Ecstasy implies a passing beyond all the conceptual thinking of the discursive reason (q.v.). It may sometimes be marked by a state of trance, or by a loss of normal consciousness; but such psycho-physical accompaniments are in no way essential. Occasionally the term *ekstasis* is used in a bad sense, to mean infatuation, loss of self-control, or madness.

FAITH (πίστις – pistis): not only an individual or theoretical belief in the dogmatic truths of Christianity, but an all-embracing relationship, an attitude of love and total trust in God. As such it involves a transformation of man's entire life. Faith is a gift from God, the means whereby we are taken up into the whole thean-thropic activity of God in Christ and of man in Christ through which man attains salvation.

FALLEN NATURE (παλαιὸς ἄνθρωπος – palaios anthropos): literally, the 'old man'. *See* Flesh, sense (ii).

FANTASY (φαντασία – fantasia): denoting the image-producing faculty of the psyche, this is one of the most important words in the hesychast vocabulary. As one begins to advance along the spiritual path one begins to 'perceive' images of things which have no direct point of reference in the external world, and which emerge inexplicably from within oneself. This experience is a sign that one's consciousness is beginning to deepen: outer sensations and ordinary thoughts have to some extent been quietened, and the impulses, fears, hopes, passions hidden in the subconscious region are beginning to break through to the surface. One of the goals of the spiritual life is indeed the attainment of a spiritual knowledge (q.v.) which transcends both the ordinary level of consciousness and the subconscious; and it is true that images, especially when the recipient is in an advanced spiritual state, may well be projections on the plane of the imagination of celestial archetypes, and that in this case they can be used cre-atively, to form the images of sacred art and iconography. But more often than not they will simply derive from a middle or lower sphere, and will have nothing spiritual or creative about them. Hence they correspond to the world of fantasy and not to the world of the imagination in the proper sense. It is on this account that the hesychastic masters on the whole take a negative attitude towards them. They emphasize the grave dangers involved in this kind of experience, especially as the very production of these images may be the consequence of demonic or diabolic activity; and they admonish those still in the early stages and not yet possessing spiritual discrimination (q.v.) not to be enticed and led captive by these illusory appearances, whose tumult may well overwhelm the mind. Their advice is to pay no attention to them, but to continue with prayer and invocation, dispelling them with the name of Jesus Christ.

FLESH (σάρξ – *sarx*): has various senses: (i) the human in contrast to the divine, as in the sentence, 'The Logos became flesh' (John 1 : 14); (ii) fallen and sinful human nature in contrast to human nature as originally created and dwelling in communion with God; man when separated from God and in rebellion against Him; (iii) the body in contrast to the soul. The second meaning is probably the most frequent. If the word is being employed in this sense, it is important to distinguish 'flesh' from 'body' (σῶμα – *soma*). When St Paul lists the 'works of the flesh' in Gal. 5 : 19–21, he mentions such things as 'seditions', 'heresy' and 'envy', which have no special connection with the body. In sense (ii) of the word, 'flesh' denotes the *whole* soul–body structure in so far as a man is fallen; likewise 'spirit' denotes the *whole* soul–body structure in so far as a man is redeemed. The soul as well as the body can become fleshly or 'carnal', just as the body as well as the soul can become spiritual. Asceticism involves a war against the flesh – in sense (ii) of the word – but not against the body as such.

GUARD OF THE HEART, OF THE INTELLECT (φυλακὴ καρδίας, νοῦ – *phylaki kardias, nou*): see Watchfulness.

HEART (καρδία – *kardia*): not simply the physical organ but the spiritual centre of man's being, man as made in the image of God, his deepest and truest self, or the inner shrine, to be entered only through sacrifice and death, in which the mystery of the union between the divine and the human is consummated. ' "I called with my whole heart", says the psalmist – that is, with body, soul and spirit' (John Klimakos, *The Ladder of Divine Ascent*, Step 28, translated by Archimandrite Lazarus [London, 1959], pp. 257–8).

'Heart' has thus an all-embracing significance: 'prayer of the heart' means prayer not just of the emotions and affections, but of the whole person, including the body.

ILLUSION (πλάνη – *plani*): in our version sometimes also translated 'delusion'. Literally, wandering astray, deflection from the right path; hence error, beguilement, the acceptance of a mirage mistaken for truth. Cf. the literal sense of sin (q.v.) as 'missing the mark'.

INCENSIVE POWER or aspect of the soul (θυμός – *thymos*; τὸ θυμικόν – *to thymikon*): *see* Appetitive aspect of the soul.

INNER ESSENCES OR PRINCIPLES (λόγοι – *logoi*): *see* Logos.

INTELLECT (νοῦς – *nous*): the highest faculty in man, through which – provided it is purified – he knows God or the inner essences or principles (q.v.) of created things by means of direct apprehension or spiritual perception. Unlike the *dianoia* or reason (q.v.), from which it must be carefully distinguished, the intellect does not function by formulating abstract concepts and then arguing on this basis to a conclusion reached through deductive reasoning, but it understands divine truth by means of immediate experience, intuition or 'simple cognition' (the term used by St Isaac the Syrian). The intellect dwells in the 'depths of the soul'; it constitutes the innermost aspect of the heart (St Diadochos, §§ 79, 88: in our translation, vol. i, pp. 280, 287). The intellect is the organ of contemplation (q.v.), the 'eye of the heart' (*Makarian Homilies*).

INTELLECTION (νόησις – *noīsis*): not an abstract concept or a visual image, but the act or function of the intellect (q.v.) whereby it apprehends spiritual realities in a direct manner.

INTELLIGENT (λογικός – *logikos*): the Greek term *logikos* is so closely connected with Logos (q.v.), and therefore with the divine Intellect, that to render it simply as 'logical' and hence descriptive of the reason (q.v.) is clearly inadequate. Rather it pertains to the intellect (q.v.) and qualifies the possessor of spiritual knowledge (q.v.). Hence when found in conjunction with 'soul' (*logiki psychi*), *logikos* is translated as 'deiform' or as 'endowed with intelligence'. Intelligence itself (τὸ λογικόν – *to logikon*; τὸ λογιστικόν – *to logistikon*; ὁ λογισμός – *ho logismos*) is the ruling aspect of the intellect (q.v.) or its operative faculty.

INTENSE LONGING (ἔρως – *eros*): the word *eros*, when used in these texts, retains much of the significance it has in Platonic thought. It denotes that intense aspiration and longing which impel man towards union with God, and at the same time something of the force which links the divine and the human. As unitive love *par excellence*, it is not distinct from *agapi*, but may be contrasted with *agapi* in that it expresses a greater degree of intensity and ecstasy (q.v.).

INTIMATE COMMUNION (παρρησία – *parrisia*): literally, 'frankness', 'freedom of speech'; hence freedom of approach to God, such as Adam possessed before the fall and the saints have regained by grace; a sense of confidence and loving trust in God's mercy.

JESUS PRAYER ('Ιησοῦ εὐχή – *Iisou evchi*): the invocation of the name of Jesus, most commonly in the words, 'Lord Jesus Christ, Son of God, have mercy on me', although there are a number of variant forms. Not merely a 'technique' or a 'Christian mantra', but a prayer addressed to the Person of Jesus Christ, expressing our living faith (q.v.) in Him as Son of God and Saviour.

LOGOS (Λόγος – *Logos*): the Second Person of the Holy Trinity, or the Intellect, Wisdom and Providence of God in whom and through whom all things are created. As the unitary cosmic principle, the Logos contains in Himself the multiple *logoi* (inner principles or inner essences, thoughts of God) in accordance with which all things come into existence at the times and places, and in the forms, appointed for them, each single thing thereby containing in itself the principle of its own development. It is these *logoi*, contained principially in the Logos and manifest in the forms of the created universe, that constitute the first or lower stage of contemplation (q.v.).

MIND: *see* Reason.

NOETIC (νοητός – *noïtos*): that which belongs to or is characteristic of the intellect (q.v.). *See also* Intellection.

PASSION (πάθος – *pathos*): in Greek, the word signifies literally that which happens to a person or thing, an experience undergone passively; hence an appetite or impulse such as anger, desire or jealousy, that violently dominates the soul. Many Greek Fathers regard the passions as something intrinsically evil, a 'disease' of the soul: thus St John Klimakos affirms that God is not the creator of the passions and that they are 'unnatural', alien to man's true self (*The Ladder of Divine Ascent*, Step 26, translated by Archimandrite Lazarus [*op. cit.*], p. 211). Other Greek Fathers, however, look on the passions as impulses originally placed in man by God, and so fundamentally good, although at present distorted by sin (cf. St Isaiah the Solitary, § 1: in our translation, vol. i, p. 22). On this second view, then, the passions are to be educated, not eradicated; to be transfigured, not suppressed; to be used positively, not negatively (*see* Dispassion).

PRACTICE OF THE VIRTUES (πρακτική – *praktiki*): *see* Contemplation.

PREPOSSESSION (πρόληψις – *prolipsis*): *see* Temptation.

PROVOCATION (προσβολή – *prosvoli*): *see* Temptation.

REASON, mind (διάνοια – *dianoia*): the discursive, conceptualizing and logical faculty in man, the function of which is to draw conclusions or formulate concepts deriving from data provided either by revelation or spiritual knowledge (q.v.) or by sense-observation. The knowledge of the reason is consequently of a lower order than spiritual knowledge (q.v.) and does not imply any direct apprehension or perception of the inner essences or principles (q.v.) of created beings, still less of divine truth itself. Indeed, such apprehension or perception, which is the function of the intellect (q.v.), is beyond the scope of the reason.

REBUTTAL (ἀντιλογία – *antilogia*; ἀντίρρησις – *antirrisis*): the repulsing of a demon or demonic thought at the moment of provocation (q.v.); or, in a more general sense, the bridling of evil thoughts.

REMEMBRANCE OF GOD (μνήμη Θεοῦ – *mnimi Theou*): not just calling God to mind, but the state of recollectedness or concentration in which attention is centred on God. As such it is the opposite of the state of self-indulgence and insensitivity.

REPENTANCE (μετάνοια – *metanoia*): the Greek signifies primarily a 'change of mind' or 'change of intellect': not only sorrow, contrition or regret, but more positively and fundamentally the conversion or turning of our whole life towards God.

SENSUAL PLEASURE (ἡδονή – *hidoni*): according to the context the Greek term signifies either sensual pleasure (the most frequent meaning) or spiritual pleasure or delight.

SIN (ἁμαρτία – *hamartia*): the primary meaning of the Greek word is 'failure' or, more specifically, 'failure to hit the mark' and so a 'missing of the mark', a 'going astray' or, ultimately, 'failure to achieve the purpose for which one is created'. It is closely related, therefore, to illusion (q.v.). The translation 'sin' should be read with these connotations in mind.

SORROW (λύπη – *lypi*): often with the sense of 'godly sorrow' – the sorrow which nourishes the soul with the hope engendered by repentance (q.v.).

SPIRITUAL KNOWLEDGE (γνῶσις – *gnosis*): the knowledge of the intellect (q.v.) as distinct from that of the reason (q.v.). As such it is knowledge inspired by God, and so linked with contemplation (q.v.) and immediate spiritual perception.

STILLNESS (ἡσυχία – *hesychia*): from which are derived the words hesychasm and hesychast, used to denote the whole spiritual tradition represented in the *Philokalia* as well as the person who pursues the spiritual path it delineates (*see* Introduction, vol. i, pp. 14–16): a state of inner tranquillity or mental quietude and concentration which arises in conjunction with, and is deepened by, the practice of pure prayer and the guarding of heart (q.v.) and intellect (q.v.). Not simply silence, but an attitude of listening to God and of openness towards Him.

TEMPERAMENT (κρᾶσις – *krasis*): primarily the well-balanced blending of elements, humours or qualities in animal bodies, but sometimes extended to denote the whole soul–body structure of man. In this sense it is the opposite to a state of psychic or physical disequilibrium.

TEMPTATION (πειρασμός – *peirasmos*): also translated in our version as 'trial' or 'test'. The word indicates, according to context: (i) a test or trial sent to man by God, so as to aid his progress on the spiritual way; (ii) a suggestion from the devil, enticing man into sin.

Using the word in sense (ii), the Greek Fathers employ a series of technical terms to describe the process of temptation. (See in particular Mark the Ascetic, *On the Spiritual Law*, §§ 138–41, in vol. i of our translation, pp. 119–20; John Klimakos, *Ladder*, Step 15, translated by Archimandrite Lazarus [*op. cit.*], pp. 157–8; Maximos, *On Love*, i, §§ 83–84, in vol. ii of our translation, pp. 62–63; John of Damaskos, *On the Virtues and Vices*, also in vol. ii of our translation, pp. 337–8.) The basic distinction made by these Fathers is between the demonic *provocation* and man's *assent*: the first lies outside man's control, while for the second he is morally responsible. In detail, the chief terms employed are as follows:

(i) *Provocation* (προσβολή – *prosvoli*): the initial incitement to evil. Mark the Ascetic defines this as an 'image-free stimulation in the heart'; so long as the provocation is not accompanied by images, it does not involve man in any guilt. Such provocations, originating as they do from the devil, assail man from the outside independently of his free will, and so he is not morally responsible for them. His liability to these provocations is not a consequence of the fall: even in paradise, Mark maintains, Adam was assailed by the devil's provocations. Man cannot prevent provocations from assailing him; what does lie in his power, however, is to maintain constant watchfulness (q.v.) and so to reject each provocation as soon as it emerges into his consciousness – that is to say, at its first appearance as a thought in his mind or intellect (μονολόγιστος ἔμφασις – *monologistos emphasis*). If he does reject the provocation, the sequence is cut off and the process of temptation is terminated.

(ii) *Momentary disturbance* (παραρριπισμός – *pararripismos*) of the intellect, occurring 'without any movement or working of bodily passion' (see Mark, *Letter to Nicolas the Solitary*: in our translation, vol. i, p. 153). This seems to be more than the 'first appearance' of a provocation described in stage (i) above; for, at a certain point of spiritual growth in this life, it is possible to be totally released from such 'momentary disturbance', whereas no one can expect to be altogether free from demonic provocations.

(iii) *Communion* (ὁμιλία – *homilia*); *coupling* (συνδυασμός – *syndyasmos*). Without as yet entirely assenting to the demonic provocation, a man may begin to 'entertain' it, to converse or parley with it, turning it over in his mind pleasurably, yet still hesitating whether or not to act upon it. At this stage, which is indicated by the terms 'communion' or 'coupling', the provocation is no longer 'image-free' but has become a *logismos* or thought (q.v.); and man is morally responsible for having allowed this to happen.

(iv) *Assent* (συγκατάθεσις – *synkatathesis*). This signifies a step beyond mere 'communion' or 'coupling'. No longer merely 'playing' with the evil suggestion, a man now resolves to act upon it. There is now no doubt as to his moral culpability: even if circumstances prevent him from sinning outwardly, he is judged by God according to the intention in his heart.

(v) *Prepossession* (πρόληψις – *prolipsis*): defined by Mark as 'the involuntary presence of former sins in the memory'. This state of 'prepossession' or prejudice results from repeated acts of sin which predispose a man to yield to particular temptations. In principle he retains his free choice and can reject demonic provocations; but in practice the force of habit makes it more and more difficult for him to resist.

(vi) *Passion* (q.v.). If a man does not fight strenuously against a prepossession, it will develop into an evil passion.

THEOLOGY (θεολογία – *theologia*): denotes in these texts far more than the learning about God and religious doctrine acquired through academic study. It signifies active and conscious participation in or perception of the realities of the divine world – in other words, the realization of spiritual knowledge (q.v.). To be a theologian in the full sense, therefore, presupposes the attainment of the state of stillness (q.v.) and dispassion (q.v.), itself the concomitant of pure and undistracted prayer, and so requires gifts bestowed on but extremely few persons.

THOUGHT (λογισμός – *logismos*; νόημα – *noīma*): (i) frequently signifies not thought in the ordinary sense, but thought provoked by the demons, and therefore often qualified in translation by the adjective 'evil' or 'demonic'; it can also signify divinely-inspired thought; (ii) a 'conceptual image', intermediate between fantasy (q.v.) and an abstract concept; this sense of *noīma* is frequent in the texts of St Maximos, where the rendering 'conceptual image' is normally adopted.

WATCHFULNESS (νῆψις – *nipsis*): literally, the opposite to a state of drunken stupor; hence spiritual sobriety, alertness, vigilance. It signifies an attitude of attentiveness (προσοχή – *prosochi*), whereby one keeps watch over one's inward thoughts and fantasies (q.v.), maintaining guard over the heart and intellect (φυλακὴ καρδίας/νοῦ – *phylaki kardias/nou*; τήρησις καρδίας/νοῦ – *tirisis kardias/nou*). In Hesychios, *On Watchfulness and Holiness*, §§ 1–6 (in our translation, vol. i, pp. 162–3), watchfulness is given a very broad definition, being used to indicate the whole range of the practice of the virtues. It is closely linked with purity of heart and stillness (q.v.).The Greek title of the *Philokalia* is 'The

Philokalia of the Niptic Fathers', i.e. of the fathers who practised and inculcated the virtue of watchfulness. This shows how
central is the role assigned by St Nikodimos to this state.

WRATH, wrathfulness: *see* Appetitive aspect of the soul.

INDEX

[Major entries are given in bold type]

AUTHORS AND SOURCES

SUBJECTS

Intelligent aspect of soul, 356, **360**; soul's sovereign aspect, 21–2; through it God is worshipped, 277

Intense longing, 360–1. *See: Eros*

Intimate communion, 361

Iron in the fire, metaphor for incarnation, 143

Isaac, meaning of name, 276

Israelite: means intellect that sees God, 180

James, meaning of name, 276

Jannes and Jambres, 300

Jerusalem: noetic, 17; vision of the heavenly, 175, 241, 321

Jesus Christ: *see* Christ

Jesus Prayer (invocation and remembrance of Jesus), 15, 16, 25, 26, 33, 44, 45, 56, 57, 73, 167n., 359, 361; and the continual remembrance of God, 15; gathers together the intellect, 15, 27; Jesus as the name of salvation, 129

Job, 87, 184, 222, 231, 251

John the Baptist, St, 130–1

Joy, **260–3**; and sorrow, 20, 234; and contemplation, 55

Judas, 185, 222, 229

Judgment: judge no one, 86, 160–1; moral judgment (*phronisis*), 36–7, 39, 273–4; one of the four principal virtues, 23, 36, 100–1, 115, **256–7**; last judgment, 75, 104, 115–16, 136, 262–3, 312–13

Justice: one of the four principal virtues, 23, 100–1, 115, **258–9**; meeting-place of all the virtues, 39

King, earthly and heavenly, 60, 307–8

Kingdom: inner, 60; of the heart, 17, 26; of heaven within us, 25, 30, 126, 305; anticipated in this life, 292; prayer as the key to the kingdom, 45

Knowledge, spiritual (*gnosis*), 363; of God, 255; natural spiritual knowledge, 273–4; natural knowledge of God, 76, 166; *gnosis* as a gift of grace, 154; an all-embracing term, 236–7; signifies dispassionate contemplation, 134; to be combined with the practice of the virtues, 34–5, 103; with grief, 24; with humility, 28; not to be sought prematurely, 138; set between six diabolic pitfalls, 134, 170, 233; active

gnosis, 101; and the higher kind of faith, 213; know yourself, 85, 239; secular knowledge, 154; spurious knowledge, 101, 156, 191

Laity, 104

Law: natural, 55, 83; law of intellect and of sin, 28; Jewish Law, 341

Laziness, 102

Learning, secular, 154, 211, 266, 267–8, 276

Light: the divine, 32, 33, **45–6**, 47, 284, 313; ineffable, 67, 311, 317, 321; boundless, 321; creation of light, 159, 193; sensible and spiritual light, 43; light of intellect, 33, 43, 44; luminous reflection of Jesus in soul, 25; the vision of divine light is not merely metaphorical, **347–8**; soul and body transfigured by light, 45, 311, 312; glory of Adam before fall, 300; light shining from Moses' face, 300, 312, 331, 347; Paul's vision of light, 348; intellectual light from God or devil, 304; delusive visions of light, 81, 91; Satan as angel of light, 237, 250, 270, 304, 339. *See* Fire

Listlessness, 155, 156

Logoi: see Inner essences

Logos, 361. *See* Christ

'Lord, have mercy', repetition of, 145, 199

Lord's Prayer, 167

Love, **253–4**; for God and neighbour, 17, 62, 163, 175–6, 180, 184, 288–9; highest of virtues, 57, 253; greatest commandment, 288; our labour useless without it, 293; natural, 253; disinterested, 346; linked with dispassion, 96, 115, 253, 357; *agapi* and *eros*, 361. *See* Eros

Luke, St: author of Acts, 181

Lust: *see* Desire

Magicians, 300

Male and female, 50

Man: *see* Person, the human

Manna, 132–3; means simple prayer, 54

Marriage: and virginity, 83; self-restraint within, 231. *See* Nuptial symbolism

Martha and Mary, 104, 127, 298

Martyrs, 123, 146, 343; meditation on, 108, 131; the forty martyrs, 111; outward and inward martyrdom, 161, 281, 343. *See* Death

father, 140; test our free will, 249; test
our faith, 274; positive value, 31, 77, 162,
234, 268, 311; source of joy, 31, 139; to be
seen as blessings, 172, 273; to be embraced actively, 239; lead to dispassion,
333; we are tested by both affliction and
relaxation, 346–7. See Endurance, Suffering, Temptation
Trinity, the Holy, 61, 84, 143, 166, 192, 255,
334. See God
Trisagion, 119
Troparion, 107n.
Truth, 34, 36, 37, 39, 41, 52

Veil of the temple, 45, 142
Vices, linked to each other, 79, 291. See
Passions
Vigils, 90–1; limited value, 335
Virgin Birth: *see* Mother of God
Virginity, 83, 136, 238
Virgins, wise and foolish, 238, 293–4, 313
Virtues: list of, **203–4**; interdependent, 78,
88, 290, 345; of soul and body, 220; bodily
virtues, tools for those of soul, 103; moral
virtues, 225; three most comprehensive
virtues, 49; the four principal, 23, 36,
100–1, 209, 256; the six principal, 36; in
the three aspects of the soul, 110; virtue
defined as all-embracing self-control, 21;
as mean between two extremes, 88, 101,
162, 171–2, 256, 258; practice of virtues,
not enough by itself, 30; acquisition of,
162, 181, 183, 195; through forcefulness,

344–5; passions transformed into virtues
(and *vice-versa*), 269; dual fruits of virtue
and vice, 286. See Practice of the virtues
Vision: of God, 16, 142–3; spiritual visions,
46, 333; deluding visions, 81, 91, 235
Vocation, from God, 195–6

Warfare: inner and outer, 16, 18, 23–4, 25,
28, 30, 331, 351; against demons, not men,
258
Warmth of heart, 67
Watchfulness (*nipsis*), 15, 17, 18, 26, 100, 105,
220, **365**. See Attentiveness
Water, 90, 151
Wealth: *see* Possessions
Wedding garment of soul, 328–9. See Nuptial
symbolism
Will: of God, embodied in commandments,
18, 21; as eternal life, 215; human will, to
be cut off, 82, 83, 84, 87, 149, 162, 172,
194, 196, 215, 243. See Flesh, Free will
Wine, 90
Wisdom: spiritual, 199, 211, 256; hidden,
274; secular, 276
Withdrawal from human society, 88, 89. See
Stillness
Work: spiritual and physical, 44; noetic, 17
World: may mean the passions, 260; world
ruler, 229, 299. See Creation, Nature
Wound of love, inflicted by God, 50, 33?
Wrath: *see* Anger
Wrestling with a temptation, 207